Crimes Against Humanity

A Normative Account

Crimes Against Humanity is the first booklength treatment of the philosophical foundations of international criminal law. Its focus is on the moral, legal, and political questions that arise when individuals who commit collective crimes, such as crimes against humanity, are held accountable by international criminal tribunals. These tribunals challenge one of the most sacred prerogatives of states – sovereignty – breaches of which can be justified only in limited circumstances, following what the author calls a "minimalist account" of the justification of international prosecution.

The book is divided into four parts. Part A provides a definition of international crime and justifies the existence of norms that can achieve a universal binding force. Part B identifies and defends several principles of international criminal law. Part C turns to institutional arrangements for prosecuting group-based crimes. Part D looks at defenses, as well as alternatives, to international criminal prosecutions, such as amnesty and truth and reconciliation programs.

Written in a clear and accessible style, *Crimes Against Humanity* will appeal to anyone with an interest in international law, political philosophy, international relations, and human rights theory.

Larry May is Professor of Philosophy at Washington University in St. Louis.

Cambridge Studies in Philosophy and Law

Some other books in the series:

Crimes Against Humanity

A Normative Account

Larry May

Washington University

CAMBRIDGE
UNIVERSITY PRESS

PUBLISHED BY THE PRESS SYNDICATE OF THE UNIVERSITY OF CAMBRIDGE
The Pitt Building, Trumpington Street, Cambridge, United Kingdom

CAMBRIDGE UNIVERSITY PRESS
The Edinburgh Building, Cambridge CB2 2RU, UK
40 West 20th Street, New York, NY 10011-4211, USA
477 Williamstown Road, Port Melbourne, VIC 3207, Australia
Ruiz de Alarcón 13, 28014 Madrid, Spain
Dock House, The Waterfront, Cape Town 8001, South Africa

http://www.cambridge.org

First published 2005

Printed in the United States of America

Typeface Times Roman 10/12 pt.   *System* LATEX 2$_\varepsilon$ [TB]

A catalog record for this book is available from the British Library.

Library of Congress Cataloging in Publication Data
May, Larry.
Crimes against humanity : a normative account / Larry May.
p.   cm. – (Cambridge studies in philosophy and law)
Includes bibliographical references and index.
ISBN 0-521-84079-1 (hbk.) – ISBN 0-521-60051-0 (pbk.)
1. Crimes against humanity.   2. International offenses.   I. Title.   II. Series.
K5301.M39   2005
345′.0235–dc22   2004045112

ISBN 0 521 84079 1 hardback
ISBN 0 521 60051 0 paperback

Contents

Acknowledgments

This book has taken me a long time to write, nearly twice as long as any of my previous books. Part of the problem was that first I had to learn quite a bit of international law before I felt competent enough to provide philosophical reflections on international criminal law. As an undergraduate, I had sat in classrooms at Georgetown's School of Foreign Service, enthralled by developments in the emerging field of international law. Eventually, I put those interests aside to pursue a career teaching moral and legal philosophy. I only occasionally dabbled in international law until I found myself in a law school classroom, again as a student. This book began life as I sat in these classes realizing how much the world had changed in the twenty-five years since my undergraduate days. My long-dormant interests in international law were rekindled. I am grateful to Steve Legomsky and Peter Mutharika for igniting that spark and for putting up with that older and troublesome student who took more and more of their courses.

As I finished my law school studies, I was bitten by the criminal law bug, and I have subsequently helped in the defense of several defendants accused of murder. My emerging interest in this field of legal practice dovetailed with my intense interest in the newest field of international law – international criminal law. Here was a hothouse experiment in how to derive *legal* prescriptions from *moral* ones, and hence a field ripe for philosophical exploration and for discussions of individual and collective responsibility. It was also a field in need of a defendant-oriented approach. I am grateful to Peter Joy and Bob Wolfrum for helping to fuel my general interest in criminal law, and to Leila Sadat for providing me with such a rich introduction to the field of international criminal law.

As always, my greatest debt of gratitude goes to those theorists who have read and commented on my work. Carl Wellman read the entire manuscript in early draft and gave me valuable feedback and encouragement. Jack Knight, James Bohman, and Andrew Rehfeld read big chunks of it at crucial early points in the drafting. Thad Metz assigned several chapters in his graduate course and conveyed very helpful information about how his students responded to my arguments. I have also benefited from all-too-brief conversations with the following scholars of international law: Richard Goldstone, Robert Wise, Ruth Wedgewood, and M. Cherif Bassiouni, who convinced me that I had something important to say. In addition, at a crucial point, I received significant advice and support from Allen Buchanan, whose generous comments on a late draft of the book have improved it immeasurably.

As the project neared completion, I received an extraordinary opportunity. Kit Wellman invited me to present the book manuscript at a summer workshop held for Atlanta-area philosophers and political theorists. For two extremely intense days, and in a spirit of deep cooperation, eight theorists mulled over the penultimate version of the manuscript and made an enormous number of excellent suggestions and objections. The book could never have gotten into its current form without the collective efforts of this group, whose members included Andrew Altman, William Edmundson, Peter Lindsay, George Rainbolt, Andrew Valls, Kit Wellman, Clark Wolf, and the Washington outsider David Luban. Luban has been especially generous with his sympathetic criticisms.

I have read various versions of all of these chapters at meetings of the American Philosophical Association and American Political Science Association and at conferences in Albuquerque, Amsterdam, Belgrade, Boston, Calgary, Chapel Hill, Cleveland, London, Lund (Sweden), Portland, Washington, DC, and St. Louis University Law School. I wish to thank the organizers of these various conferences for inviting me to present early versions of these chapters. One of the chapters has been translated into Italian and published in *Ars Interpretandi* (an annual journal of legal hermeneutics). Another chapter was published by Wilfred Laurier Press in Canada. One chapter will soon be published in Serbian.

Many, many other people contributed helpful comments on particular chapters. I would especially like to thank the following: Bat-Ami Bar On, Marcia Baron, Alyssa Bernstein, Jovan Bobic, Susan Brison, Matthew Cashen, Frances Foster, Trudy Govier, James Harold, Thomas Hill, Pauline Kleingeld, Aleksandar Jokic, David Lyons, Geoffrey Sayre-McCord, Angelika Means, Lukas Meyer, Christopher Morris, Ian Mueller, Peter Mutharika, James Nickel, Thomas Pogge, Eric Rovie, Mortimer (Tim) Sellars, Wayne Sumner, Roy Tsao, Steve Viner, Jeremy Waldron, and Iris Young.

The editor of Cambridge University Press's Philosophy and Law series, Gerald Postema, read several versions of this book. He has acted in the best traditions of an excellent editor. At an early stage of the book's development, he expressed strong interest and encouragement. At later stages, he insisted that I make the book as good as I possibly could. I will always be in his debt. I am also indebted to Ronald Cohen, whose copyediting greatly enhanced the clarity of the arguments in this book. Nancy Viner provided the index.

Finally, I would like to thank Marilyn Friedman, who discussed most of these chapters over many dinners and who helped me out of many a pickle I had gotten myself into. I dedicate this book to our daughter, Elizabeth, whose own emerging interest in criminal justice, stemming from a deep concern for the victims, kept me honest.

This book is the first volume of a projected multi-volume work on the normative foundations of international criminal law. The next volume will concern war crimes. It is hoped that these volumes will spark the interest of both political philosophers and practitioners of international law.

PART A

UNIVERSAL NORMS AND MORAL MINIMALISM

1

Introduction

Given the inherent costs of criminalization, when a particular legal prohibition oversteps the limit of moral legitimacy, it is itself a serious moral crime.

Joel Feinberg, *Harm to Others*, p. 4

This book provides a philosophical analysis of some of the most difficult issues in international criminal law, most importantly how to justify international interference in one of the traditional prerogatives of a sovereign State – the decisions about whether to engage in criminal punishment of its citizens. International criminal law involves the prosecution of individuals according to international law, often in international tribunals, rather than according to domestic law. The problems of sovereignty that arise are said to be outweighed by the denial of impunity to State leaders and even minor players, who would not normally be prosecuted for serious human rights abuses. The defense of human rights is a powerful weapon used to curtail unbridled State action taken against individuals, thereby promoting global justice. But when we turn to the use of criminal law to protect human rights, we need to focus precisely on what some individuals did to others, and whether those actions met the elements of specific crimes.

Consider the charge of genocide, for example. Genocide is a powerful moral category of rebuke – indeed the most powerfully evocative of all of the current charges in international criminal law. Prosecutions for genocide, especially at the trials in The Hague and Arusha, were very important cultural markers that identified when grave injustice had been committed. But the moral outrage against genocide, despite how much I would otherwise support it, does not easily translate into the specific elements of a crime that must be proven in a court of law. We cannot prosecute on the basis of our moral outrage alone. This is especially true of cases in which a minor player is accused of genocide because his or her acts were part of a larger genocidal campaign, and yet the individual defendant did not personally have the intention to destroy, in whole or in part, an entire group of people.

This was driven home to me as I sat in the gallery of the Yugoslav Tribunal in mid-June of 2001. The prosecution had just completed its case in chief, and one of the judges asked the prosecutor what evidence had specifically been presented that proved the charge of genocide. The judge said that most of the evidence had actually established the elements of persecution, a crime against humanity. The prosecutor responded with a largely moral argument: The defendant had engaged in especially gruesome acts against Muslims, and the world expected that he would be prosecuted on the most serious of the charges – namely, genocide, not merely persecution. I went to lunch with several newspaper reporters who were unanimous in agreeing that the defendant must be convicted of genocide to mark his horrible acts. I disagreed, as did the judges, who dismissed the genocide charge against the defendant for the prosecutor's failure to present a prima facie case establishing the elements of genocide.

This book attempts to provide a broad philosophical defense of such trials in international criminal law. To be defensible, though, international criminal law must move beyond honoring the victims of horrific harms and embrace norms that support an international rule of law. Throughout this book, I argue that victims' rights should not be the overriding concern of international criminal law. If international law is to achieve the respect and fidelity to law that is the hallmark of most domestic law settings, defendants' rights must be given at least as much attention as victims' rights. Philosophically, we are justified in applying universal criminal norms in the international arena only when the scope of international crime is restricted to those crimes and criminals that are truly deserving of international sanctions. We need to pay much more attention than we have to the justification of international prosecutions, especially to the kind of in-principle justification that has been the hallmark of normative jurisprudence and philosophy of law. International moral outrage over atrocities must be tempered with international protection for the rights of defendants, so that the defendants in international criminal trials are not themselves subject to human rights abuse.

In this introductory chapter, I will discuss the idea of sovereignty, which has created such difficulties for discussions of international law, especially international criminal law. By the end of this chapter, I will offer a preliminary solution to the problem of sovereignty that will itself require much more supporting argumentation in later chapters to be fully plausible. The problem for international law is that States are sovereign by virtue of having exclusive legal authority over matters within their borders, whereas international law sweeps across the borders of States. In a world of absolute State sovereignty, international law would have no place. But this would be problematical, since there would then be no way to adjudicate disputes among States, especially those arising when one State's forces cross the borders of another and attempt to subjugate the other State's citizens.

There is a long history of debate about the philosophical and moral justification of international law. There are two main difficulties with justifying international law: one centered on sovereignty, and the other on toleration. First, is it ever justifiable for the international community to violate a State's sovereignty in order to protect that State's own subjects? Second, shouldn't the international community be willing to tolerate wide diversity in the way one State treats its subjects? In what follows, I present a Hobbesian answer to these philosophical problems, showing that Hobbes is not necessarily the great adversary of international law, contrary to what is often claimed by international law scholars today. Indeed, a Hobbesian position, or what I later call a moral minimalist position, can even support the concept of international criminal law. This is because a Hobbesian would be forced to admit that when a State sovereign cannot protect its subjects, that sovereign no longer has the right to exclusive control over the affairs of those subjects, nor a claim for the tolerance of other States. In this chapter, I provide a Hobbesian approach to sovereignty that supports some international criminal prosecutions.

In Section I, I provide a brief account of the types of international crime. In Section II, I provide an argument, largely drawn from the work of Hugo Grotius, as to why sovereignty is important and should be given a contingent moral presumption. In Section III, I discuss the value of sovereignty in more contemporary terms by relating it to the value of tolerance. In Section IV, I turn to the work of Thomas Hobbes in order to give us a more developed understanding of the problem of sovereignty. And in Section V, I turn (perhaps surprisingly) back to Hobbes to give us a solution to the problem of sovereignty. The Hobbesian solution I sketch opens the door to the legitimacy of international criminal trials, although the legitimacy is more limited than many contemporary natural law theorists would like it to be. In Section VI, I give a brief summary of the main arguments advanced in the rest of the book.

I. Identifying International Crimes

Historically, international law was thought to concern the regulations of the interactions of States, which included one State's transgression of the borders of another sovereign State and the mistreatment of that State's civilian citizens. One of the few types of crimes involving individual human persons instead of States were so-called war crimes, crimes committed by soldiers against civilians and prisoners of war. Prosecutions for war crimes effectively involved intervention in the affairs of one State in order to punish the individual human persons as agents of a State for intervening in the affairs of another State. On the analogy of war crimes, other offenses against a State that did not involve a State's acting against another State, but nonetheless involved one State's suffering a harm, such as in piracy cases, were also thought to be subject to international criminal sanctions. Since the Nuremberg Trials, the idea has been recognized, although not systematically defended, that the leader of, or even a minor player within, a State can commit international crimes by the State's abusive treatment of a fellow subject. In this book, I shall mainly focus my attention on crimes of this sort, especially what have come to be called "crimes against humanity," and the crime of genocide, crimes committed by individuals against other individuals that are so egregious as to harm all of humanity and hence to call for international prosecution.

The two most influential listings of international crimes were set out roughly fifty years apart. The 1945 Charter of the Military Tribunal at Nuremberg identified three classes of international crime:

Crimes Against Peace
War Crimes
Crimes Against Humanity[1]

The 1998 Rome Statute of the International Criminal Court (ICC) lists four categories of crime:

The Crime of Genocide
Crimes Against Humanity
War Crimes
The Crime of Aggression[2]

The Nuremberg Charter's "crimes against peace" are pretty much the same as the Rome Statute's "crime of aggression." "Crimes against peace" have never fared well in international law, since it has been so hard to figure out what counts as an *aggressive* war as opposed to a *defensive* war. At Nuremberg, genocide was treated as a crime against humanity, but the Rome Statute singles out genocide as a separate, and the most egregious, crime. Hence, the list of international crimes has been relatively constant over the fifty-year period from Nuremberg to the ICC.

It has been hard to figure out how to put into the dock whole States, which are principally the entities that violate the peace. War crimes and crimes against humanity are the main, although not the only, crimes prosecuted today. Traditionally, war crimes were crimes committed by soldiers of one State's army against the soldiers or the civilian subjects of another State. The classic examples of war crimes are the torture of prisoners of war or the slaughter of non-combatants. "Crimes against humanity" is a category of crime largely invented in the early twentieth century to capture a range of crimes that one person commits against another person, that are directed against a population, and are organized by a State or State-like entity, not necessarily during war.

For justificatory purposes, I will suggest that there are three bases for prosecuting international crimes:

Crimes that will not be prosecuted domestically because of a weak State
Crimes that are committed by the State or with significant State complicity
Crimes that target a whole group, not merely a solitary human person

These justificatory bases ground prosecutions for the main categories of international crime identified at Nuremberg and Rome. I will shortly say something brief to introduce each of these bases of prosecuting international crime. Before beginning that task, let me say something, also introductory, about a different category of crime that I will largely ignore.

There is a wide category of crimes that are amorphous, and are often highly contested.[3] I am thinking of those crimes that have occasionally been prosecuted as international crimes for convenience sake. Included in this category are:

Piracy
Hijacking
Trafficking (in drugs, women, or slaves)
Money-laundering

These crimes do not fit into the standard Nuremberg or Rome categories but have been, or might be, prosecuted because they are crimes that cross State borders[4] in their execution, or occur outside the confines of State borders altogether (such as on the high seas) and have been thought to be best dealt with as international crimes. These crimes are considered international crimes largely as a matter of convenience. It is notoriously hard to justify these crimes as deserving of international prosecution except on pragmatic grounds, and today such crimes are largely left off the list of international crimes.

My aim here is to provide an in-principle, morally minimalist, account of the justification of international prosecutions. I will largely ignore the amorphous category just described, and stick to the two main group-based categories of international crime identified at Rome – crimes against humanity and the crime of genocide – also devoting some time, but considerably less, to war crimes. According to the grouping I proposed earlier, I will not focus on those crimes that are justifiably prosecuted internationally because of a weak or non-existent State. Such prosecutions are not normally seen as controversial, even by those who are generally opposed to international criminal law. Instead, I will focus on those crimes that are deserving of international prosecution because they are directed at a group. These crimes, which are thought to harm humanity in some sense, are certainly the most controversial cases. I will also spend some time discussing crimes that are committed by or with State complicity. Both of the last two justificatory bases of international crime are related to what I will call the international harm principle.

Today, there are two types of crime that might harm humanity. One category is genocide, now treated as the most serious of all international crimes. The other is what is called "crimes against humanity," and includes such things as murder, torture, and rape that are aimed at a certain population and that are widespread or systematic. These crimes will be the primary focus of this book because they seem to be the hardest to justify and yet the crimes most often pointed to today as paradigmatic of international crimes. I will spend some time also discussing the category of war crimes, although mainly in considering what defense to these crimes should be allowed. There is little controversy about how to justify counting war crimes as international crimes, since there is often a literal crossing of borders by members of one State to harm members of another State, the earlier paradigmatic idea of truly "inter" national crimes. The harder thing to justify is crimes that are "intra" national crimes – that is, crimes that are committed by a State against its own subjects or allowed to occur by one subject's assaulting another. These crimes – that is, genocide and crimes against humanity – are especially hard to justify as deserving of international criminal prosecution because they so clearly violate State sovereignty.

International law achieves its first, and perhaps most plausible, justification by acting as a forum for adjudicating disputes arising from one State's crossing of another State's borders. For without such adjudication by peaceful and impartial means, States would be in a state of constant warfare among each other that would resemble Hobbes's "war of all against all." Grotius called this "a common law among nations, which is valid alike for war and in war."[5] Today, international criminal law is often seen as at least as great an assault on State sovereignty as that of outright war, since it involves the prosecution of a State's subjects by a legal authority that sits, in effect, as a higher authority than the State, and thereby seemingly infringes directly on the sovereignty of the State. In the next few sections of this chapter, I will explain the problem of sovereignty and how that problem might be solved so as to allow for prosecutions of international crimes.

II. The Contingent Presumption Favoring Sovereignty

In this section, I will explain why sovereignty should count as a strong presumption that must be rebutted if international law, especially international criminal law, is to make any sense. I will here draw on the ideas of Hugo Grotius, ideas that will also begin to provide us with a way to justify legitimate restrictions on sovereignty if international law is to get off the ground. I draw on the work of Grotius (as well as that of Hobbes in later sections) in order to find inspiration from the first early modern discussions of international law, both because they are still good arguments and because it is important to find the historical roots of our debate that will mainly be located in quite recent literature and that might appear too focused on specific contemporary facts.

State sovereignty is important, and has been seen to be so, largely because there is no world State that can easily protect individuals from the attacks by enemy and competing States. In 1625, Grotius provided a very good definition of sovereignty that also makes reference to some of its initial plausibility:

> That power is called sovereign whose actions are not subject to the legal control of another so that they can be rendered void by the operation of another human will . . . [T]he State which we have defined above as a perfect association, is the common subject of sovereignty.[6]

For Grotius, States are "perfect associations" in that they are grounded in both natural justice and expediency. According to Grotius, "the law of nature has the reinforcement of expediency."[7] States have as their chief aim the offsetting of the natural inclination of humans to seek only after their own advantage. States are created with the aim of "maintenance of the social order."[8] The State is a perfect association in that it meets the needs of humans for peace, and also provides a just basis for the settlement of disputes by instituting systems of law in which disputes are adjudicated by those who are not themselves interested in the results.

Grotius is best known for the way that he links his conception of the law of nature to what he calls "the law of nations." Municipal or domestic law has its origin in the consent of the individuals to be bound, but the bindingness of what we have consented to is itself based in the law of nature, especially in our natural desire for peace and sociability. Similarly, international law is based in the consent of States, but again the bindingness of what States have consented to is based on the branch of the law of nature Grotius calls "the law of nations." Grotius envisions a "great society of states" that is bound by certain laws "between all States."[9] But Grotius is not a dreamer; he realizes that such an international society and its law is largely "without a sanction," and hence significantly different from municipal law. Nonetheless, he argues that a great society of States may be realized when people come to see that the concept of justice that governs *municipal* law also governs *international* law. In both legal settings, humans are bound by their natural desires and by their duties to God.

The obligations that States owe to each other according to the law of nations are most strongly binding in times of war, according to Grotius, especially concerning the enforcement of rights of those "too weak to resist."[10] Natural justice operates in such instances, even when the municipal laws of nations are silenced. The laws of nations are laws of "perpetual validity and suited to all times."[11] Grotius argues that the natural law applied to States is part of what he calls "the natural and unchangeable philosophy of law."[12] Grotius also then goes on to outline a new field of jurisprudence that will govern the rightful bases of nations going to war as well as in waging war. For Grotius, this jurisprudence is premised on a universal base, but such a base, contrary to what is sometimes thought, is itself grounded in the two equally sufficient bases of human's sociable nature and God's divine commands. This dual grounding gives Grotius's views much more contemporary plausibility than earlier natural law views, such as those of Thomas Aquinas.

Grotius, anticipating Hobbes, also gives one of the best explanations for possible limitations on sovereignty:

> The kingdom is forfeited if a king sets out with a truly hostile intent to destroy a whole people ... for the will to govern and the will to destroy cannot coexist in the same person.[13]

Grotius thought that such a condition would rarely arise, at least among kings who are possessed "of their right minds."[14] In any event, sovereignty for Grotius can be alienated when the aim for which that sovereignty was instituted is abrogated.

Drawing on Grotius's remarks, we begin to see why a presumption in favor of sovereignty should exist, at least contingent on there not being a world State, as a means to provide protection and support for individual subjects. Since States are constituted to aim at the social order and to maintain harmonious dealings among the citizens of the State, a kind of moral presumption is given to States: As long as they are conforming to this normative aim, they should not be interfered with by other States. Social stability requires exclusive legal control over a population. Such a presumption is contingent, since it might turn out that a world State might come into being that could better maintain social stability. But until such a time, States are to be given a moral presumption in favor of non-interference, for the sake of their subjects and for the overall peace and harmony of the world. Both justice and expediency require that States be afforded this presumption, but that remains a rebuttable presumption.

One can also begin to see why it would make sense to make the presumption a rebuttable one, since it is certainly possible that a sovereign ruler could attack rather than protect its subjects. It might also turn out that a given sovereign becomes incapable of protecting its subjects, as is increasingly true today in central Africa, especially in the Congo, where all of its neighbors have made incursions across its borders for their own gain. Grotius also said, again anticipating Hobbes, that sovereign rulers can never be so strong that they would not sometimes come to need the help of other States: "[T]here is no state so powerful that it may not sometime need the help of others outside itself, either for purposes of trade, or even to ward off the forces of many sovereign nations united against it."[15]

Contemporary writings on this topic often follow in a similar vein. One of the most common arguments in favor of sovereignty, or what some call intrastate autonomy, is that States do a reasonably good job of protecting the well-being and freedom of individual subjects. This argument is obviously based largely on an empirical claim that could be rebutted. I will not attempt to defend this view, but in light of my moral minimalism that seeks the least controversial assumptions, I will simply assume that there is quite a bit of empirical support for thinking that many, if not most, States do a reasonable job of protecting the well-being and freedom of their subjects.

There is another, much more recent, argument that I wish to mention as well. Allen Buchanan argues that giving a kind of presumption to State sovereignty can also be defended by reference to group rights. Individual humans have chosen to associate together, or to remain associated together, in distinct nation-states. We owe a certain moral presumption to States out of respect for the rights of group self-governance that is embodied in respecting State sovereignty.[16] Of course, this is also a rebuttable presumption in that it can turn out not to be true that individuals or groups have chosen, or would choose, to form just the States that currently exist. But if we ignore, or violate, the sovereignty of States, we also risk violating the right of individuals and groups to decide what associations they wish to form, where one of the most important characteristics of such associations is that criminal prosecution and punishment be under the control of these associations, not under some foreign control.

So we begin with a general presumption in favor of sovereignty that must be rebutted if international law, especially international criminal law, is to be justifiable. For international law seems most especially to be concerned with the legality of what the individual agents and subjects of sovereign States do. And yet attempts to assign legality or illegality to what these individuals do is itself to subject them "to the legal control of another," and thereby to violate State sovereignty, at least according to Grotius's reasonable-sounding definition of sovereignty. But as we will see later in this chapter, there is also a plausible resolution of the problem of sovereignty for international criminal law, a solution that we have already seen anticipated by Grotius's remarks concerning those clear cases in which a State indicates that it will not protect the well-being of a group of subjects.

III. Sovereignty and Toleration

Other than a concern about whether defendants will be treated well, there are two main reasons why one might be opposed to trials by international tribunals. First, one might say that such trials violate State sovereignty in that they violate the right of a State to the exclusive adjudication of matters that affect only its own citizens and that take place within its borders. Second, one might say that such trials fail to display tolerance toward the diverse practices of States and their members. These reasons are related in that tolerance is often the value appealed to when defending State sovereignty. In addition, tolerance and sovereignty are often both justified by reference to the value of reasonable restraint. Concern for the liberty of States and their subjects leads to the conclusion that one should not interfere unduly, if at all, in the internal affairs of a sovereign State. Such concern is said to lead us to tolerate societal differences both in setting moral standards and in making and enforcing laws.

I will defend a moral minimalist position in international law where the limit of toleration and sovereignty is reached when the security of a State's subjects is jeopardized. Support for the values of tolerance and sovereignty is premised on the willingness and ability of a State to protect its subjects, either by not attacking them or by not allowing them to be attacked. If a society or a State fails to secure the safety of its members, then tolerance and sovereignty have reached their limit, and may justifiably be infringed. The limit has been reached practically in the case in which the State can no longer protect its subjects – for then the State is simply no longer sovereign over its people. International tribunals take the place of domestic tribunals that cannot be maintained by the weakened State. The limit has been reached normatively when a State can, but chooses not to, protect its subjects when it should. International tribunals are instituted because it is thought that the State will not conduct a fair trial since it was complicit in the harms being prosecuted, or when the interests of humanity will not be served. This position is itself limited in that not just any injustice or violation of human rights will warrant the claim that a State has no right to resist international intervention. I will spend considerable time later arguing that only the violation of basic human rights to security and subsistence will warrant the violation of State sovereignty and the principle of toleration, as well as warrant international criminal prosecutions. In Chapter 4, I refine this point by defending what I will call the "security principle." In addition, I will argue that there must also be some sort of harm to the international community, a violation of what I will call the "international harm" principle, for international tribunals to be fully justified, a position I defend in Chapter 5.

Unlike recent philosophical discussions of international law and politics, my focus will be on the justification of an international tribunal that prosecutes individuals for crimes, rather than a discussion of what would justify one State's directly intruding into another State.[17] In addition, unlike John Rawls, in his book *The Law of Peoples*,[18] I will not primarily be concerned with peoples and types of society, but will rather try to provide an argument for limitations on State sovereignty that is independent of type of society and that focuses on individual persons rather than nations or peoples. The key question for the justification of international criminal law is how to justify prosecutions before international tribunals of individuals who will not be effectively or fairly prosecuted by their home States. This will involve enforcing norms that are non-consensual. The enforcement of non-consensual norms is key because unlike other aspects of international law, international criminal law cannot operate effectively if it must wait for the consent of States to its prosecutions. It must overcome the problem of sovereignty as well as the problem of toleration.

John Rawls provides us with a good place to begin when he says that toleration involves the core idea of refraining "from exercising political sanctions . . . to make people change its way."[19] In this sense, toleration protects a realm of autonomous action on the part of peoples, and calls for civility and restraint, especially concerning the practices of people who are not like us. One of the chief things liberals should want to avoid is the charge of moral or political imperialism. Liberals especially need to avoid the appearance of trying to foist their values on the rest of the world. Toleration is a virtue that must be protected to make the liberal project legitimate. As a result of taking toleration seriously, Rawls says, we need to limit the domain of rights abuses that will warrant international intervention into the affairs of a State.

For Rawls, there are limits to the toleration of people even in liberal societies. Human rights, at least those that Rawls regards as properly human rights rather than merely rights more generally conceived, set the limits of toleration. If a State violates human rights, then other States are not required to display toleration toward that State. For Rawls, among the most basic of human rights are the rights to subsistence and security, including the security of property.[20] Rawls unfortunately says very little about why the violations of these rights are the ones that might subject a State "to forceful sanctions and even to intervention."[21] While my own list of basic human rights is narrower than Rawls's, especially concerning economic rights that are not necessary for subsistence, my view on this point is similar to his. In the next section, I will present my own argument, heavily influenced by Hobbes, in favor of seeing these human rights as providing a basis for justified interference with the sovereign affairs of a State, and for thinking that other forms of human rights abuse will generally not be enough to make it true that a State has no right to prevent the "crossing of its borders" that international tribunals might call for.

Before proceeding to my solution to the problem of sovereignty, I wish to explore the relationship between sovereignty and toleration. The problem of toleration is that in a pluralistic world, there seems to be a premium on letting individual societies establish their own moral or legal codes, such that toleration is seen as a kind of local sovereignty, even approaching the limit as to where an individual person's peculiar moral beliefs need to be tolerated as if that person were fully sovereign over his or her own life. John Stuart Mill talks of sovereignty this way when he says:

In the part which merely concerns himself, his independence is, of right, absolute. Over himself, over his own body and mind, the individual is sovereign.[22]

But in this limiting case, we can also begin to see a way out of the predicament, since surely we do not think that we need to tolerate all forms of oddness in others, especially when their oddness risks harm to us – the limit of my right wildly to swing my arm is when it hits your nose. Let us explore the parallels between the limits on sovereignty and the limits on toleration.

To see the parallel concerns of toleration and sovereignty, one need only look at two dimensions of toleration. Consider the first: that a group be left alone to pursue autonomously its own conception of the good. Michael Walzer notes that multinational empires – Persia, Egypt, and Rome, for instance – were the first to discuss toleration. "The various groups are constituted as autonomous or semi-autonomous communities that are political or legal as well as cultural or religious in character, and that rule themselves across a considerable range of activities. The groups have no choice but to coexist with each other."[23] Groups may be forced to tolerate each other in case that is what is necessary for a multinational state to exist. Here we see that tolerating a group is co-extensive with granting that group a kind of autonomy or sovereignty over its own affairs. As Walzer says, this is not so much a matter of fairness as of survival in a deeply divided multinational state.[24]

Another dimension of toleration is that people not maintain an attitude of censure and anger toward one another. Simon Blackburn illustrates this when he says: "A moralistic society is one in which a large variety of things arouse anger and censure of others; a tolerant or tranquil society is one in which only certain behavior does so."[25] Of course, this is meant to be a general comment, and not one that rules out all forms of censure and anger. Rather it is only that in a tolerant society, the number of things that will arouse censure and anger are specific and small in number. Sovereignty also is made more secure by restricting the domain over which people consider themselves entitled to feel aggrieved. The key consideration will be to find a reasonable limit to toleration and to sovereignty, beyond which it is appropriate to display anger and censure, without undermining the general sense of tolerance.

IV. Hobbes and the Pursuit of Security

In this section, I suggest that Thomas Hobbes's ideas can supply us with some of the support for the idea that toleration and sovereignty can be legitimately abrogated when a person's security is jeopardized. Many theorists would consider such a proposal odd since Hobbes is normally portrayed as the great defender of the position that moral laws are not laws properly so called, and "states could be bound by no higher law."[26] This view is based on Hobbes's claim that the relationship among States in international affairs is like the relationship among people in the state of nature, where the natural human condition can be described as the "war of every man against every man."[27] As Hobbes says at the end of Chapter 30 of *Leviathan*:

The Law of Nations and the Law of Nature, is the same thing. And every Sovereign hath the same Right, in procuring the safety of his People, that any particular man can have, in procuring his own safety.[28]

It is thus contended that Hobbes is the great defender of the use of violence, especially in situations where there is no sovereign, and most especially in the relations between States. It is often forgotten, though, that in the very paragraph where Hobbes speaks of the war that exists in any state of nature, he also declares that the first branch of the "first, and fundamental law of nature" is "to *seek peace and follow it.*"[29] The more Hobbesian-sounding law of nature, "by all means we can, defend ourselves," is said to be only the second branch of the first law of nature.[30] Hobbes has been often unfairly characterized as the defender of the right of States to use any means, including violence, in their relations with one another and with their own subjects. This is because in the state of nature, while individual persons have the right to do everything, this is not a reasonable position in which to remain.[31]

Hobbes is also often portrayed as the main critic of a strong domain of international law. This is because Hobbes seemingly argues that it is irrational for any person to initiate trust in others to sustain peace unless that person has a guarantee that others will also act peacefully. Such a guarantee comes from having a sovereign power that keeps all subjects in awe by instilling fear into their hearts. In international relations, no such sovereign exists, and so no guarantee of others' peacefulness exists. Hence, there seems to be no reason for States to act peacefully. But Hobbes's argument is more subtle than this. In the state of nature, all people are roughly equal. Even the strongest must sleep, and then even the weakest can drive a knife into the back of the strongest. All people fear this loss of life, and any sign of weakness in the state of nature will risk such a loss of life. If two people make an agreement to trust each other, and not to use violence against the other, then each person renders himself or herself vulnerable to the other. Yet, by rendering oneself vulnerable, one risks that loss of life that is most feared. Hobbes's position takes on a subtlety, though, when he admits that it is just this sense of trust that is absolutely crucial for cooperation and commerce, and that trust is also crucial for overcoming the miserable conditions of the state of nature. For this reason, while it is always unreasonable to be a first performer of the social covenant, it is also unreasonable not to want to join cooperative associations that could protect us.[32]

It seems reasonable to argue that if Hobbes rejects the desirability of first performance to the social contract, he should also be opposed to the attitudes of cooperation and trust that are essential to an international rule of law. Yet, in Chapter 14 of *Leviathan*, Hobbes indicates that the first performance of contracts is only conditionally irrational in the state of nature – that is, only when cooperation jeopardizes self-defense.[33] But Hobbes also counsels that we should always pursue peace over war and that it is reasonable to go to great lengths to create a situation in which people feel bound to keep their promises and contracts. Indeed, Hobbes defines the law of nature as a dictate of right reason that counsels against the use of force and violence.[34] Civil society, along with the domestic rule of law, is created so as to provide just the sort of mutual enforcement of agreements that will make first performance reasonable.

The first performer is faced with a dilemma. She desperately wants the commerce and cooperation of her fellows, and yet she also fears that they will try to overwhelm her at the first sign of weakness on her part. This first performer is driven by self-interest, but self-interest pulls in two opposing directions. The state of nature, because of everyone's right to use violence, is "solitary, poor, nasty, brutish, and short,"[35] hardly the position that anyone would prefer from the standpoint of self-interest. Yet, in order to get out of the state of nature, she needs to give a sign that she is trustworthy and not likely to engage in violence against her fellows. But, as soon as she would give such signs of cooperativeness in order to entice others into cooperation with her, she risks a great loss. Any showing of cooperation on her part risks an act of violence, resulting in loss of liberty or even loss of life, at the hands of others who will see her weakness as a basis for their own gains. Hence, the first performer is paralyzed – pulled in different directions by two equally strong motivations, both connected to self-interest.

We can view Hobbes's parable about the first performer in the state of nature as a model for States that resist forming agreements in international law that would limit their sovereignty, or that would not recognize the right of international criminal tribunals. International civil society, with its corresponding international rule of law, seems initially just as fraught with insoluble problems of first performance as that in the state of nature. As the events of September 11 2001 have shown, even the most powerful member of the world community, the United States, can be harmed by one of the weakest members, a small band of Muslim militants. When the United States slept, the weak were able to drive a knife into its back. The United States would clearly gain from being a party to a multilateral treaty that would force its enemies to restrain themselves. Yet, the United States continued to worry that it would so weaken itself by agreeing to the terms of the Rome Treaty (establishing the ICC) that it would not be able to defend its subjects against criminal sentences issued by the ICC. The United States was thus paralyzed by the hope of world peace and the fear that joining an international organization, the ICC, would open itself up to harm by those who seek to exploit the weakness that comes from displaying a cooperative spirit.

A Hobbesian position on international relations sets the stage for seeing what would make it rational for the United States, or other States, to join the treaty creating the ICC. After all, in the original state of nature scenario, people do find their way out of the state of nature by establishing organizations and enforcement mechanisms that will diminish the likelihood that displays of cooperativeness will result in harm to the cooperators. Hobbes is often interpreted as holding that only a single monarch can supply the needed enforcement mechanism. But this is an oversimplification of his view that misses his main point. In the frontispiece of *Leviathan*, Hobbes portrays the sovereign as a king but only in outline, filled in by the individual people who have given their consent to the social contract. Indeed, at the beginning of Chapter 18 of *Leviathan*, Hobbes says that the "sovereign power is conferred by the consent of the people assembled."[36] These people are the ones who will stand behind any individual king or other leader, and it is their might, not that of the king, that is crucial for peace to be secured, since the king is the stand-in for the collective will of the people.

In contemporary international law, enforcement mechanisms do not necessarily depend on there being a world "king" or president. We do not need a world monarch or other world sovereign, but only sufficient agreement among the States to provide enforcement for the rulings of such international organizations as the ICC. Joining the ICC is only problematical for the United States if there is no good enforcement mechanism in place. If the ICC has teeth, then joining it is a reasonable strategy even for, and indeed especially for, States such as the United States that fear that other States will try to take advantage of them. For the best strategy to gain peace for oneself is to try to bind others not to be aggressors; but such binding almost always means also binding oneself. This is just what the multilateral Rome treaty that set up the ICC has attempted to do.

A Hobbesian position on international law would support a systematic set of laws of nature that can be derived from the two-pronged principle: Seek peace where you can, and otherwise be ready to resort to war. What is lacking in Hobbes's account, from a contemporary perspective, is a strong defense for human rights. Indeed, Hobbes famously argues that in the state of nature, "every man has a Right to every thing; even to one another's body. And therefore, so long as this natural Right of every man to every thing prevails, there can be no security to any man (how strong or wise soever he be) . . ."[37] Indeed, Hobbes argues that the laws of nature are mere theorems for what "conduceth to the conservation and defense of themselves."[38] For this reason, natural laws are not laws properly so-called: they are binding "*in foro interno*," not "*in foro externo*."[39]

Nonetheless, for Hobbesians, natural laws are no less binding in terms of their reasonable restraint on violent action because of their "*in foro interno*" status. These secular natural laws bind in the conscience, and this is a true bindingness.[40] But they do not bind as laws often do – that is, they do not bind because of the fear of punishment at the hands of the law-givers. Fear of the person who could punish creates a bindingness that is externally motivated. Yet the internally motivated bindingness of conscience, while weaker than such things as fear, is still a motivation for most people. And a Hobbesian can follow Hobbes in arguing that it is reasonable for humans to place restraints on what they can bargain away: "[T]here be some rights that no man can be understood by any words, or other signes, to have abandoned or transferred . . ."[41]

Because Hobbes did not clearly recognize a category of moral rights that could be used to ground fundamental legal norms, and because he did not think that the laws of nature were laws properly so-called, he is normally seen as the first strict legal positivist rather than as a defender of natural law theory. But it seems to me that the Hobbesian, although non-standard Hobbesian, position on international relations I have been sketching blurs the distinction between *positivist* and *natural law* theories in significant ways and sets the stage for a moral minimalism that lets in a minimal conception of natural law.[42] For while the laws of nature only bind in the conscience, they do still bind, and can form the basis for restraint of violence, even in the international arena. A secularized and minimalist natural-law theory is one that derives constraints on the use of violence from principles of human psychology and morality.

V. Solving the Problem of Sovereignty

In this section, I will say more about the problem of sovereignty, a problem that has greatly vexed theorists of international law for centuries, and that has posed the major impediment to the institutionalization of international law, especially at the criminal level. Writing in the early nineteenth century, John Austin had claimed that law was simply what the sovereign commanded it to be, and where there was no domestic sovereign, there were no domestic legally binding norms.[43] Similarly, since there was no international sovereign, there were no binding international legal norms. Universal international norms would, at best, be moral norms with no legal legitimacy. Since Austin's time, it has become common to refer to this problem as the "problem of sovereignty." It is one of the most obvious objections that can be made to the very idea of international law – namely, that there is no law-giver in the international arena, and hence no law properly so-called.

I want to consider two responses to Austin's famous argument against international law. One response to his challenge is an argument by analogy, commonly heard today by international lawyers, but which unfortunately does not succeed. There are a large number of international treaties and a large number of international customs that States adhere to. States behave toward these "legal" norms in roughly the same way that individual humans behave toward legal norms in a domestic setting. Hence, here is the argument for international law from analogy – namely, if it looks like a law and everyone behaves as if it is a law, then it is a law. Since States and State leaders behave as if they are bound by international laws, then regardless of what these norms are called, they are international laws.

An obvious objection to this view is that even the routine adherence to norms of international law is not definitive of whether they are laws properly so-called. It is not enough that humans routinely behave in certain patterns for their behavior to be governed by law. For their routine behavior may be governed by habit and not at all consciously governed by laws. And if it is not based on habit, then the routine nature of the behavior has no long-lasting status that could ground a belief in the bindingness of international law. Felt bindingness is about all that one can hope for in the domain of international law since there is no international lawmaker. But this will not support a claim that international law is law properly so-called. The problem of sovereignty cannot be solved by reference to behavior alone. It is not sufficient merely to point out that the behavior of States and State leaders, as well as international lawyers, is of the sort that is normally explained by reference to law. It may indeed quack like a duck, but in fact it may be something else, perhaps a goose; it may look just like law, but it may be something else, perhaps only a moral or customary norm. In Chapters 2 and 3 we will see that we need some other argument in order to establish the principle that international law really is law, given that there is no international sovereign.

Human rights theorists provide us with the key insight that in order for there to be any hope of world peace, there must be what Grotius called a "law of nations." In addition, the vulnerable deserve, as a matter of justice, to have their rights protected from offending States. These two important claims help us see the need for some form of international law. A Hobbesian perspective then provides us with two other components. It is always reasonable for a State to be motivated by the desire for peace. And law, properly so-called, occurs where there are sanctions sufficient for people to respect and to fear the consequences of breaking the law. International law makes sense both conceptually and practically on this revised Hobbesian position, but only in a world where States recognize that cooperation and peace are to be prized above all else, and where enforcement mechanisms are reliable and fair. Obviously, at certain points in history, international law will flourish, and at other times it will have to go underground, as a practical matter. But conceptually, this revised Hobbesian position is that the so-called problem of sovereignty is not insoluble: States can recognize that it is worthwhile, especially for their own self-defense, to restrain themselves in order to achieve peace and cooperation. And justice will also be sought in such an order since it, according to Hobbes, is itself necessary for the establishment of "mine and thine," thereby limiting what one person will feel entitled to do to other persons.

The problem of sovereignty can be solved insofar as it is indeed reasonable to see peace as desirable and insofar as people can then meld their wills into a force that will promote and protect the peace. Multilateral agreements about such things as international criminal law may be more than merely a replacement for sovereignty. Hobbes suggests – by the image of people that filled the outline of the monarch in the frontispiece to *Leviathan* – that the will of the people can substantively create a sovereign. If they all give to another person or entity the power to enforce law, then there is indeed a form of sovereignty. This may not be the kind of full-blown sovereignty of Jean Bodin – namely, where there is no other competing or superior power. And it is also obviously not yet a world State or even a world governmental structure. It can be minimally rather like a police force that is popularly accepted, where the populace is the community of States. But this is still a form of sovereignty in the sense of an enforcement mechanism for the law.

International sovereignty need not be equated with a world government. The agreement to promote and protect peace may constitute the loosest of federations among the States of the world. Indeed, as M. Cherif Bassiouni and Edward Wise[44] have suggested, it need only be an agreement to prosecute, or extradite to a State that will prosecute, those individuals who have violated international law. A very loose federation is just what we have when there is consensus in favor of the Rome Treaty creating the ICC. An agreement to prosecute or extradite is different from an agreement on what norms are binding in the international arena. While, especially, universal international norms need not be based on agreement, the establishment of sovereignty, or a replacement for it, requires a fair degree of popular support. A loose federation may provide enough sovereignty for an international court's opinions to constitute binding international law, at least in the Hobbesian sense that violations of the norm will indeed be sanctioned.

There remains the problem of whether international law is law properly so-called. There are various kinds of things that are called law: individual laws, sets of laws, legal systems, and so on. Some will argue that law properly so-called is one that is part of a system of law. But others are willing to recognize law, even properly so-called, that is merely part of a set of laws. I here follow H. L. A. Hart, as I indicate in the next chapter, in distinguishing between a set and a system of law in terms of whether there is a rule of recognition. In federations, there are various levels of law, with many of the levels not being based on commands issued by a proper sovereign. Things have gotten more complicated since the time when Hobbes first discussed these issues, but the changes can be accommodated by the idea that when people are sufficiently motivated to seek peace, they will find forms of international law that facilitate cooperation and deter violence.

So we have come to the point of seeing how there might be valid, binding law without full-blown sovereignty. In this context, think of the Yugoslav Tribunal, sitting in The Hague, as a pocket of international criminal law. The court was established by a vote of the Security Council of the United Nations. It relies on the good will of member States for extraditions to be enforced. But as long as the States continue to support its efforts, then it acts like a proper court, applying law properly so-called. One does not need to support a social contract theory in order to see how the Yugoslav Tribunal has succeeded in applying law, perhaps even law properly so-called. One only need see that there can be pockets of sovereignty that arise whenever there is an enforcement mechanism that works in conjunction with a set of rules.

VI. Summary of the Arguments of the Book

In the final paragraphs of this Introduction, I will provide the reader with a sense of the overarching argument of the book. The main focus of the book is on the moral, legal, and political questions that arise when individuals who commit collective crimes, such as crimes against humanity, are held accountable by international criminal tribunals. These tribunals offer a challenge to the sovereignty of States, which had previously had exclusive jurisdiction over the putative criminal conduct of their individual members. Because of the vast diversity of types of crime, rules of evidence, and standards of proof, the question is raised as to whether there is any common global ground for identifying and prosecuting truly "international" crimes.

Part A takes up the challenge of providing an understanding of international crime that is not merely what most States at a given time have agreed, by treaty, to call international crimes. In Chapters 2 and 3, I continue the task, begun in Chapter 1, of arguing that there are some norms that cross borders and achieve universal binding force. A Hobbesian, or moral minimalist, position that is between legal positivism and robust natural law theory is articulated and defended. Even given my moral minimalism, certain norms are *jus cogens* – that is, norms with universally binding force, the violation of which can be the basis of international prosecutions. I also argue that such norms cannot be grounded in consensually based custom. Custom, even when followed by nearly all States, merely provides an indication of which norms are likely to be universally binding. Custom standing alone does not provide a justification of these norms. Rather, universally binding norms can be justified only by normative philosophical arguments.

Part B identifies and defends several principles of international criminal law. In Chapters 4, 5, and 6, I provide the normative philosophical basis of universal norms of international law by reference to two principles. I argue for the security principle, which holds that certain human rights abuses – namely, the assaults on physical security and subsistence perpetrated by a State against its own citizens or allowed to occur by the State – can deprive a State of its right to prevent an international body from "crossing its borders" to protect the victims or to remedy their harms. I also argue for the international harm principle that holds that group-based harms are normally necessary to justify truly "international" prosecutions. International prosecutions for both war crimes and crimes against humanity are increasingly defended by reference to human rights, a strategy I follow myself. But I also argue that only human rights abuses that are sufficiently serious can be prosecuted by international tribunals because of a concern for the rights of the defendants. In this way, I defend another kind of minimalism concerning which rights are properly the subject of international law. The security principle limits State sovereignty, whereas the international harm principle delineates a type of crime that can legitimately be prosecuted by international as opposed to domestic tribunals.

Part C turns to institutional arrangements for prosecuting the group-based crimes that I argue are definitive of international criminal law. In Chapters 7, 8, and 9, I argue that when minor players are prosecuted for collective crimes, there must be some explicit link between what the individual intentionally did and the international aspect of the crime. I consider three important international defendants: Dusko Tadic, Augusto Pinochet, and Adolf Eichmann. I defend the view that discriminatory intent must be proven for minor players to be justifiably convicted of these crimes – it is not enough that the minor players knew that their acts formed a part of a larger plan of ethnic violence, for instance. When the leaders of States are prosecuted, it is easier to show the connection between their acts and the group-based harms, because of a revised understanding of command responsibility as a form of collective responsibility that I defend. But intent is still key.

Part D looks at defenses as well as alternatives to international criminal prosecutions. In Chapters 10 through 13, I consider both substantive and procedural defenses that can be raised in such criminal proceedings, and I also consider alternatives to international trials, such as amnesty and truth and reconciliation programs. I argue that the "superior orders" defense is more problematical than normally thought, but that some of the problems with this defense can be overcome by reference to a revised understanding of the defense of duress. In addition, I argue that respect for the international rule of law means that the procedural defenses of retroactivity, selective prosecution, and lack of proportionality of punishment also provide a much more serious challenge to international tribunals than is normally thought. In addition, I argue that, in some cases, trials are not the only possible remedies for group-based harms. Other reconciliatory strategies will provide what victims are owed, and also sometimes better exemplify the principle of equity that is crucial, especially for crimes that involve large segments of the population as both victims and perpetrators. Nonetheless, I continue to maintain that international criminal tribunals can be justified in certain cases.

Throughout this book, I argue that international prosecutions for crimes against humanity, genocide, and war crimes can be philosophically justified. For this justification to succeed, a much clearer idea of the nature of international crime needs to be articulated than has so far occurred in contemporary debates. In addition, as in debates about domestic criminal law, we need to move beyond the simple claim that a crime is merely an act that a society has agreed to call a crime. Especially for international punishment to be justified, there needs to be some coherent basis for thinking that certain acts are deserving of international punishment. I have provided such grounding by reference to the security principle, the international harm principle, *jus cogens* norms, and the international rule of law. Other bases of justification might be possible. What is needed is a vigorous debate about the foundations of international criminal law. I hope that this book, at the very least, stimulates that debate.

The discussions in the following chapters are a mixture of philosophical analysis and assessment of often very current developments in international criminal law, with the most detailed discussion given to the first few cases to be decided by the International Criminal Tribunal for the Former Yugoslavia (ICTY), and to the debates concerning the formation of the permanent International Criminal Court (ICC). In this respect, the book plows new ground in trying to provide the beginnings of a conceptual and normative basis for the relatively new field of international criminal law.

2

Jus Cogens Norms

When an international tribunal is set up to address mass murder or ethnic cleansing perpetrated by members of a State against fellow members of the same State, a relatively new form of international law is put on the table. This is the most controversial forum for international law. It is the most controversial because it implies that there are international normative standards that govern how States act within their own borders and toward their own subjects. Such standards imply that there are norms that hold true for all States, perhaps at all times. If the standards in international law are merely what States agree about, then all a State has to do to get its own genocidal practices taken out of the international law domain is to declare that this State does not agree to be bound to a normative standard that proscribes genocide, in a similar way that a rapist could avoid prosecution simply by denying the jurisdiction of the court. International prosecutions often occur on the basis of what is called "universal jurisdiction" – that is, on the basis of norms that hold for all States regardless of where they or their subjects act, yet it is often unclear what the basis of this universal jurisdiction is.

In this chapter, I argue that there are some principles that transcend national borders and achieve universal binding force. In international law, some crimes so clearly harm the international community that they must be proscribed in all societies.[1] Such crimes are often said to violate *jus cogens* norms, norms that can be clearly known and understood by all as universally binding.[2] One of the main justifications for prosecuting war crimes, crimes against humanity, or genocide is that they violate these *jus cogens* norms. I take up the difficult task of showing how even a moral minimalist could admit the existence of *jus cogens* norms, and hence to recognize a beginning basis for international law. My argument in this chapter is initially drawn in prudential, rather than explicitly moral, terms, although I will begin to sketch a minimal moral basis for such universal norms. In this sense, I will continue to follow Hobbes in providing a basis for international criminal law.

Jus cogens norms were first identified in the international law of treaties. The Vienna Convention on the Law of Treaties said that certain treaties should not be respected since these treaties violated "peremptory norms of general international law." The Vienna Convention then said that "a peremptory norm of general international law is a norm accepted and recognized by the international community of States as a whole as a norm from which no derogation is permitted..."[3] A peremptory rule is normally defined as "an absolute rule; a rule without any condition or alternative of showing cause."[4] While *jus cogens* norms are somewhat controversial, I will assume that they are norms that have universal scope, or, as I will often say, *jus cogens* norms are universal norms that ground "universal jurisdiction" in international law.[5]

Jus cogens norms – literally the laws or norms that are known and binding throughout humanity – form the clearest basis for identifying distinctly international crimes as violations of international law. These norms are often said to involve "principles which are recognized by civilized nations as binding on states, even without any" express obligation based on convention or treaty.[6] *Jus cogens* norms are peremptory, and give rise to obligations *erga omnes*, obligations that extend to all people.[7] The idea that there are *jus cogens* norms is unique to the twentieth century, but its roots go back at least to the time of Grotius,[8] and are also based in several quite different philosophical traditions.

In this chapter, I show that a philosophical view, which I call "moral minimalism," can be a justificatory basis for certain prosecutions in international criminal law. This view holds that there is a basic minimum of individual rights that States must protect if their subjects are to owe the State obedience to law. The general defense of *jus cogens* norms is also often drawn in more than minimalist natural law terms. I argue against an expansion of the domain of *jus cogens* norms to include nearly all human rights abuses, a proposal that has been supported by certain natural law theorists. While I provide reasons to reject such an expansion, I do nonetheless argue that *jus cogens* norms should be the principal basis for the justification of international prosecutions for genocide and crimes against humanity. In Chapters 4 and 5, I provide a relatively new way to justify *jus cogens* norms of international criminal law, by reference to a group-based international harm principle linked to the principle of security. Chapter 2 sets the stage for that substantive argument. Chapter 3 refutes the main alternative view in international law – namely, that customary norms can ground international criminal law.

In the first section of the chapter, I survey some of the most important documents on *jus cogens* norms to see what sort of theoretical position is needed to justify *jus cogens* norms in international law. In the second section, I consider two twentieth-century thinkers – one who provides key components of a foundation for *jus cogens* norms, and the other who provides explicit support for such norms while remaining wedded to the legal positivist tradition. In the third section, I sketch my own version of a moral minimalist, or Hobbesian, position that can provide a foundation for *jus cogens* norms. In the fourth section, I examine the contemporary natural law perspective on *jus cogens* norms, as expressed most forcefully by Justice Robert Jackson at the Nuremberg Trials. I then consider some serious conceptual challenges to this view that have been articulated by Third-World and Socialist theorists. I consider this anti-colonialist approach in some detail, and then employ it to offer some cautionary notes about the way the new natural law theory is being used to support *jus cogens* norms. I set the stage here for a positive defense of *jus cogens* norms, and then rely on the argument in Chapter 3 to undermine the chief rival view. Throughout, I stress the importance of seeing some norms as universally binding. When States or their citizens violate such norms, this will provide an initial reason for why international tribunals – for the prosecution of crimes against humanity, for instance – might be justified.

I. Universal Norms in an International Setting

A turning point in the international conceptualization of *jus cogens* norms occurred in the 1969 Vienna Convention on the Law of Treaties. There it was acknowledged that the right of States to disregard unconscionable contracts was a right that was largely non-consensual – that is, not modifiable even by the consent of the States. Here is what is said in Article 53 of the Vienna Convention:

A treaty is void if at the time of its conclusion it conflicts with a peremptory norm of general international law. For the purposes of the present Convention, a peremptory norm of general international law is a norm accepted and recognized by the international community of States as a whole as a norm from which no derogation is permitted and which can be modified only by a subsequent norm of general international law having the same character.[9]

The Vienna Convention here allows States to disregard their own properly executed treaties, if conforming to the treaty would violate fundamental norms, without waiting for the consent of the other parties to the treaty.

Various minor conceptual puzzles occur in this, by now famous, defining moment for the idea of *jus cogens* norms. For example, what is meant by a "subsequent norm"? Is it a norm that has been recognized later in time than the recognition of the norm that is now being modified? If so, is it contemplated here that the norms are only prima facie binding, where norms of later recognition can override? Yet the use of the term "no derogation" seems to imply that these norms are not prima facie but rather absolute expressions of duties and rights. Perhaps the norms are absolute and cannot be overruled, but they can be modified nonetheless. Also, what is the source of general international law? Can it be made by treaty, such as the Vienna Convention itself? If so, then why not call these norms *consensual* rather than *non-consensual*?

This last puzzle points to a major conceptual problem. The peremptory norms, which are called *jus cogens* norms, are themselves often said to be based on the acceptance and recognition of the international community. "Acceptance" introduces an element of consent into norms that conceptually are supposed to be non-consensual. This is one of the most important conceptual problems with the idea of *jus cogens* norms, and that will spur our attempts to provide a coherent and systematic approach to the conceptualization of *jus cogens* norms in later sections of this chapter. It will be contended that acceptance cannot ground what end up being universal norms. Only non-consensual principles can ground universal principles of the sort envisioned by the Vienna Convention drafters. I will return to this issue in Chapter 3, where I consider the possible customary basis for *jus cogens* norms.

To get a better sense of what is at issue, let us turn very briefly to the Barcelona Traction case.[10] In this 1970 case, the International Court of Justice (ICJ) recognized the central issue at stake in disputes involving *jus cogens* norms.[11] The case concerned Spain's nationalization of a Canadian corporation whose stockholders were primarily of Belgian nationality. The question arose as to whether Spain owed compensation to the Belgian nationals. To answer this question, the court first held that "[w]hen a state admits into its territory foreign investment . . . [it] assumes obligations concerning the treatment to be afforded them."[12] The obvious question was: What kind of obligation does the State have? The answer given by the court, while not completely clear, seemed to point to non-consensual obligations that were presumed whenever certain kinds of situations arose.

In Barcelona Traction, the ICJ distinguished between two kinds of obligation. The first kind concerned "obligations of a State towards the international community," whereas the second kind involved "those arising vis-à-vis another State in the field of diplomatic protection."[13] The claims of the Belgian nationals, expressed by the government of Belgium, were held to be at most only of the second kind – that is, claims based on whatever terms had been agreed to between the respective States, Belgium and Spain. But since there was no treaty on this matter between the two States, Belgium had no legal basis for its demand to be compensated. Thus the Belgian nationals were owed nothing by the Spanish government because there was no consensual diplomatic arrangement between these parties.

The obligations of the first kind – those held not to apply even potentially to the Belgian nationals – are here called "obligations *erga omnes*." According to the court,

[s]uch obligations derive, for example, in contemporary international law, from the outlawing of acts of aggression, and of genocide, as also from the principles and rules concerning the basic rights of the human person, including protection from slavery and racial discrimination. Some of the corresponding rights of protection have entered into

the body of general international law . . . others are conferred by international instruments of a universal or quasi-universal character.[14]

Notice that some of these obligations are not described as based on the consent of the parties. Rather these obligations, which roughly correspond to the *jus cogens* norms addressed earlier, are based on principles of general international law, or other sources of a universal or quasi-universal character. The court does not explicitly say that the obligations themselves are based on universal norms, but this idea seems consistent with what the court is saying. So, at least on one interpretation, obligations *erga omnes* are based on universal norms, either *jus cogens* norms (which are, as we saw earlier, norms admitting no derogation that are part of general international law), or norms that are consensual but have achieved some kind of universal character.

The Barcelona Traction opinion can be read as identifying two types of international obligation: (1) those that are part of general international law, and (2) those that have been agreed to by all, or nearly all, of the people in the world community. The first of these obligations constituted a decidedly different basis to which Belgium might have been able to appeal than those norms that were based on explicit treaty arrangements. If there are any norms beyond treaty-based contractual norms, such norms were said to be part of general international law. Norms that specify obligations *erga omnes*, seemed to be based on *jus cogens* norms, the supposedly universal norms of general international law that could be appealed to in disputes between two sovereign States.

In order to justify certain kinds of obligations owed to States or non-State entities concerning foreign investment issues, the ICJ in Barcelona Traction turned to a non-consensual basis of international legal norms. The court implicitly recognized that if obligations are said to attach to all States, and yet the underlying support for these obligations is itself a matter of consent of these States, severe conceptual difficulties arise. For then how can a State be declared to be bound if that State can abrogate that obligation subsequently by declaring its non-consent?[15] Unfortunately, what has just been quoted here is all that the court says about such norms, leaving us in need of a theoretical justification for obligations that States incur but not by treaty or other forms of agreement, and that States cannot relieve themselves of by similar consensual means.

There are two answers to the problem I have posed that have been offered in international law: one is historical, the other conceptual. The first answer, the subject of Chapter 3, is that universal norms of international law arise by some magical process out of the long traditions and consensual customs of States. The second answer is conceptual and normative – namely, that a norm must be identified that is binding non-consensually, perhaps in terms of what all people reasonably must seek. In a later section of this chapter, I will provide the beginnings of a conceptual and normative answer, drawn in terms of prudence, a rudimentary understanding of human nature, and minimal moral considerations, by building on the insights gained from my discussion of Hobbes in the introductory chapter. A non-consensual grounding for *jus cogens* norms, of the sort provided in the following sections of this chapter, is just what is needed for the United Nations and its ICJ, as well as for the new ICC. Let us briefly consider the views of an international legal theorist on this point.

Maurizio Ragazzi suggests that there are norms of customary international law that are legally binding on States "irrespective of whether or not [the state] has expressed its consent to be bound."[16] Ragazzi says that this principle is widely shared among other international legal scholars. Of course, that it is widely shared does not yet tell us if it is plausible. If States can relieve themselves of the international obligations related to *jus cogens* norms, then such important matters as basic international human rights cannot be secured against the actions of States that claim not to recognize the legitimacy of a given human right.[17] But if the express consent of States is not required, then it is hard to see how the norms in question can originate in what is consensually customary or conventional. But perhaps what Ragazzi is suggesting is that part of so-called customary international law is not grounded in the consent of States. Whether *jus cogens* norms are conceptualized as a non-consensual part of customary international law, or as part of the general principles of international law, it remains clear that they cannot be consensual, or they will lose any claim to be universal and inviolable (not subject to derogation).

II. Contemporary Legal Positivism

Contemporary legal positivists have generally not acknowledged the legitimacy of international legal norms, let alone universal or *jus cogens* norms. As I indicated earlier, John Austin had claimed that law was simply what the sovereign commanded it to be, and where there was no sovereign, there were no legally binding norms.[18] Since there was no international sovereign, there were no binding international legal norms. Universal or *jus cogens* norms would be, at best, moral norms with no legal legitimacy. But a more recent legal positivist, H. L. A. Hart, embraced what he called a "minimum content of natural law" that provided support for both moral and legal norms in any society, and that could provide us with a key idea in grounding international legal norms, even though Hart himself would undoubtedly have been skeptical of such norms.[19]

According to Hart, some legal positivists, "Hobbes and Hume among them, have been willing to lower their sights: they have seen in the modest aim of survival the central indisputable element that gives empirical good sense to the terminology of Natural Law."[20] The minimum purpose of survival is what brings people together to form societies. "In the absence of this [minimum] content men, as they are, would have no reason for obeying voluntarily any rules."[21] On this account, the human need for survival, and the corresponding desire for security, are facts that provide a natural basis, and perhaps a limit, for both legal and moral rules, at least as long as humans are vulnerable to attack by one another. The rules that Hart attempts to derive from this minimum content include requirements prohibiting killing and bodily attack, mandating a system of mutual forbearance, and respect for property. Hart here seems to support the kind of Hobbesian position about the importance of security and self-preservation that I discussed in the introductory chapter.

For Hart, citizens must be able to view the State as providing a minimum of security from external threat, and from possible abuse by their own State, in order for the State effectively to require of its subjects obedience to its laws.[22] Contrary to the way he is normally read, I believe that Hart provides a good bridge between traditional natural law theory and traditional legal positivism. He talked *explicitly* of a minimum content of the natural law on which legal norms based their efficacy, although not their justification. Thus, unlike his positivist predecessors, Hart was willing to acknowledge a certain legitimacy of natural law concepts in his generally positivistic theory. As he said: "Such universally recognized principles of conduct which have a basis in elementary truths concerning human beings, their natural environment, and aims, may be considered the *minimum content* of Natural Law."[23]

Hart argued that law was best understood as an intersection of primary and secondary rules. Primary rules stipulated what subjects were obligated to do, whereas secondary rules spelled out how primary rules were to be identified, interpreted, and changed. Mere commands, even when conjoined with regularity of adherence to those rules, did not indicate that there was an extant legal system. Primary rules, such as the prohibition against murder, may be laws, but until they were joined with secondary rules specifying how interpretation, addition, and change of rules could occur, there was no legal system. Hart was at pains to argue that mere regularity of behavior does not indicate that there is a legal system. For there to be a legal system, as opposed to a mere set of rules, there had to be a system of rules that incorporated both primary and secondary rules, especially a rule of recognition that allowed for the clear identification of primary rules as part of the system of law.[24]

It bears noting that Hart thought that international law lacked a basic norm that could allow one to identify primary international legal rules. Hart argued that international law differed from domestic law, with international law most plausibly seen as a collection, or set, of rules that did not form a unified system.[25] We could not answer questions about the ultimate source of legitimacy of an international legal principle, or about any other secondary rules that governed interpretation, change, and addition of the primary rules of international law. Nonetheless, Hart claimed that this does not mean that "there is some question about [international] rules or their binding force which is left unexplained . . . The rules . . . [are] binding if they are accepted and function as such."[26]

For Hart, international legal norms had not achieved the same status as typical domestic legal norms, even though the binding force of international norms is generally unquestioned. When there was a question of what the norms of international law are, definitive answers could not be given. Nonetheless, Hart recognized that international law was changing, and might some day constitute a system of law, like a domestic or municipal legal order. But at the time he was writing, international legal norms got their legal character from their acceptance by States, not from more basic norms. It is possible that for Hart, the charter of the ICC, along with the system of courts it creates, would provide the sort of multilateral agreement that could provide a rule of recognition for international criminal law.

Importantly, Hart did not accept a universal moral basis for international legal norms, although it is important to point out that Hart did not accept a universal moral basis for domestic legal norms either.[27] I have been arguing, though, that Hart may have recognized a basis for international legal norms grounded in an understanding of human nature. In the next section, I will link Hart's exposition of international law to the Hobbesian approach I sketched in the introductory chapter. I will argue that a Hobbesian position grounds legal norms in minimal moral notions. Hart did not do this. But he did, nonetheless, provide an interesting piece of this account by clearly articulating the link between minimal natural law principles and rudimentary rules governing societies of humans, such as we know them to be.

We should take note of two parallels between Hart's characterization of international legal norms and the contemporary discussion of *jus cogens* norms. First, the definition offered by the Vienna Convention also talked of "acceptance" as the key component to *jus cogens* norms. Second, Hart's conclusion that there is no international "rule of recognition" helps explain why so many contemporary theorists disagree about the substance, or even the existence, of *jus cogens* norms in international law. Indeed, Ragazzi says that the failure to agree on "the precise content of *jus cogens*" is both regrettable and also dangerous in that this uncertainty provides "States with an excuse for escaping from their international commitments."[28] Perhaps because of this uncertainty, one would not expect contemporary legal positivists to employ the concept of *jus cogens*, and by and large they do not, with one exception.

It is surprising that one of the most influential accounts of *jus cogens* norms in international law was provided sixty years ago by Alfred von Verdross, who was a self-described legal positivist. Verdross embraced what he called "an ethical minimum" embodied in *jus cogens* norms. He distinguished two groups of *jus cogens* norms: (1) "single, compulsory norms of customary international law," such as that a state can occupy and annex *terra nullius*,[29] and

(2) norms *contra bonos mores* – that is, norms contrary to "the ethics of a certain community." Concerning the latter category, Verdross claimed that there is a common ethical minimum for all communities – namely,

maintenance of law and order within the state, defense against external attacks, care for the bodily and spiritual welfare of citizens at home, protection of citizens abroad.[30]

Verdross supplied the idea that at its core, *jus cogens* norms provide a *moral minimum* that all communities must meet if they are to issue binding laws.

Verdross's list of what is included in the moral minimum is very similar to the list of things that Hart included in the minimum content of the natural law. Both lists are based on the idea that security is the chief good that people would expect legal systems to provide for them. Verdross, unlike Hart, was explicit in describing a *moral* minimum for any legal system, and thought that it applied to domestic as well as to international law.[31] The minimal moral content of law provides the rationale for obedience to law and for the obligations thought to attach to membership in a political society. The key idea for both Hart and Verdross was the normative claim that a State should not act to jeopardize the security of its citizens. For Verdross, this claim was explicitly moral. If a State could not provide for the security of its subjects, its subjects were not obligated to obey the State's laws. Verdross extended this idea to the international domain. If a State did not protect its citizens, that State's sovereignty was not due international respect either.

III. Moral Minimalism

My own view draws on legal positivism, but like Verdross, it has an explicit moral core. Contrary to standard legal positivism, moral minimalism holds that there are basic moral rights that undergird the system of mutual forbearance[32] that States should promote. A moral minimalist sees *jus cogens* norms as providing a protection from treatment by a State that would jeopardize the security of its subjects, or, as I will say in Chapter 4, that would violate the security principle. The respect that one State is owed by the "international society" cannot occur if a State allows for the mistreatment of a whole segment of its society. This was the guiding idea that led to the Genocide Convention after World War II, as well as to the international conventions condemning apartheid and torture.

Moral minimalism holds that when States act so as to undermine their subjects' security, a moral minimum of acceptable behavior by States has been violated, and it may not be unjust for international tribunals to take action that would otherwise be unjust violations of a State's sovereignty. While I believe that certain aspects of this idea are consistent with a moderate legal positivist position, neither Hart nor Verdross explicitly endorsed this implication. Rather, Hart denied that there were currently such international norms, although he did famously hold that "if there are any moral rights at all, it follows that there is at least one natural right, the equal right of all men to be free."[33] And Verdross felt that the chief implications of his view concerned the nullification of treaties rather than the direct intervention of international criminal tribunals into the affairs of a sovereign State. We will later explore what might be needed in addition to the violation of the security principle in order to justify such international intervention. The aim of this section is to begin to defend the idea that certain minimal substantive moral norms are universally binding, the violation of which is a key component in the justification of international trials against individual human persons.

In my view, Hobbes supplies some of the best arguments in favor of moral minimalism. On the basis of his state of nature scenario, Hobbes argues that what is universally desired is "prevention of discord at home, and hostility from abroad."[34] Without the preservation of such goods, the individual person has no reason to obey the laws, but instead should follow the second rule of nature – namely, to do all that one can, even by means of violence, to preserve one's life. Restrictions on the individual's use of violence constitute a large part of obedience to the law. Moral minimalists start from the point that all people desire to be protected, but proceed from that to a moral right of self-preservation and self-defense. For Hobbes, this move was justified because of retained rights that all people held and could not be understood to consent away. In this sense, certain natural rights for Hobbes form a set of non-derogable norms quite similar to the *jus cogens* norms we examined earlier in this chapter. As we will see in subsequent chapters in greater detail, this Hobbesian position leads to the idea that when the State attacks or fails to provide for the protection of the individual person, then that person can appeal to international entities for that protection.

It is notorious that Hobbes's "laws of nature" are seemingly only "Conclusions, or Theorems concerning what conduceth to the conservation and defense of themselves,"[35] but this is nonetheless a ground on which Hobbes discusses rights as well. For Hobbes distinguishes law properly so-called from these mere theorems, but the laws of nature are immutable moral laws for Hobbes, as he says in the final paragraphs of Chapter 15 of *Leviathan*, and elsewhere. The minimal moral rights are immutable and universal norms that coincide with, but are not the same as, what prudence dictates. There are very distinct advantages to this view. Most important of all, this conception of universal norms will not fall prey to the skeptic who doubts the authority of God or of religion or any secularly based moral authority. This is especially important today since the fact of pluralism has made such skepticism even more rampant.

Hart recognized a limitation on the moral minima embodied in Hobbes's laws of nature – namely, that these norms are really contingent on how humans are at the moment, and so far have been in recorded history. If humans had hard shells, things would be different, and protection from external assault would not be acknowledged as a prerequisite for obedience to law. The "empirical good sense" of the terminology of natural law is embodied in the idea that humans, as a contingent matter of how they are, have no basis for obeying law if they are not secured in their persons and property by the sovereign, as we saw previously. In the end, though, Hart does not recognize that this is already a moral minimum for universally binding norms. I will leave open the question of whether security is a norm of universal scope or merely a quasi-universal norm, based only on what we have known humans to be like. For what follows in my larger argument, all that matters is that there be a philosophical basis for universal or quasi-universal norms, grounded in basic human rights, on which the norms of international law might rest. This is the basic insight of moral minimalism as I conceive it.

We are now in a position to begin to see how *jus cogens* norms could be grounded in moral minimalism. What is most appealing about moral minimalism is that it explains the nearly universal recognition of such norms as self-preservation and self-defense. The drive for self-preservation is indeed a feature of humans, at least as we know them now and as they have been known. Of course, there are situations in which self-preservation is overcome by other motivations. But societies are not structured on such exceptional cases. Rather, there is a general recognition of the importance of minimal moral maxims that support self-preservation. And such a basis could very plausibly explain the appeal of the idea of *jus cogens* norms.

Moral minimalism stands in sharp contrast to traditional natural law theory in many respects. What interests me here is the way that universal norms are grounded. Traditional natural law theory grounded such norms in a higher order law or law of God. Insofar as legal positivists took a position on this matter at all, it was to be highly skeptical of such a project. I follow legal positivists in such skepticism. As I have indicated, there is at least one self-described legal positivist who did not shy away from talk of moral minima, but who saw such ideas as themselves corresponding to human nature. Rights that are grounded in the moral minimum are crucial for explaining both the authority of sovereigns and the limitation on sovereignty that occurs when sovereigns cannot, or choose not to, protect basic human rights. This points to the need for international criminal law as a source of protection for those individuals who are either attacked by their States, or whose States fail to protect them from other individuals or groups. For as Hobbes said, "[T]here is no man that can hope by his own strength, or wit, to defend himself from destruction, without the help of Confederates."[36] This was meant to be as true a principle of the law of nature for individual humans as it was a law of nations. We can here see the beginnings of a possible justification for international intervention into the affairs of a sovereign State. Such international intervention is not based on a concern for wide-ranging human rights. As I will argue later, only those human rights that protect the security of the individual can, when abused, trigger justified international intervention.

IV. Contemporary Natural Law Theory and its Critics

The reluctance of legal positivists to provide a set of basic international norms that could conclusively mandate international legal intervention for a wide array of human rights abuses, such as prosecuting Nazi war criminals, led many theorists to look back to the natural law tradition.[37] Justice Robert H. Jackson, the chief American prosecutor at the Nuremberg trials, said that he saw himself representing all of humanity as he sought to punish those Nazi leaders who had committed "atrocities and persecutions on racial or religious grounds."[38] Jackson argued that the Martens Clause of the Hague Convention of 1907 provided two related sources of international law from which a defense of international tribunals could be derived. International interventions are justified by reference to "the principles of the law of nations, as they result from the usages established among civilized peoples, [1] from the laws of humanity, and [2] the dictates of public conscience."[39]

On this view, there are principles of natural law that are somehow enshrined in the public conscience. What offends the public conscience in international crimes is that humans are treated in ways that no human should have to bear – namely, to be made to suffer arbitrarily. Arbitrary suffering is here treated as clearly wrong from the natural law perspective since it violates the most basic standards of how humans are to regard each other, and how humans know, in the light of reason, that they should behave. Humans are supposed to treat each other with minimal decency based on the idea that human personhood has a core of intrinsic value that must always be respected. According to this view, an act of torture victimizes humanity as well as the individual who is made to suffer because of the disrespect that is shown to the intrinsic value of the person. While I find this position to be largely plausible, and will defend a view somewhat similar to it later under what I call the international harm principle, there are serious conceptual difficulties, as we will see next.

I support the general movement toward increasing the protection of human rights in international law. In this sense, I see my own project as not incompatible with the new so-called natural law theorists, especially those in international criminal law. But I urge that we distinguish carefully between those human rights that protect physical security and subsistence, and those rights that protect less important interests, including both civil rights and economic rights that, while important, will when violated not provide a basis for international prosecutions. Again, my reason for taking this somewhat more conservative stance regarding human rights in international criminal law, even as I would support this expansion in other domains of international law, is based on a concern for the legitimate sovereignty interests of States as well as for the rights of defendants. Setting the bar too low weakens sovereignty and also puts defendants in unfair jeopardy unless the harms they are accused of committing are at least as important as those that they themselves now risk.

Jerzy Sztucki has clearly indicated why natural law theory has been recently in ascendance in international law. He says that "[t]he only difference between a religious doctrine and the concept of *jus cogens* in international law is . . . [that] a religious doctrine does not lose its *ratio existendi* by the fact of being adhered to by only some people, while the concept of peremptory norms of general international law is rendered senseless if their content is not universally (or quasi-universally) adhered to."[40] If State practices that employ torture are to be considered a violation of *jus cogens* norms, it seems that *jus cogens* norms cannot be based on the consent of the States in question, since so many States have engaged in torture over the years.[41] In addition, to overcome serious problems concerning ex post facto prosecution, norms must be knowable and binding in advance of being articulated by international tribunals that attempt to prosecute these crimes. If *jus cogens* norms are indeed readily apparent to most people, then there are seemingly strong normative reasons for supporting a natural law basis, especially a religiously motivated natural-law basis, of *jus cogens* norms to justify prosecutions of international crimes.

Initially, the new natural law theorists were inspired by the need to provide an international legal framework that would condemn the horrific immorality of genocide. More recently, those new natural law theorists sought to characterize apartheid as a violation of moral norms that were so basic that they should also be legal norms in any system of law. And when the delegates met in 1998 to form an international criminal court, they were inspired by the horrific acts of ethnic cleansing that had recently occurred in the Balkans, as well as genocide in Rwanda. In all these cases, the "laws of humanity and the dictates of public conscience" were said to be so offended that a permanent international tribunal needed to be formed to take action. The natural law theorist's account of *jus cogens* norms was said to be able to provide theoretical support for what even the moderate legal positivists would not – namely, an international tribunal for the prosecution of those accused of war crimes and crimes against humanity.

The principles of natural law, though, embraced by traditional natural law theorists, focused on assaults to civil and political rights of individuals, rather than to economic and social rights, failing to see that both could involve a denial of security. For this and other reasons, Socialist and Third World theorists were, and have remained, skeptical of the traditional natural law theorist's account of *jus cogens* norms. From the early negotiations among the Allied powers at Nuremberg concerning the nature of crimes against humanity, the Soviets insisted on tying crimes against humanity to "initiation and waging of aggressive war rather than the violation of human rights."[42] Grigory I. Tunkin is the Soviet legal theorist who had perhaps the most developed conception of *jus cogens* norms. Tunkin proceeds from the assumption that "[c]ontemporary international law is in its essence anti-colonial. It is a law of equality, self-determination, and freedom of peoples."[43] Norm creation is a matter of struggle between economic classes. On this model, "there is no other means of creating rules of law binding upon these states except the co-ordination of the wills regarding the content of the rules and their recognition as legally binding."[44]

From a consensual base, the anti-colonialist perspective is willing to grant *jus cogens* norms a special status, but it will be more limited than that often ascribed to these norms: "[A]n agreement which brings into being a principle of *jus cogens* differs in its content from agreements creating 'ordinary' norms of general international law."[45] But Tunkin and others deny that *jus cogens* norms have any independent moral weight behind them.[46] Rather, it is the special agreement on these fundamental norms that gives them their weightiness. For this reason, *jus cogens* norms are clearest when they are applicable to regional or local questions. Tunkin argues that if there is no higher moral authority to these norms, then *jus cogens* norms cannot "prohibit the establishment of local norms which are different from them in their social contents."[47]

It is surely right to think that *jus cogens* norms must be applied with reference to differences in context and circumstance. These norms need to be applied and adjusted to particular cultural situations. It is also right to think that *jus cogens* norms, as general principles of international law, can be easily linked to anti-colonialist principles. But these elements of *jus cogens* norms cannot be normatively supported by a purely consensual foundation, as we will see in the next chapter. Even within a given region, the norms will not be peremptory if they can be changed by the consent of States or regional entities involved. In this respect, natural law theory is superior to anti-colonialist theory.

The anti-colonialist perspective provides us with a rather different and rich way of partially conceptualizing *jus cogens* norms. Such an understanding of the concept of *jus cogens*, and especially of its difficulties, mirrors the conception of *jus cogens* norms held by various contemporary Third World countries. Many Third World States worry that a country such as the United States might try to enforce its own idiosyncratic notion of *jus cogens* norms on the rest of the world.[48] This is also what fueled Tunkin's insistence that one cannot move from a particular culture's idea of ethical norms to international legal norms. I take this as a strongly plausible cautionary warning for anyone who is inclined to support natural law theory, or even a moral minimalist position.

The anti-colonialist account of *jus cogens* norms cannot remain grounded in purely consensual foundations, as we will see more clearly in the next chapter. Indeed, Tunkin seemingly recognizes this when he allows that *jus cogens* norms are not like normal consensual norms in international law. As general norms of international law, *jus cogens* norms are themselves foundational, and any societies that reject them risk conceptual incoherence in their legal systems. So the question arises as to what sets *jus cogens* norms apart from standard, consensual norms in international law? At least part of the answer given by Tunkin is that, *in a given region*, they are regarded as peremptory. The next question is why certain norms, even if restricted to within the confines of a given region, would be considered binding independently of the consent of the States?

The answer that the anti-colonialist perspective provides refers to the common regional understanding of the seeming rightness of these norms. So, in some respect, this perspective provides a similar account of *jus cogens* norms to that of the views we addressed earlier. But there are important differences that give the anti-colonialist perspective its uniqueness. The anti-colonialist perspective is different from the natural law perspective in that *jus cogens* norms are grounded in the specific conditions, especially the harms inflicted on those who can least resist the attacks by their sovereigns, of peoples in a given region rather than in an account of eternal law universally instilled in all people. It is this aspect of anti-colonialism that I will build on in Chapter 5. The anti-colonialist perspective also differs from the version of legal positivism espoused by Verdross, since his general principles derived from *jus cogens* norms are binding on all legal systems, not just those that exist in a given region of the world.[49]

Tunkin and other anti-colonialists are adamant that *jus cogens* norms not be grounded in human nature. Indeed, following Marx, these theorists deny that there is a fixed human nature at all. But, at least partially following Hart, it may be possible to recognize the contingency of human nature and yet see a basis for *jus cogens* norms, at least for humans such as we have come to know them, that is not merely regional but exists across regions and borders. Such a view could turn on what some Marxists have called "species being" rather than "human nature."[50] The anti-colonialist account has provided strongly cautionary advice against rushing to presume too much about human nature or about natural law. But as some of these theorists also recognized, such caution does not rule out the idea of *jus cogens* norms altogether.

In this chapter, I have begun to set out a crucial foundational concept of international criminal law – namely, the idea that there are universal norms that States should adhere to, and the violation of which might justify "universal jurisdiction" for international prosecutions. The discussion has focused on a three-way debate between (1) moderate legal positivists such as Hobbes, Hart, and Verdross, (2) natural law advocates such as Justice Robert Jackson, and (3) anti-colonialists such as the Soviet theorist Gregori Tunkin. I have sketched a view of some universal norms, called *jus cogens* norms, that provide a non-consensual basis for international criminal law that are binding on all States regardless of express agreements to the contrary. I began to defend a moral minimalist position on the justification of *jus cogens* norms. I argued that *jus cogens* norms can begin to ground international prosecutions, but *jus cogens* norms do not proscribe all human rights abuses.

What I have attempted to do so far in this chapter and in the introductory chapter is to provide a novel way to begin to defend international norms – namely, by reference to *jus cogens* norms grounded in very minimal moral premises. To do so, I have resurrected Hobbes, the philosopher most commonly associated with the critique of the very idea of international law. Such a strategy will be seen as both an advantage and a disadvantage.

The advantage is that a Hobbesian, or moral minimalst, position is itself often the starting point for critics of international law, and if my view is plausible, those critics will be confronted on their own turf. Policymakers who avow Hobbesian worries about international criminal law will have to take my arguments much more seriously than they would have to take traditional natural law arguments in support of international law.

The disadvantage is that a Hobbesian, or moral minimalist, position cannot justify as wide a conception of international criminal law as some theorists seem to want. Perhaps some will then urge that more robust natural law ideas will have to be grafted onto a Hobbesian tree. In any event, that tree is considerably sturdier than the traditional natural law basis for international law in general, and will better withstand the winds of nationalism and isolationism that often threaten to blow down the whole edifice of international criminal law.

In the next chapter, I turn to the most common way to justify *jus cogens* norms – namely, by reference to international custom. I offer a set of criticisms of this strategy. Then, in Chapters 4 and 5, I explore further the possibility that there is a common core to *jus cogens* norms that is used to limit the actions of States and State-like actors. I identify two principles – the security and international harm principles – that capture this core idea. Such a common core would help rebut the charge that *jus cogens* norms are simply Western moral ideals imposed on the rest of the world. If we can identify a common core to *jus cogens* norms in international criminal law, then we would have a basis for international condemnation of such practices as genocide, apartheid, and slavery. And we would have a basis for international prosecutions that does not rely on a potentially problematical version of natural law theory that anti-colonialists and Third World states have complained about.

3

Custom, *Opinio Juris*, and Consent

It is often said that many universal norms at the international level derive their authority from custom.[1] One of the leading textbooks on international criminal law asserts:

Unlike international agreement as such, customary international law is of a universally obligatory nature. Thus, what was at one time an international agreement binding merely signatories and their nationals can later become customary law for the entire international community.[2]

Jus cogens norms are here said to be non-consensual, and yet sometimes to be also customary. But customary international norms are said to begin life as simply a matter of agreement – that is, arising from the acceptance of States over time.

Initially, it might seem that consensual norms of international law are a nice fit with my moral minimalism. Custom does not seem to be based in the questionable metaphysics of the natural law tradition, and custom seems to provide an easy way to limit the extent of binding norms – that is, to only those norms that reach a near-universal acceptance over time. Custom does indeed seem to limit the reach of international norms in a somewhat plausible way, thereby appealing to one aspect of my moral minimalism – namely, the substantive worry that we not overreach in proscribing every rights violation as a violation of international criminal law. But custom, as a source of *jus cogens* norms in international criminal law, is not consistent with another aspect of my moral minimalism – namely, that we not rely on controversial assumptions. As this chapter will show, customary international criminal norms are indeed suspect, even though not appealing to natural law principles, since they are initially grounded in consent, and yet are said to give rise to non-consensual norms.[3]

How can consensual norms give rise to non-consensual obligations? In this chapter, I take up this conceptual puzzle, ultimately arguing that if *jus cogens* norms are to be understood as truly universal norms, then they cannot be grounded in consensually based customs alone. More than acceptance, even over a long period of time, is necessary for having some norms in the international legal system that are to be treated as allowing no derogation, even by States that have not recognized these norms as legally binding. In the next two chapters – Chapters 4 and 5 – I provide what is missing in consensually based customary accounts of *jus cogens* norms. The present chapter, though, is mainly negative, arguing that consensually based custom is not a firm basis for *jus cogens* norms of international criminal law.

In international law, it is well established that for a customary norm to rise to the level of a *jus cogens* norm,[4] all or most States must recognize that norm as universally binding, they must behave as if they are bound by this norm, and they must meet the *opinio juris* test – namely, such felt bindingness must be based on a sense of legal or moral obligation.[5] The question posed in this chapter is whether such additional elements in an account of consensually based custom can ground *jus cogens* norms. I argue that consensually based custom and *opinio juris* cannot ground universal norms. The main reason is that such international custom, even when it meets the *opinio juris* test, remains a consensual basis for legally valid norms, yet what is needed for the justification of universally binding norms is a non-consensual basis. I also argue that while consensually based custom, standing alone, cannot supply the justification for such universally binding norms, consensually based custom, including the concept of *opinio juris,* can at least supply evidence of the existence of such norms. As we will see in the next chapter, an international harm principle could provide the support lacking in consensually based custom for universal norms in the international realm. But it is simply a mistake to think of universal *jus cogens* norms as merely arising from consensual customary international law. At the end of this chapter, I will consider what a non-consensually based custom might look like, and what it might be grounded in.

In the first section, I begin with some cautionary remarks drawn from the work of David Hume, who considered the attempt by his contemporaries to ground obligations in consent. Hume argued that such attempts were hopeless unless they were conjoined with non-consensual considerations. In the second section, a non-criminal model of understanding international customary norms is analyzed. I consider two cases concerning international contracts and property rights: the Texaco/Libya Arbitration[6] and the Kuwait/Aminoil Arbitration.[7] These cases were adjudicated by reference to international customary norms. In the third section, I will examine the case of Iraq, which had invaded Kuwait in 1990 to gain its oil resources, and was repelled by an international military force headed by the United States. In this third section, I will critically examine the supposed customary basis for the UN-imposed sanctions against Iraq after the Gulf War that were aimed at deterring Iraq from future aggression and punishing Iraq for its harmfully exploitative behavior toward Kuwait. In the fourth section, I will examine the conflicting opinions presented by two international judges on the role of custom and *opinio juris* in adjudicating international disputes concerning the use or threat of nuclear weapons.

In the fifth section, I directly confront the attempt to portray consensually based customary international law as providing universal norms that all states should obey. I argue that such custom, standing alone, cannot supply the justi- fication for such norms, but that custom, including the concept of *opinio juris*, can at least supply evidence of the existence of legally valid norms. In the sixth section, the relationship between *jus cogens* norms and international custom- ary law is further explored. I briefly examine six ways to save the consensual customary basis of universal norms, rejecting each in turn. By the end of this chapter, we can see the need for a non-consensual basis for universal norms of the sort we began to explore in Chapter 2, and that is then continued in Chapters 4 and 5.

I. Some Lessons from Hume

In David Hume's famous essay, "Of the Original Contract,"[8] several mistakes are identified among political philosophers of the eighteenth century. It seems to me that these mistakes have been repeated by contemporary theorists of international criminal law. I begin with a short discussion of Hume's arguments against the attempt to ground obligation in consent. Like Hobbes, Hume grants that one of the salient features of a state of nature is that all people are roughly equal. Since they are roughly equal to one another, "we must necessarily allow, that nothing but their own consent could, at first, associate them together, and subject them to any authority."[9] Consent is, on Hume's account, the obvious source of authority for binding obligations in the state of nature. But over time, as new people who had never consented come on the scene, problems arise for a consensual account of obligation.

We can also think of contemporary disputes in international criminal law as similar to the state-of-nature scenario that Hume envisions. As I argued in Chapter 1, there is a rough equality among States, giving rise to the problem of how one State can bind another State. Initially, the most obvious way to do this is through the mutual consent of States. This is why most of the major sources of international law in the twentieth century, such as the Charter of the United Nations or the Statute of the International Criminal Court, were initially established by multilateral treaties – that is, by States binding themselves, and thereby creating a basis by which one State could claim that another State is bound even given the rough equality of States. Hume and Hobbes are in agreement at this stage.

For Hume, the problem of consent arises from those philosophers who "assert not only that government in its earliest infancy arose from consent or rather the voluntary acquiescence of the people, but also even at present, when it has attained its full maturity, it rests on no other foundation."[10] In a telling analogy,

Hume says that these same philosophers would be repelled by the idea that the "consent of the fathers" in one generation could "bind the children, even to the most remote generations."[11] Consent cannot provide a basis for binding universal norms, argues Hume, because with "every man every hour going out of the world, and another coming into it," original consent will not clearly bind all.[12] There must be some other ground of continuing obligation of non-consenting persons other than mere original consent.

Here, there is a similar problem to that of retroactive legislation.[13] In retroactive legislation, as we will see in much greater detail in Chapter 11, a person is held accountable for actions taken in the past that are held to have violated a law only passed in the present. To say that one has violated a law that did not exist when one acted is to engage, at best, in a sleight of hand. There is now a law that exists, and on which prosecution proceeds. But if one could not have known about the law when one acted, it is patently unfair to use that law as a basis for judging past behavior. Similarly, to bind a State on the basis of an agreement or treaty that that State had not agreed to is similarly problematical. If a State did not sign on to the treaty, it is patently unfair to use the terms of the treaty to judge the behavior of a non-signatory State.

Hume argues that moral duties and obligations arise from sentiment "restrained by subsequent judgment or observation."[14] The "general interests or necessities" are sufficient to create the bindingness of such duties and obligations. For our purposes, this recalls the Hobbesian point of the previous chapter that all people have a general interest in self-preservation and self-defense, and that such an interest can ground binding universal norms. Hume seems to be operating in a similar mode when he argues that moral duty arises out of general interests or necessities. The main point here is that the consent of others cannot replace these interests. The consent of some people cannot bind other people, and hence universally binding norms cannot be generated out of consensual norms.

Now, recall the quotation from a leading textbook on international criminal law with which I began this chapter. There the authors claim that customary international law is of "a universally binding nature." They claim that the support for such customary international law comes from binding international agreements. This is not itself problematical. States obviously think, with justification, that their treaties create binding obligations on one another. But Paust et al. go on to say that these treaty agreements later become binding for the "entire international community"– that is, even for those States that were not a party to these treaties. Yet from what they say, it is at best mysterious as to how such a transformation occurs. Again recall Hume's remark that such arguments seem to be like the argument that the consent of fathers binds successive generations of children. Why think that the consent of some States can come to bind other States, even those that explicitly decided not to sign on to the original agreement? This is the topic I will be exploring in the remainder of this chapter.

Of course it might be, as Hume seems to have held, that there are non-consensual customs that are binding on all, and that derive their bindingness from interest and necessity. Perhaps the test of *opinio juris* is supposed to allow us to pick out just such customs. This would all be fine if theorists of international criminal law had a clear idea of what it was that *opinio juris* added to original agreement to transform consensually based customs into non-consensual ones. But as we will see, *opinio juris* merely adds that some States not only consent but then act as if they are morally or legally bound. Then, once enough States so behave, binding universal norms arise. It often seems as if the sheer length of time by which a consensually based custom has lasted is sufficient to transform such a custom into a non-consensual, universally binding custom. Such a view obviously falls prey to the set of Humean objections I have just recited.

How does this Humean position square with the moral minimalist position with its Hobbesian leanings discussed in the previous chapter (and to be discussed in subsequent chapters)? It is interesting to note that in a quotation from H. L. A. Hart mentioned earlier, Hobbes and Hume are linked as those who have understood the empirical good sense of a minimalist understanding of the natural law doctrine. And even from such a brief discussion of Hume so far, one can hopefully see why Hart linked Hume and Hobbes together. Hume diverged somewhat from Hobbes in thinking that it was the strong interest that individuals had in self-defense that ultimately was the rationale for the sovereign's authority, not merely what people actually consented to.

I wish to highlight a general lesson to be learned from our discussion of Hume. Consensually based custom does not mysteriously transform itself into non-consensual custom, even as it stands the test of time. Indeed, custom does not seem to be a very good basis at all for a stable understanding of what people are obligated to do, and much less for a universally binding set of norms. In what follows, I will build a parallel argument against deriving *jus cogens* norms from consensually based custom by reference to several major disputes in international law generally, and international criminal law in particular. Much confusion will be uncovered, as well as significant conceptual difficulties, when theorists of international law discuss the customary basis of *jus cogens* norms. I will illustrate the strains of that confusion, and then argue that other attempts to save the idea that custom can produce binding universal norms are also likely to fail.

II. A Non-Criminal Model: The Oil Nationalization Cases

The first problem with seeing consensually based custom as a source of universal legal norms is that it is too weak to justify these norms. Certain forms of custom are meant to pick out those norms that are universal, and yet the test for custom seems to rely only on the consent of the parties involved, at least those that are most directly affected by the claimed rights and duties. Let us consider how an international arbitrator used the notion of custom to analyze Libya's right to nationalize a private corporation's assets to prevent exploitation of Libya's natural resources. The non-criminal *jus cogens* norm in question concerned the prohibition of the destruction of a State's natural resources. When custom originates from, and is justified by reference to, the empirical fact of consent, it cannot provide a ground for *universal* norms. At the end of this section, we consider the normative argument that is needed, and was supplied, in the second Libya case. By analyzing how this case succeeded and failed, we will find a rough model for how to proceed from consensual custom to universal legal norms.

In 1974, Texaco and Libya sought arbitration to resolve disputes stemming from Libya's contract deeding oil fields to Texaco in 1955. The deeds contained the following clause: "[C]ontractual rights expressly created by this concession shall not be altered except by mutual consent of the parties."[15] Yet, in 1974, Libya "nationalized the totality of the properties, rights, assets and interests of California Asiatic Oil Company and Texaco Overseas Petroleum Company arising out of the 14 Deeds of Concession held by those companies."[16] The ensuing dispute centered directly on the right of Libya to nullify a contract that had expressly guaranteed that no changes in the contract were allowed unless both parties consented. Libya argued that as a sovereign entity, it had the right to dispose of its natural resources as it saw fit. But Libya did allow for an international arbitrator to resolve its dispute with Texaco.

In the Texaco/Libya Arbitration case, the arbitrator cited approvingly UN General Assembly Resolutions that confirmed "that every State maintains a complete right to exercise full sovereignty over its natural resources and recognizes Nationalization as being a legitimate and internationally recognized method to ensure the sovereignty of the State upon such resource."[17] Although the arbitrator recognized that General Assembly resolutions are not legally binding, he declared that when the States most likely to be affected by the resolution have voted for the resolution, then these resolutions become a customary legal basis for obligations.[18]

Here we have a clear basis for determining international legal obligations – namely, look to the General Assembly resolutions, and also to the votes taken in that body. The General Assembly is treated like a legislative body duly authorized to make binding law. But since there is no international State, it is not clear who has authorized the General Assembly to make binding law. Indeed, as the arbitrator admitted, the General Assembly itself does not recognize its resolutions as anything other than advisory. This is why the arbitrator says that the case actually concerns whether there is a basis in customary international law for nationalization of resources. The arbitrator seemingly held that the General

Assembly can establish a customary basis for binding law when a State both (1) is likely to be affected by the resolution, and (2) has voted for the resolution. If both these conditions are met, then a State is bound by the resolution.[19]

This opinion is conceptually unsettling in several respects. The most obvious conceptual difficulty concerns the favorable reference to General Assembly Resolutions about inherent or universal rights, and the failure to regard these Resolutions as creating binding legal obligations unless the States consent to them. There are two difficulties. First, ether the General Assembly votes create binding custom – that is, new law – or the General Assembly votes merely acknowledge an already existing custom. In the former case, it is the consent of the parties that creates custom, and it is not clear why we need to talk of custom as playing a role at all. In the latter case, the General Assembly is largely irrelevant since the non-consensual custom would exist whether positive votes were taken by the General Assembly or not. Second, either the rights are universal or inherent, in which case they do not require the vote of the General Assembly or the consent of State parties most likely to be affected in order to be binding, or the Resolutions require the consent of State parties that are likely to be affected, in which case the rights declared in the Resolutions are consensual and not inherent or universal.

The arbitrator's opinion does in one sense conform to Hume's cautionary warnings, for the parties bound by the General Assembly votes are those States that voted positively and that understood they would likely be affected by the ensuing Resolution. But it is surely not the case that "universal" rights were created by these acts of "original" consent. It displays a serious conceptual confusion to think that the limited scope of what one consents to be bound to can create universally binding norms. We turn next to a much more successful attempt to ground a universal obligation not to exploit another State's natural resources, also at least begun in considerations of consent.

In another case, Liamco v. Libya,[20] Libya had first nationalized 51 percent of Liamco's concessions. Then, when Liamco failed to reach agreement with the new Libyan government concerning the use of natural resources in Libya, the remaining 49 percent of Liamco's concessions was nationalized.[21] Libya again claimed that its actions were justified in order to protect its natural resources from exploitation. Liamco claimed that the actions of the Libyan government were "politically motivated, discriminatory and confiscatory."[22] Both sides agreed to submit to international arbitration.

In the Liamco/Libya Arbitration, the international arbitrator specifically addressed one of the hardest questions: If a State owns natural resources and transfers ownership to another party, why does that other party not have the right to exploit those natural resources as part of its property right? According to the arbitrator, a property right has been defined since Roman times, as the right to use or abuse a given thing. The ancient notion of property rights granted to the property holder a right that could not be taken away without the property holder's consent. "In the light of that classical definition, the State could not expropriate any private property."[23] But the arbitrator does not follow this logic to its obvious conclusion.

In both Western conceptions of property and those that arise out of the Koran, "public necessity" is a ground for violation of property rights.[24] The Liamco arbitrator relies on an old Muslim legal maxim: "Private damage has to be suffered in order to fend off public damage." On the basis of such an understanding of property rights, the arbitrator says that a modern "social" view of property has emerged that sees a natural resource as property that is "subservient to the public interest of the Community represented by the State."[25] Nationalization of private property in order to advance the community interest can thereby be defended.[26]

The Liamco arbitrator concludes that "most publicists today uphold the sovereign right of a State to nationalize foreign property," even in contravention of "international treaties."[27] The writings of publicists are one of the chief sources of determining customary norms. As in the Texaco case, the principle that a State can abrogate private property rights for the community good is justified by reference to customary international law. In both the Texaco and Liamco Arbitrations, customary international law is considered the source of the legitimacy of nationalization. Nationalization becomes a legitimate response to exploitation of a State's natural resources by a foreign company. In both cases, customary international law is said to protect a State's right that its economic resources not be exploited. Since the advent of the Vienna Convention on Treaties that gave voice to the idea that there were non-consensual, *jus cogens* norms, such norms have been held to override those consensual rights and duties established by contracts and treaties.

The Liamco arbitrator seemed to acknowledge this point. An additional element was added to the analysis of State practices in order to determine the existence of a universal right of a State to protect its natural resources from exploitation. The arbitrator sought justification of universal rights by reference to normative arguments concerning property rights. Such arguments were then conjoined with the evidence of State practices, thereby putting the arbitrator on considerably firmer ground for claiming that economic exploitation was proscribed by universal (*jus cogens*) principles, not merely by reference to consensual customary practices. Thus the Liamco decision avoids the conceptual problems of the Texaco decision. The arbitrator appealed to non-consensual principles in order to justify the claim that universal prescriptions existed. Consensually based custom, standing alone, was not thought to be sufficient to ground universal rights and duties. So we have here a rough model of how to solve the main problem of this chapter. Something other than consensually based custom, perhaps a normative argument, seemed to be needed in order to make of certain consensually based customs a source of non-consensually binding international law.

III. Iraq's Invasion of Kuwait

The second problem with seeing consensually based custom as a source of international rights and duties is that it does not provide a clear basis to obligate those States that have not consented. A classic example of this problem comes in the various recent problems in Iraq. One of the most interesting aspects of the UN enforcement actions in Iraq is the attempt to justify the idea that non-member States, and hence States that have not explicitly consented to the United Nations Charter, can be obligated to act when Security Council resolutions call for universal adherence. How can the actions taken by the United Nations bind States that are not members of the United Nations? The answer cannot be drawn in the simple terms of consensually based custom.

In 1990, Iraq invaded Kuwait, laying claim to Kuwait's rich oil fields. The United Nations, through the Security Council, was quick to condemn Iraq's actions, and to call upon member States to defend the rights of Kuwait. A military response from a United States-led military force followed closely the Security Council resolutions.[28] Ten days after Iraq invaded Kuwait, the United States announced an interdiction policy – actually, a naval blockade – against Iraq. Eventually, a U.S.-led military force confronted the Iraqi armies, and repelled them. The United States claimed to be justified in its military action by reference to Article 51 of the United Nations Charter. This action spurred the Security Council to pass another resolution, 665, authorizing such a use of force against Iraq.[29] It has been argued that Article 51 merely provides a codification of customary international law, and hence does not require explicit UN endorsement of a State's defensive acts. Indeed, Article 51 specifically says that the right of collective self-defense is an "inherent right" of member States.[30]

The recognition of a customary international norm condemning the use of economic exploitation and armed aggression by one State against another is an important development in international law. The Nicaragua case had clearly articulated the principle that armed aggression was a violation of *jus cogens* norms.[31] In the Iraq resolutions, the Security Council makes it even clearer that all States are obligated to aid the UN in preventing such aggression. While this statement does not apply to all human rights abuses, preventing armed aggression is here placed on the same footing with the *jus cogens* norms condemning slavery, genocide, and apartheid.

Security Council Resolution 661 decides that "all states" shall participate in the sanctions against Iraq. In Resolution 670, pursuant to Chapter VII of the UN Charter, the Security Council called "upon all states to carry out their obligations to ensure strict and complete compliance with resolution 661." In effect, the Security Council declared that cooperating with the UN in stopping unjustified State aggression is an obligation *erga omnes*, an obligation on all States based on universal *jus cogens* norms.[32]

Here we see some of the same problems as in the oil nationalization cases. The Security Council, like the General Assembly, acts by means of votes taken by its member States. The Security Council is not in a privileged position to identify universal norms, nor to create them. In addition, we have the problem of understanding how consensually based custom, standing alone, can bind those States that are not members of the United Nations, and hence could bind States that were not part of the Security Council's deliberative process. Iraq was one such non-member State. And to make matters worse, Iraq claimed that its rights were also violated by the various Security Council actions.

After Iraq removed its troops from Kuwait, the Security Council passed additional resolutions creating continuing economic sanctions against Iraq. Yet Iraq complained vigorously about the denigration of its sovereignty by Resolution 687, which extended sanctions after the U.S.-led forces left Iraq. Specifically, Iraq complained that it had been deprived "of its lawful right to acquire weapons and military materiel for defense . . . thus endangering the country's internal and external security."[33] Such a claim, as well as the claims that Iraq had acted unjustly, seem to me to be best defended not by reference to what Iraq had consented to do, for Iraq had consented to do very little. The issue seems to be better drawn in non-consensual terms: what Iraq owed to the other members of the international community, and what those members owed to Iraq as a matter of minimal morality.

One possible basis for Iraq's complaints, as well as the complaints made against Iraq, can be found in the universal right of a State to defend itself from external attack, and the universal obligation of a State to care for the bodily and spiritual welfare of its citizens. If this right and duty defended by Verdross, and also clearly recognized in the United Nations Charter, is indeed a *jus cogens* norm, it is very hard to see how it could be grounded in what Iraq or any other States consented to. What underlies Resolution 687 is that Iraq has violated the moral minimum of acceptable behavior of States. Such a basis for the claims against Iraq would not turn on whether Iraq was at the time a member of the United Nations and hence subject to the resolutions of the Security Council.

In the first two sections of this chapter, we have seen that the main problem of consensually based custom as a source of universal legally binding norms is that such a consensual source of putative law is not binding on States that have not consented. In addition, it is unclear how conflicts of custom can be adjudicated. Appeals to custom alone will not allow for the resolution of such problems. At most, customary practices of some States will tell us what those States think they are legally bound to do, not what other States that have rejected these customs are legally bound to do. In this sense, it is right to think that Security Council resolutions get their bindingness from the fact that they do, sometimes, reflect non-consensual norms of international law. Such resolutions also make binding norms, but only for those States that remain members and only for as long as the votes of the Security Council continue to declare such norms to be binding on its members. Non-consensual norms that could bind non-member States have to gain their justification from a source other than consensually based custom.

IV. The Threat to Use Nuclear Weapons

The third problem with seeing consensually based custom as a source of universal norms is that custom is not only normatively too weak to be much of a justification at all, but it is also so hard to meet the test for custom that custom will rarely be able to resolve disputes. The test for custom requires that all or most States engage in practices consistent with recognizing the norm as binding, and the *opinio juris* provision adds the notion that all or almost all States must indicate that they are motivated to follow the norm out of a sense of legal or moral obligation. Yet rarely, if ever, can such a high standard be achieved. Consensually based custom will then not be very useful in articulating duties and obligations in international law. And once again we see that consensually based custom will not provide a basis for non-derogable duties of the sort required for universal *jus cogens* norms.

In the ICJ's opinion on whether the threatened use of nuclear weapons can be justified to defend the rights of an aggrieved State, we see this problem in stark relief as two prominent international jurists disagreed about what is customary international law, and how if at all custom could resolve a dispute. In lodging dissents in the nuclear weapons case, Judge Schwebel and Judge Weeramantry debated the issue. Both of these jurists are highly respected as international law scholars. But, as will emerge, both failed to understand the difficulties with the concept of *opinio juris*, the concept that is supposed to provide a test for whether a norm rises to the level of customary international law with universally binding force.

According to the ICJ's majority opinion in the Advisory Opinion on Nuclear Weapons Use, the threat or use of nuclear weapons is generally contrary to international law. But the court left open the possibility that the threat or use of nuclear weapons might be justified "in an extreme circumstance of self-defense, in which the very survival of the state would be at stake."[34] The ICJ took up the issue of tactical nuclear weapons in paragraph 95 of its advisory opinion, and said, "the Court does not consider that it has sufficient basis for a determination on the validity" of the threat or use of tactical nuclear weapons. Thus the ICJ did not declare this use of nuclear weapons to be illegal. What is more important, though, is that the dissents spawned by this opinion give a rather clear idea of the conceptual problems that continue to plague the idea of customary international law.

Judge Schwebel, a United States judge sitting on the ICJ, argued in dissent that State practices and *opinio juris* demonstrate the support in customary international law for the legality of the threat or use of nuclear weapons. To support this claim, Schwebel points to the U.S.-led war against Iraq in 1990. Citing statements by Iraqi Foreign Minister Tariq Aziz, Schwebel contends that the U.S. threat of nuclear strikes deterred Iraq from using its chemical and biological weapons during the war with Iraq.[35] Schwebel argues that the threat of nuclear weapons allowed the United States to win the war, and thereby allowed the United Nations effectively to sanction Iraq for invading Kuwait. This shows that the threat of nuclear weapons can be rational, and acceptable to all. If Iraq had not been deterred by the threat, the United States would have been justified in using nuclear weapons in order to prevent the use by Iraq of prohibited weapons of mass destruction. According to Schwebel, it would be imprudent to prohibit the use of nuclear weapons as long as there are rogue States and terrorists who will only be deterred by nuclear threats.[36]

Judge Schwebel's use of the example of the invasion of Iraq does not support his claim that State practices and *opinio juris* favor the legality of nuclear weapons. First, there is no consensus that the United States would have been justified in using nuclear weapons to counter Iraq's use of chemical or biological weapons. Schwebel can cite no one outside of the United States who agrees with him about this point. Hence he is unable to show the nearly unanimous State practices he needs in support of his point, let alone the additional dimension of *opinio juris*. If the United States believed that it was justified in threatening the use of nuclear weapons, why was there then, as well as now, very little public discussion of this strategy. The United States may have been willing to use nuclear weapons, but it is unclear from what Schwebel shows that the United States felt it was clearly legally or morally justified in doing so.

Second, arguments about what would be prudent are not adequate for establishing *opinio juris*, which requires that a State act out of a sense of moral or legal obligation. Schwebel's argument misses the mark by failing to establish anything like the *opinio juris* dimension of customary international law. The chief conceptual problem with customary international law illustrated by Schwebel's opinion is that States often do things for unclear motives, and yet *opinio juris* requires a showing that a State's practice is based on a felt sense of legal or moral obligation. It is very hard to isolate the intentions and motives of a State, but it surely cannot be assumed that if a State clearly acts on prudential motives, it is thereby acting on the basis of a felt legal or moral obligation.

Prudence might provide a normative basis for a *jus cogens* norm, but only if prudence were linked to a moral minimum. Schwebel tries to make prudence a basis of custom, and then posits custom as a basis of a *jus cogens* norm. Such a strategy is simply confused. Prudence could motivate a state to support a custom, but the fact of consent is ultimately an empirical matter of whether many, or perhaps all, States support the custom. Even if all States support a custom on the basis of prudence, it is the prudence, as a normative matter, not the custom, as an empirical matter, that might ground a *jus cogens* norm.

Judge Weeramantry, also arguing in dissent, tries to counter Judge Schwebel's argument, by appealing to custom and *opinio juris* as well. Weeramantry bases much of his opinion on the Martens Clause of The Hague Convention in arguing that the threat or use of nuclear weapons "represents the very negation of . . . the structure of humanitarian law."[37] Such ultimate human values risk being wiped out, or at least massively and quite horribly destroyed, by "the advent of nuclear war."[38] Weeramantry says that the cornerstone of that branch of international customary law called humanitarian law is the Martens Clause's requirement that the dictates of public conscience must not be violated.[39] Here we see Weeramantry adding moral considerations to the arguments about State practice.

The part of the Martens Clause that seems most important to Weeramantry is the role that the "dictates of public conscience" play in filling the gaps left because we don't have a complete code of the laws of war. The "test" of what satisfies public conscience is "that the rule should be 'so widely and generally accepted that it can hardly be supposed that any civilized state would not support it,' "[40] and hence is contrary to common decency. And Weeramantry says that the public conscience has spoken many times, in the most unmistakable terms, that the threat or use of nuclear weapons is unacceptable.[41] Weeramantry here seems to be influenced by natural law arguments, not by simple appeals to custom. The Martens Clause is presented as affirming a normative principle, not merely as one part of a previous multilateral treaty. In Chapter 5, I will explore the "public conscience" basis of *jus cogens* norms. But it should be here noted that this basis is not itself consensually customary, but rather morally normative, since what counts as a matter of public conscience is not simply a matter of what most States happen to believe.

While I share many of Weeramantry's sentiments, his argument leaves something to be desired. If we give a literal interpretation of his test for ascertaining when custom becomes a universal norm, there will then be no rule favoring or disfavoring the threat or use of nuclear weapons if there is just one civilized country that does not support it. But we know that several, if not many, "civilized" States do not support this rule. Indeed, the majority opinion in this case[42] also cites the Martens Clause. And the same is true of Judge Schwebel's opinion that mentions the Martens Clause approvingly on its very first page. Hence it seems that Weeramantry has set too stringent a test for what is necessary to ground universal international norms. He is right that whatever threatens the advent of nuclear war is indeed one of the worst of human disasters to be avoided at nearly any cost. But he is confused in thinking that the consensual practices of States plus *opinio juris* is unequivocal in supporting this idea, or is likely ever to be. The upshot is that the addition of *opinio juris* to consensually based custom does not help to arrive at *jus cogens* norms of international law.

V. What is the Relationship Between Custom
and Universal Norms?

Customary international law is said to have two elements. First, there must be reasonably consistent and nearly universal practices of States to act in a certain way, such as not torturing people. Second, there must be *opinio juris* – that is, a general sense of legal or moral obligation on the part of the States that motivates them not to engage in a certain practice. As the ICJ held in the North Sea Continental Shelf Cases: "[t]he States concerned must therefore feel that they are conforming to what amounts to a legal obligation. The frequency, or even habitual character of the acts is not in itself enough."[43] Mark Janis calls *opinio juris* a "magic potion" that is added to the frequency of State practice. Janis says that the best sources of *opinio juris* are the statements made by jurists and judges because it is hard to tell what the motivation is for State action or practice.[44] As we saw earlier, even with the statements of jurists, there is often no consensus.

When a large number of States not only consent to be bound by a given custom, but also behave in ways that indicate that they have a sense of moral or legal obligation to obey that norm,[45] the customary norms are supposed to bind not only those States but also other non-consenting States. How is it possible for one State to bind another State by means of consent? Think of the prohibition of torture. What started out as a matter of mere consent by some States is said to have evolved into a norm that is binding on all States, and that cannot now be overturned by the express agreement of States. And this is supposed to be due to the fact that these States not only consent to the norm, but behave as if they are bound by it from a sense of obligation. But how can it happen that a norm that is based on the consent of various States can itself be transformed into a norm that is universally binding?

At least part of the answer is that in addition to the original consent, it must now be that all, or almost all, States regard a given norm as a universal norm. This appears to be a way to determine universal norms by asking all States what they think are universal norms, and this is indeed partially what is going on. But in addition, all, or nearly all, States must demonstrate by their behavior that they regard the norm as binding. And the bindingess needs to be one that is recognized as universal or somehow necessary in a sense that makes the norm a priori, as the ICJ recognized in the North Sea Continental Shelf Case.[46] In that case, the question was whether the equidistance principle was a "natural law of the continental shelf" evidenced in the customs of nations. The court asks: "[W]as the notion of equidistance . . . an inherent necessity of continental shelf doctrine?"[47] It answers that this cannot be, since States have recognized two competing principles for determining the extent of a State's continental shelf.

The court then considers whether nonetheless "this emerging customary law became crystallized" as a result of being recognized in various treaties.[48] The treaties, though, would normally only provide a consensual basis for a given norm – after all, treaties are just elaborate contracts. But if the treaties recognized an existing norm thought to be universal, then this would be evidence for the existence of such a norm. Again, it would not be sufficient for the norm to be merely "accepted," but the States would also have to behave as if the norm were indeed a universal norm. So we are still left wondering how consensually based customary norms could become universal norms, and what might be the "magic potion" that could transform the former into the latter in international law.

At this stage, we need to draw an important distinction that will help us understand the relationship between customary and universal norms. We need to distinguish between *evidence* for the existence of a universal norm, and *justification* of that norm. Consensually based custom could provide evidence, although certainly not conclusive evidence, of the existence of a universal (*jus cogens*) norm, but consensually based custom cannot justify a *jus cogens* norm. The main reason for this is quite simple. Even if all States once consented to be bound by a given custom, and behaved as if this custom were universally binding, that would not make the norm universally binding since the States could change their views toward this custom. Paust et al. recognize this point when in their recent textbook of international law they assert that "customary law can be dynamic . . . What once was custom can change to non-custom . . . and what was not customary law can grow into customary law . . ."[49]

Let us say that a State is confronted with a supposedly universal norm based on a near-unanimous consensus among States. And a State is able to deny the universal bindingness of the norm merely by declaring that it does not now agree that the norm is binding. If even a small number of States change positions and now declare that they no longer acknowledge the norm as universal, then by these very declarations the norm would seem to lose its universal status.[50] Yet surely this cannot be. If the norm is to be universally binding now, it cannot also be true that now States can make that norm not universally binding. Either the norm is universally binding or it is not. States cannot make a norm currently more or less universally binding by their votes or by their practices, even if based on a sense of obligation.

This simple argument is not meant to deny that *opinio juris* may be the best evidence we have of the existence of a universal (*jus cogens*) norm of international law. If all or most States do acknowledge a norm as universally binding, and their behavior also displays such an acknowledgment, then this is indeed evidence of the existence of such a norm. Such evidence becomes even stronger if the reason that States do acknowledge such a norm is because of a sense of legal or moral obligation. And if States stop acknowledging a norm as universal, then this is very good evidence that such a norm may never have been universally binding. But in neither case is this evidence conclusive for establishing that a norm is or is not a universal legally binding norm.

So what might count as conclusive evidence of a universal legally binding norm? It might be conclusive if there is a morally normative argument based, for instance, on what reasonable States would accept. The very best evidence we have of a universal norm of international law is when there is both *opinio juris* and normative justification for such a norm. Normative justification may be enough, at least in the abstract, but in a highly diverse world, where the very premises of such a conceptual argument are highly contested, it is prudent to look to *opinio juris* in addition to normative justification in order to determine what the *jus cogens* norms of international law are. It is prudent because even if fully justified, the norm may not be respected by States unless it already also has fairly widespread support seen in the customary practices of these States. But such appeals to consensual custom, standing alone, cannot ground these norms. A norm cannot be said to be universally binding if, at the moment of a State's falling under the obligation, a State can evade this bindingness merely by declaring itself not bound.

VI. Defending Custom

The kind of custom we have been examining – namely, that which starts off as based in a multilateral treaty – is seemingly either justified by long-standing norms that reach back in time for their justification – that is, to the acceptance of certain norms at those historically distant times[51] – or is justified by the current acquiescence of States. In both cases, the customary norm is justified by the acceptance, and hence the consent, of States. Such norms cannot mysteriously change themselves into non-consensual norms unless something else is added. Perhaps the custom is based on hypothetical rather than actual consent. But in such cases, it is the morally normative argument underpinning the hypothetical consent that does the work, not the practices of States. In this section, I will explore various ways that one could still try to argue that consensually based custom might ground universal or inherent norms.

First, let us consider the "historical" argument. Customs are often defended on the grounds of having stood "the test of time" – namely, that the justification of the norm is acknowledged over different historical eras. Most customs start out as consensual in the sense that people regard the custom as binding because they accept it, or acquiesce in it. As a custom displays a staying power – that is, as generation after generation accepts or acquiesces in it, that custom demonstrates that it is acceptable to a broad constituency. In other words, customs gain in stature, and perhaps also in legal bindingness, the longer they last and as they gain more and more adherents. The more diverse the States that effectively "sign on" to a custom, and the longer those States remain "signatories," the stronger is the custom's bindingness. Having stood "the test of time," the custom demonstrates its "universal" acceptability. At some point, perhaps at that mystical point identified by Mark Janis, the custom itself ceases to be consensual and becomes non-consensual.

One significant problem with the historical argument concerns what have been called "persistent objectors."[52] Certain States may have dissented from the custom from the very beginning of the custom's history, and their dissent continues into the present day. By so objecting, these "persistent objectors" establish something like a counter-custom of their own. By the same reasoning as that provided by the consenters, the dissenters can claim that their dissent also gets stronger the longer it lasts, and perhaps also crystallizes into a countervailing non-consensual custom that is as strong as the original custom itself, since it is based on the same "test of time." Once it is acknowledged that the "persistent objector" is not bound by the customary norm to which it dissents, then the universal bindingness of the original customary norm is rendered suspect. This objection shows that a single State can, counter-intuitively, disrupt the move from historical consensual custom to universal norm.

Second, let us consider the "fairness" argument. Such an argument has its strongest support in reaction to the problem of the "persistent objectors." Take, for example, the custom that people not take advantage of those who are in vulnerable positions. If such a custom is not treated as universally binding, then some will choose not to follow the custom, and yet may well benefit from the custom, for instance, if they themselves are ever in a vulnerable position and hence in need of the restraint that the custom calls for. Those who do not follow the custom – the dissenters – will feel free to take advantage of the vulnerable to their own benefit, and yet will also count on the restraint of others if these dissenters are ever rendered vulnerable. In the parlance of social choice theory, this will allow the dissenters to become "free riders" in a society where most of the people restrain themselves. And because the dissenters benefit from their exploitation of this custom, it is unfair. The dissenters benefit from the adherence of others to a custom to which they themselves do not adhere. Fairness calls for the dissenters to be subject to the custom to avoid the free rider problem.

The fairness argument gives us a reason to treat some consensually based customs as universally binding norms, but it does not establish the principle that these customs, as opposed to any others, really are universally binding. Instead, we are given fairness-based reasons to apply certain norms to all, but no reason to think that the norms so applied have a special character by virtue of having been backed by custom. Indeed, we have merely pushed the skeptical question back one level. Instead of asking why "persistent objectors" should be held to a custom that they dissented from, we now ask why the custom itself is thought to be so important that dissent from it is not to be allowed, even on the very good grounds provided by the "persistent objectors?" And the answer to this question cannot rely merely on the fact that a norm is supported by custom, but must appeal to fairness, or some other ground for thinking that the norm must be considered binding for all. Yet, such an argument is no longer basically a customary or historical argument but rather one of normative principle.

Third, a related strategy is to argue that customs should be seen as universally binding in order to solve certain coordination problems. Here it is not fairness but efficiency that makes the custom universally binding. On this strategy, perhaps custom is itself grounded in just one consensual principle – namely, a single rule of recognition that says that any norm that has satisfied the *opinio juris* criteria for being a custom is a proper basis of legal obligation. If all States accept such a rule, then any norm that meets the criteria becomes a binding norm on all States. If enough States accept a custom, then the other States are bound because all States have accepted the rule of recognition "tipping principle": as soon as n-number of States accept a norm, then, so as to solve a serious coordination problem, all other States accept that norm as binding on them, even those States that have not previously accepted it. And the basis for such a rule of recognition is that the world is simply a better place if there is a stable pattern of conduct than if there is not. Here is a way to link prudential considerations with morally normative ones that one would expect a moral minimalist like me to endorse.

Yet I still find myself skeptical. We would seem to need universal agreement to the rule of recognition, and yet this is not the case in international law. There has not been anything like the acceptance of an international rule of recognition, as Hart and others have pointed out.[53] Think of those States that never accepted the UN Charter or who never ratified the Rome Treaty. We have not solved the problems identified earlier since there are still persistent objectors to the rule of recognition, and yet these persistent objectors would find themselves nonetheless bound by the norms endorsed by that rule of recognition. As Hart also said, a rule of recognition is merely a fact. If some States do not accept a given rule of recognition, then it is not a rule of recognition for them.

Fourth, rather than being based on consent, perhaps custom derives its authority from a set of interdependent habits in a given population. These interlocking habits create a web of normative behavior in a society that is meant to ground *jus cogens* norms. Interdependent habits are not the same as consent. Indeed, it would be as odd to say that custom has been established by consent as it is to say that tradition has been established by a deliberate act. Rather, customs are established over time as more and more States find themselves acting in ways that are consistent with the custom. According to this defense of custom, it is not consent but a certain kind of implicit acceptance over time that is key, and the acceptance is seen in a State's behavior, not in some "mythical" consent. As long as States behave in interdependent and habitual ways, these habits are themselves a basis of custom that has normative force.

Whether acceptance is inferred from behavior or based on explicit consent, there is still the problem of how some States that behave in ways supportive of a custom can bind other States that do not behave in this way. I suppose it can be said that these other States simply already do behave this way (although perhaps unself-consciously) or that they will come to behave in this way down the road. Such a view denies the possibility of true "persistent objectors" to a given custom, and yet history is full of such examples. Persistent objectors consistently behave in ways that are opposed to a given custom. States that reject the custom against torture behave in ways, although probably not very often, that mark their objection to the custom. Of course, part of this is an empirical matter concerning how States actually do behave. But shifting to how States behave, and away from what States explicitly consent to, does not help account for the bindingness of certain norms, especially the bindingness for the persistent objectors.

Fifth, custom could be considered to provide us with "as if" universal norms in the same way that scientists act as if they had "discovered" a new physical element – call it krypton. The act of those who accept the custom, and the act of the scientist, are similar in that they merely give us the best evidence of the existence of a universal norm. This position is attractive in that it actually plays off my earlier discussion of the difference between evidence for, and justification of, a norm. Just as science doesn't need any more support, so also is this true for international norms. Here it is claimed that custom is the best evidence we can seek, and is not in need of supplementation by additional bases. Custom is then like a scientist's discovery of krypton in that custom is a kind of recognition by a society that a norm is binding. The society's recognition is not what makes the norm binding, just as the scientist's discovery of krypton is not what creates krypton. Both the norm and the krypton were already there. The society recognizes the existence of the norm by agreeing to, or acquiescing in, a custom, just as the scientist recognizes the existence of krypton by "discovering" or naming it.

Yet I would want to insist that, even as evidence, consensual custom still does not provide a basis for a universal norm in the sense of providing a justification. Indeed, by the way this third position is articulated, it is clear that the custom does not provide a justification of the norm for those who would doubt that the norm does in fact exist, just as the skeptic is not answered by the scientist's reference to the "discovering" or naming of krypton. The skeptic will want to hear the reasons, and not just trust the scientist's word, just as the skeptic will not trust the "word" of the custom. Once again, our skeptical question is merely pushed back another level. Certainly no one denies that there are such putative customs and discoveries. The question is rather whether any putative custom or discovery really does pick out the universal norm or the krypton. To answer a skeptic at this level, one needs a different kind of argument than one that merely makes reference to some evidence. One needs an independent reason for the skeptic to trust that the society or the scientist is a reliable finder of actual, as opposed to illusory, norms or krypton.

Sixth, one could merely suggest that the defenders of *jus cogens* norms have simply overreached. *Jus cogens* norms are no different from norms in most societies proscribing murder or rape. That just these acts are proscribed is based on custom. That the proscription extends to all members in a society is based on utility, or some other value. In the international "society," *jus cogens* norms on this understanding would be simply those norms that are considered most fundamental, in terms of the benefits, or other values, that adherence to those norms is thought to provide for the world community. Once again, there are various ways to help pick out which of the international norms should have this designation. But the justification for them as universal or fundamental norms is simply that adherence to them does indeed benefit, or provide some other value to, that community. It is the value of these norms that gives them their universal bindingness and that goes beyond the mere criteria of identification of the norms.

Here we finally come to a position that is likely to produce a justification for universal norms in international law. But in the end it is a justification that is independent of the existence of the consensually based custom itself. For the justification is really based entirely on the utility, or other moral value, of a given norm, regardless of what its form happens to be, or regardless of its history. Hence this last attempt to save the customary basis of *jus cogens* norms either fails outright, or points us toward the type of justification that is based on moral principles, such as the principle of utility. In the next chapter, I will offer just such a justification of *jus cogens* norms as universally binding norms. But this sixth attempt fails if it is thought to provide a justification based solely on the evidence of the existence of a norm rather than on the underlying justification for having the norm.

Consensually based customs thus do not justify the norms that they express. This said, it is also true that customs play a role in giving recognition to norms, perhaps even to universal norms. The custom of condemning murder can be said to give voice to the universal norm against the premeditated taking of innocent life. Therefore, to say that *jus cogens* norms are part of customary international law is not quite as odd as it first seemed. *Jus cogens* norms can be part of customary international law and still be non-consensual as long as the non-consensual nature of these norms is not thought to derive from their being originally consensual, as we learned from David Hume. That universal *jus cogens* norms are customary is merely due to the way that they are sometimes recognized rather than anything having to do with their nature or justification.

The *opinio juris* test adds an important dimension to custom as a basis for international rights and duties. It is not enough that States behave as if there are universal rights and duties at stake. *Opinio juris* requires that the States behave in this way out of a sense of moral or legal obligation. Meeting this test will indeed greatly help in the identification of those customary norms of international law that are universally binding. But rather than looking at the behavior of States, and at the motivation of those States, why not look at the obligation itself, and ask whether there are good arguments based on normative principles to support such an obligation. Such a grounding will give us a direct basis for the identification and justification of non-consensual norms that does not depend on magically creating them out of consensually based customary norms.[54]

The non-consensual basis of *jus cogens* norms is especially important for practices that involve exploitation. Many States find themselves contractually bound to acquiesce in violating their own subjects' right not to be exploited. Because of the treaties and accords that those States have consented to, as was true in the two Libya cases discussed earlier, States are seemingly forced to exploit their subjects. If *jus cogens* norms are consensual, then they cannot easily be used to override other consensual norms, such as those imposed by treaty or contract.[55] Yet, as in the case of unconscionable domestic contracts, it is well recognized in international law that States do have a basis for rejecting exploitative treaties and contracts.[56] If this is to be a part of international law as well, the norms necessary for such an overriding will have to be non-consensual.

The conclusion to the argument of this chapter is that there is a serious conceptual confusion about custom and *opinio juris*, the supposed basis for universal *jus cogens* norms, in international law. Consensually based custom, standing alone, is not a clear basis for justifying the universal international norms, the violation of which will warrant international prosecutions. As in most justificatory matters, there is no substitute for moral support. I have hinted at what that normative support might look like, but the main point of this chapter has been a negative one: Consensually based custom and *opinio juris* are not sufficient bases for the condemnation of rights abuses and the ensuing crossing of borders to redress those rights violations. The most significant finding of this chapter is that there remains serious conceptual confusion about *opinio juris* as a cornerstone of universal *jus cogens* norms in international law. In the next two chapters, we will turn to the philosophically normative support for, and limitations on, universal *jus cogens* norms.

PART B

PRINCIPLES OF INTERNATIONAL CRIMINAL LAW

4

The Security Principle

In this chapter, I will provide a moral argument that grounds *jus cogens* norms and that partially justifies international prosecutions. In the last chapter, we saw that the attempt to ground universal norms in consensually based custom is doomed, unless custom, including *opinio juris*, is combined with moral support. In this chapter and the next, I will supply that support by arguing that a norm of international law is *jus cogens* if it satisfies two principles – the security principle and the international harm principle.

The argument of this chapter begins with a return to moral minimalist principles having to do with self-defense and self-preservation as the support for the security principle. This principle opens the door for otherwise prohibited intrusions into State sovereignty. Then, to justify fully international criminal prosecutions, I turn to another principle, the international harm principle, which will justify specific intrusions into a sovereign State to prosecute certain crimes. The main basis of the international harm principle is the requirement that if there is a fully functioning State, in order for a crime to be prosecuted in an international tribunal, that crime must be group-based, in one of two senses I will later discuss. Violations of the security principle may be sufficient to justify humanitarian intervention into the affairs of a State. But in order to justify the likely infringement of liberty of individuals that comes from trials, satisfying an additional justificatory principle is necessary.

International law is premised on the idea that there are norms that all States should embrace. Typically, these norms are described as justice-based or in some manner connected to human rights. In order to promote justice or to protect human rights, certain State practices need to be interfered with. Most of international law is consensual and cooperative, merely facilitating the coordination of interests of various States. International law is most controversial when it sanctions or even requires intervention by a State or international body into the affairs of another State. These intrusions can take the form, among others, of armed military action or the required extradition of a State's nationals to an international tribunal. International tribunals, which prosecute and punish individuals rather than States for various crimes, require different justificatory schemes than is true for military action directed against the offending State itself, since it is individuals rather than the State directly that is the target of the prosecution.

In the first section of the chapter, I examine various strategies for understanding the nature of international crimes. Many theorists of international law have recognized that there is a need for some kind of codification of international crimes. But most have also said that it is not possible to have a set of theoretical criteria for what counts as an international crime. In this section, I challenge that view. I argue against those who say that we should give up on finding a theoretical rationale for international criminal prosecutions. I argue that an explicit moral justification is needed for jeopardizing the loss of liberty of a defendant in a criminal trial. In the second section, I set out a version of the security principle, and begin to provide a defense of that principle. I explain why international tribunals should be limited to violations of basic human rights – that is, to violations of the right to physical security and subsistence, and not to the panoply of human rights listed in various international documents. In the third section, I provide an additional, Hobbesian, argument in defense of the security principle, comparing the security principle with the more general right of self-defense. In the fourth section, I respond to five objections to my defense of the security principle.

I. International Crimes and Moral Legitimacy

International crime, like international law itself, is at best an ambiguous concept. It can refer to crimes that States will enforce domestically as a result of treaty obligations that those States have incurred. Or it can refer to what is customarily accepted as criminal by the community of nations. Or it can refer to the acts that are clearly proscribed by so-called *jus cogens* norms, norms of such transparent bindingness that no individual can fail to understand that he or she is bound by them, and no State can fail to see that it should either prosecute such acts or turn the perpetrator over to another institution that will prosecute.[1] These differing conceptions of international crime result from the differing sources of international criminal law. In this section, I will argue that, especially with the institution of the new International Criminal Court, we need a clear basis for identifying international crimes, distinguishing them from domestic crimes, and, most importantly, explaining why the prosecution of these international crimes has moral legitimacy.

In 1995, M. Cherif Bassiouni pointed out that the "term 'international crime' or its equivalent had never been specifically used in international conventions."[2] Yet in 1998, a multilateral convention established an International Criminal Court, where the name of the court signifies that the term "international crime" has now come into use. It is thus of pressing concern that the idea of international crime be explored explicitly. In one sense, "international crime" is easy to define. International crimes are simply those crimes recognized in international law. As Bassiouni puts it, "[t]he criminal aspect of international law consists of a body of international proscriptions containing penal characteristics evidencing the criminalization of certain types of conduct."[3] But beyond this simple point, it is not so easy to see what should evidence international criminalization.

Let us begin by considering domestic criminal law. John Stuart Mill asked the salient question: What are "the nature and limits of the power which can be legitimately exercised by society over the individual."[4] His answer was that more was needed than merely showing that a valid law was in place. From standard liberal principles, where liberty is one of the highest values, it is obvious that when the law seeks to incarcerate a person, thereby taking away that person's liberty, a very strong rationale is needed. It is always legitimate to ask not only whether a criminal law exists but also whether it is morally legitimate. A similar question can be asked at the international level, but now the question is not about the legitimate exercise of the power of a particular State, but the legitimate exercise of the collective power of all States. Since Nuremberg, there has been a healthy debate about what would legitimate the international community's punishment of a person or State.

My focus in this section is on the moral legitimacy of the exercise of the collective, coercive power of States in international criminal trials. The idea of legitimacy in criminal law, writes Joel Feinberg, "is not an invention of arcane philosophy. It is part of the conceptual equipment of every man and woman on the street."[5] Domestic criminal statutes are legitimated by moral principles, and those moral principles are least controversial when they are ones that nearly any person would find reasonable. Moral legitimacy is crucial for any type of law since the law's effectiveness is so closely linked with a person's sense that the law is legitimate and the corresponding sense of obligation that a person feels. Without this sense of the binding effect of the law, there is nothing of moral importance that motivates people to obey the law in the first place.[6]

Law's effectiveness is dependent on the moral legitimacy of the law.[7] In this, as will be clear later, I follow Lon Fuller, a paradigmatic moral minimalist, who attempted to provide a middle ground between legal positivism and robust natural law theory. In the last chapter, we saw that consent or acceptance alone will not ground *jus cogens* norms. But we also saw that, especially in a pluralistic society or world community, it makes prudential good sense to link wide-scale acceptance to normative justification. For law to be effective, there must be such acceptance, but the acceptance is not what justifies the norms. Rather it is the moral legitimacy of law that both provides a justification for its enforcement and also creates wide-scale acceptance. There is a minimum moral or natural law content that laws must display to be legitimate. This is what I am calling the "moral legitimacy" of the law. The morality of law does not need to be robust for law to be legitimate. Here there is a set of moral principles, recognized in virtually every legal system, that makes a law worthy of being enforced. Such moral principles ultimately protect the inner normative core of law by guaranteeing that the law is, in some rudimentary way, fair.[8]

One moral principle that seems crucial to the legitimacy of international (or any other) criminal law is that a person should not be prosecuted for something that either wasn't a crime or couldn't be known to be a crime at the time the defendant acted. This principle of fair dealing has been well known since Roman times, and is often cited by the Latin phrase: *nullum crimen sine lege*. This moral principle seemingly requires that international crimes have a well-recognized and easily accessed source that will allow individuals to figure out what is required of them. In this respect, international law's traditional emphasis on custom is especially problematical. It is for this reason that many theorists of international criminal law have urged that the legitimate sources of international crimes be restricted to only special kinds of customary law – namely, that which is uncontested.[9]

In the last chapter, we explored the idea of customs that are based on *opinio juris* as providing evidence of *jus cogens* norms. Rather than requiring such a theoretical core, some have argued that it is sufficient that there be a codification of crimes in international law.[10] Such a view misses the point behind the call for moral legitimacy. Again, consider the analogy with domestic criminal law. Just because a State has statutorily required that people act a certain way does not mean that the statutory law is morally legitimate. It is always an open question as to whether a duly passed law is itself legitimate. This is readily seen in the debates about whether statutes prohibiting pornography or other so-called victimless crimes have sufficient legitimacy for the State to punish those who do not conform.[11]

It is not enough that what is criminal is known or knowable, but it also must somehow make sense as to why just these acts are proscribed. Without such a requirement, the actual or hypothetical consent of the citizens cannot be reasonably inferred. If there is no rationale to the laws, then they appear as potentially arbitrary exercises of State power. And here we need a second moral principle – namely, that the restrictions on individual liberty required by conformity to criminal law achieve some highly valuable purpose. Merely codifying laws does not guarantee that the laws are morally legitimate in this sense.

Many philosophers have settled on the idea that society has an interest in preventing harm, and that only those acts that are aimed at the prevention of harm should be criminalized.[12] Indeed, I would argue that all criminal laws are legitimate only if they address the prevention of harm, or something of equal importance. If something as significant as a harm is not involved then, as is true in the debates about the nature of domestic crime, there would not be sufficient justification for the serious interference with liberty that is involved in criminal punishment. If, for instance, people risk imprisonment for calling each other derogatory names, something has gone seriously awry.[13] The harm potentially inflicted by the defendant is greatly disproportionate to the harm that the defendant will be made to suffer by imprisonment. And here we also need to comment that this is yet another moral principle of legitimacy well recognized in all legal systems – namely, that the punishment must somehow fit the crime.[14]

Harm can be understood in terms of interests, in that a harm is a "setback to interests," which is also somehow a denial of rights.[15] For international criminal law, the difficult question concerns whose interests are to be taken into account. If we say that it is the interest of any person, the setback of which constitutes a sufficient harm for criminal punishment, then we have no basis for distinguishing domestic crimes from international ones. But before we discuss that issue, it is of course legitimate to ask whether "setback to interest" is the best way to understand harm. Why not, for instance, make international crime depend on preventing a person from getting what he or she wants? My response is that many wants are not significant enough to justify infringement of liberty, for each of us also wants to be free from punishment, and this want is often more important than the wants of another person concerning the disposition of his or her luxury goods, for instance. Similar worries can be expressed about letting any harm-prevention justify criminal punishment. We look to interest setback as the threshold for legitimate punishment because interests are conceived as non-trivial. It is not legitimate to punish someone for trivial acts, given that punishment itself is not a trivial matter, even if those trivial acts are clearly proscribed in a code of crimes, and may even cause minimal harm.

Why shouldn't codification be all we can expect, especially in our morally pluralistic and fractious world? As I said earlier, many theorists of international criminal law bemoan the attempts to give an underlying rationale to the list of crimes that count as international crimes. In many respects, these theorists are taking a post-modern approach to international criminal law. They think that it is misguided even to attempt to provide a theoretical structure, because it will somehow do violence to the historical reasons why specific acts have come to be listed as international crimes. Specific contexts have given rise to the international community's directing its attention in various ways toward perceived wrongs, and creating crimes in order to capture the insights of those historical moments. Think of piracy, for instance. Piracy is one of the oldest recognized international crimes. And yet, so it would be claimed, it does grave injustice to such a crime to strip it from its historical context and to try to find an underlying principle that will capture this act, piracy, as well as other acts such as apartheid, genocide, and torture, which have also been proscribed in other historical contexts.[16]

I agree that the reason why societies criminalized acts of piracy may be very different from the reason societies criminalized acts of apartheid, genocide, and torture. But if people are still today to be punished for committing these acts, now long after the time has passed during which these acts were first condemned as criminal, then we need a current account of what makes these acts legitimately punishable now. And more importantly, we need some basis from which people can see that such acts are indeed worthy of criminal sanction at the international level, and not merely anachronistic manifestations of bygone prejudices. Unless we give up on the search for moral legitimacy of criminal punishment, and argue that the international community is right to prosecute any crimes that it can, it is not sufficient merely to codify international crimes. We must also explain why each of these things listed in the code are non-trivial matters, the violation of which merits the serious loss of liberty involved in punishment.

I believe that one reasonable strategy, as we will now see in greater detail than in the previous chapters, is to restrict international crimes to those that involve a violation of *jus cogens* norms understood as a violation of both the security and the international harm principles. Bassiouni has commented that linking international crime to *jus cogens* norms has the advantage of setting the stage for the new ICC, which will presume universal jurisdiction and application to all humans, not just to those in a particular region or particular historical time.[17] In the remainder of this chapter, I set out and defend the security principle, leaving to the next chapter an exposition and defense of the international harm principle. The security principle will provide a moral minimalist basis for understanding *jus cogens* norms in international criminal law.

II. The Security Principle

In this section, I explore "the security principle," the principle by which international criminal law is initially made plausible, and by which limitations on tolerance and sovereignty are also partially justified. I have already discussed this principle in an informal way in previous chapters. The security principle can be stated more precisely as follows:

If a State deprives its subjects of physical security or subsistence, or is unable or unwilling to protect its subjects from harms to security or subsistence,

a) then that State has no right to prevent international bodies from "crossing its borders"[18] in order to protect those subjects or remedy their harms;

b) and then international bodies may be justified in "crossing the borders" of a sovereign State when genuinely acting to protect those subjects.

Sovereignty is premised on the willingness and ability of a State to protect its subjects. If a State fails to provide physical security and subsistence to its subjects, then that State has no right to prevent international legal bodies from justifiably infringing that State's sovereignty. An international body may be justified in then acting to protect those subjects. Neither sovereignty nor toleration require that a State be left free to deprive its subjects of the basic human rights of physical security and subsistence.

I should say just a bit here, although it is not the focus of this book, about why, at least initially, it is international bodies rather than other States that may be justified in interfering with the sovereign affairs of a State that acts against its subjects. I rely on the plausible assumption that State sovereignty is more jeopardized when another sovereign State "crosses its borders" than when an international body does so. Another State's interference risks the complete overturning of State sovereignty to a much greater extent than is true when an international body does so. At least for the foreseeable future, international bodies are not very likely to turn into conquering States, whereas past and recent history is replete with examples of State's moving from protector to colonizer. The concerns about sovereignty expressed in earlier chapters lead me to be cautious, and so it is international bodies rather than other States that are the most plausible entities that may be justified in crossing borders to protect individuals when the security principle has been violated.

That a State has no right to prevent an international body from "crossing its borders" does not yet mean that a particular international body does have the right to do so.[19] I leave until later chapters the question as to what are the conditions that must be satisfied for a specific international body actually to have the right to "cross a State's borders" to protect that State's subjects. In general, such a body must itself meet certain threshold conditions, such as conforming to another principle – what I will call "the international rule of law." At the end of the book, I raise questions about whether criminal trials by international bodies are always better than amnesty or reconciliation programs. Such considerations could also deny to a particular international body the right to "cross a State's borders" to conduct criminal trials of those accused of crimes against humanity, genocide, or war crimes.

The security principle is involved in the justification of the three main forms of international criminal prosecution recognized since Nuremberg: war crimes, genocide, and crimes against humanity. In war crimes, the State whose soldiers are mistreated seems to have the best claim on prosecuting the offending State's war crimes perpetrators. If a State is unable or unwilling to prosecute the perpetrators of war crimes committed against its own subjects, then that State is not adequately protecting its subjects. In such cases, the security principle will give us grounds for having an international body take up these prosecutions. The failure of a State to protect its own subjects/soldiers from war crimes can trigger the security principle, although not as obviously as in the case of genocide or crimes against humanity.

Crimes against humanity and genocide normally involve a State's choosing to attack its own subjects outright, or choosing to allow attacks on its subjects to occur within its own borders. For obvious reasons, this type of international crime is most clearly a violation of the security principle. We do not in this case have a State that is too weak, but paradoxically a State that is strong and yet willing to allow for whole groups of its subjects to be subject to attack or to be deprived of basic subsistence. One could even say, although I will not defend this claim here, that the problem is that the State is *too* strong – that is, able to turn against a portion of its own subjects whom the State would normally need to sustain its power. In such situations, it will often require interference with a society's or a State's autonomy to provide international legal remedies for these harms, since the State that has attacked its own subjects, or let these subjects be attacked, normally has little interest in prosecuting the agents of the State's own policies.

The security principle opens the door for international prosecutions for war crimes, genocide, and crimes against humanity by indicating how the State's powerful claim to the authoritative, exclusive control over its own internal affairs can be rebutted. But the security principle alone does not provide a justification for these international prosecutions, for violations of the security principle may not be serious enough to warrant international prosecutions of individuals. This is because international criminal prosecutions risk loss of liberty to the defendants, a loss that is of such potential importance that it should not be risked unless there is also a harm to the international community. I take up this topic in the next chapter. What the security principle does is to make potentially justifiable what would otherwise be considered an unjustified violation of a State's sovereignty when its border is crossed, but does not yet justify a particular prosecution.

In my moral minimalist view, the most plausible philosophical basis of *jus cogens* norms draws on the moral foundation that supports any society – namely, protection from violations of the security principle. Security is an obvious interest or need – indeed, I would argue that it is necessary – for the fulfillment of any rights. As Henry Shue has argued:

No one can fully enjoy any right that is supposedly protected by society if someone can credibly threaten him or her with murder, rape, beating, etc., when he or she tries to enjoy that right . . . In the absence of physical security people are unable to use any other rights that society may be said to be protecting without being liable to encounter many of the worst dangers they would encounter if society were not protecting the rights.[20]

Without the protection of security of the individual, whatever good the State provides to a person will be subject to the most serious of threats that will effectively nullify those other goods. In fact, this is the situation in certain places in the world today where, for instance, women are constitutionally not denied certain goods such as professional jobs but where they fear for their physical security if they in fact take those jobs.[21] Here, the ability of the State arbitrarily to threaten, or to allow others to threaten, certain persons, renders the promise of these other goods a sham. We will encounter a number of examples of Shue's point in Chapter 6.

On my moral minimalist account, basic respect for the security of people is the key to universal international criminal norms. In this context, consider McDougal et al.'s classic book on international human rights.[22] They argue that a much broader notion of respect is "the core value of all human rights," since protecting the value of respect will make it possible to realize "human dignity on the widest possible scale."[23] Their perspective is that of "citizens of the larger community of humankind, who identify with the whole community, rather than with the primacy of particular groups."[24] McDougal et al.'s approach comes out most clearly when they discuss *jus cogens* norms, norms that they say are explicitly meant to apply to a "global bill of human rights."[25] McDougal et al. say that their views are inspired by the "natural law and natural rights tradition,"[26] although they also make reference to Verdross.[27] On their view, *jus cogens* norms provide a basis for reciprocal respect, "both individually and among groups."[28] But having said this, they provide no basis for drawing the distinction between the perspective of humankind and other perspectives,[29] since their perspective seems to take in all norms – indeed, their list of universal *jus cogens* norms covers seven pages of small print.[30]

Here is the nub of my worry about an expansive natural law approach to international criminal law. The Universal Declaration of Human Rights lists such things as "the right to . . . periodic holidays with pay" as universal human rights.[31] I take it as uncontroversial that no one would think that an international criminal trial should be conducted when agents of a State fail to provide paid holidays for their employees. The most obvious reason for this is that a criminal trial puts the defendant's basic liberty in jeopardy. Yet, in the case of certain human rights denials, the defendant's liberty is more significant than the substance of the human right that the defendant has supposedly denied to the victim. What we need is some principle, what I call the "security principle," which, in combination with the international harm principle examined in the next chapter, warrants us to distinguish human rights that are relevant to international criminal law from those human rights that are important but not relevant to international criminal law. Failure to make this distinction means that people will be tried, and will risk serious deprivation of their liberty rights, even though their acts did not cause a corresponding deprivation of liberty rights, or their moral equivalent, for their victims. I realize that no one seriously maintains that deprivation of the human right to paid holidays should trigger an international criminal trial. My point is that recognition of the absurdity of this position should motivate us to think seriously about a more deflationary moral basis for international criminal law than one that is based on any and all human rights abuses. Rather, only violations of the security principle in terms of deprivation of basic rights to subsistence and physical security should be the basis for international criminal prosecutions.

III. A Hobbesian Defense of the Security Principle

To provide a fuller account of the security principle, let us first think about how an international body can be justified, based on international law, in interfering with the sovereign affairs of one State that decides to wage aggressive war against another State. From a Hobbesian perspective, the State that has been attacked has something like a right of self-defense against the aggressing nation. States can be analogized to individual persons, and rights ascribed accordingly. Of course, there are many points of disanalogy as well, not the least of which is that the borders of States can shift over time, and revolutions can change the identity of States, in ways completely different from the strong stability over time of the identities of most human persons. Despite these points of disanalogy, States that have attained a minimal legitimacy have something like a right of self-defense that would justify their demanding that the attacks cease, in asking other States to come to their aid, and in suing for redress of these harms.

The best way to justify this right of a State to self-defense is simply an extension of the right of self-defense of the subjects of that State. Again from a Hobbesian perspective, there is a sense in which, at least hypothetically, subjects can be understood to have given up their own rights (although not the right of self-defense) in exchange for the mutual giving up of rights on the part of all other members of the State. The artificial person that embodies State sovereignty has its right to rule by virtue of having accepted the role of enforcer of the mutual transferring of right. As Hobbes says, this gives the sovereign the duty (or "office") of preserving the safety of the people. Indeed, Hobbes says that the duty of preserving the safety of the people is the chief duty of the sovereign. Whether it is a strict duty or not, this duty is that which defines the office of sovereign.[32]

My own "Hobbesian" argument is probably a blend of Hobbes and Locke. The central idea is that the sovereign ruler of a State in effect promises to hold the safety of the people as his or her chief duty. The sovereign's right to rule derives from a hypothetical transfer of right from subjects to sovereign. Subjects have a right to self-defense – a moral minimum – and they entrust to the sovereign the right to enforce such a right. On the assumption that the sovereign will indeed protect its subjects from attack or assault, and will certainly not attack or assault these subjects, they temporarily give up their right to exercise violence against their potential attackers. If the sovereign displays an inability or unwillingness to continue to protect its subjects, then the sovereign loses the exclusive right to the means of violence or adjudication that can protect those subjects.

Hobbes gives a wide meaning to the duty of the sovereign to preserve the safety of the people.[33] "But by safety here is not meant a bare preservation, but also other contentments of life, which every man by lawful industry, without danger, or hurt to the commonwealth, shall acquire to himself."[34] Embedded in this quotation from Hobbes is a version of what I call "the security principle."

For Hobbes, the two key components of such a principle are (1) that bare preservation be secured, and (2) that one not be subjected to danger in ways that disrupt one's pursuit of contentment or happiness. The first component might be called security of existence; the second, security of welfare or well-being. When either of these components of the principle cannot be, or are willfully not being, protected, then the artificial person that embodies sovereignty has not satisfied the duties of the office of sovereign. In the case of attack from another State, the attacked State's right of self-defense is based on the transferred right to protect the individual persons who comprise it.

I wish to separate my own view from the Hobbesian position I have generally been defending so far. While it may be true that people all expect that their sovereign will not only protect their physical existence, but also provide for their contentment, this latter consideration should not ground the claim that when contentment is not provided, the State in question has no right to block interference with its affairs, especially in the domain of international criminal law. The reason for this is that international prosecutions risk serious deprivation of the liberty of the accused. The loss of liberty that comes from incarceration is not at all comparable to the loss of contentment faced by one who remains outside of the confines of a jail or prison. Of course, I have already indicated that there can be serious deprivations of economic interests – such as occur when subsistence is jeopardized – that would be comparable to the loss of liberty one experiences from incarceration. My point is that if a State leader, or other person acting in behalf of the State, is put in the dock, it should be for having done something truly egregious. Failing to provide for the broad contentment of the members of a State should not be given equal weight to the risk to liberty that is involved in international criminal prosecution.

The right to lead a contented life is important. But of even greater importance is the liberty interest of those who would be subject to international criminal prosecution. This is not to say that individual liberty can never be overridden by other considerations. I here rely on an assumption about the primacy of avoiding serious deprivations of individual liberty by contrast with not-so-serious deprivations of other interests. I am making a relatively weak claim consistent with my moral minimalist project. I take no stand on the conflicts between serious deprivations of liberty and serious deprivations of welfare. If a State leader is accused of stealing huge sums from the State treasury, thereby seriously jeopardizing the economic interests of his subjects, I am willing to consider this crime as one that is serious enough to risk the deprivation of liberty involved in the prosecution of that State leader. For the State to have no right to block international prosecutions of its subjects, there must be as much harm risked by what was done *by* that subject as harm risked *to* that subject from successful prosecution.

Especially when we consider international intervention to prohibit a State from attacking its own subjects, we have an even clearer basis than in cases of war for thinking that sovereign States are not allowed to violate the safety of their own people. The same is true of international intervention to prohibit a State from allowing some of its subjects to deny the rights of existence and physical security to other subjects. Crimes against humanity have the disturbing character of normally involving a State's effectively attacking its own subjects, or choosing to allow such attacks to occur unpunished.[35] As I said earlier, what is particularly disturbing is when a State is so strong that it can disregard a whole segment of its population and actually use its power to the detriment of that population group. When this occurs, the subjects are, in some sense, no longer bound to obey the laws of the sovereign State. To see this point, let us turn to the example of a State's use of capital punishment.

Even Hobbes is quite clear in saying that a person is not bound to follow laws that risk one's life:

If the sovereign command a man, though justly condemned, to kill, wound, or maim himself; or not to resist those that assault him; or to abstain from the use of food, air, medicine, or any other thing, without which he cannot live; yet hath that man the liberty to disobey.[36]

The reason for this is that no "man is bound by the words themselves, either to kill himself, or any other man."[37] And this claim is supported, a few pages later in *Leviathan*, by the following principle:

The obligations of subjects to the sovereign, is understood to last as long, and no longer, than the power lasteth, by which he is able to protect them.[38]

Thus, for Hobbes, any law that calls for a person to give up his or her right of self-defense is not a law people are obligated to obey.[39]

The power to protect the subjects is somewhat different from the will to attack these same subjects. It is of course possible that a State can attack its subjects even as it retains the power to protect them. Such a distinction is especially important in cases of the State's imposition of the death penalty against its subject for a crime the subject has been convicted of. Here it matters that the State continues to have the power to protect, but chooses to attack the subject anyway, usually for the reason that such an attack on an individual subject is thought to render the rest of the individual persons in the State more secure. Nonetheless, even when justly condemned, the subject retains the liberty to disobey the sovereign. What is crucial is whether our resistance or disobedience "frustrates the end for which sovereignty was ordained."[40] The Hobbesian position, while perhaps not the same as Hobbes's actual position, is that State attacks on the subjects of the State generally trigger that State's loss of the protections of sovereignty and toleration, perhaps even in the case of capital punishment.

I would urge that some consideration of human rights be incorporated into the Hobbesian project. The introduction of human rights ideas into a Hobbesian framework is not nearly as odd as it may sound. As we have seen in this chapter,

Hobbes was acutely aware of the problems for sovereigns who act in ways that clearly show an unwillingness to protect their subjects. And while Hobbes does not explicitly recognize that the claims of the subjects are based on human rights, he does the next best thing by recognizing that such claims are grounded in the natural rights that these subjects held in the state of nature and that the subjects have never really lost. The element that human rights ideas add is the explicit recognition that there are rights that people have by virtue of being human, and that certain of these rights cannot be waived. These rights rise to the surface in those cases where sovereigns clearly indicate that they are acting contrary to the security interests of their subjects.

In crimes against humanity or genocide, the sovereign representative is the one who seemingly acts in ways that frustrate the purposes for which sovereignty was ordained. By attacking the very subjects that sovereigns are "ordained" to protect, the prerogatives of sovereignty are called into question. And this, then, is the opening that is needed to justify international intervention. The principle of security is now effectively addressed to a person's own State: If the State attacks its own people, or chooses not to prevent attacks on them, then the State loses the right to keep international agents outside of its borders. Subjects can appeal to the principle of security in order to seek international help to secure themselves against various attacks, including attack by their own sovereigns.[41] The principle of security thus provides a basis for international prosecutions in cases of crimes against humanity or genocide. Indeed, given my account here, there is almost as firm a basis for interfering with a sovereign State that attacks its own subjects as there is for interfering with a State that attacks the subjects of another State.

According to a Hobbesian understanding of the right of a State to control its own affairs, that right must be seen as limited. When a State fails to protect its own subjects' basic human rights, either by attacking its subjects or by choosing to allow attacks to occur unprosecuted, then that State loses its right to exclusive adjudication, as well as its right to keep other bodies from crossing its borders to protect those subjects or to redress their harms. But I have also argued that this is only true of violations of the most basic human rights, including the right to physical security and subsistence, not to a panoply of rights that some groups think important. And this is because we should set an especially high standard for international proceedings that effectively take control of criminal matters out of the hands of the State. In addition – and this is also true of domestic tribunals – the individual State leader or citizen, when placed in the dock, risks the loss of liberty that is itself important in terms of justice and human rights. For these reasons, only the most egregious harms warrant international prosecution. Upon these theoretical arguments can be built the beginning of an account of international criminal law that can then be applied to various conceptual problems concerning the prosecution, defense, and remedies for such international crimes as crimes against humanity.

IV. Objections to the Security Principle

In this final section, I will take up five objections that could be made to the security principle. The first objection is that, given a state of nature scenario of the sort I have myself embraced, it is not clear why all members of such a state of nature do not have the right to punish any transgressors. Why is there a need for a special justificatory principle, such as the security principle, if everyone already has a Lockeian right to punish transgressions of the laws of nature? According to this objection, once people are thrown back into the state of nature, then the laws of nature authorize everyone to punish any transgressors of the laws of nature. There is no need for a specific justification to warrant the "crossing of borders" in order to prosecute and punish transgressors of the laws of nature. This objection is an extension of the position taken until 2003 by Belgium, which claimed to have the right to prosecute anyone who committed genocide or crimes against humanity anywhere in the world.

I am somewhat sympathetic to this objection. In one sense, what the security principle says is that once a State fails to protect a subject, then the State has no right to prevent other entities from protecting that subject. But this does not mean that we are forced into a true state of nature, for the offending State still exists. It is important to point out that the kind of international vigilante justice that would result from giving any State the right to prosecute an international crime would surely be even more abhorrent than having a single forum, such as the ICC, established for such prosecutions. It is true that there is a kind of international state of nature, but that concerns the interactions of States, not of individual human persons. The State borders remain a problem to get around as long as there is a State that is generally providing protection of its subjects, even as it fails to protect some others. International prosecutions occur generally against the backdrop of coherent States, but States that seem to deprive specific subjects, or groups of subjects, of protection of their security and subsistence rights. We are not in a Lockeian state of nature in which anyone can justifiably prosecute and punish those who cause harm. We are in a situation where there are States and where State borders have a contingent moral presumptiveness, as I argued in Chapter 1. Some sort of principle is needed to justify international prosecutions.

A second objection concerns the way in which I have seemingly blurred the distinction, often thought to be absolutely crucial in domestic criminal law, between jurisdictional considerations and the elements of the crime. International crime could be merely crime that falls within a given jurisdiction, and that within that jurisdiction meets the statutory elements of a particular crime of that jurisdiction. If a State has agreed to enforce international law, the only relevant question is whether that State then has jurisdiction over a given defendant. And questions of jurisdiction do not require a justificatory principle such as the security principle. Rather, what is needed is that a State show that the crime occurred within its territory, or that it was committed by, or directed against, one of the State's subjects.

My response here will probably not satisfy those who are schooled in the long-standing tradition of distinguishing jurisdiction from elements of crimes. Nonetheless, it needs to be said that international law is, and is likely to remain, jurisdictionally infirm. All of the standard ways to establish jurisdiction in international law, except for the principle of universal jurisdiction, do not establish a basis for a truly international tribunal to have jurisdiction. For example, according to the nationality principle, one way to establish jurisdiction is to show that the perpetrator was a subject of the State that now claims jurisdiction. Another example is the principle of passive personality, whereby international jurisdiction is established by showing that the victim is under the protection of a State. These principles of "international jurisdiction" really only establish that one State may legitimately prosecute someone whom that State would normally not be entitled to prosecute.[42] Only the principle of universal jurisdiction is strong enough to establish that an international tribunal can prosecute. The principle of universal jurisdiction actually blurs the distinction between jurisdiction and the elements of international crimes in just the way that my security principle does. In both cases, what seems to be salient is whether a truly international crime that violates a *jus cogens* principle has been committed. If this has been established, then prosecution by an international tribunal may be justified.

A third objection is that I have overstated the importance of the potential harm done to an international defendant by the loss of liberty involved in criminal punishment, and hence that one does not need the kind of justification for international prosecution and punishment that I endorsed. Punishment comes in degrees, and is not of such overriding importance that it requires special justification. In any event, there is no reason to think that a very serious crime must be committed before punishment can be justified. Punishments can be harsh or lenient or many steps in between, and hence punishments can be calibrated to fit the degree of importance of the offense. If international punishments can be lenient, then there is no reason to think that only the most serious of harms can be legitimately prosecuted and punished by international tribunals.

My brief reply to this objection begins by pointing out that even minor loss of liberty is a significant loss. This is why minor domestic crimes are generally not punished by jail sentences but by loss of privileges (such as the privilege to drive or to hunt). In the international arena, there are few such privileges whose loss could be substituted for jail time. In addition, the harm to the defendant is not the only harm in question when considering international prosecution and punishment. There is also a kind of harm to the State whose subject is the defendant in the international prosecution. This second type of harm, best characterized as a "loss of sovereignty" harm, means that only serious offenses should be prosecuted – that is, those that violate the security principle. Finally, as will become increasingly clear in the next two chapters, I would point out that the international community only has an interest in prosecuting crimes that are likely to have an effect on a large number of people. The Rome Statute similarly sets the limit of the ICC's jurisdiction as involving "the most serious crimes."[43]

The fourth objection questions the need for there to be crossing of borders along with its special justification, the security principle, for international prosecutions to occur. My initial idea was that international prosecutions were significantly different from domestic prosecutions, because the former but not the latter required a crossing of a State's borders. I said when first discussing this point that it was not necessary that borders literally be crossed, but only that a potential abridgement of State sovereignty be involved in the process of extradition necessary to begin the process. It could be objected, though, that many of the cases that are quite prominent – and that I will consider later – do not involve a crossing of borders and hence do not require the kind of special justification I have been at pains to develop, because no forced extradition was necessary. In the Tadic[44] and Pinochet[45] cases, for instance, no borders needed to be crossed because the defendants were found outside their home States, and the States in which they were found were willing to extradite them. Even in the case of Eichmann,[46] who was captured in Argentina and effectively kidnapped to Israel, there was no longer a Nazi State that could have complained.

I would reply by pointing out that if sovereignty involves a State's exclusive purview over the criminal prosecution of its subjects, then it is a violation of State sovereignty to try a State's subject without that State's consent. For this reason, there will be at least a metaphorical crossing of borders with all international tribunal actions that occur without the consent of the defendant's home State. And this language of "metaphorical crossing of borders" is meant to signal that a violation of State sovereignty of the magnitude that is felt when a State's borders are literally crossed has occurred. Of course, it is not a violation of literal or metaphorical crossing of borders if a State consents, or perhaps does not dissent, from the proceedings. But when Pinochet was arrested in London, and Chile objected, a "metaphorical" crossing of its borders occurred that required the kind of justification that this current chapter addresses. Even in Eichmann's case, Argentina complained about Israel's actions.

A fifth objection is related to the fourth. Even after establishing the notion that someone may "cross a State's borders" I have not settled the question of why an international tribunal such as the ICC, rather than another domestic tribunal, should now prosecute. One could argue that I have confused the issue of what makes something an international crime with the question as to which forum should be used to prosecute international crimes. I will only say something brief here because the next chapter is designed to provide the full answer to the question by indicating why certain crimes are such that the international community has an interest that would warrant prosecution by an international tribunal. But I will say something here about my seeming to have confused the question of what is an international crime with the question as to which forum should prosecute.

Most of international criminal law of the last fifty years has been prosecuted in domestic tribunals. This trend is likely to continue since the ICC has adopted the principle of "complementarity."[47] According to this principle, the international criminal tribunal sitting in The Hague will only take a case if the State whose subject has allegedly committed the crime does not investigate or prosecute the defendant, or does not have good reasons not to prosecute, based on a thorough investigation of the charges.[48] Nonetheless, I think that the best way to think of these prosecutions is as if they were taking place in an international tribunal. After all, the various crimes that fit under the heading "crimes against humanity" are not normally recognized as crimes by the criminal statutes that govern domestic tribunals, and are not clearly crimes that affect the domestic community in the way that they do affect, and create an interest in, the international community. So it makes sense to see these trials that occur domestically as really stand-in trials for trials of international tribunals.

In this chapter, I have presented and defended the first of the two most important normative principles for justifying international prosecutions – namely, the security principle. In the next chapter, I will present and defend the second normative principle, the international harm principle. Both principles are normative principles, with an explicit moral dimension. Their defense rests at least in part on the plausible system of international justice that results from accepting these principles. Since the principles are linked, the supporting arguments for the security principle will get clearer and stronger when we come to consider what conditions will specifically warrant an international trial – namely, an additional violation of what I will call the international harm principle. It is to this task that we turn in the next chapter.

5

The International Harm Principle

In this chapter, I focus on the normative justification of international criminal tribunals, especially those that prosecute crimes against humanity or genocide. Because of that focus, I am especially interested in determining the limits of international law that might themselves be based on considerations of justice or human rights. I am interested in investigating what sorts of norms, once violated, warrant international criminal tribunals to prosecute a State's leader or a subject of a State that participated in serious human rights abuses, especially where the abuse was directed at fellow subjects of that State. These are especially tough issues because what is at stake in international prosecutions is the restriction of liberty of the accused, which itself risks violations of justice or human rights. To offset the possible injustice done to defendants by incarceration, there must be a correspondingly important injustice to the international community that is being prosecuted, and ultimately redressed. International criminal trials that risk the loss of a defendant's liberty require a special form of justification.

The security principle opens the door for such things as international tribunals by countering the claim of abridged sovereignty by a particular State whose subjects would be the defendants in an international trial. Another principle, the international harm principle, is needed to counter the claim made in behalf of the defendant that his or her liberty is jeopardized by such an international trial. The international harm principle will set out a rationale for such trials based on the nature of the harm: either the group-based status of the victim or the group-based status of the perpetrator. An argument is advanced to show that group-based harm violates a strong interest of the international community, and can even be said to harm humanity. The international harm principle is ultimately connected with the idea that international crimes are those that are widespread or systematic. In this chapter, I make this connection by reference to the idea of group-based harm. In the next chapter, I explain in greater detail why it is that individualized crimes should normally not be prosecuted by international tribunals.

It is interesting to note that the trials that are most frequently cited as paradigmatic of international criminal law – those concerning crimes against humanity or genocide – turn out to be the hardest to justify. Typically, there is no weak or non-existent State, but rather, as I said earlier, the problem is often that a State is too strong, perceiving itself to be so strong that it can attack segments of its own population. When this occurs, there is not only the question of why some entity might legitimately cross that State's borders to help the victims, but also the question of why it is the international community that has an interest in what is going on within the State's borders. It is to this second question that this chapter is addressed.

In the first section, I provide a preliminary articulation of the second normative principle of international criminal law – namely, the international harm principle – that will modify the security principle and, combined with it, provide a justificatory basis for international criminal tribunals. In the second section, I explain how it is that certain actions violate the international harm principle by harming humanity through focusing on a non-individualized feature of the victim, and thereby risking widespread harm. In the third section, I explain how it is that certain actions harm humanity when the perpetrator of a harm is an agent of a State, or the State in some way actively participates in the harm, thereby making the harm systematic. In the third and fourth sections, I provide a more nuanced understanding of the international harm principle by discussing two types of group-based action that could count as international crimes. In the fourth section, I deal with various objections to the principle, including one objection that asks whether we need both the security and the international harm principle, or only the latter.

I. Harming Humanity

When the security of a person has been jeopardized, especially by that person's own State, then it is permissible for sovereignty to be abridged so as to render the individual secure. But when we ask about international tribunals that hold some individuals criminally liable for the violations of the security of other persons, more needs to be shown than just that a person's security has been breached. There must be some compelling reason why the international community is warranted in prosecuting individuals as opposed to States. I will defend here the second principle of international criminal law – the international harm principle. A discussion of this principle will provide the positive, moral argument for thinking that group-based rather than individualized harms are the proper subject of international prosecutions. I will also develop a detailed discussion about the kind of harm that would warrant international criminal tribunals directed against individuals.

Harm generally concerns a serious setback to an important interest of a person.[1] One of our most important interests is that we not be deprived of life, liberty, or property in an arbitrary manner. Requiring a violation of the harm principle is a well-recognized way to delimit the kind of things that it is legitimate to prosecute people for. The idea behind the harm principle is that since significant harm is risked to the defendant in a criminal trial, such trials should only be conducted when the defendant is accused of causing similarly serious harm to others. And not all serious harm to individuals should be prosecuted as a violation of international law. We should be very reluctant to countenance international tribunals prosecuting individualized crimes rather than those concerning groups of people and protected classes of people.

As I will argue in this chapter, what sets paradigmatic international crimes apart from domestic crimes is that, in some sense, humanity is harmed when these crimes are perpetrated. Given what was shown in the last chapter, the question is how certain jeopardizing of a subject's right to self-defense or self-preservation could also constitute a harm to humanity. In my view, humanity has interests. One interest of humanity is that its members, as members, not be harmed. This is similar to the claim that a club has an interest that its members, as members, not be harmed. For when the club's members are harmed in this way, the harms adversely affect the reputation of the club, and even the ability of the club to remain in existence. Of course, humanity is not a club, or even a community properly so-called. But analogizing humanity to a community may help us make initial sense of how humanity could be harmed by certain crimes. Another interest of humanity is that its members not be assaulted by the agents of States or with the active participation of a State or State-like entity, since such harms are systematic and also likely to affect people in non-individualized ways.

In domestic settings, criminal prosecutions should only go forward when group-based individual harm is alleged – that is, harm that affects not only the individual victim but also the community. This is why criminal law is a subset of public law – the harms that are the subject of prosecution are not private but public in the sense that the public is harmed when the individual is harmed by certain crimes. In international criminal law, harms that are prosecuted should similarly affect a public – what could be called the world community, or humanity. It is hard to figure out exactly what causes harm to such a public, but often this is no harder than figuring out what exactly causes harm to a domestic community – for instance, the State of Missouri. Often what is meant is that Missouri's residents are made less secure by the crime. If the harm is committed by one person against another for largely personal reasons having to do with a long-standing grudge or a series of insults, the criminal law will often not get involved, and this is because the interests of the State of Missouri are not clearly affected. But if the harm is conducted randomly, so that any Missouri resident could have been harmed, then the State of Missouri will be quite likely to prosecute the crime, as if it were standing in for all of those potential victims.

If international criminal prosecutions are to be considered legitimate, my moral minimalist position holds that there must be some sense in which there has been harm to the entity that stands in for a particular community; it is not enough that an individualized crime has occurred. While the nature of the crime may be difficult to determine, the international community is likely to be harmed when the perpetrator of a crime does not react to the individual features of a person, but rather to those features that the individual shares with all, or very many others, or if the perpetrator of the harm is, or involves, a State or other collective entity rather than being merely perpetrated by an individual human person. Thus I will subscribe to the following principle of group-based harm:

To determine if harm to humanity has occurred, there will have to be one of two (and ideally both) of the following conditions met: either the individual is harmed because of that person's group membership or other non-individualized characteristic, or the harm occurs due to the involvement of a group such as the State.

In the rest of this chapter and in Chapter 6, I will defend the view that group-based, as opposed to individualized, crimes should be the focus of international prosecution.

In international prosecutions, I propose that we embrace the following version of the international harm principle:

Only when there is serious harm to the international community, should international prosecutions against individual perpetrators be conducted, where normally this will require a showing of harm to the victims that is based on non-individualized characteristics of the individual, such as the individual's group membership, *or* is perpetrated by, or involves, a State or other collective entity.

This principle will be shown to be consistent with the common claim made by international courts that they only prosecute harms that are systematic or widespread. The idea I will develop in the rest of this chapter is that international prosecutions require a showing that harm that is group-based has occurred. Group-based harms are either group-based in terms of the nature of the crime or in terms of the status of the perpetrator(s). Group-based harms are likely to be either more widespread, in the sense of being not restricted to isolated victims, or more systematic, in that they display more than just motivations of hatred or cruelty, than harms that are individually based. Group-based harms are of interest to the international community because they are more likely to assault the common humanity of the victims and to risk crossing borders and damaging the broader international community.

The international community takes a special interest in certain categories of acts because these acts seem to affect humanity adversely: This is the basis of the international harm principle. M. Cherif Bassiouni has said that the only way to make sense of *jus cogens* norms is to recognize that "certain crimes affect the interests of the world community as a whole because they threaten the peace and security of humankind and they shock the conscience of humanity."[2] In the next section, I will look more closely at Bassiouni's idea, taken from The Hague Convention's Martens Clause, that *jus cogens* norms are grounded in the laws of humanity, and the dictates of public conscience.[3] I will separate this issue into two parts: First, I will investigate the group-based nature of the victim or target of the harmful act, and then turn to the group-based nature of the perpetrator.

II. Humanity and Widespread Harm

Let us begin with the victim or target of the harmful act. On first sight, there appears to be a difference between the two rationales often mentioned for international prosecution – namely, the rationale based on the peace and security of humankind (which is most at home with *legal positivism*), and the rationale based on shocking the public conscience (which seems to derive from *natural law theory*). It could be argued that an especially vicious act of rape could shock the conscience of the international community, even if it did not threaten the peace and security of humankind. The possibility that an individualized crime could rise to the level of an international crime merely by shocking the conscience of humanity does not seem to be countenanced in any of the definitions of crimes against humanity that have been formulated in recent years.[4] There are obvious pragmatic reasons why States would be uncomfortable thinking about international crimes in this way, since then State sovereignty about internal criminal matters might be threatened. As we will see in the next chapter, if individualized rape counts as an international crime, then there is no way to limit international crimes and prevent them from completely overlapping with domestic crimes.

Theoretically, though, a "shocking the conscience of humanity" test may very well apply to individualized crimes that have no collective nature and are not part of a "State plan." To assess this possibility, we need to think hard about how "humanity" can have its conscience shocked in the first place. Since humanity is not the sort of entity that is generally thought to have a conscience, humanity's conscience must be either a shorthand or metaphorical expression.[5] "Conscience of humanity" could be shorthand for what would shock many humans. But if an international crime is one that shocks the conscience of many humans, then that crime is merely a crime that shocks the conscience of humans, not humanity, and we do not have a basis for distinguishing international crimes from domestic crimes.

Another way to draw a distinction between acts that are international crimes and acts that are domestic crimes has to do with whether the act risks harming humanity in that it risks disrupting the peace and security of humanity. Humanity is harmed because of the risk of harm to the members of humanity concerning their peace and security. There are three distinct ways of thinking of "harm to humanity." First, a member of humanity is harmed, and thereby the larger whole of which the individual is a part is, in some sense, harmed along with that individual. Second, some significant characteristic of humanity is harmed, perhaps by harming it within each member of humanity. Third, all of humanity is harmed, say by a nuclear holocaust that destroys humanity. The first approach fails to be a basis for international crime unless there is some reason to think that the harm to the individual does, in some non-trivial way, harm the whole of humanity. The third is useless except in the most extreme of cases in which humanity is truly harmed directly. The second approach is the most promising.

If an individual person is treated according to group-characteristics that are out of that person's control, there is a straightforward assault on that person's humanity. It is as if the individuality of the person were being ignored, and the person were being treated as a mere representative of a group that the person has not chosen to join.[6] The civil rights movement in the United States has been premised on the idea that such treatment toward racial groups is a clear harm to the person and also to a larger community of persons. According to this analysis, discriminatory treatment is based on the common characteristics rather than the unique features of the victim. In some sense, it doesn't matter that the acts are taken against named, discrete individuals. It may as well be that the acts were taken against anonymous individuals, since their individuality plays so little a role in the treatment. When harm occurs in the way I have just described, it can be called group-based, not merely individualized.[7]

In a 2000 Missouri Supreme Court decision, a distinction is made between random acts of violence and acts directed at the specific identity of the victim. The court says that the "fact that Ferguson's selection of his victims was random demonstrates a callous disregard for the sanctity of all human life."[8] On the other hand, if Ferguson had chosen his victims on the basis of their unique identity, then he would not have displayed a callous disregard for all of humanity but merely animus toward certain particular humans. I am suggesting a similar argument in this chapter, but with reference to the distinction between group-based attacks versus attacks on individuals based on their unique characteristics. Group-based harms have in common with random acts of violence the characteristic of callous disregard for the individuality of the person, and hence an assault on what is common to all humans and hence to all of humanity. As I will argue, the international community has more of an interest in group-based acts of violence than in random acts of violence.

In my view, humanity is normally harmed in a way that the international community should care about when an act is committed against individuals because of their group affiliations – that is, according to things that are beyond their autonomous agency. And, as I will argue next, the international community should care about such acts because of the harm risked to members of humanity, as members. Humanity is a victim when the intentions of individual perpetrators or the harms of individual victims are based on group characteristics rather than on individual characteristics. Humanity is implicated, and in a sense victimized, when the sufferer merely stands in for larger segments of the population who are not treated according to individual differences among fellow humans, but only according to group characteristics. When acts have this structure, then it is clear that non-individualized treatment has occurred, and it is of the sort that should be internationally proscribed by *jus cogens* norms. The international community thus enters the picture, in order to vindicate humanity through its international legal tribunals.[9]

I would here offer a further distinction between what *offends* humanity and what *assaults* humanity. Assaults on humanity are a class of offenses that are especially egregious and deserving of sanction. Humanity is offended when there is any non-individualized treatment of an individual, but humanity may be sufficiently vindicated by a domestic trial. The security principle gives a reason why States cannot legitimately object to certain kinds of violations of their sovereignty by international bodies such as international tribunals. The international harm principle then gives reason for that intervention. But such intervention should be exercised cautiously – that is, only when the harm is very serious and when there is an assault rather than a mere offense.

The key component of this harm principle is that a person be treated in a way that is individuality-denying. The type of harm that most readily meets this criterion is group-based harm of the sort that we will see graphically exhibited when crimes against humanity or genocide occur. One of the most salient norms in this context is that individual persons should not be harmed because of their group memberships. A 1997 international court opinion states this point quite succinctly when it says that acts rise to the level of the international crime of persecution when "the emphasis is not on the individual victim but rather on the collective, the individual being victimized not because of his individual attributes but rather because of his membership in a targeted civilian population."[10] The point of this analysis is that international *jus cogens* norms protect individuals from a certain form of non-individualized treatment that is group-based.

International courts have held that international crime manifests the condition of widespreadness. How does this condition relate to the assault on the victim's individuality by group-based harm? At least one explanation is that when attacks on individuals are based on group characteristics rather than the individual characteristics of the victims, there is a much greater likelihood that the harms will be spread throughout a population rather than focused exclusively on a particular victim. Indeed, we have seen just this pattern in the ethnic cleansing that has spread in various parts of the world in the last decade. Genocide is a good example of a crime that is group-based, and likely to be widespread, as we will see in greater detail in Chapter 9. Widespreadness makes the most sense when understood as a tendency – that is, the tendency of various assaults, because of their nature, to be spread throughout a particular population and not merely restricted to certain individuals.

There will occasionally be harms that assault the victim's individuality, and hence are likely to be widespread, and yet are not strictly group-based. Think of a case such as the bombing of Hiroshima.[11] This bombing of civilians with widespread horrible casualties was arguably not group-based. While all of the victims were of the same nationality and most of the same ethnicity, the bombing was not aimed at these features of the group assaulted. Rather, the assault was politically motivated in the sense that it was designed to bring Japan to its knees, and to end World War II more quickly. But it could be argued nonetheless that the bombing of Hiroshima was an international crime, indeed a crime against humanity. The argument would be similar to what we just saw – namely, that the individuals killed were treated not according to their unique characteristics, and the sheer scope of the harm threatened to spill over borders. Of course, those who argue that the bombing of Hiroshima was not a crime against humanity usually do so by reference to the fact that the bombing actually diminished rather than increased the risk of further harms (by Japan) across its borders. While not attempting to resolve this dispute here, I am willing to admit that it is not necessary that harms be group-based for them to rise to the level of international crimes. Nonetheless, I think the examples in which the victims suffer non-group-based harms will be very few in number, and have been so historically, and when these cases have occurred, there has been another sort of group-based harm – namely, that the perpetrator was connected to a State or other group.

Consider the short list of practices thought to violate international *jus cogens* norms, or obligations *erga omnes*[12] – namely, genocide, apartheid, slavery, and torture. At the top of that list is genocide, where clearly the emphasis is on the group, the destruction of a people, not merely the individual victim. Apartheid can be easily seen in the same light, as clearly directed against a racial group. Slavery is the mistreatment of a people, including the denial of a people's right to self-determination. Torture is the only practice currently seen as condemned by *jus cogens* norms that does not readily have a group orientation. But the form of torture condemned by *jus cogens* norms is that practiced by the State, or a State-like actor, and it is this element of State action that makes torture also group-based when it is prosecuted at the international level.[13] Although it is now in the domain of a different form of group-based harm, torture is still group-based, as I will show in the next section.

III. Group-Based Actions and Systematic Harm

Let us now discuss the second prong of the international harm principle – namely, when the actor or perpetrator is also somehow group-based. In this section, I will begin to discuss particular practices that might satisfy the criteria of international harm. I will continue this discussion in more detail in the next chapter, where I focus on various kinds of rape and sexual violence as putative international crimes. In this second way that harms are group-based, it is not that the victim is experiencing group-based harm but rather that there is State involvement, or similar group involvement, in the harmful acts, thereby making these acts systematic rather than random. As the Yugoslav Trial Chamber recognized, implicit in some of the *jus cogens* justifications of international crimes "is the fact that the conduct in question is the product of state-action or state-favoring action."[14]

If rapes are part of a State-sponsored plan to eliminate an ethnic group within that State's borders, or as a State-accepted way for some individuals to intimidate a sub-group of women in a given community, then that individual crime rises to the level of an international crime because of its systematic and invidious nature. The actions of States, or State-like actors, have given the international community its clearest rationale for entry into what would otherwise be a domestic legal matter. And this is true in two senses of the term "domestic": The actions are not merely between two individuals, but involve the larger society, and the actions are no longer merely appropriately prosecuted at the domestic level, since the domestic State is itself a party to the violence, as we will see later in the chapter.

In our earlier discussions of *jus cogens* norms, the conceptual basis for these norms was identified as the demand for security that can be lodged against States. When it is the State that is assaulting a person, either through an official representative of the State (such as a member of the army or the police), or because of some State-sponsored plan, then there is a very clear violation of a *jus cogens* norm since security of the individual is so clearly not being protected by the State. According to my earlier Hobbesian analysis, State sovereignty is linked to the provision of protection for the State's subjects. So when the State is involved in the assault on individuals, there is an opening for prosecution by an international tribunal. In addition, when it is the State that is the victimizer, and not merely that the State allowed the attacks to occur, then it normally makes little sense to argue that a domestic tribunal should prosecute the crime since it is so unlikely that the State could impartially prosecute itself.

Certain kinds of State action can mark a crime as international in that there is coordinated systematic harm, which then assaults people for reasons not based on their individual characteristics. We could treat the notion of a government plan of rape – for instance, as a part of an ethnic cleansing campaign – the way that we treat a corporation or university in terms of its policy of sexual harassment. Here, the chief question is whether the plan has been formulated by the collective entity or whether there is knowledge of the illicit practice, and whether any efforts have been made to stop it. When harm is systematic in that it is carried out by a State or State-like entity, there are likely to be other people who will be victimized on the basis of the characteristics picked out by the plan since the harms being planned are aimed at more than a single individual. The international community then would have a legitimate basis for intervention so as to protect the larger community also likely to be harmed by the plan.[15]

I wish now to modify my proposal that if either the target of the act is group-based (in the sense that the victim is chosen for harm as a result of having common characteristics), or the perpetrator is group-based (in the sense that the perpetrator is an agent of a State or State-like entity, or is attempting to advance a plan of the State), then international prosecution is appropriate. My modification is that, ideally, both of these conditions should be satisfied – that is, the harm should be both widespread *and* systematic. I will call this the "ideal model." The ideal model of international crime will best secure the rights of the defendants, the importance of which I will explore in later chapters. In some cases, though, it may be justifiable for prosecutions to go forward even with only one of these two factors present. For example, if the group-based harm is very widespread, then it may be sufficient for international prosecution even without direct State involvement, because of fears that the harm will spill over borders.

In international criminal law, acts are inhumane and humanity is implicated when the intentions of individual perpetrators or the harms of individual victims are connected to group-based characteristics rather than to the unique characteristics of the individual perpetrators and victims. Humanity is implicated when the individual actor or sufferer merely stands in for larger segments of the population, who attempt to deny individual differences among fellow humans and look only at group characteristics. This is the specific purview of international criminal law and where prosecutions by international tribunals can be most easily justified. In the next chapter, I provide additional arguments to this effect by discussing in detail various ways that some forms of rape can be considered an international crime, as well as why it is not legitimate to see other forms of rape as prosecutable before international tribunals.

In this and the last chapter, I have argued that international criminal prosecutions can be justified by reference to two principles – the security principle and the international harm principle. The security principle provides a reason why State sovereignty may be abridged – namely, when the physical security or subsistence rights of an individual are jeopardized by that State's action or inaction. But this initial basis for international criminal law should be limited to rights abuses that are especially egregious because of a parallel concern that the risk of punishment to the individual perpetrators of these crimes is also important and can only be justified if the harm to the victim is equally serious. In addition, though, the international harm principle also must be violated in order for prosecutions by international tribunals to be justified. The international harm principle calls for a showing that the crime in question is group-based either in terms of the nature of the victim's harm or the character of the perpetrator of the harm. This additional principle is necessary because individualized harm to victims that violates their physical security or subsistence is still not sufficiently the subject of international interest to warrant prosecuting individuals in international tribunals. Justified international prosecutions require either that the harm must be widespread in that there is a violation of individuality of a certain sort epitomized by group-based harmful treatment that ignores the unique features of the individual victim, or the harm must be systematic in that it is perpetrated in pursuance of a plan by an agent of a State or with active involvement from a State or State-like entity. These group-based considerations provide a basis for thinking that the international community has a special interest in these cases that would warrant prosecution by an international rather than a domestic tribunal.

In explaining the idea behind the international harm principle, I have distinguished two considerations – the nature of the victim's harm, and the character of the perpetrator of that harm. I initially argued that either of these considerations could provide a sufficient basis for international interest to warrant prosecution by an international tribunal. The group-based nature of the harm provides a basis for the widespreadness of the harm in that there is a tendency of the assaults to spread throughout a population because they are aimed at group characteristics rather than individual ones. Group-based harm fails to treat the victim in terms of his or her individuality in a way that is owed to all human agents. I also argued that if the character of the perpetrator is group-based, in the sense that the harm is based on a systematic plan carried out by an agent of the State or with active involvement by a State or State-like entity, then international prosecutions could also be justified. In addition, I suggested that ideally we should look for both a group-based harm to a victim and also State or State-like involvement in that harm – what I called the ideal model of justification. As we will see in the next chapter in a detailed consideration of the case of rape, international tribunals normally should prosecute mass rape and sexual violence when humanity is harmed or when the harm is State-based, and ideally when both of these factors are present.

IV. Objections to the International Harm Principle

In this final section, I consider various objections to the international harm principle that I set out in this chapter. The first objection is that the two types of group-based harm that I identify in this chapter – the group-based nature of the victims and the group-based nature of the perpetrator – are so different from one another as to call for two different analyses rather than the confusing attempt to provide a single analysis of two so different phenomena. Simply because the term "group" features in the description of both of these conditions does not mean that they are significantly related to each other. Indeed, so much confusion results from the use of the same term for such different bases of international crime that it would be better not to use the term "group" at all in the discussion of the international harm principle. This confusion calls into question the very notion of speaking of an international harm principle at all. Unless some common conceptual basis can be found, it would make sense to think of widespreadness and systematicity as two distinct bases of international crimes.

I agree with the general point of this objection. There are indeed two quite distinct group-based conditions here. The victim is the subject of group-based harm in the sense of being treated as merely a member of a group and not according to that individual's unique identity. The perpetrator is a member of a group, most notably a State, where the group membership is crucial for the perpetrator's ability to commit the harm in question. While membership in a group is crucial for each of these aspects of the international harm principle, there are differences. For these are indeed two distinct ways that groups feature in the exposition of the international harm principle, and it would be a mistake to refer to both of them as part of the category of group-based harm if it misled people into thinking that we are talking of only one type of phenomenon.

Nonetheless, the two types of group-based harm have quite a lot in common. For membership in a group is crucial to both, whether it is membership of the victim in an ethnic group or membership of a camp guard in a State-sponsored ethnic cleansing campaign. Group membership is key to understanding both why the victims are selected or why the perpetrators acted as they did. As we will see in the next chapter, it is not sufficient to point out that the rapes in an ethnic cleansing campaign were directed against women victims, but one must also see that the rapes were directed against these women because of their ethnic identities, not because of their unique identities. Similarly, it is not enough to note that it is men who are perpetrating these rapes in an ethnic cleansing campaign, but one must also see that these men were members of armed units under the direction of a single leader who was following a plan to use rape as a means of intimidation. In this sense, there is a significant commonality between the first prong of the international harm principle – that the harm to the victim be group-based – and the second prong – that the harm be committed in a group-based way. Even though some conceptual confusion is risked, more clarity that would offset the possible confusion can be achieved.

A second objection is that we do not need the group-based status of the victim, and in general all of the attention to what it means to "harm humanity," since so many of the harms in question are perpetrated by members of a State that provides crucial support for the individual perpetrator to engage in the harm that the perpetrator is indeed able to accomplish. Why not simply say that when there is significant State involvement in various harms, there is a sufficient international interest to warrant international prosecutions? In Chapter 7, we will discuss a case, Prosecutor v. Dusko Tadic – indeed the very first case prosecuted by the Yugoslav Tribunal – in which the crime was not perpetrated by a member of a State. It is true, as we will see, that there was State involvement. But since the perpetrator was not a member of that State, it is hard to link him to the international crime.

To be legitimately prosecuted in international tribunals, perpetrators must be linked to an act that is proscribed in international crime. One could say that Tadic was just doing the bidding of the State, even though he was not a proper agent of the State, but such a strategy will not be available in other cases, especially where there is persecution, one of the most significant crimes against humanity. But to say that of Tadic would be to do him a grave injustice, for while he shared some of the goals of the Republik Srbska, he was not merely an unpaid soldier in the army. He manipulated the larger campaign of ethnic cleansing to his benefit. And as we will see in Chapter 7, it is the intention to discriminate that is crucial, rather than the official or unofficial role he played in the ethnic cleansing.

Indeed, to prosecute Tadic at all requires a different showing than that he was a cog in the State-sponsored ethnic cleansing campaign. Instead, it needs to be shown why the international community has a special interest in ethnic cleansing. And to do this, or at least to do it in a convincing manner, one needs something like the first prong of the international harm principle that I have just explicated. Or failing this, we will be thrown back on the other prong of the international harm principle, which cannot be satisfied in the case of Tadic. It bears repeating that there is a third option (not properly part of the international harm principle) that can be met if the State whose subject allegedly committed the crime is either too weak to prosecute or ineffectual in doing so. I discussed this option in the very first chapter, only to set it aside as not being the main conceptual focus of the book. But in some cases, this is indeed a reasonable basis for international prosecution.

The third objection is that I have put too much weight on the potential loss of liberty that the defendant will suffer, and not nearly enough weight on the original harm that was suffered by the victim. If we worried as much about defendants, as I suggest we should, then domestic prosecutions would also be much harder to justify than is currently thought possible. Crimes against humanity and genocide focus on some of the most horrible things that individuals can do to one another. Victims of oppression and torture, to say nothing of victims of systematic attempts to eliminate whole groups of people from the face of the earth, are some of the most downtrodden of victims. They need protection, and we should not fail to give as complete protection as possible out of a misplaced concern for the defendants as potential victims of a "false positive" prosecution.

My inclination is to bite the bullet here and admit that my point could sweep more broadly and call for stiffer justificatory principles for domestic prosecutions. I am inclined in this direction because of my belief that the concerns of victims are simply being given far too much weight across the board. I am also inclined to admit that I have not emphasized the harm to victims, at least in part because the contemporary international criminal law literature has been so thoroughly victim-oriented already. Nonetheless, I do not wish to diminish the importance of the suffering of the victims of international crimes such as crimes against humanity or genocide. People have suffered grievously from these crimes. But this is no reason to ignore or diminish the rights of the alleged perpetrators of these crimes. And, as I will argue in Chapter 11, adherence to the rule of law demands as much.

Current formulations of international criminal law have also taken a conservative stand on what counts as an international crime. As I have indicated, the Rome Statute, for instance, says that the jurisdiction of the ICC will be limited only to "the most serious offenses."[16] In this book, I provide the normative support for such a position. Of course, one can disagree, and argue for a larger domain of crimes prosecutable by international tribunals. But to do so, one cannot ignore the defendants who stand in the dock before these tribunals. I will take up the most serious concerns about such tribunals from the standpoint of the rule of law in Chapter 11. Unfortunately, not all harms can or should be prosecuted by international tribunals. But there are other possible avenues of approach, as I indicate in the final chapter of the book.

A fourth objection is that certain kinds of group-based crimes are not captured by my international principles, but should be – such as various forms of persecution that do not threaten physical security or economic subsistence. Think of a minor official in a State who enforces the statutory requirement that the State's Jewish subjects wear yellow armbands. It would be odd indeed if no further harm came to these subjects than merely this indignity, and I cannot think of any such real-life cases, since such persecution is normally only the prelude to much more egregious forms of persecution. But even if this were all there was to it, it would be odd not to count this as persecution under crimes against humanity. For aren't all group-based crimes ones that harm humanity, and hence are deserving of international prosecution and punishment? If the very idea of crime against humanity is to make sense, how can we not include a much wider array of cases than I have suggested are captured under the international harm principle.

There are several dimensions to this objection. First, this objection asks about the necessity of satisfying both the security principle as well as the international harm principle. For without the requirement that the security principle be violated, it does indeed look as though this practice violates the international harm principle, and violates it twice – that is, it violates both of the two prongs since the victim suffers harm as a result of his or her group membership, and the perpetrators commit the harms with group – that is, State – involvement. Let us remember that the point of the security principle was to allow us to overcome the presumption in favor of State sovereignty. Just because the international community has an interest in a certain kind of crime does not mean that the international community can justifiably violate a State's sovereignty by trying a subject of that State in an international tribunal for an international crime. The presumption in favor of State sovereignty has moral weight, as we saw in

Chapter 1, and there must be a sufficiently weighty countervailing consideration to offset it.

Another question asked by the objection is whether this practice rises to the level of an international crime by being sufficiently weighty morally. And here there is room for disagreement. In one sense, I would admit that all group-based crimes are deserving of international oversight, since the crime assaults humanity. But in another sense, I would insist on maintaining a distinction between assaults and offenses, where only the latter are serious enough to offset the risk to the liberty of a defendant that occurs in prosecutions, as well as the previously mentioned violation of the State's moral presumption of sovereignty. I would not dispute the fact that the international community has an interest similar to that which occurs with more serious forms of persecution. My point is only to dispute how weighty this particular form of persecution is. When persecution does not jeopardize the security or subsistence rights of an individual victim, I think that normatively such harms do not rise to the level of being international crimes prosecutable by international tribunals.

A fifth related objection is that the international harm principle has the effect of too greatly restricting the domain of international criminal law, thereby making it ineffective against a wide range of human rights abuses, and making it too hard to add new international crimes as the need arises. The whole point of the developing field of international criminal law has been to counteract the impunity by which various parties have acted, and to make sure that victims are not forgotten just because their perpetrators were in States that were obscured from view by the larger international community. Those who assert this objection could argue that we need to expand rather than contract the domain of international criminal law, perhaps encompassing the amorphous cases I described in the first section of Chapter 1. Today, for instance, many people want to include hijacking as a specific category of international crime. The international harm principle stands in the way of such progress. Hijackers are often not associated with States, and they do not normally target people because of their group membership. Because hijacking is difficult to capture under the international harm principle, that principle should be dispensed with so that all human rights violations will be prosecuted and punished.

My response to this objection will only be the beginning of an answer that will be supplemented by various discussions later in the book. The Rome Statute lists four categories of crime under its jurisdiction that are of concern to the international community as a whole: genocide, crimes against humanity, war crimes, and aggression.[17] As I pointed out in Chapter 1, the Rome Statute's list is virtually identical to the one that formed the basis of the jurisdiction of the Nuremberg Tribunal – namely, war crimes, crimes against humanity, and crimes against peace. The Nuremberg Tribunal's "crime against peace" and the Rome Statute's "crime of aggression" are virtually the same. And the crime of genocide was not recognized as a unique category at Nuremberg but discussed under crimes against humanity. The point here is that we have already more than fifty years of consensus that international criminal law, if it exists at all, should be limited to the most serious of crimes that concern the international community, not all of the possible crimes of concern to that community.

Normatively, once again adopting my moral minimalism, I urge that we remain cautious about expanding beyond relatively clear limits. But I am not opposed to increasing the list of international crimes. Indeed, in the next chapter I turn to an elaborate discussion of one type of crime, rape, that was until fairly recently thought not to fit in the category of international crimes. I will examine a number of different cases in which rape can be seen as an international crime as a way to get much clearer about the usefulness and legitimacy of the two principles I have described and defended in the last two chapters. At the end of the next chapter, I return to the issue of why individually oriented crimes should not be prosecuted, attempting once again to explain why group-based crimes are the international crimes that should be prosecuted by international tribunals.

6

International Crime: The Case of Rape

International criminal law is currently faced with a defining moment: how to understand the truly international character of certain kinds of crime while providing an expanded forum for the prosecution of many egregious harms in the world. In this chapter, I extend the arguments of the previous two chapters by considering a specific example, the crime of rape. I focus on the very difficult case of how rape and other forms of sexual violence, typically understood as paradigmatically individualized crimes, should be handled in international criminal law. In light of the discussion of the last two chapters, I argue that unless there has been a complete breakdown in the rule of law in a particular country, international tribunals should only be concerned with prosecuting individuals for rapes that are group-based in that the harms are directed against individuals because of their group memberships or where there is some kind of State (or State-like) involvement. I argue that isolated acts of rape should not normally be subject to international prosecution, but examples such as the "comfort women" of World War II, and recent examples of mass rape in Yugoslavia, would be properly prosecuted internationally.

Until very recently, most theorists of international law ignored the possibility that international tribunals could be used to prosecute rape. Perhaps because of critical reaction to this omission, some of these same theorists now consider rape a proper subject of international prosecution.[1] But the possibility that international tribunals could be used as an alternative forum to domestic tribunals for rape prosecution has raised the specter of sovereignty usurpation once again, contributing to the difficulty of justifying the use of international tribunals for what many think are strictly domestic affairs. Of course, part of the problem is that international trials are not generally supposed to be substitutes for domestic trials. International trials are supposed to prosecute distinctly international crimes. Prosecuting rape as an international crime as opposed to a domestic crime seems to blur this distinction between international and domestic crimes. So here is the chief conceptual puzzle: How can the very same act, rape, be both a distinct international crime and also a distinct domestic crime? Our first answer is that rape can be perpetrated for different reasons – for instance, as an assault against a particular woman or as a strategy of war. Even though it is the same act, in some sense, it can be conceptualized differently and prosecuted differently because of the differences in why it is perpetrated.

In this chapter, I provide an answer to the question: How should international crimes be distinguished from domestic crimes? Once the International Criminal Court (ICC) is fully operating, will it usurp domestic courts? In statements such as those made by U.S. State Department officials and Senate Foreign Relations Committee members, the argument was advanced that the ICC had dangerously broad jurisdictional powers.[2] One strategy for addressing this concern is to mark out clearly the extent and rationale of prosecutions by international tribunals concerning crimes that historically have been the exclusive purview of domestic tribunals. Rape and other forms of sexual violence provide a good test case for drawing such a distinction.

In the first three sections of this chapter, I consider the example of rape, and ask why this crime, which is normally prosecuted under domestic law, should also be prosecuted as an international crime. I discuss three examples of rape, each drawn from different areas of the international law of sexual violence. In the first section, I begin by briefly addressing sexual violence in war. In the second section, I examine the conceptualization of rape as a crime against humanity, with specific attention to a recent case from the Yugoslav Tribunal. In the third section, I turn to an example of sexual persecution from asylum law, the intersection of international human rights law and domestic immigration law. For all three cases, conceptual difficulties with the use of international law to remedy these harms are identified. At the end of the third section, I return to the discussion of the previous chapter. By examining in detail the interests of humanity and the status of perpetrators, an argument is advanced that group-based harm, perpetrated against an individual because of group membership or as part of a State plan, is exactly the sort of crime that should be prosecuted in international tribunals.

In the fourth section, I argue that individually oriented crimes should not generally be included as international crimes. I argue against those who defend a more expansive domain of international crime. I take an explicitly defendant-oriented approach to this topic, arguing that it is not a good argument to urge a more expansive approach to international crimes merely because victims' rights are at stake. Offsetting considerations of defendants' rights argue for restraint in our approach to defining and prosecuting international crime, although this does not mean, as I argue at the end of the chapter, that victims' rights should not also be taken seriously.

I. Rape as a War Crime

One reason that rape was ignored in international criminal law was because it seemed to be merely an "ancillary crime" incident to war. Rape was not itself seen as a violation of international peace the way that genocide, apartheid, and slavery were. Rather, rape was seen as merely something that soldiers did on their own, thus making it no different from the countless rapes committed by non-soldiers in cities and villages across the globe. International tribunals were supposed to concern themselves with harms that violated international peace and shocked the conscience of humanity. Rape seemed too ordinary to shock the conscience of humanity.[3] For a crime to be international, it was thought that it had to be more than a garden-variety domestic crime. Yet, recently we have seen rape elevated into a clear strategy of war, seemingly justifying several high-profile international prosecutions for rape,[4] and also raising again the questions of why and whether rape should be seen as an international crime.

Over the past decade, issues of sexual violence have begun to take center stage in international law. Mass rape has been the subject of a few trials before international and domestic criminal tribunals.[5] Along with the new international interest in combating sexual violence has come a renewed discussion of the sources of norms that could justify such intervention by international tribunals.[6] Throughout the following sections, I will focus on conceptual difficulties that have arisen in justifying international action against sexual violence. I will here continue to refine the case, begun in the last two chapters, for thinking that it is group-based acts and not isolated individual acts that should be the focus of international tribunals.

The first conceptual question to be investigated is why rape should ever be seen as anything other than a personal, domestic crime. I begin with the most plausible basis for answering that question – namely, that where rape occurs during wartime, it may constitute a war crime, not merely a domestic crime. Indeed, it has been common to see rape as merely a domestic crime in two senses of that term: both as a domestic (or private, household) crime as opposed to a public crime, as well as a domestic (or municipal, State) crime as opposed to an international crime. For centuries, rape has been considered one of the spoils of war, something that male soldiers expected as partial payment for their courage and bravery on the battlefield. The attempt to characterize rape as an international war crime, on the same level as the murder or torture of innocent civilians by enemy soldiers, is not new. In 1646, Hugo Grotius said that rape "should not go unpunished in war any more than in peace."[7] Today, this seems uncontroversial, although it took 350 years before international tribunals recognized the wisdom of Grotius's remarks. Rape is no longer one of the spoils of war, regardless of how brave or courageous the soldiers have been on the battlefield.

While the category of war crimes is not the primary focus of this book, I wish to say something about it, certainly the oldest of the distinctly international crimes.[8] The Just War tradition, which traces its origins back at least to the writings of Augustine, recognizes that the international community has a strong interest in preventing certain kinds of harm from occurring even in – and especially in – those circumstances where States are engaged in warfare that is designed to cause harm to one another's soldiers. Grotius, for instance, devotes the whole of Book III of his *The Law of War and Peace* to considerations of "what is permissible in war." He says that if a soldier has been forced into battle, he may not rightly be killed.[9] More importantly for our purposes, Grotius argues that in wartime, the death of innocent persons must be prevented "so far as is possible."[10] The murder, or rape, of a civilian is seen as wrong in wartime just as much as it is wrong in peacetime.

A male soldier who rapes a civilian woman in a town just captured by his army unit engages in an individual act somewhat similar to, but importantly different from, that of a male assailant who rapes a woman whom he follows home from work. Arguably, the male soldier's act of rape is different from more "normal" cases of rape in that the soldier's act is facilitated by the larger organized use of force against a whole civilian population, whereas the "normal" rapist acts in a way that is opposed by the organized use of force of the larger society. The soldier's act of rape is made easier by the fact of the war, especially by the way that war tends to disrupt the power of the police and army that would normally protect civilians from such acts of violence. The soldier's act of rape may be raised to the level of a war crime, not merely a crime of an isolated individual, for two quite different reasons. First, wartime conditions are often so damaging to the internal legal institutions of a country that it is many years before that country's institutions can be said to embody the rule of law. As a result, for rape to be prosecuted at all in such cases, it must be done internationally. But, as we saw in Chapter 1, this justification for international prosecutions is not an in-principle justification but one only based on purely pragmatic considerations.

Second, in light of what we saw in the last chapter, rape can be seen as a crime requiring international prosecution because of some international interest affected, rather than merely being prosecuted at the international level because no domestic tribunal is likely to prosecute it. Rape has not only been perpetrated in an indiscriminate way by victorious marauding troops who do not fear the rule of law, but it has also been used in quite a discriminate way either as a means to terrorize civilian populations or to perpetrate some form of genocide or ethnic cleansing.[11] The question arises as to whether rape and other forms of sexual violence should be seen as true war crimes. In the Just War tradition, war crimes have been treated as violations of international law in the sense that the security of peoples is adversely affected when inhumane acts are committed against vulnerable people. Here, the international interest is rather simply explained. On the assumption that wars are inevitable, the international community has a

strong interest in minimizing harm to civilian populations during war, especially since such harm runs the risk of becoming widespread. The rape of
civilians during wartime is clearly one such harm that should be the subject of
international prosecution, although, as I said earlier, not many theorists have
recognized this point.

Whereas rape is criminalized in nearly every society, it has not been viewed in
the same way as other violent crimes – the crime of torture, for instance. Torture is seen as a war crime because of its utterly disruptive effects on the
peace and stability of a society. Rape during war was not thought to have a
similarly disruptive effect, supposedly because of the "privacy" in which it is
conducted.[12] Because of the "private" nature of the act, primarily thought to be
one involving sex between a man and a woman, the crime was not thought to
have the kind of wider implications and consequences that would jeopardize the
peace and stability of the international community. In the next section, I begin
to explain the somewhat unusual way that rape may disrupt international peace
and hence affect the interests of the world community, and of humanity itself.

II. Rape as a Crime Against Humanity

The second conceptual question to be investigated is why one would think that
rape could be the kind of crime that adversely affects the international community, and hence is to be prosecuted as an international crime. To answer this
question, I turn to examples in which rape has been alleged to be a crime against
humanity, in order to connect directly with the discussion in previous chapters.
As we have seen, the designation "crime against humanity" is supposed to pick
out a heinous form of crime, a crime that shocks "the public conscience" of the
world community or that violates "the laws of humanity."[13] International prosecutions are conducted not because domestic prosecutions are unlikely, but in
order to signify the importance or magnitude of the offenses for all of humanity.
Thus, just as in the case of United States federal crimes, crimes against humanity signal that a larger constituency than normal has been assaulted because of
the way that the victims have been treated.

The most recent definitions of crimes against humanity (in the Rwanda
Tribunal Statute and the ICC Statute) include rape and other forms of sexual
violence,[14] in large part due to the recognition that ethnic and racial persecutions
have increasingly employed sexual violence as part of a plan of intimidation
and terror. Indeed, according to the most recent definitions of crimes against
humanity, the act of rape, or any other of the listed acts, must be conducted as
part of a systematic and widespread plan directed against a civilian population.
This is the significant backdrop of this chapter. When rape and other forms of
sexual violence are treated as crimes against humanity, they are treated very
similarly to murder and torture as crimes against humanity – that is, they are
prosecuted not as individualized crimes, but because of the group-based nature

of the crime. Yet, little attention is paid to the rationale for insisting that rape be linked to group-based harm for it to be an international crime, and less attention yet to why group-based crimes should be seen as harmful to humanity.

In a case before the Yugoslav Tribunal, sensitivity was shown to the plight of women in the ethnic cleansing campaign in the Balkans. The ICTY Trial Chamber decided the case of Prosecutor v. Anto Furundzija in December 1998.[15] The accused, Furundzija, was the local commander of the Jokers, a special unit of the military police of the Bosnian Serb regime. A Muslim woman was arrested and brought to the Jokers' headquarters for questioning. Furundzija forced the woman to undress, and threatened her by rubbing a knife along her inner thigh and stomach. The woman was moved to another room, where she was beaten and forced to have oral and vaginal sex with a soldier while Furundzija stood by, doing nothing to prevent these acts.[16] This and similar acts were committed as a form of intimidation of the Muslim community in Bosnia, as part of a general plan to forcibly remove Muslims from most of Bosnia, thereby extending the domain of "Greater Serbia" to include increasingly large tracts of the former Yugoslavia.

The court concluded that there has evolved "universally accepted norms of international law prohibiting rape as well as serious sexual assault. These norms are applicable in any armed conflict,"[17] not just in times of war. Interestingly, though, the court did not go further and call the norms proscribing rape and sexual violence in armed conflicts *jus cogens* norms, as it had done concerning torture, for which the accused was also charged.[18] We will return to this issue later, where I will argue that rape can be seen as quite similar to torture. One should only note here that the accused was tried for both rape and torture, and the charges of torture were considered to be conceptually different and somehow more serious than the sexual violence charges. Thus, even in this landmark trial, where rape is prosecuted as a crime against humanity, there is still some reluctance to see rape as comparable to torture and murder, the paradigmatic crimes against humanity.

Kelly Dawn Askin has argued that many rapes should be seen as violations of *jus cogens* norms on the same level of seriousness as torture. She urges that rape and other forms of sexual violence be considered crimes against humanity if they are part of a systematic attack made on gender grounds, not merely on racial, ethnic, political, national, or religious grounds.[19] I agree with Askin that rape can be just as serious as torture, and that especially if it is directed at women as a group, it should be subject to international prosecution. But there is a conceptual problem in characterizing many cases of mass rape as being directed at women as a group that helps illustrate something about the nature of international crimes, and also the conceptual problems with understanding otherwise individualized crimes as international crimes.

Consider the case of the so-called comfort women. These women were captured by the Japanese army during World War II and forced into a kind of sexual slavery to provide "comfort" for the Japanese troops. The enslavement and rape of these women was so heinous that, for many people, it called out for international prosecution. The question, though, was what the rationale for the prosecution should be. Various theorists, such as Askin, argue that this is a case in which there should be international prosecution because of the harm done to women as a group. I agree with Askin about this case, although my reasons are different, and more complicated, than hers. There are deep conceptual problems with seeing such cases as examples of group-based harm if the group in question is the group of women – an amorphous group that spans all economic classes, religions, races, and ethnicities.

The comfort women were chosen because they were women, but it is hard to argue that the Japanese army, or any particular member thereof, intended to enslave these women as a way of harming women as a distinct group.[20] The comfort women were drawn from Korea, China, the Philippines, and Indonesia, and they were not restricted to any particular ethnic group. Nonetheless, it is important to note that Japanese women were not selected to be comfort women, and this was largely true of European women as well. So it is hard to characterize the sexual violence involved in the treatment of the comfort women as directed at women as a group, but rather to a particular subset of women. They were sexually exploited because they were non-Japanese Asians, but not merely because they were women, and not clearly so as to harm the group women.[21] If there was a message being sent to a larger group at all, it is much more likely that these women were persecuted in order to send a message of intimidation to their national communities, rather than to send a message to all of women.

There is often a parallel problem in characterizing rape or sexual violence today as a crime based on membership in the group "women." In the Balkans, Serb paramilitary forces raped Muslim and Croat women; these Serbian men did not generally rape Serbian women. I do not wish to rule out the possibility that a State or State-like entity could order mass rapes in order to harm women as a group. My point is that the recent cases illustrate the fact that nationality or ethnicity is normally more important than "gender" from the standpoint of the perpetrators of mass rape and sexual violence. Krishna Patel points out that even where State-sponsored forced impregnation occurred, the harm is directed at "Bosnian women," yet "non-Bosnian women are not systematically and repeatedly raped by Serbian forces." For this reason, Patel says that the case is a difficult one conceptually because these women "share two immutable characteristics: their gender and also their ethnicity as Muslims."[22] In this case, I am sympathetic to Patel's point that these women have two related group-based harm claims, and that it is hard to determine which is the primary target of the attackers.[23] Regardless of which of the group-based forms of harm are involved in these cases, there is nonetheless non-individualized treatment of the sort that was identified in the last chapter as justifying international prosecutions.

There is yet a third group-based claim that these women can make, and it is this claim that is in many ways the most persuasive. If there is State involvement in rapes and other forms of sexual violence, then there is also a group-based claim for international prosecution. I argued in the last chapter that State involvement is a group-based characteristic of the crime that could transform a crime such as rape into an international crime. Even if cases such as those of the comfort women or the mass rapes of Bosnian women do not fit under the first prong of my international harm principle as establishing group-based crimes against women, we can turn to the second prong of the international harm principle, and look at the character of the perpetrator. As we will see in the next section, the involvement of the State will nonetheless make it possible to see these crimes as deserving of international prosecution.

If the Serb militia did attack women of all ethnicities, or if the attacks were aimed at degrading the women as women, then I would agree with Askin's basis for seeing how these rapes could count as gender-based violations of *jus cogens* norms. But if they are more ambiguous, more aimed at degrading the ethnic community than at degrading the women, then it is less clear that they should count as gender-based violations of *jus cogens* norms, although they would probably still be ethnic-based violations of *jus cogens* norms. I remain sympathetic to the movement that seeks to add gender to the group-based characteristics that can trigger international prosecutions, even as I remain somewhat skeptical that there will be many cases of this sort. The most important issue here is why group-based harm is indeed the key to justified international prosecutions.

To confront this problem, we need a more nuanced understanding of international crimes and their relationship to *jus cogens* norms than international courts have provided so far. The last chapter began this task, and the end of this chapter will continue it. Before undertaking that task, it will also be instructive to examine one other area of international law where rape seems to be of sufficient interest to the international community to call for an internationally sanctioned remedy, a category of crime that is also recognized as a crime against humanity but one that is different from what we have just considered.

III. Rape as Persecution

The third conceptual question concerns why only rape that is group-based, and not individual rapes, should be of sufficient interest to the international community to count as international crimes. To begin to answer this question, I will examine a case that is outside international criminal law, but in which the group-based nature of harms is key – namely, the intersection of domestic immigration law and international human rights law. When recent rape victims have brought asylum claims under U.S. immigration law, rape, like torture or genocide, must be linked to membership in a social group (or sufficiently based on a kind of political opinion) if it is to count as persecution. For asylum to be granted, a person needs to be a refugee, and a refugee is defined as a person fleeing persecution in his or her home country. The relevant form of persecution for asylum is that "on account of race, religion, nationality, membership in a particular social group, or political opinion."[24] But why should this be the only basis for establishing an asylum claim in such cases?

If one has been subjected to individual isolated acts of persecution, asylum will generally not be granted in the United States, or in many other countries. One likely reason for this is that the proper recourse is through the domestic courts of one's home country. On the other hand, if the harm to the victim is group-based, then it is likely to be pervasive and not merely directed at the individual person. As with persecution as a crime against humanity, the basis of persecution in asylum cases has to be something beyond what is harmful to discrete individuals, unless there is also State involvement. I identified this element earlier as that of widespreadness, although in persecution as a crime against humanity one can also refer to the second prong of the international harm principle having to do with the perpetrator's involvement with a State or State-like entity.

Consider the case of Olimpia Lazo-Majano, an El Salvadoran woman who sought asylum in the United States. She had been the victim of long-term abuse at the hands of her former employer, Rene Zuniga. Zuniga was a sergeant in the Salvadoran military. He had used his gun, as well as grenades held against her head, to force Lazo-Majano to submit to intercourse. Zuniga also threatened to bomb her home if she did not submit to him. Zuniga fled her home country and sought asylum in the United States. Various courts considered her asylum claim. According to the United States Ninth Circuit Court of Appeals, "Zuniga told Olimpia that it was his job to kill subversives."[25] The court held that "Zuniga is asserting the political opinion that a man has a right to dominate [a woman] and he has persecuted Olimpia to force her to accept his opinion without rebellion."[26] In the court's estimation, this involved "a cynical imputation" of a political opinion to Lazo-Majano. The court concluded that "[e]ven if she had no political opinion and was innocent of a single reflection on the government of her country, the cynical imputation of political opinion to her is what counts . . . one must continue to look at the person from the perspective of the persecutor. If the persecutor thinks the person guilty of a political opinion, then the person is at risk."[27]

The key difficulty in Lazo-Majano is to see how persecutions by males of females could be more than individually based. From the perspective of her attacker, this case had all of the appearance of a personal problem – Zuniga seemingly did these things to her because he wanted to force her to have sex with him. If, though, there is a pattern of such behavior directed against members of a group in a given country, then it is no longer merely personal. And the international community steps in, represented by the country that grants asylum, because the persecution is more serious for being group-based. But why should group-based sexual violence, and not individualized sexual violence, be seen as important to the international community? Part of the answer is that this form of sexual violence is seen as sufficiently similar to genocide, slavery, and apartheid to demand international attention. But why are genocide, slavery, and apartheid given this status? To answer this question, and the questions from the two previous sections of this chapter, I have been developing a nuanced understanding of the concept of *jus cogens* norms.

Returning to the issues at the forefront of international criminal law – namely, the nature of *jus cogens* norms – we have seen several conceptual problems illustrated in the three cases discussed here. First, why think that any form of rape should be seen as anything other than a personal (domestic) crime? Second, why think that certain types of rape harm the interests of the international community, and hence should count as an international crime? Third, why think that only group-based types of rape, such as genocide, slavery, and apartheid, are of sufficient interest to the international community to count as international crimes? And why think that genocide, slavery, and apartheid should be of special interest to the international community?

When an isolated incident of rape occurs in a given country, it is difficult to prove that the rape is group-based, in either of the two senses I developed in the last chapter. When there is mass rape in a given country, especially directed at a sub-section of the female population of that country, then it is easier to show that the acts of rape are group-based and that they are likely to be widespread. In addition, if these rapes are seemingly directed at certain types of women because of a State plan, then there is again a non-individualized treatment of an individual person that, because of its systematic nature, will surely be harmful to a larger segment of the population as well. Here the "State plan" in these cases gives the international community an additional basis for international prosecutions. So when rape is widespread or systematic, it is not aimed at a particular woman. As part of a plan, or as intentionally aimed at a specific group, the rape is such that there is not only a harm to the particular woman but also a harm to humanity of the type I described in Chapter 5. It is for this reason that some rapes are not only domestic crimes but also instances of international crime.

In the most egregious examples of mass rape and sexual violence, something very much like a plan or policy is afoot. As Catherine MacKinnon has put it, the difficulty is that "[r]ape has so often been treated as extracurricular, as just something men do, as a product rather than a policy of war."[28] While it may be very difficult to show that there was an affirmative governmental plan or policy to use rape as a means of persecution of non-Bosnian women by Serb forces, it is considerably easier to show that there was a negative policy to allow it to occur. All that needs to be shown is that the relevant governmental units were aware of the widespread practice and did nothing intentional to prevent it.[29]

I do not wish to rule out international prosecutions of rape or sexual violence that lack governmental complicity, but merely to suggest that these will be considerably harder to justify as condemnable by *jus cogens* norms and subject to prosecution by international tribunals. Individuals who are not part of the State structure can engage in group-based harm that could rise to the level of international concern. But in such cases there would need to be something, provable through direct evidence, that linked the individual perpetrator to the State, or perhaps to the larger society. The individual normally must be either some kind of official representative of the State or clearly attempting to advance the State's, or the society's, goals. In Chapter 7, I will argue that discriminatory intent on the part of the perpetrator may be sufficient to link a non-State actor to the larger community's plan of harmful group-based treatment.[30] But the clearest cases of international prosecution will remain those in which the perpetrator is a leader, or at least has a role in the State structure, as was true in all of the cases discussed earlier in the chapter.[31]

Do the acts need to be systematic in the way discussed at the end of the last chapter in order for the acts to rise to the level of international crimes?[32] Not necessarily. But if we are talking about a single incident of rape, even by a State official, it will be hard to show that such an act is to be imputed to the State rather than merely to the individual perpetrator. For the officials have two persona – their truly official or artificial persona and their personal or natural persona.[33] In order to show that a member of the police was indeed acting in his or her official capacity, it is often necessary to show that there was a pattern of such behavior and no one in authority over the police officer did anything to stop it, and often that other police were also acting in a similar manner. Even better would be the showing that there was an explicit policy, as there appeared to have been in Bosnia, of the Serbian police using sexual assault as a means of intimidating ethnic Muslims.

It is the main practical thesis of this chapter that when rape and sexual violence are targeted at a group or are part of a State policy, then these forms of sexual exploitation are also clearly violations of what ought to be regarded in international law as *jus cogens* norms, and for this reason legitimately prosecuted by international tribunals. Mass rape and sexual violence clearly violate moral minimalism since they are assaults against the bodily security of the women who are assaulted. This would satisfy the security principle. And when the assault is either directed at a group or involves a State (or State-like) actor, and ideally when both conditions are met, then it is sufficiently linked to the international harm principle to call for international prosecutions.[34] In the next section, I consider five additional objections to my group-based model of international crime.

IV. Why Not Individualized International Crimes?

The first objection to my view of the nature of international crime is that it turns the clock back. International human rights activists have fought for several generations to get international courts to focus on individuals rather than States as the victims, and to focus on individuals as perpetrators rather than States and other international organizations as perpetrators. The idea is that meaningful progressive human rights change can occur only when individuals are front-and-center such that we cannot ignore who is the victim, and where perpetrators cannot hide behind their States or other groups, and are forced to become individually accountable for their heinous deeds. The ICC is similarly inspired by the push toward individual accountability and away from merely State-based and other forms of group accountability.[35] It might be thought that a group-based approach to international criminal law moves us away from individual accountability.

I have two responses. First, as I stated at the beginning of the chapter, if we fail to distinguish international crimes from domestic crimes, the ICC and similar international tribunals will continue to experience difficulties with those who fear usurpation of domestic tribunals, and hence of State sovereignty.[36] This is a pragmatic point, but it is very important. If international criminal law is to progress, multilateral agreements such as the ICC treaty must have widespread support. Such support will not be forthcoming if courts such as the ICC are seen as potentially usurping the sovereignty of domestic States. And if the multilateral agreements do not gain sufficient support, then these international criminal tribunals will fail. So even if one thinks that international criminal law should have a wider purview than I have proposed, extending that purview will actually make it less likely that there will be effective international criminal courts at all.[37]

This first response is practical. The critics of international tribunals, such as former U.S. Senator Jesse Helms, are worried about just such a conflation of international and domestic legal norms, and as a result have blocked the United States from implementing major human rights treaties. Without some basis for distinguishing among these types of legal norms, Helms and his friends will have a powerful argument against U.S. participation in these treaties. But if a clear, in-principle distinction between domestic and international crimes can be maintained, then the encroachments on U.S. sovereignty caused by these treaties will not appear to be so great. And the world will gain by being able to hold the U.S. accountable for some especially egregious and widespread human rights abuses.

My second response is theoretical, and has been rehearsed in some detail in the preceding pages. For the international community to prosecute certain crimes, those crimes must be shown to violate some security interest of the victim and in some sense constitute a harm to the world community. Here the task of defining just what is involved in truly international crimes becomes urgent. If international crimes are not cast in group-based terms, it will be very difficult to draw a distinction between international and domestic crime. And even if such a distinction can be drawn, it will lack a moral foundation that allows a perpetrator to see why what he or she did was indeed something deserving of punishment.

The second objection to my view asks why it is important for international law to be premised on group-based norms rather than individualized norms. The main reason I adopt a group-based approach is to be able to make a principled distinction between international legal norms and domestic ones. One could challenge this idea by arguing that in an ideal world, there would be no need to make such a distinction between international and domestic legal norms. Indeed, it could be argued, there is no in-principle basis for distinguishing rights at either level, and much harm can be done by maintaining the distinction in terms of further entrenching unjustified notions of sovereignty when human rights abuses occur. I would only point out that we do not live in an ideal world. As we will see, fairness to defendants requires relatively clear lines to be drawn between what is punishable and what is not.

It is important to continue to maintain a distinction between international and domestic legal norms. I agree that ideally there is no need to draw this distinction. In one sense, all rapes harm humanity in the sense that the individual is a part of humanity. But in another sense, individualized rapes, where the harm is not group-based or not perpetrated by a State or State-like actor, do not directly harm the interests of humanity. Only when these acts are based on something more than individual characteristics is there a strong threat to the peace and security of humanity that would warrant international concern. As long as there are functioning domestic courts, we should leave the prosecution of most rapes to these courts. The international courts should be used only in highly unusual circumstances, not as a replacement for what domestic States are able to prosecute.

The third objection to my view asks why defendants' rights can only be secured by limiting the status of international crimes. Rather, what is needed is only for good procedural safeguards to be instituted that make sure that defendants are not subjected to violations of the rule of law. Procedural safeguards, such as making sure that there is indeed a clearly expressed law that a defendant is being prosecuted for having violated, is the main thing that is owed to defendants and that will ultimately secure the rights of defendants. By focusing on limitations on the nature of international crime, one only makes it more likely that human rights abusers will act with impunity and avoid prosecution for – or at least not be sufficiently deterred from committing – international crimes.

My reply is to point out that the line between procedural safeguards and careful limitation of what counts as international crimes is not always easy to draw. If defendants who have no State involvement are going to be tried in international courts for normally highly individualized crimes such as rape, rather than for clearly group-based crimes such as slavery, these defendants should have been able to see, at the time they acted, that what they were doing was a violation of international law, as well as why the provisions of the law were deserving of respect and obedience. As explained earlier, this is one of the main moral principles conformity with which is necessary for law to have moral legitimacy. Moral legitimacy is not achieved merely by making sure that defendants have narrowly conceived procedural safeguards such as the right against self-incrimination. For if this were all that were needed for moral legitimacy, then it would not be clear that broader considerations of fairness in the rule of law are met, such as that no defendant be prosecuted unless he or she could have ascertained what he or she needed to do to avoid prosecution.

Fourth, as I suggested earlier, some would argue that it is enough that there exist a list somewhere of which crimes are indeed international ones. The ICC statute provides such a list. Perhaps one could follow H. L. A. Hart's suggestion that international law encompasses just those rules that the world community accepts as legitimate.[38] Statutes such as that of the ICC set out a list of those crimes whose violations are to be recognized as international crimes. Once the ICC statute had been ratified by enough States, then it was easy to pick out which crimes are considered to be international ones. And the most obvious objections based on the rule of law – namely, those having to do with ex post facto prosecutions – can be met.

The simplicity of the "list of international crimes" proposal belies its chief drawback. For those States that do not agree to the list, or who do so but later change their minds, there is no clear reason for regarding those crimes as anything other than what some States and interest groups managed to insert into an international criminal statute.[39] There will be no in-principle basis for seeing these crimes as "deserving" of international prosecution. This problem can be illustrated by the plight of some of the Bosnian Serb "small fry" now in jail at The Hague who had no hint that their acts, as unspeakable as they may be, were even remotely likely to land them in jail and awaiting trial before an international tribunal.[40] This is not to say that one should have sympathy for them given their horrendous deeds. Rather, my point concerns the rule of law (the subject of Chapter 11). The ICC will resolve some of this difficulty by supplying a list of international crimes for the world community, and hence putting future perpetrators of these crimes on notice that they risk international prosecution. But the ICC statute will not solve the problem discussed at the beginning of the chapter of showing that a given list of crimes contains those crimes morally deserving of international prosecution and punishment.

From a victim's rights orientation, it makes sense to have an expansive domain of international crimes, so that no victimizer can get away from his or her responsibility with impunity. But from a defendant's rights approach, we must exercise more caution. Most importantly, there must be some underlying rationale for the claim that a certain crime is an international crime. As is true in domestic criminal law, if crimes are merely a collection of prescriptions, then defendants will not know what they are supposed to do, or, more importantly, why it is considered morally important to avoid certain kinds of conduct. Such an understanding is important for the general sense of moral legitimacy of the law and for a proper attribution of responsibility to those who commit egregious acts in the world. For it is moral legitimacy that is the true hallmark of the rule of law, not the mere retribution garnered on behalf of the victims of horrendous crimes.[41] We will not gain respect for the international rule of law until international crimes are conceptualized as more than mere lists of acts that some States and interest groups once thought to be criminalizable.

Fifth, another related objection is that such a "list of offenses" could be pruned according to the principle that only those crimes that are sufficiently "serious" are allowed on the list. Such a view has an obvious simplicity to it. Of course, it still remains for us to establish which crimes are of sufficient seriousness. But the convergence of views on what counts as "serious" over the last fifty years, from the Nuremberg Charter to the Rome Statute, seems to support the idea that the degree of seriousness can do the job that my much more elaborate "normative principles" are designed to do. So, according to this objection, there is no need to have complex philosophical justifications for each crime on the list. Such a list would not necessarily constitute a system of international criminal law, but it might still be a sufficiently coherent set of laws to make them deserving of respect as a fair list of international crimes for which defendants can legitimately be prosecuted.

This fifth objection is harder to meet than was the fourth. If one could construct a list of international crimes all of which were the most serious of human rights abuses, one might indeed overcome the objection that a defendant needs to know not only what is proscribed but why certain acts are indeed proscribed. But how are we to decide which human rights abuses are truly serious enough to be justifiably prosecutable by international tribunals? It will not do merely to look at what has been considered serious over the last fifty years, since then we will only know what was *once* considered serious, not what *now remains* of serious concern to the international community. This response harkens back to my discussion of the problems with custom. For this fifth objection really asks why we cannot merely rely on custom to weed out which human rights abuses are most serious and justifiably proscribed. But it is not clear at all that appeals to such custom have any moral legitimacy. So we are then thrown back to the question with which we began Part B of the text – namely, what normative principles are the most plausible in limiting the domain of international criminal law so that only the most serious of offenses are prosecuted. An appeal to seriousness, by itself, does not resolve the question of which principles one should appeal to in order to determine which crimes are indeed most serious. So I must agree that this objection is right on the mark, but that it also actually paves the way for seeing the value of the approach I have taken in these last three chapters.

In this chapter, I have elaborated on my in-principle basis for distinguishing between international and domestic crimes. I have used various examples of rape to illustrate my claim that such crimes must normally be group-based either in terms of the status of the perpetrators or the character of the harm. Even those who disagree can regard my efforts as at least providing a preliminary way of sorting, where a core basis for deciding which are international crimes is established in a way that meshes with the uncontroversial international crimes. My critics might choose to use this model as a basis for deciding which additional crimes are to be added to the current lists codified in international instruments, where other putative international crimes can be added on the basis of special justification, by analogizing from the core crimes. And even if this much is rejected, I hope, at the very least, to have spurred a philosophical debate about the concept of international crime. The defendants who will be subject to serious risk of loss of liberty are owed a clear answer to the various conceptual questions I have posed in this chapter.

In the third part of the book, we turn to specific normative and conceptual problems that arise out of the prosecution of people accused of international crime. But we will not leave behind the general philosophical issues we have been addressing. Those issues will be given a more concrete context in the next three chapters as we investigate conceptual issues that have arisen out of the Tadic, Pinochet, and Eichmann cases. These cases of prosecutions for crimes against humanity and genocide will illustrate some of the most famous examples of seemingly justified international prosecutions. Yet we will see that these cases were fraught with conceptual problems that the normative principles I have articulated and defended in Part B are meant to resolve. It is in the consideration of such cases that the plausibility of the general theoretical arguments of the last three chapters will be enhanced. We will see how the theory works itself out in difficult cases, and how those cases raise ever more conceptual problems for rival views of the normative account of international criminal law I have been defending.

PART C

PROSECUTING INTERNATIONAL CRIMES

7

Prosecuting "Minor Players" for Crimes Against Humanity

Whom should international tribunals prosecute for crimes against humanity? In the case of ethnic cleansing in the Balkans, should it be the Serbian leaders who orchestrated the forced migrations in Bosnia and Kosovo?[1] If "minor players"[2] are prosecuted, what must the prosecution show in order to link these individuals to the larger ethnic cleansing campaign? The first people prosecuted at the Nuremberg Trials were the leaders of the Third Reich who had, among other things, planned and orchestrated the Holocaust.[3] In contrast, because of the difficulty in capturing the leaders, the first people prosecuted by the International Criminal Tribunal for the Former Yugoslavia (ICTY) are the "minor players" rather than the leaders of the ethnic cleansing campaign.[4] This chapter will address the conceptual justification of prosecuting these minor players.[5] The next chapter will address the justification of prosecuting the leaders of States. In both chapters, we will seek a link between individual action and group action.

If the individual minor players are to be prosecuted by international criminal tribunals, what makes their acts crimes against humanity[6] rather than merely crimes against a particular State?[7] Is there a conceptually sound basis for prosecuting these individuals for having committed acts that are only loosely connected to the larger ethnic cleansing program?[8] Following from the earlier chapters, the argument of this chapter takes an explicitly defendant-oriented approach. From this perspective, an element of a crime should not be rejected because it is hard for the prosecutor to prove.[9] In addition to paying attention to the rights of the victims, we must not lose sight of the rights of the defendants, who stand in much peril as they are confronted by the full force of "foreign" courts in which even their lawyers are often unaccustomed to appearing.

The focus of this chapter will be the grounds for prosecuting minor individuals, as opposed to State leaders, for ethnic cleansing as a crime against humanity.[10] Initially, the difficulty is deciding which individuals are to be prosecuted. In whose actions should the international community take a special interest?[11] If we stick only to the second prong of the international harm principle, then it will be very difficult to prosecute minor players, because they are often not State agents. For successful prosecution of minor players, the first prong of the international harm principle will have to be employed – namely, it will have to be shown that the victims suffered a group-based harm. Here, one of the most difficult conceptual problems is how to link the crimes of an individual to the larger plan or scheme that is said to have harmed humanity.[12] One single act of murder does not seem to be an act of ethnic cleansing, and yet it is the relatively minor perpetrators of single acts with which recent international criminal courts have concerned themselves.[13]

The first part of this chapter will analyze the concept of ethnic cleansing, with special emphasis on the facts of the case of Prosecutor v. Dusko Tadic. This was the first prosecution of an individual for ethnic cleansing as a crime against humanity. The trial was conducted against a minor player, not an official responsible for planning the overall scheme of Serbian ethnic cleansing against Muslims and Croats in Bosnia-Herzegovina.[14] The second part of the chapter will describe and critically assess three of the four elements of crimes against humanity as they were identified by the ICTY – that the crime be (1) directed against a civilian population, (2) systematic or widespread, and (3) part of a State or group policy. The thesis of the second section is that these elements do not sufficiently link an accused minor player to the larger criminal endeavor so as to prove that the individual's act was clearly an international crime. These three elements establish that an international crime has been committed, but another element is needed to show that a minor player is guilty of committing that group-based crime.

The third part of the chapter will examine the most controversial dimension of the ICTY's elements of a crime against humanity – namely, (4) discriminatory intent. The thesis of the third part is that the element of discriminatory intent is necessary to link the acts of a minor player to a group-based crime, such as ethnic cleansing. This part of the chapter argues in favor of the ICTY's inclusion of the element of discriminatory intent. An argument is offered against the current view, as was expressed in the new permanent ICC, that this element be eliminated from the elements of crimes against humanity. The fourth part of the chapter will tackle one of the most difficult objections to my proposal – why shouldn't certain minor players be at least partially responsible for these crimes if these individuals knew of the group plan and willingly participated in it? I modify my original position somewhat, arguing that if there is an intent to participate in a plan that is known to be discriminatory, then a transferred discriminatory intent can be established.

The final part of the chapter examines in more detail how the Trial and Appellate opinions in the Tadic case attempted to resolve the conceptual difficulties outlined earlier as it prosecuted Tadic for the crime of ethnic cleansing. The overarching thesis of this chapter is that discriminatory intent is a necessary element of crimes against humanity when certain minor players are prosecuted for crimes such as ethnic cleansing. Yet, if this additional intent requirement is recognized, then it will be very difficult, although not impossible, to convict minor players, as opposed to State leaders, for such crimes.

I. Ethnic Cleansing and the Acts of Dusko Tadic

The Commission of Experts for the former Yugoslavia, established by the UN Security Council, defined "ethnic cleansing" as "rendering an area ethnically homogenous by using force or intimidation to remove persons of given groups from the area."[15] More specifically, the Commission said that ethnic cleansing involved "a purposeful policy designed by one ethnic group to remove by violent and terror-inspiring means the civilian population of another ethnic or religious group from certain geographic areas."[16] The Commission of Experts said that ethnic cleansing involved murder, torture, arbitrary arrest and detention, extrajudicial executions, rape and sexual assaults, confinement of civilian population in ghetto areas, forcible removal, displacement and deportation of civilian population, deliberate military attacks or threats of attacks on civilians and civilian areas, and wanton destruction of property.[17]

In 1992, the United Nations condemned "ethnic cleansing" in the former Yugoslavia.[18] The Secretary-General of the United Nations said:

Both in Bosnia and Herzegovina and in Croatia, minority families driven from their homes and farms are replaced, sometimes apparently with official assistance, by persons of other ethnic groups displaced from other regions. The purpose is to create areas overwhelmingly populated by a single ethnic group, a practice that has come to be known as 'ethnic cleansing' ... what is required is energetic official action to end the excesses which are being carried out by ethnic chauvinists of all communities.[19]

The ICTY was created to prosecute those responsible for ethnic cleansing.[20] Although the ICTY has treated ethnic cleansing as a war crime, a crime against the Geneva Conventions, and a crime against humanity, this chapter will focus only on the latter category of crime, the category that the ICTY spent the most time discussing in its first case.[21]

The idea of a crime against humanity is unique to the twentieth century.[22] For an act to be so heinous as to be called a "crime against humanity," that crime must be directed not merely against individuals but against social groups and, in a sense, the whole of humanity.[23] Today, those individuals who perpetrated the "ethnic cleansing" campaigns in the former Yugoslavia have been charged with having committed crimes against humanity.[24] The ICTY is one of the very first courts to prosecute individuals who committed the specific murders, rapes, tortures, and so on, by which crimes against humanity were effected.[25] Previously, only the leaders of an army or political unit would be so connected to the larger plan to be guilty of such crimes.[26] Indeed, it is only very recently that international courts have begun to prosecute minor players at all.[27] In its first trial, the ICTY chose to prosecute the individual acts of Dusko Tadic as crimes against humanity.[28]

Dusko Tadic, a Serbian former saloon owner and automobile mechanic, became the first person prosecuted by the ICTY for violations of humanitarian law, including crimes against humanity, associated with ethnic cleansing in Bosnia.[29] Tadic was certainly a heinous individual, who stood accused of truly horrific acts. The indictment against Tadic mentions the following acts, among others:

1. Participating in the destruction and plunder of Bosnian and Croat residential areas.[30]
2. Killing and beating men and women who were seized or detained.[31]
3. Killing, torturing, beating, and sexually assaulting concentration camp inmates.[32]
4. Participating in the seizure, selection, and transportation of individuals into concentration camps.[33]
5. Killing and cruel treatment of prisoners.[34]

In addition, it was alleged that Tadic ordered one Muslim concentration camp inmate to bite off the testicles of another inmate, surely one of the more gruesome charges of the entire war.[35]

By some accounts, Tadic claimed to have been motivated in his actions because he was seeking revenge for the rape of his wife by a Muslim from Tadic's town. According to Michael Scharf, this accusation was almost surely fabricated by Tadic for his own self-serving ends.[36] Nonetheless, Tadic is indeed the first person prosecuted and convicted by the ICTY. Tadic was the first to be prosecuted because he had fled to Germany and was hence easier to capture than those who still remained in Bosnia and the wider Yugoslavia and who were initially protected by political and military leaders openly contemptuous of the ICTY.[37]

To get a sense of the difficult conceptual issues faced by the prosecution, one needs to realize that the prosecutors themselves treated the Tadic case as involving much larger crimes than the acts of a heinous individual. In his opening statement, prosecutor Grant Niemann said that the trial was not just about "what occurred between the accused and the victims of these crimes" but "about the tragic destruction of that once proud and beautiful country, Yugoslavia."[38] The defense counsel argued that Tadic had been made a "symbol" of all that had gone wrong in Bosnia, and the specific case against Tadic risked being "blown out of all proportions."[39]

The ICTY struggled with the question of whether Tadic was connected closely enough to the larger ethnic cleansing campaign to be prosecuted by the International Tribunal. Indeed, at one crucial juncture, the Trial Chamber admits that Tadic "has not been charged nor has the Prosecution proved, that the accused was engaged in the operation of the [concentration] camps."[40] Tadic was at best a minor player, a part-time karate instructor and saloon keeper who realized that he could extract revenge and twisted pleasure from using his contacts at the concentration camps to abuse long-time enemies and others whom he brutally treated in a kind of "blood lust."[41]

The conceptual question is not whether Tadic was a particularly ignoble criminal, but whether his terrible criminal acts rose to the level of international crimes, especially crimes against humanity. Before attempting to answer this question, Parts II and III of this chapter will discuss the conceptual difficulties that have arisen in the attempt to delimit the elements of crimes against humanity. Throughout these two parts, the issue is whether the acts of individuals who did horrible things can be prosecuted as international criminal acts, even though the individuals prosecuted were themselves not the instigators or directors of the larger plan of violence. I argue that discriminatory intent must be shown for minor players such as Tadic in order for them to be justifiably prosecuted and convicted for crimes against humanity.

II. Three Uncontroversial Elements of Crimes Against Humanity

There have been three significant attempts to define crimes against humanity. In 1945, the Nuremberg Tribunal defined crimes against humanity for the first time, saying that they involved such individual criminal acts as murder, extermination, or enslavement committed against any civilian population "before or during the war."[42] In 1993, the Statute for the International Criminal Tribunal for the former Yugoslavia (ICTY) defined crimes against humanity as acts of murder, torture, rape, and so on, "committed in armed conflict, whether international or internal in character, and directed against any civilian population."[43] And in 1998, the Rome Statute created a permanent international criminal court, defining crimes against humanity as certain acts "committed as part of a widespread or systematic attack directed against a civilian population, with knowledge of the attack."[44]

The history of attempts to define crimes against humanity displays a progressive movement away from thinking that these crimes must be conducted during wartime. For the Nuremberg Tribunal, crimes against humanity were effectively a sub-set of war crimes. For the ICTY, crimes against humanity also seemingly had to be connected to war, although the war could be a civil war, and hence need not be a war between two sovereign States. The Rome Statute defined crimes against humanity as a sub-set of crimes conducted against a civilian population, regardless of whether the attacks constituted war at all. Crimes against humanity are now no longer merely a sub-category of war crimes, but rather especially egregious crimes directed against a civilian population.[45] In 1995, the ICTY Appeals Chamber ruled that "it is by now settled customary international law that crimes against humanity do not require a connection to international armed conflict . . . [and] may not require a connection to any conflict at all."[46]

The ICTY's Trial Chamber said that the requirement of a connection to war has now been replaced by the requirement that the acts be "directed against any civilian population."[47] The connection, or "nexus," with war, or with some kind of large-scale attack, meant that crimes against humanity were to be distinguished from isolated acts, even those isolated acts that were especially atrocious in character.[48] Now that the nexus with war has been broken, serious conceptual and practical problems have arisen in cases where minor players such as Tadic are prosecuted for crimes against humanity.[49]

The thesis of this part of the chapter is that the three uncontroversial elements of crimes against humanity do not sufficiently link the acts of an accused minor player, such as Tadic, to the larger international crime. These three elements are that the crime be (1) directed against a civilian population, (2) part of a State or group policy, and (3) systematic or widespread.[50] These elements all make reference to collective categories such as civilian populations, group plans, and systematic and mass action. Yet, none of these elements clearly links the acts of an individual to the collective crime in a way that will support prosecution of that individual.[51] In analyzing these elements, international courts and legal theorists have continued to try to fit crimes against humanity into the mold of domestic criminal law categories that were designed to establish the elements of individual criminal acts. These three elements of crimes against humanity will be analyzed and their conceptual problems will be set out next.

A. The First Element: Directed Against a Civilian Population

All of the major definitions of crimes against humanity stipulate that these crimes must be directed at a civilian population.[52] In the Tadic case, the ICTY's Trial Chamber offered this as the guiding idea behind the "population" element:

> [T]he "population" element is intended to imply *crimes of a collective nature* and thus exclude single or isolated acts . . . the emphasis is not on the individual victim but rather on the collective, the individual being victimized not because of his individual attributes but rather because of his membership in a targeted civilian population.[53]

The key conceptual difficulty is that this element of the crime concerns something "of a collective nature," yet the act being prosecuted is individual in nature.

The ICTY's Trial Chamber has affirmed that a single act can constitute a crime against humanity if it is committed as part of a widespread or systematic attack on a civilian population.[54] If a "nexus" to a war were still required, things would be slightly easier. One could look at whether the individual act in question was commanded by the leaders of one of the parties to the war, or at least countenanced by those leaders in their overall plan of war. Wars are, after all, best seen as organized efforts of many individual acts. But State policies outside of wartime are often harder to conceptualize as transforming individual acts into acts that have a "collective nature."[55]

What does it mean for an individual act to have a collective nature? This question will be explored in various ways over the following sub-parts of the chapter. As a preliminary answer to the question it should be pointed out that many individual acts are instances of types of acts that have a collective nature. Consider the act of writing this chapter. This individual act might be an instance of the collective act of scholars writing about crimes against humanity.[56] On even a higher level of abstraction, the act of writing this chapter is itself an instance of "writing" in general, arguably a category that ranges over many acts, and can be characterized as a part of a distinct activity of humanity.

When individual acts of murder, torture, or rape are said to be directed against a civilian population, there must be a clear causal connection between what the accused individual did and what happened to that civilian population. It would not be sufficient for the victim of murder, torture, or rape merely to be a member of a larger civilian population. Not every attack on a member of a group is also an attack on the group itself. As will be explored later, when the intentions of a perpetrator are personal – for instance, attempting to seek revenge for a personal slight – an attack on a member of a civilian population may be merely an attack on that person alone. For an assault by an individual to be directed at a civilian population, more is needed than merely showing that the person attacked was a member of a population group.[57]

This sub-part of the chapter has argued that an element that specifically links the accused individual to the population that is under attack is needed. The population element is meant to allow for the transformation of otherwise isolated acts into something else – namely, acts that are instances of attacking a whole population, of which the defendant's attacks on individuals are a part.[58] Yet it is unclear how the population element does in fact link the acts of a minor player to the international crime. An additional element must be included to show how an attack by one individual on another individual could be seen as also an attack on a whole population, and ultimately an attack on humanity itself. The ICTY Trial Chamber said that the population element is closely related to the element of State or group policy.[59] We turn next to this element in search of the basis for transforming the individual act into a crime against humanity.

B. The Second Element: State or Group Policy

The ICTY, as well as the drafters of the 1998 Rome Statute, said that a State or other group policy is another main element of a crime against humanity.[60] This element is said to be implied by the ICTY Statute's stipulation that crimes against humanity must be "directed at" a civilian population.[61] For the attack to be directed at this population, there must be some group policy or plan to that effect. The ICTY's Trial Chamber said that the act in question must not be merely a random one – namely, "that there must be some form of policy to commit these acts."[62] The conceptual question, though, is whether the existence of such a plan is sufficient to link an individual defendant to the larger harm.

The ICTY contended that the policy necessary to raise an individual crime to the level of a crime against humanity "need not be the policy of a state."[63] Groups other than States – namely, "private individuals with de facto power or organized in criminal gangs or groups – might also commit the kind of systematic or mass violations of human rights covered by the article . . ."[64] Once again one can see the importance of the group context in understanding crimes against humanity. The individual actor accused of a crime against humanity is not required to be the one who directs the attack on the civilian population. Rather, this major element of the crime refers to a larger group that encompasses the individual actor.

Conceptually, the group policy or plan cannot itself be a feature or element of the individual's act. There can be policies or plans of individuals, such as when one makes it one's policy not to force one's children to eat things they do not like.[65] However, in the context of crimes against humanity, it is not the plan of an individual perpetrator of a crime that constitutes this element of the crime. Rather, this element concerns a policy of a group, a "State or group policy." The question then arises: How can an individual's act manifest a group plan? As in the argument advanced earlier about the population element, it is not sufficient to show that the individual's act is indeed a part of that plan. For an individual act to manifest the group plan, the individual must do something so that the plan can be characterized as his or hers. Otherwise, it may be that the individual's act only coincidentally forms part of the larger action.

This sub-part of the chapter has argued that the group plan element does not sufficiently link the acts of the accused individual to the international crime. There must be some additional showing that the minor player's acts are sufficiently linked to the group plan also to allow the group plan to be seen as the plan of that individual actor. As will be shown in subsequent sections of this chapter, it is also not enough that the individual know about the plan; rather, the individual must intend that the acts fit into that plan. Before turning to those arguments, let us turn to the third of the uncontroversial elements of crimes against humanity to see whether this element will sufficiently link the individual actor to the larger international crime.

C. The Third Element: Systematicity or Widespreadness

A third uncontroversial element of crimes against humanity is that they be carried out in a systematic way or by means of mass or widespread action.[66] Systematicity is said to refer to the quality of the act, whereas widespreadness or "mass action" refers to the sheer number of people who are affected.[67] The rationale for the "systematic or widespread" element is that it is necessary to make sure that truly isolated acts are not captured under the "crimes against humanity" label.[68] However, as will be demonstrated, an individual act of murder, torture, or rape that is being prosecuted as a crime against humanity cannot itself have either systematicity or widespreadness.[69]

Grammatically, a single act is not "systematic or widespread" outside of a group context.[70] There must be a background of other acts that this act fits into for the idea of "systematic or widespread" to make sense.[71] So, properly speaking, systematicity or widespreadness cannot capture the collective nature of individual acts of ethnic cleansing without reference to some other element. Individual acts cannot be either systematic or widespread, at least not in the way that crimes against humanity are characterized;[72] rather, the individual acts are a part of that which manifests this element. The question is not whether this act is systematic or widespread, but rather whether the collection of acts organized by a given plan has the feature of systematicity or widespreadness.[73]

Ratner and Abrams, in a highly influential 1997 book, mistakenly understand the idea of systematicity or widespreadness. They say that the

requirement of action "against a civilian population" suggests that even the most atrocious acts are not crimes against humanity if they have an impact on only very few people. To regard the state-sponsored execution of a handful of political opponents as a crime against humanity because their murders constitute "an act against a civilian population" risks suggesting that their lives are worth more than others for purposes of international law.[74]

Ratner and Abrams here seemingly are trying to find a way for systematicity or widespreadness to account for the "collective nature of individual acts." Ratner and Abrams seem to think that a crime against humanity must be an act that has consequences well beyond the individual person who is the victim of the crime.[75] In their view, if a State orders the execution of only "a handful of political opponents," the acts of the State should not be considered to be crimes against humanity because the acts lack systematicity or widespreadness.[76]

Ratner and Abrams give a conceptually flawed understanding of the element of systematicity or widespreadness. The key is not that an individual act has "an impact" on very few or very many people, but whether that act fits or does not fit into a group's plan, which itself has an impact on few or very many people. It is the plan that has to have the systematic or widespread effect. If this were not so, it would be hard to see how an individual act of murder, directed at a member of an ethnic minority, could meet the elements of widespreadness or systematicity. An act could coincidentally, and unbeknownst to the perpetrator, have widespread effects on an ethnic population, but the putative widespreadness would not be linked to the plan that would make the individual act part of a larger enterprise that would be deserving of international punishment.

The ICTY recently recognized the point in 1996 that Ratner and Abrams fail to see when it provided the following argument:

[A]s long as there is a link with the widespread and systematic attack against a civilian population, a single act could qualify as a crime against humanity. As such, an individual committing a crime against a single victim or a limited number of victims might be recognized as guilty of a crime against humanity if his acts were part of the specific context identified above.[77]

The acts of murder may indeed be carried out in secret, and hence have little or no consequences for others in the population (who do not know of the murders). But if the murders are part of a larger plan, and that plan has widespread and systematic effects, then an individual act of murder, rape, or torture could constitute a crime against humanity.[78]

Ratner and Abrams are clearly on the right track conceptually when they assert that the element of widespreadness or systematicity needs to be an element in the individual's act itself if the perpetrators are to be held responsible for an international crime.[79] But it is too much to expect that acts of murder, torture, and rape will be carried out in such a way that they have themselves widespread or systematic consequences. How can an individual criminal act have the characteristic of widespreadness or systematicity? This can only happen in one of two ways. Either the act must itself have very wide consequences, which has a serious conceptual problem – namely, it will not capture what the category of crimes against humanity is aimed at.[80] Or the individual act must be seen as part of a group plan. However, the element of widespreadness or systematicity does not link the individual acts of murder, torture, or rape to the group plan. In addition, as was shown in Section II, the group plan element does not sufficiently connect the individual act to the larger international crime.

This sub-part of the chapter has argued that on the most plausible reading, the element of systematicity or widespreadness is not an element of individual acts but of collections of acts, or of acts by groups of people. The element of widespreadness or systematicity cannot link the act of an accused individual to the larger international crime. Hence, given what has been shown previously, none of the three uncontroversial elements discussed so far manifests the "collective nature" of the individual acts. For this reason, we must turn to another element, an element that is hotly debated in contemporary international criminal law.

III. Discriminatory Intent

The most controversial element in the ICTY's elements of crimes against humanity is that non-State actors must have a discriminatory intent. Beth Van Schaack has argued that the inclusion of this element, which she calls discriminatory motive, makes the idea of crimes against humanity conceptually problematical. Specifically she argues:

> The requirement that the defendant act on the basis of other than personal motives threatens to revive the war nexus requirement by repackaging it in terms of the motivational state of the defendant. The discriminatory motive requirement adds nothing to the international nature of the offense and threatens to exclude from the rubric of crimes against humanity inhumane acts involving non-enumerated motives... [T]he drafters [of the ICC Statute] wisely excluded the Tribunal's extraneous motive requirements.[81]

This part of the chapter will provide an extended argument against the position advanced by Van Schaack, especially against the view that the discriminatory intent element adds nothing to the international nature of the offense.[82] I will argue that discriminatory intent is conceptually necessary to link the acts of "minor players" to the larger crime of ethnic cleansing.

Discriminatory intent is ambiguous between "intent to harm a group" and "intent to harm an individual because of that individual's group membership."[83] In most cases, I will use the term "discriminatory intent" in the second sense. But there will inevitably be some slippage throughout the section, since it is often true that people who have discriminatory intent in this second sense do so out of having discriminatory intent in the first sense. But for my argument to succeed, it is only necessary that discriminatory intent in the second sense be proved in order for there to be a link between the individual act of the perpetrator and the international nature of the crime in question.

The idea of a discriminatory intent element for crimes against humanity has been hotly debated.[84] In the debates about the ICTY Statute, France, the United States, and Russia argued for discriminatory intent as an element.[85] But by the time the Rome Statute was debated, only France spoke in favor of the element.[86] As a result, the Rome Conference rejected the element of discriminatory intent.[87] Even though the Rome Treaty drafters did not include discriminatory intent in the common elements of crimes against humanity, there is a special knowledge requirement nonetheless – namely, that the perpetrator have "knowledge of the attack" on the civilian population of which his or her act is a part.[88] The ICTY Statute did not explicitly contain either a discriminatory intent or knowledge element, but the Trial Chamber has required discriminatory intent nonetheless, whereas the Appeals Chamber rejected that element, as we will see later in this chapter.[89]

The main reason for thinking that there should be some additional mental element (either discriminatory intent, or knowledge of a larger plan) is because, especially in cases of minor players, the other elements discussed here do not distinguish isolated criminal acts from crimes against humanity.[90] The need for an additional mental element has been recognized in trials conducted in the 1990s, before the ICTY was instituted. In 1992, the French Court of Cassation considered the case of a Vichy officer who had killed seven Jews. The charges were dismissed because the officer in question, Touvier, lacked the requisite intent – namely, "a specific motivation to take part in the execution of a common plan by committing in a systematic manner inhuman acts or persecutions in the name of a State practicing a policy of ideological supremacy."[91] In 1994, the Canadian Supreme Court stated the principle somewhat differently when it held that "with respect to crimes against humanity, the additional element is that the inhumane acts were based on discrimination against or the persecution of an identifiable group of people."[92] But the Canadian court went on to hold that "it would not be necessary to show that the accused knew that his or her actions were inhumane."[93] In both cases, discriminatory intent was recognized as an element of a crime against humanity, although to date this is only a minority view in international law.

The main issue is this: What sort of intent or knowledge does a minor player have to have in order for his or her acts to be sufficiently connected to a group plan of attack on a civilian population so that the individual act counts as a crime against humanity? A crime against humanity typically involves an act of torture, rape, or murder that already violates the criminal laws of a given country and that is raised to the level of an international crime because of the nature of the crime.[94] When the accused is a minor player, the additional intent or knowledge elements are necessary to transform an otherwise isolated act into an act with a collective nature.[95] Crimes against humanity are thought to involve such egregious conduct that the crime is raised to a level above that which offends a domestic community. What seems to matter is that the perpetrator knows about, or intends to participate in, the larger crime – for instance, intends to participate in massive human-rights abuses against an ethnic group.[96]

The *discriminatory intent* element better links the minor player's individual acts of murder, torture, or rape with the larger crime than does the *knowledge* element. As we will see in the next section, if a person merely knows that there is a larger systematic and widespread plan of civilian attack, there is little reason to hold that person responsible for the larger criminal plan, for that knowledge may be completely incidental to why the person so acted, and hence would not necessarily affect that person's guilt. On the other hand, if a minor player intends his or her acts of murder, torture, or rape to be part of a wider ethnic cleansing campaign, for instance, then his or her acts of murder should be treated differently.[97]

For a minor player to share responsibility with others for a larger crime, such as ethnic cleansing, that individual needs to be linked to the larger crime. If the individual perpetrator is a leader who also planned or orchestrated the ethnic cleansing campaign, then the intentional act of planning or orchestrating links the individual with the ethnic cleansing.[98] Without such a link, the individual only has a "guilty mind" concerning the *particular* act of murder, torture, or rape. If the individual perpetrator is a "minor player," it cannot be assumed that this individual has a "guilty mind" concerning the larger crime. For individual responsibility to be ascribed to the minor player for the larger crime – the crime against humanity – a "second" or "specific" mental element is needed – namely, the intent to participate in that larger crime in addition to the intent to perpetrate the individual acts in question.

When an individual shares responsibility for a crime against humanity, the key consideration will be what role was played. How much he or she shares in responsibility depends on how significant a role that person played in the harm to the group. Normally, the individual perpetrator will not be responsible for all of the harm caused by the larger crime, since many others were also perpetrators. The additional intention links his or her act of murder or rape, etc., with the larger events so that he or she can be held at least partially responsible for that larger crime.[99]

The kind of evidence, and the very kind of inquiry, needed to determine whether a crime against humanity has been committed, launches one into an investigation of what groups have done, and what the members of groups intend to do in concert with one another.[100] The closest parallel in domestic criminal law concerns conspiracies or hate crimes. Crimes that refer to what groups have done can be conceptualized as group-based crimes.[101] As we have seen in Chapter 5, the first prong of a group-based crime is one that is perpetrated against an individual victim, but that is perpetrated because of the characteristics or features of the individual victim that are also characteristics or features of a group, not because of features that are unique to the individual victim.[102]

Group-based categories of assessment fall in between purely individual cat-egories of assessment and truly collective categories of assessment. Individual assessment looks to the act and state of mind of individual humans to determine responsibility or liability. This is the norm in the criminal law systems of many countries'.[103] Collective assessment looks to the group and treats the group as having a guilty act and state of mind. This is the norm in Anglo-American con-ceptions of corporate responsibility and liability.[104] Group-based assessment is a hybrid category that looks to the characteristics or features of an individual that are shared in common with other members of a given group.

A good example of a group-based assessment can be seen when a human individual is held responsible for engaging in an act of racial discrimination. The perpetrator's act of not hiring, for instance, is made on the basis of an applicant's characteristics or features that are shared with others – that is, on the basis of his or her racial identity, not on the basis of unique features of the applicant.[105] In order for an act of not hiring to be also an instance of racial discrimination, it must be that the perpetrator decides not to hire because of the person's common features, and not, for instance, because of the person's unique talents or skills.[106] Discriminatory effect is sufficient for certain purposes, such as establishing that compensation is owed a victim. But when an individual is said to be guilty of a crime involving discrimination, more than discriminatory effect is needed.

Beth Van Schaack's position, quoted at the beginning of this section, fails to see that crimes against humanity are group-based crimes, not collective ones. For minor players to be prosecuted for crimes against humanity, an element that connects the individual's act to the group crime must be proved. This element must be both a characteristic, or feature, of the individual person, and also somehow connected to the group harm. Mere knowledge of the larger crime is not sufficient. It does refer to the individual, but it does not sufficiently link the individual to the group plan.

The discriminatory intent element is much closer to the standard elements of domestic crimes than are the elements of population, group plan, and systematicity or widespreadness, since it refers to the mental state of the accused.[107] These three uncontroversial elements call for an analysis of what the group is doing, and contradict the individualistic model of responsibility upon which criminal liability is normally based.[108] In the Anglo-American system of criminal law, for instance, the elements of criminal acts concern the "conduct" of the accused, specifically, "(1) the act, or the omission to act where there is a duty to act; and (2) the state of mind which accompanies the act or omission."[109] The three uncontroversial elements of crimes against humanity are significantly different from the elements of crime in the Anglo-American system of criminal law, elements such as malice aforethought.[110] The chief exception concerns crimes of conspiracy, which are already treated as group-based crimes, and to which we shall return in the next chapter.

Neither the knowledge element, nor any of the three uncontroversial elements, can link an individual minor player to a crime against humanity. The knowledge element is insufficiently linked to the larger crime, and the three uncontroversial elements are not rooted in the characteristics or features of the accused individual. Instead, a group-based element is needed, such as discriminatory intent, to justify prosecution of an individual for a group-based crime, such as a crime against humanity. To see this point more clearly, the final part of this chapter examines the way an ICTY Trial Chamber justified the conviction of Dusko Tadic, a minor player accused of ethnic cleansing, and why an ICTY Appeals Chamber reversed the decision. Before turning to that task, a serious objection to my proposal needs to be addressed.

IV. Knowledge of the Plan

A serious objection can be raised to my proposal. Why shouldn't certain minor players be held at least partially responsible for crimes against humanity if these individuals knew of the group plan and willingly participated in that plan, but didn't intend that discrimination occur? And why not treat the intent to participate in such a plan as meeting the *mens rea* requirement for criminal culpability of these minor players?[111] I will address this objection, which I will treat as two distinct proposals, in this section. It is one thing merely to have knowledge of

a plan that one willingly participates in, and quite another to intend to participate in such a plan. The difference between these two positions will be clear
if we think about the typical soldier who normally intends only to do what his
or her country, acting through a commanding officer, says he or she should do.

The analysis is somewhat different if we are asking, as in Chapter 10 we
will be asking, about what will excuse a soldier from personal responsibility,
as opposed to what would count as not meeting the elements of the crime and
hence establishing a prima facie case against the accused. A soldier could meet
all of the elements of the crime in question and still have an excuse – namely,
that he or she had been ordered to do the act that seemingly met the elements
of a crime. *Intention* is not as important as is *knowledge* in the superior orders
defense, but intention, in my view, is more important than knowledge in the
elements of a crime against humanity. The knowledge that is key in the defense
is whether a soldier knew that it was wrong to follow the order, or whether he
or she knew that the order was not legally valid. The knowledge that a minor
player's actions are merely part of a larger plan is not sufficient for meeting
the elements of the crime, and hence for establishing prima facie culpability. I
return to this point by considering the first of two objections to my claim that
discriminatory intent, not mere knowledge of a larger plan, is necessary for
establishing prima facie culpability.

Let us begin with the objection that knowledge of a plan and willingly participating in the plan are enough for international culpability of minor players.
One basis for this claim is the reasonable point that the international community
has a strong interest in deterring these minor players from such participation.
If minor players can be deterred from following such orders, then the orders
will not be followed, since surely the leaders of States will not perform the
acts of rape and torture themselves and thus dirty their own hands. In addition,
the minor players morally seem to be part of a conspiracy or concerted effort,
and hence should at least share responsibility for the harms they cause by their
participation. The minor players certainly are morally guilty for the role they
play in these harms, and so it is not unreasonable for us to see them also as
legally culpable and subject to international sanctions.

As I have argued throughout this book, moral guilt does not translate directly
into legal culpability, even at the international level, where law and morality
sometimes seem to merge. The main reason for this is that when legal culpability
is alleged, there are serious consequences concerning loss of liberty that are not
necessarily at stake when moral guilt is alleged. This is the reason why so much
emphasis is placed on *mens rea* requirements. In law generally, there must be
a clear intent to do wrong, in addition to actual participation in wrongdoing,
before criminal culpability, as well as punishment, can be established. For such
crimes, merely having bad motives is not sufficient for such criminal culpability.
In U.S. law in major crimes such as rape and murder, there actually has to be
a double intent: the intent to do something wrong and the specific intent to

rape or murder a person. Merely intending to do something that is wrong is not sufficient for legal culpability, even though it may be enough for moral guilt.

Here is where the connection between motive and intention is a key concern. For it may be that the motive of a given soldier or other minor player is merely to do his or her duty, or perhaps to advance through the ranks. Such an individual does not have any particular reason to do this act as opposed to hundreds of others open to the agent. But this act is the one that he or she has been instructed, or commanded, to do.[112] In Chapter 10, I will consider in more detail the relevance of superior orders to culpability in such cases. Here, I merely wish to raise the issue of the connection between the motive and the intent of the minor player. Often there is such a connection, so that the desire to advance through the ranks is a motivation that is connected to an intention to do whatever is necessary to satisfy that desire.

When a personal motivation or desire stimulates an intention, it is hard not to see the intention as also completely personal, rather than also public. This can be seen when one realizes that most soldiers and other minor players will willingly do whatever they are commanded to do. But why not attribute a constructive intention to the minor players whenever they willingly participate in a plan that is discriminatory? Or, to put it differently, why not hold minor players culpable for what their superiors intend to do, and what those minor players willingly carry out? Just as there is "command" responsibility, why should there not also be "commanded" responsibility? At least part of the answer to these questions is that there is a serious disanalogy afoot: The minor players do not normally benefit from State plans the way that leaders of States do. In addition, there are also serious differences in control between commanders and commanded. The combination of the two makes for very different assessments of culpability. The commanders control the decisions about what plan to pursue, and often set things up so that that plan benefits them in some way. The commanded do not have such control over the plans, and do not normally benefit from the plans. So we can conclude that it may be true that minor players will think they can be relieved of culpability and hence are not inhibited from doing what they know to be wrong. And while this is a strong moral point, it does not necessarily establish legal culpability. There should be an intention to do something specific that is proscribed by international law in order for minor players to be justifiably deprived of their liberty for international crimes.

Next, let us return to the other variation of this objection – namely, why not hold culpable those minor players who intended to participate in a plan that was discriminatory? Why insist that the minor players have discriminatory intent themselves? I would tentatively agree that this could be a basis for culpability for minor players in international crimes. One strategy is to accept what I rejected in a different case earlier – namely, that there is a kind of constructive intent here. If one merely knowingly participates in a plan, this is different from intending to participate in that plan. In the latter case, the intent to participate may transform itself into a constructive intent to do what the plan sets out to do, especially where a person fully understood what the plan entailed. Indeed, rather than thinking of this as *constructive* intent, we might say that this is a case of *transferred* intent: By intending to participate in a plan that one knows to have certain consequences, one's intent is transferred to that which one knows will occur.

Philosophically, there has been much discussion about such transferred intent. Jeremy Bentham, for instance, distinguishes between direct and oblique intention in the following passage:

> A consequence . . . may be said to be directly or lineally intentional, when the prospect of producing it constituted one of the links in the chain of causes by which the person was determined to do the act. It may be said to be obliquely or collaterally intentional, when although the consequence was in contemplation, and appeared likely to ensue in case of the acts being performed, yet the prospect of producing such consequence did not constitute a link in the aforesaid chain.[113]

For Bentham, it matters that the contemplation of a given consequence was not the reason why one did a certain thing. But it is still true, for Bentham, that this contemplation was a form of intention, although oblique or indirect, in that by intending to do that which one knows to have a certain consequence, the intent to bring about that consequence is transferred to the person. Bentham helps us see the relevant distinction that is at stake in this second proposal we are considering. And from Bentham's remarks, it is also relatively easy to see that an intention, even when oblique, is still an intention. Perhaps oblique intention of this sort is sufficient for criminal culpability.

In the Just War tradition, oblique intentions are exculpable if there are sufficient reasons for thinking that the consequence directly intended is of overriding importance. In the classic case, a bombing mission may be justified even though it is clear that innocent lives will be lost if it can be shown that there was no other way to meet a military objective, such as destroying a supply depot, and that the objective was itself necessary for the successful conduct of a just war. But in our case, we do not have a clear countervailing positive consequence that is directly intended. Indeed, as in the example suggested earlier, the soldier or other minor player merely has as his direct intention that an order be obeyed. For these reasons, the oblique intention of the soldier or other minor player may establish the *mens rea* element of criminal culpability. Without excusing conditions that conform to something like the Just War necessity conditions, minor players will have their oblique intentions count as meeting the *mens rea* element of criminal culpability.

In this section, I have considered two serious objections to my proposal. The first objection was that soldiers and other minor players who willingly participate in a plan that has a discriminatory intent could be held criminally liable for the consequences of that plan. I have argued that there is no good reason to complement the "command" responsibility with a "commanded" responsibility since the commanded did not benefit from the plan and were not in control of it. The second objection was that soldiers and other minor players who intend to participate in a plan that they know has a discriminatory intent are criminally liable. Here, I agreed that it might make sense to talk of a transferred intent, in much the same way that Bentham talked of an oblique intent, and that such an intention could count as satisfying the *mens rea* element of criminal culpability. In the next section, I will explore these various points further by reference to the case with which we started this chapter – the case of Prosecutor v. Dusko Tadic.

V. Prosecuting Ethnic Cleansing as a Crime Against Humanity

This final part of the chapter examines Dusko Tadic's responsibility for ethnic cleansing. Specific attention is given to the ICTY's contention that discriminatory intent is a necessary element for prosecuting Tadic for ethnic cleansing as a crime against humanity. The ICTY called for a showing of a special intent element – namely, the intent to discriminate against the members of a group by removing them from a geographical or political area.[114] Such an intention clearly would establish the collective nature of Tadic's individual acts. But practical problems arise, such as evidentiary difficulties of showing that an individual defendant, who killed or raped or tortured a member of an ethnic minority, truly intended to harm an ethnic group rather than attacking an individual who merely happened to be a member of such a group.

As was seen earlier, there is much confusion in international law about how to understand the distinctively collective nature of individual acts that are called crimes against humanity. The paradigm case is supposed to be a genocide, such as the Holocaust, where there was a clear State policy to cause harm to a sub-set of a State's population.[115] As we will see in Chapter 9, discriminatory intent is uncontroversial as an element in cases of genocide. There is ample evidence to think that ethnic cleansing in the former Yugoslavia was similarly part of a governmental plan.[116] The individual criminal acts of murder, rape, torture, and so on, were organized in a way so as to achieve a larger goal – namely, the terrorization of an ethnic group by an arm of the State, causing that ethnic group to flee.[117] The individual crimes are raised to the level of international crimes because of the way they are organized and perpetrated, especially because of the fact that it is a State that has done the organizing.

A 1992 United Nations General Assembly resolution connects the notion of "ethnic cleansing" with that of "racial hatred," calling both "totally incompatible with universally recognized human rights and basic freedoms."[118] Yet the Statute of the ICTY does not mention discriminatory intent in the characterization of crimes against humanity, even though ethnic cleansing was the very impetus for the establishment of the ICTY.[119] Nonetheless, as mentioned earlier, the Trial Chamber of the ICTY required discriminatory intent,[120] although this was reversed on appeal, as we will see. But racial hatred alone, in my view, does not link the acts of an individual with the collective action in question. Rather, something more is needed in cases of minor players – namely, discriminatory intent, the intent to discriminate against a person on racial grounds, for example.[121]

In the Tadic case, it is interesting that, after preliminaries, the first twenty-five pages of the Opinion and Judgment of the Trial Chamber of the ICTY are devoted to background considerations concerning the character of the armed conflict between Serbia and Serbian-backed forces in Bosnia, on the one hand, and other ethnic minority groups in Bosnia, principally Croats and Muslims, on the other hand.[122] Then another twenty pages are devoted to the condition of the concentration camps where Croats and Muslims were taken by Serb forces for terrorization by torture, rape, killing, and other forms of inhumane treatment.[123] Not until sixty six pages into the opinion is the accused individual, Dusko Tadic, discussed.[124] The widespread or systematic nature of Tadic's acts are thus addressed in a general way by addressing the larger armed campaign of ethnic cleansing occurring at the time that Tadic acted.

Tadic's acts are connected to the larger ethnic-cleansing campaign in two paragraphs on page 208 of the opinion, where the ICTY Trial Chamber makes two arguments.[125] First, Tadic is accused of being involved "in the take-over of Kazarac and the villages of Sivci and Jaskici."[126] Because of a nexus between Tadic's acts and the take-over of these areas, his acts are said to be sufficiently part of the larger plan.[127] Second, Tadic is accused of engaging in acts within the concentration camps "with the connivance and permission of the authorities running these camps and indicat[ing] that such acts were part of an accepted policy toward prisoners in the camps of Opstina Prijedor."[128] The court concludes that Tadic thereby "effected the objective of Republika Srbska to ethnically cleanse, by means of terror, killings, or otherwise, the areas of Bosnia . . ."[129]

Ethnic cleansing is seen as part of "widespread violations of international humanitarian law occurring within the territory of the former Yugoslavia."[130] The vast majority of the evidence in favor of the widespread or systematic nature of Tadic's acts, cited at his trial, has little or nothing to do with Tadic. When Tadic is mentioned, the "nexus" between his acts and the ethnic cleansing comes largely from the way he participated in acts of armed aggression in the villages and acts of torture, rape, and killing in the concentration camps.[131]

Tadic is accused of having committed "ten counts of crimes against humanity."[132] According to the Trial Chamber,

if the perpetrator has knowledge, either actual or constructive, that these acts were occurring on a widespread or systematic basis and does not commit his act for purely personal motives completely unrelated to the attack on the civilian population, that is sufficient to hold him liable for crimes against humanity.[133]

Note that the nexus is only broken if the individual acts for "*purely* personal motives *completely* unrelated" to the civilian attacks.[134] The nexus between individual act and group plan is thus fairly meager.

Here the court comes close to realizing that there must be a group-based crime for there to be a crime against humanity. But the court seems to allow that Tadic could be *mainly* acting out of personal motives, as long as some of the motivations were related to the civilian attacks – that is, to the group-based harm.[135] The meager nexus between individual motivation and the group-based harm is unsettling. It is possible that Tadic could have been convicted of a crime against humanity merely for having, as one very weak motivation, some kind of ethnic hatred. This is unsettling because the international aspect of the crime epitomized by the ICTY's construal of the intentional element is so meager. It is not clearly a crime against *humanity* for someone to act with such a weak motivation to harm an ethnic group. Indeed, it is even possible to have no such intention and yet to meet the ICTY's standard, since the lack of weak personal motives does not necessarily entail any specific intent at all. One should at least be grateful that the Tadic Trial Chamber does not think that it was sufficient that Tadic merely possessed the knowledge that there is a wider campaign of ethnic cleansing.

In an important admission, the Trial Chamber says that Tadic "has not been charged nor has the Prosecution proved, that the accused was engaged in the operation of the camps."[136] The obvious conceptual question arises: Why think that Tadic's acts were of a "collective nature" sufficient to justify prosecuting *him*, rather than those who did operate, or plan, these concentration camps? The answer comes when the Trial Chamber discusses the crime of persecution, one of the crimes against humanity of which Tadic is accused.

The ICTY Trial Chamber says that Tadic participated in activities in the concentration camp "with the intent of furthering the establishment of a Greater Serbia and that he shared the concept that non-Serbs should forcibly be removed from the territory, thereby exhibiting a discriminatory basis for his actions and that this discrimination was on religious and political grounds."[137] Only at this point in the 300-page Opinion does the court show how Tadic's acts might have had a collective nature, and thus that it was justifiable for *him* to be prosecuted. One could have hoped that this point was not buried, as it was, in the middle of the Opinion. For this reason, it remains unclear whether the ICTY recognized the significance of this point.

It is because of Tadic's discriminatory intent that his acts are linked to the wider ethnic cleansing campaign, thereby providing a justification for effectively convicting him for crimes against humanity.[138] In the earlier discussions of his acts as crimes against humanity, the court does not make its case because the sheer knowledge of the wider ethnic cleansing campaign does not yet show that Tadic should be held responsible for that campaign. Once it is shown that he intended to advance the campaign by his acts, or, as was argued in the previous section, that he intended to participate in such a plan, then his acts can be said to produce group-based harms for which an international tribunal could hold him accountable.[139]

Conceptually, the prosecution of Tadic for crimes against humanity is made plausible by evidence that Tadic had a discriminatory intent. Thus, in this case, the widespreadness or systematicity of Tadic's acts are made plausible not only because he knew that his acts were part of a larger plan, but also because he intended his acts be a part of that plan, and because he shared the idea that non-Serbs should be forced out of certain areas of Bosnia. It could thus be said that Tadic intentionally participated in the campaign of ethnic cleansing, even though he was not an instigator or director of that campaign.[140]

Tadic's participation in ethnic cleansing is not nearly as conceptually problematical as other examples of potential violations of crimes against humanity. Indeed, this case teaches the lesson that mere knowledge of a larger plan of widespread or systematic atrocity is not sufficient to establish individual legal guilt for crimes against humanity. If Tadic had merely known about the ethnic cleansing campaign, but used it as a cover for intentionally committing acts of revenge and petty personal gain, his acts would of course be wrong, and even illegal according to domestic criminal laws concerning murder, rape, and torture.[141] For those crimes, the prosecution would have to show that Tadic did intend to commit the acts in question. But for Tadic's acts to rise to the level of international crimes, as the court itself acknowledges,[142] he must have had a second intent, not merely additional knowledge. He must have intended, directly or obliquely, his criminal acts to discriminate against Muslims and Croats, thereby advancing the campaign of ethnic cleansing that harmed humanity.

In 1999, the Appeals Chamber of the ICTY overruled the Trial Chamber's holding that crimes against humanity require both a showing of discriminatory intent and that there were no purely personal motives of the defendant as substantive elements of the crime. The Appeals Chamber held that discriminatory intent was only necessary for one type of crime against humanity – persecution[143] – and that there was no requirement that it be shown that the defendant did not act for purely personal motives.[144] Instead, the Appeals Chamber held that "To convict an accused of crimes against humanity, it must be proved that the crimes were *related* to the attack on a civilian population (occurring during an armed conflict) and that the accused *knew* that his crimes were so related."[145] Part of the reasoning here has to do with an interpretation of the ICTY's Charter – not of particular relevance conceptually. But the Appeals Chamber also offers some reasoning in support of its claim that is independent of the statutory interpretation issue. I wish to address two of these reasons in order further to buttress my case in favor of the original Trial Chamber ruling that discriminatory intent is necessary in cases of prosecuting minor players such as Tadic for crimes against humanity.

First, the ICTY Appeals Chamber holds that "motive is generally irrelevant in criminal law."[146] To support this claim, the court quotes approvingly an argument made by the Prosecution in its brief:

For example, it does not matter whether or not an accused steals money in order to buy Christmas presents for his poor children or to support a heroin habit. All that we're concerned with is that he stole and he intended to steal ... here is the same sort of thing. There is no requirement for non-personal motives beyond knowledge of the context of a widespread or systematic act into which an accused's act fits.[147]

Intent to commit the crime is normally sufficient in criminal law, and *motive* is not necessary for conviction, although it does play a role in the sentencing phase of a trial.

My response is to point out that the Trial Chamber required discriminatory *intent*, properly conceived and defended, not discriminatory *motive*. In this context, it is important to note that it is sometimes an element of a criminal offense that the accused be shown to have two intentions: the intent to do something wrong – to engage in rape, for example; and also the intent to do something specific – namely, to rape a particular woman. What I have been proposing is not that discriminatory *motivation* be an element of crimes against humanity perpetrated by minor players (who are non-State actors), but that an additional *intent* requirement obtain. The additional intent element is that the accused not only intends to do something wrong, such as to rape, but that he or she has the added intent to rape a particular woman as a way of discriminating against her as a member of an ethnic (or other) group. Such a construal of the discriminatory intent element does not fall prey to the argument of the Prosecutor endorsed by the ICTY Appeals Chamber.

The ICTY Trial Chamber also worries that there will be some people who do horrible things and yet will not be prosecutable. The court cites to the Prosecution's contention that "requiring a discriminatory intent would create a significant normative *lacuna* by failing to protect civilian populations not encompassed by the listed grounds of discrimination," and that this would be "inconsistent with the humanitarian object and purpose of the Statute and international humanitarian law."[148] This is a variation of the problem addressed at various other points in this book that limitations on what counts as an international crime will have the effect of increasing the impunity of human rights abusers. In addition to the points I have already made here in response to this objection, I have a few more to make.

First, the ICTY Appeals Chamber itself points out, concerning the requirement that non-personal motivation be shown, that this objection is question-begging.[149] Whether such additional elements leave a *lacuna*, or create an additional onerous evidentiary burden, is irrelevant to the main question. The Tadic Appeals Chamber says, "The question simply is whether or not there is such a requirement under international law."[150] Second, I agree that there may well be a problem if we are forced to stick to just the short list of protected groups that have been recognized so far – namely, to the groups identified in the Genocide Convention: "national, ethnical, racial, or religious."[151] In Chapter 6, I indicated that I thought other groups could indeed be shown to be the sort that are deserving of protection, and hence where group-based harm to members of those groups, such as women, could be considered crimes against humanity. But the need to add to a list compiled in 1948 does not defeat my general point that discriminatory intent needs to be shown in order to convict minor players of crimes against humanity.

So the Tadic case teaches us how an individual committing an act of murder, rape, or torture could be justifiably prosecuted for crimes against humanity. But the Tadic case also shows how difficult it will be to prosecute "minor players" such as Tadic for crimes against humanity. For it is notoriously difficult to show discriminatory intent for such individuals.[152] This is one of the reasons why the Rome Statute drafters decided not to include discriminatory intent as an element in crimes against humanity.[153] But, as I have argued, the decision to postulate a special knowledge requirement instead of a second intent requirement was not a conceptually sound decision.[154] The knowledge requirement – that the accused merely knew about a larger plan of activity that was widespread or systematic – does not sufficiently link the collective activity with the individual actor's behavior in order to justify prosecution.

Ratner and Abrams see the development of individual accountability for crimes against humanity as a clear form of progress since international law thereby turns away from the idea that only States are accountable at the international level, and also away from the idea that if individuals are following orders they are relieved of responsibility for what they have done.[155] The overturning of these ideas is indeed a progressive move in international law. It is important to hold individuals accountable for the decisions and actions they take that create mass violations of human rights. It is also important for the maintenance of the rule of law.[156] But it is equally important to be aware that individual defendants risk significant prison terms as a result of these prosecutions. We should not let our zealousness in seeking to avenge harm to the victims blind us into setting the elements of international crimes too low to do justice to these defendants, whose rights also must be protected.

In this chapter, I have argued that many conceptual problems arise if one tries to prosecute minor players such as Tadic for crimes against humanity without establishing the element of discriminatory intent. If it is true that it is too difficult to prove discriminatory intent, then perhaps the international reaction to crimes against humanity such as ethnic cleansing should not be to have an international criminal trial for minor players at all. Perhaps truth commissions linked with amnesty programs are a better response to these group-based crimes.[157] Or perhaps the idea of discriminatory intent can be reintroduced into the elements of crimes against humanity, realizing that the number of people who will be prosecutable for such crimes will be few. These issues cannot be decided here. This chapter has instead presented several serious conceptual problems that face the international community's attempts to prosecute minor players such as Tadic for ethnic cleansing as a crime against humanity. The chapter has only begun the task of suggesting possible answers to these difficulties. In the next chapter, we consider the strategy of prosecuting heads of State for crimes against humanity.

8

Prosecuting State Leaders for Crimes Against Humanity

Crimes against humanity are crimes organized by a State or State-like entity against a population or other group of people. Historically, it was States that were thought to be the only parties that should be sanctioned internationally when mass crimes occurred. By contrast, international criminal law has developed in the last fifty years on the assumption that individuals should be prosecuted for such mass crimes. But how are the acts of individuals related to the actions of a State? And which individuals should be subject to punishment for such mass crimes as ethnic cleansing? In Chapter 7, I looked at non-leaders, and argued that it should be hard to convict minor players for crimes against humanity. In this chapter, I show that heads of State should not be so easily relieved of responsibility. Even though I generally take a defendant-oriented approach to prosecutions in international criminal law, I do not think that we should be sympathetic to those heads of State who claim to be immunized against international criminal charges merely because they were acting in their official capacities.

In this chapter, I will argue that the individual who should be prosecuted for a crime against humanity is normally the head of State. I will argue that the behavior of heads of State best satisfies the *actus reus* and *mens rea* requirements for being individually culpable for crimes against humanity. Establishing this thesis will provide an advantage for international prosecution in the sense that it allows these individuals to be subject to punishment in ways they were not thought to be before. But it also means that there will be a ready excuse for these individuals – namely, that they were only acting on behalf of the truly responsible party, the State itself – and hence that heads of State should have immunity from prosecution. By the end of the chapter, I attempt to solve this conceptual puzzle and thereby show that State leaders can and should be subjected to criminal prosecution and punishment for crimes against humanity.

In the first section, I discuss what additional mental element is needed for State leaders who are accused of crimes against humanity. I defend a special intent requirement that provides the individual *mens rea* requirement for the mass crime. This element is especially important in showing the *mala in se* of the acts of the leaders of States. In the second section, I discuss how States can be conceptualized as actors on the international stage. In the third section, I link the acts of leaders of States to the actions of States by reference to the special *mens rea* requirement. In the fourth section, I provide an extended example by considering the case of the Chilean leader, Augusto Pinochet, accused of brutal crimes against opposition groups of his own people. In the fifth section, I explain the rationale for excusing leaders such as Pinochet using the doctrine of "head of State immunity." I end the chapter by providing reasons for rejecting "head of State immunity" as a defense against the charge of crimes against humanity.

When prosecutions concern the leaders of various States, rather than more minor players, conceptual problems still arise. As we saw in the last chapter, one of the main problems with prosecuting minor players is that they do wrongful acts but do not clearly manifest a guilty mind for doing so. Things are reversed for State leaders. They often have a clearer guilty mind since they are often the ones that designed or set in motion a given State plan. But these leaders do not often manifest guilty acts since they do not normally engage in murder, rape, or torture, and they rarely give orders that direct specific acts of murder, rape, or torture. Like leaders of corporations, State leaders often appear to have clean hands. One strategy for confronting this problem is to adopt something like a "collective responsibility" or "conspiracy" model, currently shunned by international tribunals. Such a strategy captures the roles played by the leaders and by the minor players to determine who is most responsible. I defend such a strategy in this chapter. Along the way, I try to solve some of the conceptual difficulties with treating State leaders as responsible for crimes against humanity.

I. Command Responsibility and Group Harm

In this section, I will provide a new argument for thinking that an additional intent requirement is a necessary element in prosecuting individuals for crimes against humanity. I then discuss the type of intent requirement that is most plausible for leaders of States. M. Cherif Bassiouni, the most prominent legal theorist currently writing about crimes against humanity, has supported the requirement that for States to commit crimes against humanity there must be a discriminatory State policy of persecution.[1] Bassiouni is certainly right that if a State is to be held responsible for a crime against humanity, that State must manifest a discriminatory intent to advance the larger plan that constitutes this crime. The oddity is that if one requires a State to have a discriminatory intent, why is discriminatory intent, or some other special intent requirement, not also required for an individual perpetrator?

Bassiouni rightly points out that the main rationale for the domestic prosecution of crimes such as murder, rape, and torture is that they are considered *mala in se*.[2] *Mala in se* crimes are crimes that are "wrong in themselves" or "inherently evil," and for this reason prohibited by legislative act. On the other hand, *malum prohibitum* crimes are crimes that are wrong only because they are "prohibited by legislation."[3] Bassiouni says that the "same rationale of the *mala in se* common law crimes holds true for 'crimes against humanity,' as defined by the [Nuremberg] Charter, because the same acts are unlawful under 'general principles of law.'"[4] He fails to see that the *mala in se* requirement should be different for murder, rape, or torture as individual crimes as opposed to being parts of crimes against humanity. For crimes to rise to the level of crimes against humanity – that is, to become truly international crimes – they must be *mala in se* in some different way than they were as individual acts of murder, rape, or torture.

There are actually two, not one, *mala in se* rationales for crimes against humanity. Murder, rape, and torture are *mala in se* in that they are individual acts that are proscribed because of their immoral nature.[5] But there must be an additional *mala in se* requirement for prosecution of these acts as crimes against humanity. Murder, rape, and torture are recognized as *mala in se* nearly everywhere, as Bassiouni says,[6] but this does not yet mean that they are justifiably prosecutable as international crimes, as crimes against humanity. The justification for prosecution of these acts as crimes against humanity must involve a group-based *mala in se*. And here we would look for some additional intent on the part of the perpetrator that connects the perpetrator to the larger *mala in se* plan and makes what the perpetrator did also *mala in se*.

If the acts of murder, rape, or torture were merely crimes recognized as *mala in se* in most societies, then there would be nothing additional about these crimes that would raise them to the level of crimes against humanity. These crimes would only be *malum prohibitum* internationally, since there would be no additional immorality of the accused that would justify prosecution for a crime against humanity, as opposed to prosecution for rape, murder, or torture. Bassiouni seemingly conflates two *mala in se* elements. We need a separate *mala in se* requirement for crimes against humanity, and this is supplied by an additional intent requirement, whether in the case of minor players or State leaders.

In the last chapter, I discussed the possibility that some kind of constructive intent could satisfy the intent requirement for individual culpability in international criminal law. When dealing with minor players, I said that we should be cautious in employing constructive intent, arguing that at the very least it must be shown that the minor players intended to participate in what they knew to be an internationally criminal plan. Now, when we come to consider State leaders, I will take a somewhat different stance, allowing for constructive intent in some cases, such as when a State leader knew that his or her subordinates were carrying out an internationally criminal plan, and yet did nothing to stop them from doing it. This idea, often referred to as "command responsibility," makes sense even though I argued in the last chapter that its correlate, what I called "commanded responsibility," generally does not.

The ICTY Trial Chamber held that command responsibility is sufficient for the culpability of a leader. It is not necessary to show that the leader ordered the atrocities, but only that he or she had knowledge of the criminal activity of subordinates and failed to stop it or to punish those who so acted.[7] The failure to act to prevent, or the failure to act to punish, turns what would otherwise be a mere knowledge requirement into a constructive intention. Such a constructive intention can indeed be conceptually justified. A leader who knew that others under his command were engaged in international crimes may be culpable for those crimes if he does not act to prevent the commission of those crimes. As will be argued later, the leader epitomizes the intent of the State, and is the one who is at least presumed to intend what is allowed to be done by the members of the State.

The key justificatory question is whether a leader's intentions and actions are *mala in se* in order to establish criminal liability for that leader. To take an example, if a leader of a State knows that a plan of ethnic cleansing is being carried out by subordinates, and could have stopped it, but nonetheless decided not to, then in most cases that leader has linked himself or herself to the intentions of the subordinates. There may be personal reasons why the leader does not intervene, but because he or she is the leader, it will normally still be true that the constructive intention is appropriately ascribed to the leader. Leaders are *artificial* persons as well as *natural* persons, and even though they may have different motivations as personal leaders than as artificial leaders, there are certain limits to this idea that mean that they cannot excuse themselves from culpability by such personal motivations. As artificial persons, their failure to stop known illegal activity constructively implicates them in the illegality.

Command responsibility is not incompatible with the requirement of additional intent for prosecuting individuals for crimes against humanity. As the ICTY says, "[T]he inclusion of this additional requirement that the inhumane acts must be taken on discriminatory grounds is satisfied by the evidence discussed above that the attack on the civilian population was conducted against only the non-Serb portion of the population because they were non-Serbs."[8] Although I will partially dispute this claim later, I agree that we can reconcile the idea of command responsibility with the additional intent needed for linking individuals with the collective nature of crimes against humanity.

The International Criminal Tribunal for Rwanda (ICTR) ruled in 2000 that command responsibility is not a form of strict liability.[9] Rather, the *mens rea* must be "at least negligence that is so serious as to be tantamount to acquiescence."[10] The acquiescence is inferred from the fact that the commander had knowledge of what his or her subordinates were doing, and also had effective control over these subordinates, and yet chose not to exercise his or her control in a way that could have prevented the subordinates from acting. I have previously argued that negligence is indeed properly thought of as a form of intent.[11] In addition, there also had to be a legal duty to act to prevent such harms from occurring, as was noted by the ICTY in the Delalic case.[12] The omission, where there is a duty to act, is the *actus reus*, and the negligence that verges on acquiescence is the *mens rea* that establishes command responsibility for heads of State and other leaders.

In later sections, I will set out various models for solving the problem of how a State leader can be responsible for a group crime such as a crime against humanity. In the next section, I will show how a State can be an actor that commits a crime in the first place, as a prelude to showing how a head of State could be held responsible for a crime against humanity. I will here draw on my earlier work on the nature of groups and collective responsibility. The State will be treated as a social group that is best understood on a model that is neither individualist nor collectivist. In later sections, I will draw heavily on the analogy with conspiracies to explain both how to link the members of the State to the group action and also how to divide that responsibility among the members.

II. Group Ontology and the State

In another context, I have proposed that groups be treated as "individuals in relationships."[13] Like other social groups, States are best conceptualized as a complex set of interactions and relationships among individuals. The State is not an actor in its own right. The State does not have a mind, nor does it have body parts, and hence the State cannot be a proper agent. The complexity of interactions among individuals creates a situation such that although there is no group mind in the full-blown human sense, there are things that act like a mind within the State, as in many other kinds of groups. Various individuals perform acts in the name of the State, and their acts can be redescribed as the State's acts. Insofar as they are performing those acts in the name of the State, one can talk about those things as being *of* the State. The mental states of certain individuals can be understood, in a limited sense, as the "State's" mental states based on what is going on at the mental level of the individual members. For instance, if the legislators of a State, acting in their official capacities, intentionally set a policy or plan into effect, then that policy or plan can be redescribed as the intention of the State.

The ontological status of States is problematical because certain features of these entities cannot be understood either on standard individualist or collectivist views. My ontological account of States takes an intermediate position between individualism and collectivism. States are not sufficiently like individual persons for one to think that they have an ontological status as distinct entities, as collectivists have argued. In addition, States are not reducible to the isolated actions of discrete individual persons, as individualists have argued.

Both intention and action of a State are the kind of features that call for an analysis that looks to the individual members of the group, and that also takes into account the group's structure – that is, the way the individuals are related to each other.

Consider another social group, the corporation. Corporate intent is best seen as the collective decision of the board of directors. But this does not mean that corporate intent can be reduced to the isolated intentions of those board members. The decision-making structure of the board, something that the individual board members have neither formed nor can easily change, shapes the way these individuals will make their decisions. Because of this decision-making structure, the individual directors often end their board meeting having endorsed decisions that none of them would have endorsed outside of that structure. So, while it is true that corporate intent is really the intent of individuals, there is something important about the fact that the collection of directors achieves its decisions through an already existing structure. If we ceased to focus on the collective feature of these decisions, we would have problems explaining why these individual people reached decisions so different from the ones they would have reached on their own.

Similarly, on my view, the actions of a State are always the vicarious actions of individual members of the State. But it is a mistake to think that the vicarious feature of these actions can be reduced to features of an individual member's action. Rather, there is a collective or social dimension to the action in that the action was facilitated by the acts of members of the State, and the structure of the group plays a role in such facilitation. The interdependent actions of many people facilitate the action that is identified as the action of the State. If we were to focus only on the individuals who are acting, and ignore the relational dimension, we would lose sight of the collective nature of the action, and be unable to explain the State's behavior. Recall the ICTY's contention that crimes against humanity are crimes of a collective nature.[14] For example, when a State engages in ethnic cleansing, many members of the State act – some issuing directives, some coordinating strategy, some engaging in murder, rape, or torture. Yet focusing only on the individual acts misses the way that these acts constitute crimes against humanity, as opposed to garden-variety criminal acts. One would especially not be able to account for the way these individual criminal acts were *directed* at a specific population.

For States, as for many other social groups, intent and act are separated. One person, often a low-ranking member, a "minor player," acts for the State, thereby engaging in an *actus reus* of the State, whereas other people, normally the leaders of the State, have intentions that correspond to the *mens rea* of these State actions. There is a sense in which the State engages in intentional action that is not the intentional action of any of its members, since act and intention are divided among the members, and hence there is also a sense in which only the State itself may be fully responsible for a group harm. This does not yet rule out the possibility that individuals may be responsible as well. But since intent and act are separated among the members of a State, it may turn out that no individual person is *fully* responsible for what the State intentionally did. This will make it harder to convict individuals for such criminal conduct.

To see the legal consequences of this view, it is helpful to understand some of the current problems in corporate law. There is often a practical difficulty in corporate law: Since intent and act are separated within the corporation, not even the chief executive officer is easily shown to be responsible for the harms perpetrated by the corporation, and yet the corporation as a whole is difficult to punish or even to deter from engaging in harmful conduct.[15] To paraphrase an old adage: "The corporation has neither pants to kick nor a soul to damn." A strategic view of corporate responsibility must come to terms with the problem that the corporation is not a subject easily deterred, and yet individuals within the corporation – those who can be deterred – do not normally meet the standards of individual criminal liability. For liability to have practical effect, one needs to indicate how individuals as members of the corporation can be linked to the harms caused by the corporation, and on that basis seen as partially responsible for the harms of the corporation or the State.

My account accomplishes this practical goal by stressing the way in which the members of a social group, such as a State, are related to each other so as to enable collective intentional action. In light of my ontological analysis of group action, the first thing that a prosecutor needs to establish is that the case at issue concerns the kind of action that is best understood not in individual terms but rather in the redescribed terms of the State's intentional action. After that is accomplished, it then makes sense to ask what roles individuals played, including what roles could have and should have been played in preventing the harm in question. The idea of negligent omissions can be used to good effect once it is established that individuals were facilitated in what they did by others who, acting for the State, could have and should have prevented the harmful behavior.

It often turns out that there were negligent omissions, a type of *actus reus*, that might involve a constructive *mens rea*, by the leaders of a State. Such high-ranking members of the State would then be the most obvious individuals to be held liable for harms perpetrated by the State. Notice, though, that one only gets a sense of the guilty acts or omissions of these high-ranking members of the State if one looks at group action in terms of the structural features of the group that allow for certain members to be facilitated in what they did by what other members of the group did or should have done. My ontological account of group intentional action sets the stage for holding the leading members of a State accountable for crimes against humanity. As we will see later in the chapter, this ontological account also sets the stage for providing State leaders with an immunity from prosecution as well, but one that, justifiably, has been gradually eroded over the last century.

III. Responsibility and Punishment of States

The paradigm case of group or collective responsibility is evident when a group acts on the basis of an explicit collective decision of the members.[16] Because States have an explicit decision-making structure, States can be held accountable in many instances. Of course, it is notoriously hard to punish a State. For this reason, even though States are the ones that are primarily responsible for various group harms, there is a tendency to want to blame and punish the individual members of these States. International criminal law has made progress, many have argued, because it now focuses on punishing individuals.[17] Yet, focusing on the isolated individual acts of the members of the State loses the conspiracy-like character of what often occurs in a State. We can learn a lot about how the members of States should be treated by looking at how conspiracies have been treated in Anglo-American law.

A conspiracy is defined as "a combination between two or more persons formed for the purpose of doing either an unlawful act or a lawful act by unlawful means." The act in a conspiracy is the agreement, while the "intention to thereby achieve the objective is the mental state."[18] There is a sense in which the leaders and other members agree to accomplish certain objectives. Of course, it is rare that there is a face-to-face encounter at which this agreement is made. Rather, as is recognized in the U.S. law of conspiracy, it is more common that there is an implicit agreement that can be seen in the common behavior of the members of the putative conspiracy. Indeed, while the law often focuses on the agreement among the co-conspirators, it is the behavior of these parties from which the agreement is inferred that is the crucial element in conspiracy prosecutions.[19] The upshot of the conspiracy model of responsibility is that each of the co-conspirators is treated as an agent of the others, thereby allowing the imputation of the acts of one to the others. As LaFave and Scott say in their hornbook on criminal law, it is in this way that conspiracy law is used to strike "against the special danger incident to group activity."[20]

I propose that we adopt some of the ideas of conspiracy law to help us understand the criminal behavior of leaders of groups such as States. Rather than thinking of the discrete crime of conspiracy, let us use some of the elements of conspiracy to provide a model for conceptualizing group criminal action. If various people's acts can be conceptualized as a single activity, then we can think of a conspiracy-like arrangement among them. And we can see the acts of the individual members as parts of a larger action, with the State as a kind of placeholder for the collection of conspirator-like individuals. As in the case of conspiracies, we can then ask: Who is the person most responsible for what the group has accomplished?

In conspiracies, there are often many individual, seemingly isolated, acts that, on their own, do not normally amount to criminal behavior, or at least not to the criminal behavior one is interested in. For instance, to use an old example, one person kicks the door down, several other people cross the threshold, but only one person actually pockets the sheriff's silver buttons.[21] Often it is the leader of the group, rather than the one who actually pocketed the silver buttons, who is held responsible. Yet, the leader often did not break down the sheriff's door, cross the threshold, or pocket the silver buttons. Similarly, the individual acts of ethnic cleansing in the Balkans included acts of murder, torture, and rape of Muslims and Coats by Serbs. Yet, a State leader such as Slobodan Milosevic, who is now being prosecuted for planning the ethnic-cleansing campaign, did not engage in murder, rape, or torture. For Milosevic to be successfully prosecuted, one will need to look at the conspiracy-like arrangements between those who committed murder, rape, or torture and those who were the State leaders.

The leader of a group can be held criminally responsible for what the group does even though that individual member was not the one, for instance, who actually broke down the door or removed the silver buttons from the sheriff's trunk. The individual leader may not even be the one who entered the sheriff's house at all. Similarly, although the acts of individual members within the State themselves might not be considered criminal when viewed in isolation, nonetheless it makes sense to hold some of the leading members criminally responsible for some of the State's activities. Once it is established that there is a conspiracy-like arrangement of the members,[22] then it makes sense to ask who played the most important role. The planner of the conspiracy, as a result of his or her intent, is the person most plausibly chosen.

Another similar approach is to look to the law of corporations, especially how crimes are treated when corporations are involved. Here, one of the leading cases is U.S. v. Park. In 1975, the United States Supreme Court upheld a lower court ruling that John R. Park, the president of Acme Markets, Inc., was criminally liable for "[c]ausing adulteration of food which had traveled in interstate commerce and which was held for sale . . ."[23] While food was being stored in Acme's warehouses, Acme employees caused the food "to be held in a building accessible to rodents and to be exposed to contamination by rodents."[24] The corporation admitted guilt in the adulteration of food it then sold. Ultimately, the chief executive officer went to prison for what the corporation did.

The chief executive, John Park, had knowledge of the problems in the warehouse. The corporation had been repeatedly warned in memos from the United States Food and Drug Administration. And Park admitted that those memos had in fact reached his desk. If Park did not know anything at all about the food adulteration, the case is much harder. It could still be argued that he was at fault for some of what occurred if it could be shown that he should have known. As it turned out, Park not only knew about the food adulteration, but set the policy of the corporation that directly led to the adulteration. His criminal act was in setting the policy that led to the harm, or at least the omission of not properly supervising his employees, and his criminal intent was his negligence in failing to prevent his employees from adulterating the food in the warehouses.

An alternative to punishing people such as Park is to come up with a group-based punishment scheme. The problem here is not that I am against those schemes per se, but I do think that the consequences are often worse from group-based schemes than they are from the admittedly flawed individual-based punishment schemes. What often happens with group-based schemes is that the lower-ranking employees are the ones who are in effect punished by the group-based schemes, or at the very least the low-ranking employees are hurt disproportionately. For instance, if the corporation is forced out of business, it is often the low-ranking employees who have the hardest time finding new jobs, whereas the corporate leaders generally land on their feet. And yet the low-ranking employees are not the individuals who had the guilty state of mind, whereas the leaders are the ones with this intent.

The criminal law could punish leaders on a kind of strict liability model. This would perhaps best accomplish the deterrence goals of the law. But then another problem, based in fairness, arises. For we would be punishing people regardless of what they did or what they intended. Focusing on the acts and intentions of the leaders, especially negligent omissions, provides an intermediate position.[25] It allows for fairness to remain in the judgments that occur in the criminal law, and for the law still to be able to have a reasonable chance of deterring criminal behavior. If we only prosecute minor players who personally engaged in intentional acts such as murder, then crimes against humanity will generally be difficult to prosecute successfully in international tribunals.[26] So there are problems both with prosecuting minor players and with prosecuting leaders who did not play a direct role in the crimes. Of course, there are cases that are cleaner – for example, where the president of a State issues orders directing that harm occur to a group. Let us turn to one such case.

IV. The Pinochet Case

Augusto Pinochet provides us with a good example of a State leader who plotted the destruction of segments of his population in a way that could be construed as a crime against humanity. While Pinochet was in England for back surgery, Spain asked England to extradite him for crimes against humanity committed against Spanish nationals and others in opposition groups when Pinochet was dictator of Chile. Criminal charges were filed against Pinochet in a British court. Specifically, it was alleged that Pinochet:

1. "did murder Spanish citizens in Chile within the jurisdiction of the government of Spain;"

2. "conspired with persons unknown to intentionally inflict severe pain or suffering on another in the performance or purported performance of his official duties;"
3. "(a) detained [and] (b)... conspired with persons unknown to detain other persons ('the hostages'), and in order to compel such persons to do or to abstain from doing any act, threatened to kill, injure, or continue to detain the hostages;"
4. "conspired with persons unknown to commit murder in a Convention country."[27]

If true, these allegations make Pinochet out to be, at best, someone who let horrendous crimes occur under his watch and, at worst, the ruthless mastermind of crimes against humanity.

State leaders such as Pinochet wield enormous power within their countries. It was alleged that Pinochet ordered the assassination of the Chilean ambassador to the United States on the streets of Washington D.C. in 1976. One of the members of the British court gave a graphic account of the kinds of acts that were allegedly ordered by Pinochet:

The case is that agents of DINA [Chilean secret police], who were specially trained in torture techniques, tortured victims on a vast scale in secret torture chambers in Santiago and elsewhere in Chile. The torturers were invariably dressed in civilian clothes. Hooded doctors were present during torture sessions. The case is not one of interrogators acting in excess of zeal. The case goes much further. The request explains: "The most usual method was 'the grill' consisting of a metal table on which the victim was laid naked and his extremities tied and electrical shocks were applied to the lips, genitals, wounds or metal prosthesis; also a person's relatives or friends, were placed in two metal drawers, one on top of the other, so that when one above was tortured the psychological impact was felt by the other... or the "dry submarine" method was applied, i.e. placing a bag on the head until close to suffocation, also drugs were used and boiling water was thrown on various detainees to punish them as a foretaste for death which they would later suffer."[28]

The charge was that DINA was directly answerable to General Pinochet, and that Pinochet ordered the tortures, killings, and disappearances, or at least knew about them but did not act to prevent them. In either case, it was alleged that Pinochet set policies that intended these crimes to be committed against his political enemies.[29]

From my group-based approach to international criminal law, several problems arise, but there are clear strategies for nonetheless thinking that Pinochet should have been prosecuted for what he did while head of State.[30] One of the problems is that the various tortures and killings were not directed at an ethnic, racial, or national group. Indeed, the best that could be alleged is that Pinochet directed these acts against his political enemies. While it may be that these enemies constituted a very loose political group, it is not the kind of group that is normally thought to be the basis of international prosecution. The alleged crimes were quite widespread, and they did target individuals because of group membership, but not in the way normally recognized, at least when considering crimes against humanity such as persecutions – namely, groups that are based on racial, ethnic, or religious membership.

In Chapter 5, I argued that group-based crimes could also concern crimes that were systematic in that they were committed by a State or representatives of a State. Especially if it can be shown that Pinochet, as leader of Chile, directed the tortures and murders, then Pinochet is a paradigm example of the kind of State leader who should be held accountable for harms that occur by the agents of a State. Indeed, even if Pinochet did not explicitly direct DINA forces to torture and kill his enemies, since these forces were directly answerable to Pinochet, then the analysis in the earlier sections of this chapter would apply directly to his case, and support holding him accountable nonetheless.

Could we conceive of attacks on people merely because they were members of opposition parties to be the kind of acts that violate *jus cogens* norms and therefore become the subject of international prosecution? I believe that the answer is a qualified "yes." In principle, attacks directed against individuals because they are members of a political party could qualify as the sort of group-based harm that counts as a crime against humanity. But there are serious practical problems here since, in many cases, party affiliation is much harder to discern than is ethnicity, race, or gender. In addition, party affiliation is, in a sense, chosen, unlike the unchosen group memberships of ethnicity, race, and gender. Party affiliation is more like religion than these other sources of group-based harm. Like religion, party affiliation may be something that a person has not actively chosen, and may indeed be part of one's identity that cannot be changed easily. Because of this, party affiliation can be a source of group-based harm, but it is not as invidious as those group-based harms that are truly based on factors completely beyond one's control. Nonetheless, as in the case of gender discussed earlier, I see no reason to limit the sweep of international criminal law to group-based harms directed only at the select list of groups, based on religious, ethnic, racial, or nationality membership, that the United Nations has come to recognize. More groups than these can be the source of significant adverse treatment that international tribunals can consider. What counts conceptually is that individuals are treated invidiously on the basis of coherent group characteristics that these individuals have not chosen or cannot easily change, and there is State involvement.

In the Pinochet case, we have a clear example that meets both of the two prongs of my international harm principle. The harms were group-based in that they were directed at people merely for being members of certain political parties, and the harms were perpetrated by an agent of a State acting on the basis of a larger plan. If the charges are proved to be true, then Pinochet did indeed order the torture and execution of individuals in Chile merely because they were members of political opposition groups. And Pinochet, as head of State in Chile, seemed also to be acting for the State. While this second condition will cause potential problems in other respects – namely, concerning his counter-charge of immunity – it seems that Pinochet is a very good example of a State leader who violated international criminal law and deserved to be prosecuted for crimes against humanity.

There is this second problem, though: If Pinochet were acting as a head of state, then it seems that he is deserving of head of State immunity, but if he was not so acting, then it is unclear that his actions were sufficiently linked to the State to meet the second prong of the ideal analysis of international crimes. One way to resolve this issue is to try to link Pinochet to the harms by some other means. A plausible strategy is to argue that Pinochet was able to accomplish what he did because of the appearance that he was acting as head of State. This strategy would let us nonetheless contend that Pinochet was not authorized as head of State to order the torture and murder of his enemies, and hence that he is not covered by head of State immunity, but that he is sufficiently linked to the State to meet the second prong of the ideal analysis of international criminal involvement.

The doctrine of "apparent authority" that I relied on in this strategy is well known in U.S. domestic law. The general idea is that corporations and other organizations should not be able to relieve themselves of responsibility for what their officers or leaders have done merely because those officers or leaders were not authorized to act in this way.[31] The acts of the officers or leaders remain linked to the group if it were not possible for third-parties to tell that the officer or leader was acting beyond the scope of authority, and if the third-parties relied on the appearance of authority. This is surely true of Pinochet. As we will see in the next section, no head of State is authorized to engage in acts that clearly contravene basic precepts of international law. So, if we accept the doctrine of apparent authority, then we can say both that Pinochet's acts were sufficiently linked to the State, and that he is not deserving of State immunity for those acts.

Another issue that we will address in greater detail in Chapter 13, concerns the fact that the terms of the transfer of power that led to Pinochet's stepping down, and for free elections to be called, was that a general amnesty be granted to any government official for crimes committed during his rule. In the original Pinochet trial, Lord Lloyd of Berwick quotes approvingly the argument of the *amicus* brief filed by David Lloyd Jones. Jones argues that it is "particularly doubtful whether there exists a rule of public international law requiring States not to accord immunity in such circumstances. Such a rule would be inconsistent with the practices of many States."[32] Amnesties have been granted in similar circumstances in Algeria (1962), Bangladesh (1971), and South Africa (1990), and hence are not unusual.

The amnesty granted in Chile was claimed to be based on achieving the desired effect of smoothing the transition to democratic rule, but was probably just a deal hatched by Pinochet's cronies. Should the international community recognize such amnesties, or are they only to have validity within the State's territorial borders? There are very tricky moral and political issues intertwined in this largely legal matter that lie outside the scope of my study. I address some of the most significant moral objections to amnesties in the final two chapters of the book. Nonetheless, it does seem clear that the grant of amnesty primarily concerns the violation of the domestic laws of Chile, and cannot encompass the violations of international law since the Chilean government is not competent to grant amnesty for international crimes, no matter how important this is for reconciliation purposes. The English House of Lords, sitting as an appellate court in Pinochet's case, came to the same conclusion.[33]

One of the chief remaining questions is whether the doctrine of head of State immunity relieves British courts, as well as other national and international tribunals, of jurisdiction to try Pinochet for the charges outlined earlier. If Pinochet were doing what he was duly authorized to do, then it would seem to be more appropriate to prosecute the State than to prosecute Pinochet. Or it may be that considerations of sovereignty would dictate that neither the State nor its leader should be prosecuted by a foreign State or an international tribunal. Under what circumstances do States and their leaders have immunity from international prosecution? In order to answer this question, we will have to examine the doctrine of "head of State immunity," to which we turn in the next section.

V. Head of State Immunity

The analysis given here provides a basis for holding the leaders of States accountable for the harms those States have committed. Yet it is common for heads of State to claim immunity from criminal prosecution at the hands of other States or international tribunals. In this section, I argue against the use of the doctrine of head of State immunity in Pinochet's case and others like it. We will see that several important documents of the twentieth century have also challenged the doctrine that has allowed State leaders to evade accountability in such cases.

The doctrine of "head of State immunity" is similar to the general doctrine of "sovereign immunity," now called "State immunity."[34] Just as a State is said to have sovereignty in that other States generally cannot exercise jurisdiction over the decisions and actions taken by that State within its own borders, so the head of that State is similarly said to have immunity, because the head of State merely acts in the name of the State. The immunity is said to come from the idea that heads of State act as representatives of the State. They act as artificial persons who are bound to do what is in the interests of the commonwealth, not as natural persons acting in their own names. Hobbes gives us the classic explication of that distinction:

A person is he whose words or action are considered . . . When they are considered as his own, then is he called a *natural person*: and when they are considered as representing the words and actions of another, then he is a *feigned* or *artificial person*.[35]

According to the head of State immunity doctrine, when heads of State act as artificial persons, they should not be held accountable for what they do.

One of the main conceptual problems with the head of State immunity doctrine is that it seems to imply that there are no exceptions to what a leader can do within the State's own borders, since whatever the head of State does is really what the State does. Yet, as we saw in Chapter 1, even Hobbes recognized exceptions to the kind of immunity that States have concerning their own sovereign affairs. And Lord Steyn, writing in the Pinochet case, has pointed out that this doctrine would have made it impossible to try Hitler for the "final solution" if no exceptions were granted to the head of State immunity doctrine.[36] Lord Steyn offers a good argument for rebutting the extreme version of the head of State doctrine and for showing that the key consideration is what is included in the definition of the "functions" of a head of State:

If a Head of State kills his gardener in a fit of rage that could by no stretch of the imagination be described as an act performed in the exercise of his functions as Head of State. If a Head of State orders victims to be tortured in his presence for the sole purpose of enjoying the spectacle of the pitiful twitchings of victims dying in agony (what Montaigne described as the farthest point that cruelty can reach) that could not be described as acts undertaken by him in the exercise of his functions as a Head of State. Counsel for General Pinochet expressly, and rightly, conceded that such crimes could not be classified as official acts undertaken in the exercise of the functions of a Head of State. These examples demonstrate that there is a meaningful line to be drawn.[37]

There must be some basis for distinguishing legitimate from illegitimate acts for which a head of State can claim immunity. Such a line should be drawn in terms of what can plausibly be said to be the proper exercise of the "functions" of the head of State. Not all acts performed by a head of State are truly artificial acts since they go beyond the functions of this representative's authority. The most plausible limits on those functions concern cases in which a sovereign attacks his own subjects, as we saw in Chapter 1 and again in Chapter 3.

Since the time of the Nuremberg Charter, international law has condemned genocide, torture, hostage-taking, and crimes against humanity, and these acts have not been regarded as properly "the functions of a Head of State."[38] Article 7 of the Nuremberg Charter declared that "the official position of defendants, whether as Heads of State or responsible officials in Government Departments, shall not be considered as freeing them from responsibility or mitigating punishment."[39] A similar provision is also included in the ICTY statute. Lord Nicholls quotes the Nuremberg Tribunal as saying: "He who violates the laws of war cannot obtain immunity in pursuance of the authority of the State and in authorizing action moves outside its competence under international law."[40] Nicholls then points out that the General Assembly of the United Nations unanimously affirmed this principle on December 11, 1946. Nicholls concludes: "From this time on, no Head of State could have been in any doubt about his potential personal liability if he participated in acts regarded by international law as crimes against humanity." Indeed, by 1973, the United Nations declared that "States were to assist each other in bringing such persons to trial . . ."[41]

It is no argument against this position for Pinochet to claim that he did not personally do these horrendous things. In criminal law, it is well recognized that "there is no distinction to be drawn between the man who strikes, and a man who orders another to strike."[42] Once again, we see concepts similar to those from conspiracy law being used to explicate the responsibility of heads of State. Let me end by summarizing several of my reasons for thinking that heads of State should be the ones prosecuted for crimes against humanity.

Leaders such as Pinochet are those most likely to have the requisite *mens rea* that is necessary for international crimes such as crimes against humanity. And while it is true that heads of state normally do not do the deeds of murder, rape, or torture themselves, these acts would not occur but for the direction of these leaders. If we focus on those who do the guilty deeds, the *actus reus*, we find that often they would not do these acts if they had not been so directed or ordered. Employing the old legal doctrine of "but for" causation, it seems clear that the persons most responsible for the occurrence of the torture or murder, especially if these acts are to be understood as part of a crime against humanity, are the leaders, not the underlings.[43]

Another way to think about individual responsibility in these cases is by looking to the person who is most "State-like" – that is, most identifiable with the State that is doing the harm. If it is established that a State is responsible for various harms, then it makes sense to ask who in the State is most responsible for what the State has done. State leaders are those individuals who are normally most responsible. The "minor players" may indeed be responsible for individual acts of murder, rape, or torture. But they do not stand to gain from the coordination of these various acts in the way the leaders do. The leaders are the ones whose racial or ethnic hatred, combined with their ability to execute a plan to assault a whole population, can ground the intent and act requirements of criminality. Thus the heads of State are the ones who should normally be held responsible for crimes against humanity.

Let us think of a crime analogous to a crime against humanity – the crime of genocide. Here there is a special intent requirement – namely, that the accused intended to destroy an ethnic, racial, or national group, in whole or in part. Who is most likely, if anyone, in the society to satisfy this intent requirement when mass executions have occurred in a given State? Those who are not leaders will normally lack this intent, although in the last chapter we considered a case in which this intent requirement might have been met in the case of a minor player. Normally, while ethnic hatred may be a very strong motivator for these acts, the non-leader lacks any sense of what else is happening in the society in order to be able to form an effective intent to eliminate the population, even in part. On the other hand, the leaders are the ones whose racial or ethnic hatred, combined with their ability to execute a plan to eliminate a whole population, can ground an intent to eliminate the group, perhaps even understood by the far more stringent "in whole" prong of the crime of genocide. In the next chapter, we will consider conceptual problems in determining who is guilty for the crime of genocide.

Even when we focus on the leaders of a State rather than on the minor players, it is still not unproblematic to hold them accountable for international crimes. As mentioned earlier, the leaders generally do not straightforwardly satisfy the *actus reus* condition of criminal liability. Thus there must be some way to link those who did commit the deeds with their leaders. Often the best strategy is to focus on how the leaders facilitated, or at least did not prevent, those under their rule from engaging in acts that so clearly advanced the directives of these leaders. But this must be proved, nonetheless. It is not sufficient merely to presume that the head of state is orchestrating what occurs by those in his State, even by those under his direct supervision. Rather, for the *actus reus* condition to be met by State leaders, there must be sufficient evidence that they did expressly facilitate, or clearly acted negligently in failing to prevent, the acts of those who tortured, raped, or killed.

If someone like Pinochet did order the tortures or executions, or if he clearly knew they were occurring and did nothing to stop them, then one might be able to establish his criminal liability, but there are nonetheless other considerations. Did the leader have any excuses readily available?[44] Here we need to consider seriously the motivations of the leader. In Pinochet's case, we cannot merely dismiss his claim that he was persecuting political enemies who sought to bring the country to the brink of anarchy. And while it is true that such claims are often smokescreens, if not outright lies, such excuses in a criminal proceeding need to be carefully considered.

When States or State leaders are accused of criminal conduct by international tribunals, we should remember that considerations of due process must be adhered to, no matter how politically charged the events become. Trials are not conducted in order to accomplish a political or even a moral objective. Trials determine legal guilt or innocence and set the stage for serious penalties. As we have seen, it is even more important to remember the true nature of trials when those accused are not States or State leaders. In cases where it is minor players who are in the dock for crimes such as genocide or crimes against humanity, extreme caution needs to be taken so that these individuals do not become mere cannon fodder for politicians or for well-intentioned political and moral activists. And even when powerful heads of State, or former heads of State, are in the dock, as in the case of a Pinochet or a Milosevic, defenses must be seriously considered and, above all, trials must conform to the rule of law, subjects that we address in later chapters. In the next chapter, we complete this set of chapters on conceptual problems in prosecutions for international crimes by examining prosecutions for the crime of genocide, especially by examining the case of Adolf Eichmann.

9

Prosecuting Genocide Amidst Widespread Complicity

Genocide is a paradigmatic group crime[1]: directed against an entire group and perpetrated by a State or other organized group. But, in addition, genocides rely on widespread cooperation and complicity by many, if not most, members of a given society. Indeed, genocides are so pervasive that sometimes nearly all members of a society in some way participate, or would have participated. This raises a host of conceptual problems for the prosecution of genocide. Criminal trials seek to hold individuals accountable, yet genocide is not an individual crime. William Schabas notes: "At the drafting convention in 1948 for the Genocide Convention, the United Kingdom refused to participate because it felt that the convention approached genocide from the wrong angle, responsibility of individuals, whereas it was really governments that had to be the focus."[2] In this chapter, I will assess this criticism of genocide prosecutions, as well as the similar criticisms voiced by Hannah Arendt about the trial of Adolf Eichmann when she said: "It is quite conceivable that certain political responsibilities among nations might some day be adjudicated in an international court; what is inconceivable is that such a court would be a criminal tribunal which pronounces on the guilt or innocence of individuals."[3]

I will focus on the responsibility of individuals for genocide. Genocide involves two parts: (1) some act that promotes the destruction of a group, and (2) "the intent to destroy, in whole or in part, a national, ethnical, racial, or religious group, as such." It is unlikely that a single individual would be able to destroy a whole group.[4] But an individual could destroy a part of that group. One individual might kill another. But what makes this individual's act a political act of the sort condemned by the Genocide Convention seems to be its collective dimension, some kind of intentional connection to the action of a State or other group. Understanding the collective dimension of individual responsibility for political crimes is crucial if individuals are to be justifiably prosecuted for genocide.

In the first section of this chapter, I will indicate why many theorists regard genocide as the greatest of evils, and yet those who perpetrate genocide do not manifest the normal characteristics associated with those who cause evil. In the second section, I will explore two types of ordinariness: (1) that the individuals accused in genocides often did not act differently from the way nearly everyone else acted, or (2) that nearly everyone else would have acted as the accused did, and hence that the individuals accused in genocides did not do anything much out of the ordinary. In the third section, I will set out the "act element" in the way that genocide is currently conceptualized, and explain why what an individual does is not as important as what that individual intends. In the fourth section, I describe the intent element normally required in genocide prosecutions, and set the stage for seeing how the roles played by certain individuals in group, or political, crimes can be the basis for their prosecution. In the fifth section, I argue that it makes conceptual and normative sense to hold individuals responsible when they share responsibility in political crimes such as genocide. In the final section, I indicate why it is a mistake to punish severely minor players, whereas it does make sense to punish people like Adolf Eichmann. Nonetheless I end by criticizing Hannah Arendt's proposed rationale for executing Eichmann.

I. The Greatest of Evils

Genocide is often characterized as the greatest of evil acts. Genocide is difficult to fathom because of the sheer size of the planned assaults and murders, and because of the fact that the crimes are not directed at people based on what they have done, or even based on mere random selection. Rather, genocide involves crimes committed against people for having certain characteristics that they could not help having, and is aimed at exterminating an entire group of people. In this sense, genocide is indeed one of the, if not *the*, worst of crimes. In its consequences, genocide is horrendous, but in the performing of the act itself, various conceptual puzzles arise. In this section, I will argue that while there may be a real category of human action that corresponds to evil, when we look at those who perpetrate genocide, it does not appear to fit into the category of evil, despite the fact that genocide itself may be one of the worst evils. Indeed, I will argue that those who perpetrate genocide, and even some of the acts that constitute genocide, are so ordinary that it is unclear why *individuals* should be punished for perpetrating genocide.

At first, one would think that the people prosecuted for such heinous crimes would appear to be even worse than regular serial killers: deranged or depraved individuals who barely resemble the rest of humanity – engaged in the sort of atrocities that some think are paradigmatic of evil acts. But such is not the case. Genocide is initially unfathomable because a large number of otherwise normal people are its foot soldiers, if not also its ring leaders. As the international community focuses on this crime as the most serious crime to be prosecuted against individuals at the International Criminal Court, disturbing questions arise about individual guilt. For it is the very ordinariness of the persons accused of genocide that stands in such sharp contrast with the evil that these individuals are accused of committing.

The recent history of how genocide is conceptualized shows how serious a crime genocide is seen to be, and hence how important it is to have international trials prosecuting genocide. As already indicated, the drafters of the Genocide Convention came under harsh criticism from the United Kingdom.[5] The UK did not disagree that genocide was an evil; it only disagreed about whether individuals were the ones who should be held as the responsible parties. The influential International Law Commission issued a report in 1994 in which it "recommended that genocide constitute a crime of 'inherent' jurisdiction, the only crime so characterized. In effect, this confirmed genocide's place at the apex of the pyramid of international crimes" that individuals could be tried for.[6] The rapporteur for the International Law Commission, James Crawford, said: "Among what were described as 'crime of crimes,' genocide was the worst of all."[7] And William Schabas, the preeminent contemporary legal scholar of genocide, says that "genocide stands to crimes against humanity as premeditated murder stands to intentional homicide."[8]

Very few philosophers have worried as much about this problem as did Hannah Arendt. Indeed, Arendt employed the phrase "the banality of evil" to indicate the ordinariness or commonness[9] of evil in some cases of genocide, such as the Holocaust. Arendt's writing about Eichmann is normally cited to show that it was hard to prosecute someone like Eichmann for the crimes of genocide since he lacked *mens rea*, a guilty mind. I will discuss this important objection to genocide prosecutions in later sections of this chapter. At the moment, I want to reexamine the far more radical claim advanced by Arendt toward the end of her book – namely, that what Eichmann did was far too ordinary to count as a crime at all, in that all or nearly all other members of a given society acted or would have acted in a similar way. While generally sympathetic to Arendt's analysis of the evil of genocides such as the Holocaust, and also sympathetic with the desire to find a basis for the punishment of the individuals who cause horrendous harm, I will, in the final section of this chapter, nonetheless be critical of the justification for punishing Eichmann that Arendt offers.

Colin McGinn recently urged that the term "evil" not be flung about irresponsibly, but when used correctly, as when describing an atrocity, it is important because "it sharpens our moral reactions and stiffens our moral resolve. The idea of ruthless malice, the love of death and destruction for its own sake, constitutes a real category of human agency, and this is what the word evil is designed to connote."[10] While one might disagree with McGinn's realism about evil, the question remains as to whether genocide would fit into his class of evil acts. One reason to think that genocide is the most evil of acts has to do with the sheer enormity of the harms produced. One would expect that those who perpetrate genocides act maliciously, causing as much suffering as possible, perhaps also acting for the sake of feeling pleasure in what they have done.[11]

It is here that Hannah Arendt's work, especially her book on Adolf Eichmann's role in the Holocaust, runs so much against the grain, and if credible, is so deeply disturbing. Eichmann was one of Hitler's top henchmen, who eluded Nuremberg prosecution by escaping to South America. In the early 1960s, he was captured by Israeli commandos and forcibly transported to Jerusalem to stand trial. Arendt, who observed Eichmann's trial, simply reminds us that there was "an individual in the dock."[12] Such an individual was only one of very many people responsible for the Holocaust.[13] Indeed, from her analysis of the relevant evidence, Arendt also came to the startling conclusion that even "the German Jewish community," and especially its leadership, aimed "to negotiate with the Nazi authorities," and ultimately was "helping the Nazis to deport" fellow Jews.[14] Her charge that even the German Jewish leadership in Nazi Germany was complicit in the Holocaust remains one of the most unsettling of claims about the confusing aspects of large-scale crimes such as genocide.

Since so many members of German society, seemingly going about their normal business of being good bureaucrats, guards, judges, and religious leaders, perpetrated the Holocaust, it is also hard to see in the Holocaust the face of evil, at least as evil is understood by Colin McGinn and many other philosophers. With so many participating, it is not very likely that they were all sadists. Perhaps the leadership of that society can be understood as falling under McGinn's label of evil. Yet here, too, Arendt claims that there is no evidence that Eichmann shot or tortured any Jew.[15] In any event, there was some evidence that Eichmann directly ordered the execution of Jews, although even this evidence was scanty.

As to the person of Eichmann, it is hard to say that he was ruthlessly malicious or that he loved death and destruction for its own sake. Arendt asserts, and then attempts to prove, that Eichmann was "an average, 'normal' person, neither feeble-minded nor indoctrinated nor cynical."[16] Eichmann was also someone who very much wanted to please others, and who took his mores from those who were his superiors. He was thus no moral paragon, but hardly "the evil character" that McGinn writes about.[17] Of course, this is not to deny that Eichmann threw himself into the business of transporting Jews to their death, only that he was not malicious in doing so. Rather he was motivated by a drive to do his job well, not to hurt others. Other studies have confirmed Arendt's assessment of the banal character of those who perpetrated the Holocaust as well as other recent genocides.[18]

II. Similarity of Behavior

One of the most intriguing defenses an individual can make against the charge of genocide is that all, or nearly all, other members of a given society acted in a similar way.[19] In the first part of this section, we will examine the claim that nearly all members of a society did act similarly, whereas in the second part, we will examine the claim that nearly all members of a society would have acted similarly if given the right opportunity. These claims give rise to a defense based on what I will call the "similarity of evil" – that if this individual in the dock did not do anything different from what anyone else in a given society did, or would have done, then individual guilt is eliminated, or at least significantly diminished. For guilt is normally assigned only when there is a difference among people – one person intentionally acting wrongly where everyone, or nearly everyone, else is acting rightly – where the perpetrator is a monster and everyone else is a "normal" member of society.

Guilt is assigned when an act constitutes a transgression. There is nothing wrong in principle with the idea of assigning guilt to an entire population, assuming that everyone has indeed engaged in the same transgression. As Arendt points out, that is the situation in the Biblical story of the towns of Sodom and Gomorrah, "which were destroyed by fire from Heaven because all the people in them had become equally guilty."[20] But there does seem to be something wrong with the idea of punishing only one individual when so many others are equally guilty. This is at least problematic on grounds of selective prosecution and punishment. Those who are prosecuted or punished can rightly complain that they were singled out for no obviously relevant reason, and others who acted similarly were left alone, also without a showing of relevant differences. But a deeper problem emerges when it is not just the members of a single population who are equally guilty, but all people, all of us. For without a distinction between "us" and "them," the notion of guilt seems somehow inappropriate.

Guilt is a concept used to separate the law-abiding from the law-breakers. Many philosophers of law have argued that if all or almost all members of society are law-breakers, then this fact is a sufficient basis for thinking that the law in question is not even properly law. For certain legal positivists, law gets its legitimacy from the assent of the people. If a previously legitimate law is currently disregarded by these people, then this is reason to think that the law is no longer regarded as legitimate, and hence not something to which people would currently assent. Without the assent of the people, there is no law and no sense in which "violations" of what was previously law now constitute a transgression. If all, or almost all, disregard a previously legitimate law, it makes more sense to say that the law no longer tracks what counts as transgression rather than to say that all, or almost all, people have engaged in a transgression of law.

In addition to transgression, guilt also requires a separation between those accused and those doing the accusing. In the case of Sodom and Gomorrah, it is not only God who is judging, but also the inhabitants of the other cities at the time. For if the accuser has the same characteristics as the accused, the accuser is at least hypocritical for lodging the accusations against someone else instead of first directing accusations at those closer to home – for instance, at oneself. In principle, an accuser can avoid hypocrisy by accusing self and others, simultaneously or serially, thereby showing that no favoritism is being shown in the process of accusing. In practice, at least in law, it makes little sense to do this, since in meting out punishment, the accuser and the accused all deserve to be incarcerated – and yet who will be the jailer? We are in need of a separation of some sort, and yet it is just this separation that is seemingly blocked when all are guilty.

Whereas ordinary people do not normally commit atrocities, they do nonetheless often follow their duties and orders. In this latter sense, if not in the former, Eichmann is engaged in behavior that is similar to what most of us do. The Milgram experiments need only be mentioned as having established this point.[21] The similarity of Eichmann to the rest of us turns crucially for Arendt on this similarity of motivation and intent: to do what we are ordered or asked to do, so as to do our duty or at least so as to advance ourselves in our professional roles. It is undeniable that Eichmann carried out his orders with a great deal of imagination and enthusiasm. But even this does not make him out of the ordinary. For many of us relish the doing of what others consider to be a good job, and work hard at showing that we are not merely marking time but are working as hard as we can to meet the objectives we have been assigned to meet.

As indicated here, Arendt pointed out at great length how many members of German society in the late 1930s, for instance, were complicit in the Holocaust, even members of the Jewish leadership in Germany. The acts that were similar by all, or almost all, were not separable in terms of their effects, or at least not easily so. It wasn't just that people engaged in similar acts, some of which caused harm and some of which did not. Rather, the similar acts of many formed a situation enabling harms to occur, where it was often hard to separate out the causal influences. And for those who did not engage in similar acts, there was very good reason to think that other "normal" Germans would have done as Eichmann did, given how normal he was.

This brings us to the second possible excuse based on the similarity of evil – namely, where any of the rest would have done what the accused did if given sufficient opportunity. Of course, the tricky question is what constitutes sufficient opportunity. The fact that Jones did act badly, but Smith did not, is already some reason to think that Smith would not have done what Jones did because Smith did not do so. One has to be able to specify the relevant differences in opportunity for Jones and Smith, and then show that if Smith had had Jones's opportunities, what reasons are there for thinking that Smith would have done what Jones in fact did do? These are notoriously difficult questions to answer.[22]

One way to begin to form an answer is to point to the very similar dispositions and character traits between a person who actually participates in genocide and a person who does not. If there is such a similarity of dispositions and character traits, and if there is also a significant difference in circumstance and opportunity between these two people, then it is likely that the similarities of disposition and character traits would have moved the Smiths of the world to act like the Joneses. It then turns out that the distinction between the perpetrators of atrocities and the rest of us breaks down, and it is plausible to say that all or almost all members of a society would have perpetrated the atrocity, just as Jones did.

The separation of "us" and "them" that is characteristic of situations where accusations are made for having transgressed is made very difficult when there are no relevant differences between them and us. Arendt tried to make this as clear as she could. She has her hypothetical judges put the following words into Eichmann's mouth: "You also said that your role in the Final Solution was an accident and that almost anybody could have taken your place, so that potentially almost all Germans are equally guilty."[23] Arendt then has these judges reject such an appeal from Eichmann: "[T]here is an abyss between the actuality of what you did and the potentiality of what others might have done."[24] Arendt then acknowledges that her hypothetical judges have now moved beyond the confines of the criminal law.

Nonetheless, it is common for similar acts to be treated quite differently from one another in criminal law. What generally makes one act legally wrong and a very similar act legally right concerns whether the consequences of the act are such as to be proscribed by law, or alternatively are such as to cause harm. On this construal, all are not really "equally guilty." For while they each may have chosen to engage in "bare" acts that are similar, the consequences of these acts are different, and hence what could be described as the "full" actions are also different. Perhaps, because of this difference, we could say that those whose acts result in genocide satisfy the *actus reus* requirement of criminal responsibility, whereas those whose acts do not result in genocide can be treated as not guilty since they lack *actus reus*. We will take up this strategy in the next section.

The record of the genocides investigated by the Yugoslav and Rwanda Tribunals is replete with stories like the one that Arendt tells about Eichmann. These transcripts are full of stories of concentration camp guards and officers who were mostly doing their jobs as best they could. There is an occasional sadist, such as Dusko Tadic, who clearly liked to inflict pain on others, but the role played by these people was small in comparison with that played by "normal" people, a very large number of "normal" people, without whose complicity large-scale crimes such as genocide would not be possible. And, generally, people who do horrible things to one another, as has been confirmed by my own rather personal experience in dealing with death row cases in Missouri, are often characterized as "model prisoners" or "good neighbors," so plain looking and acting that members of their communities are often shocked when they learn that the "monster" lived next door for all of these years and took care of the neighbors' cats when the neighbors were on vacation.[25]

So Arendt's "banality of evil" thesis is that when all, or almost all, acted or would have acted as Eichmann acted, no one is legitimately able to accuse him of being guilty. Of course, one could say that the ordinariness of evil is still evil, and can legitimately be accused and punished. Arendt would accept this much. But she would nonetheless counter that to do so is to move beyond the normal purview of how guilt and innocence are conceptualized in criminal law. A radical rethinking of these concepts is first required, and many people will resist this rethinking because it might lead to a revaluing of the enterprise of blaming in moral and legal contexts. In the remaining sections of this chapter, I will examine the elements of the crime of genocide to see if there is indeed a way to characterize someone like Eichmann as deserving of prosecution for the crime of genocide.

III. The Act Element in the Crime of Genocide

Arendt often voices one of her other main concerns as follows: If individuals are prosecuted for group or political crimes, they will be held accountable for what others have done. In a sense, this is surely right. One individual's act does not constitute genocide; it is the combined acts of many that make of these individual acts an act of genocide. So when individuals are prosecuted for genocide, they are, in this sense, almost always being held accountable in part for what others have done. This would be especially worrisome either if one individual is held solely responsible for what only these other people did, or if that individual has no other connection to the acts of the others than that they happened to have a single set of consequences. But neither of these worries will apply if the act that the individual is held responsible for is his or her own act, as part of a plan that included the acts of others. Some of Arendt's worries begin to dissipate if an individual is prosecuted for what the group does, but is only held accountable for his or her role. Thus, as we will see in detail later, one of the most morally troubling aspects of prosecuting individuals for group or political crimes can be averted.

The act element in the Genocide Convention's construal of the crime of genocide should not be seen as an independent element, but rather one that must be linked with the aim, or intention, to follow a plan. It is this link to a plan that transforms the individual's act into a part of a collective act, and that makes the individual responsible for what the group does. So individual responsibility for political crimes does not have to be like holding the child responsible for what the parent has done, to use Arendt's own metaphor. Rather, the better image is that of holding one responsible only for one's contribution to a common undertaking. This makes individual responsibility for political crimes a sub-species of shared responsibility. One is held responsible for one's role or share in a larger plan. In later sections, I will develop this point into a way to answer Arendt's worries.

The 1948 Genocide Convention defined genocide as a "normal" crime – namely, one that required *mens rea* (guilty mind) as well as *actus reus* (guilty act). Yet, as we will see, the act element is best understood as subordinate to one particular type of intent. Even though the Genocide Convention called for both an *intent* element and an *act* element, the act element need not be the serious acts of directly destroying a group, or even directly killing its members. The acts that will satisfy the act-requirement of the crime of genocide include:

1. Killing members of the group;
2. Causing serious bodily or mental harm to members of the group;
3. Deliberately inflicting on the group conditions of life calculated to bring about its physical destruction in whole or in part;
4. Imposing measures intended to prevent births within the group;
5. Forcibly transferring children of the group to another group.[26]

The International Criminal Tribunal for Rwanda (ICTR) has said, in the Rutaganda case, that act 3 is to be construed "as methods of destruction by which the perpetrator does not necessarily intend to immediately kill the members of the group, but which are ultimately aimed at their destruction."[27] Of course, this brings a kind of intention element into the act element, since discerning the aim of the act means looking at the intent behind the act, making this crime very different from "normal" crimes.

The act of killing another person, or even several other persons, is not an act of genocide; indeed, it is not even an international crime at all. What makes the act of killing an instance of genocide is the intent behind it, what the ICTR calls the aim of destruction of the group. This "aim" in the crime of genocide does not refer to a person's understanding that what he or she is doing is an instance of killing or even that killing is what is directly aimed at. Such an aim is the way to characterize the intent behind the crime of killing. But for the crime of genocide, there is an additional special intent element, the intent to destroy the group.[28] This element is already a part of the act element in the "aim" mentioned in the Genocide Convention's description of the relevant acts. This "aim" transforms a normal act of killing, along with similar acts by others, and makes it into something else – namely, an act of genocide, because it is aimed at the destruction of a group. The intent element in genocide is what makes the crime an international crime at all.

The act element does not appear to be able to stand on its own conceptually as a separate element of the crime of genocide. Acts 3 and 4 refer to intention outright in the description of these act elements. Act 5 also needs some reference to intention, since it is not clear what would be meant by the notion of transferring children from one group to another without the intention to remove them permanently. Acts 1 and 2 appear to be more straightforward act categories. Killing and causing bodily or emotional harm to individuals are relatively discrete acts. But the category is not merely killing individuals but killing, or harming, members of a group. Here, there is an "aim" element that must be added to the more straightforward act element. One's aim must be that by killing Jones one is also killing a member of a given group. It is for these reasons that the act element is not conceptually isolatable from the intention element.

Two recent international court cases – one from the International Criminal Tribunal for Yugoslavia (ICTY) in The Hague and the other from the International Criminal Tribunal for Rwanda (ICTR) in Arusha – illustrate what it might mean that an individual has acted in a way that makes him or her responsible for a group or political crime such as genocide. In the Yugoslav case, a particularly vicious individual who stole into concentration camps to kill is accused of genocide.[29] In the Rwanda case, a town leader who seemingly could have stopped mass killing but did not act to do so is also accused of genocide.[30] In both cases, while there were many things the defendants could have been prosecuted for, a decision was made to prosecute these individuals for genocide. Examining these cases will shed light on how these individuals' acts contributed to the crime of genocide as opposed to the crime of murder or the putative crime of neglect (perhaps even reckless neglect) of one's duty to preserve human life. The key consideration in ultimately determining their guilt or innocence was not how they acted but what their aim was in so acting – namely, whether either of these defendants was acting in a way that was designed to harm individuals as members of a group, as a way of destroying that group.

In the Jelisic case, a Serb civilian sneaked into Bosnian concentration camps and killed at least a dozen Muslims, claiming to be the "Serbian Adolf." The Trial Chamber of the Yugoslav Tribunal (ICTY) claimed that it was "theoretically possible" that a single perpetrator could commit genocide.[31] In this case, Jelisic displayed a discriminatory motive in that he attacked these people because he hated Muslims. Nonetheless, these were seemingly random murders. Jelisic both killed people who were Muslims and had hatred against Muslims. But in order to be convicted of genocide, the accused had to act in a way that had as its aim the intention of killing members of the Muslim group, and thus destroying the group.

Here, following a plan aimed at destroying a group would indeed link the individual accused to the larger political harm and make him individually guilty of the political harm, the genocide.[32] Was Jelisic following a plan, or not? This is not merely a matter of looking at his acts, but of also considering what others were doing. If his acts were random in that while based on hatred of Muslims they were not part of a larger plan, then he could not be found guilty of genocide. If he were not following such a plan to exterminate Muslims, then his act might still meet the elements of persecution, as a crime against humanity, but not the more serious crime of genocide. The Jelisic Trial Court ruled that the defendant was not guilty of genocide since his assaults on Muslims, while directed at the group, were not aimed at the destruction of that group. The question is this: How do we tell when an act is random as opposed to being part of a plan? And the answer is that we must look to the defendant's intent. Hence, the act element appears to be subordinate to the intent element.

In the Akayesu case, a Rwandan civilian political leader apparently knew that Hutu townspeople were killing Tutsi civilians in large numbers. He himself was present at many of the killings, and participated in several of these killings. The ICTR Trial Chamber claimed that genocidal intent can be inferred "from the general context of the perpetration of other culpable acts directed at the same group, whether these acts were committed by the same offender or others." Other factors include whether one group was targeted for attack and another group was excluded from these attacks.[33] Here, command responsibility was crucial – namely, whether Akayesu knew about what was occurring, and could have, but did not, stop it from occurring. His participation in some of the killings, and his knowledge that a group was being targeted in the larger plan, plus his intentional failure to stop the killings, would make him responsible for what occurred, and ultimately for genocide. The conceptual question is: Why should we think of his failure to act as itself part of a plan? And why should we let the plans of others turn what might otherwise have been random acts of violence into acts aimed at members of a group? This is a variation of Hannah Arendt's concern expressed at the beginning of this section. The answer made reference to the defendant's aim to allow a genocidal plan to succeed.

So we have two possible avenues for linking an individual's acts to the crime of genocide. One avenue is for an individual to be intentionally following a plan of a group that had as its aim the destruction of another group. A second avenue is for an individual to be aware of an ongoing plan of a group to destroy another group that he could prevent, but that he chose not to stop. In both cases, it is the intention of the defendant that is the key to thinking that the defendant's acts constitute a kind of individual complicity in the larger political harm. The acts, considered by themselves, do not link the individual to a political crime. On the basis of the positive or negative role that the accused *intended* to be playing, it could be at least prima facie claimed that the accused was acting in a way that made him responsible for a political harm such as genocide. In the next section, I will explore in greater detail the intent element in the crime of genocide.

IV. The Intent Element in the Crime of Genocide

The key to justifying the prosecution of an individual for a group or political crime such as genocide, in addition to showing what others were doing, is to show that an individual was aiming to do a certain thing as one significant step toward destroying a group. Normally this means that the individual intended that his or her act be part of a plan that had large-scale harmful consequences. Intentional participation in such a plan makes the individual complicit in the harms that result from carrying out that plan. But various problems arise in this construal of the intent element. Not the least of these is how much of the group must the individual intend to destroy, and if it is only a small part, how is genocide to be distinguished from other group-based crimes such as persecution or discrimination? And normatively, why would we want to hold individuals accountable for this supposedly most serious of all international crimes merely on the basis of such intentions in those cases in which the defendants' actual acts were fairly inconsequential? In this section, I address the first of these questions. In the final two sections of the chapter, I address the second.

Genocide is presently an international crime that is prosecuted against individual persons. The defining intent element is this: "[G]enocide means any of the ... acts [I enumerated earlier] committed with the intent to destroy, in whole or in part, a national ethnical, racial or religious group, as such . . ."[34] It is rare that an individual person intends to destroy an entire population or group. For this reason, the 1948 Genocide Convention added the words "in whole or in part" to the definition of genocide. The ICTR specifically held that "genocide does not imply the actual extermination of a group in its entirety."[35] Yet the International Law Commission wrote in 1966 that the intention element in genocide "must be [the intent] to destroy the group 'as such' meaning as a separate and distinct entity, and not merely some individuals because of their membership in a particular group."[36]

There is another international crime – persecution (one of the crimes against humanity) – that is meant to cover murders or tortures directed at individuals because of their group membership. According to the ICTR's Akayesu judgment, the point of prosecutions for these crimes is to "protect civilian populations from persecution." On the other hand, the point of prosecutions for genocide is to "protect certain groups from extermination or attempted extermination."[37] In both cases, persecution and genocide, the individual may perform exactly the same acts; what distinguishes these crimes is the defendant's intent. More is required than the fact that an individual person participated in a genocidal plan and knew that the plan could destroy a group.[38]

The individual must also *intend* to destroy the group, at least in part. The United States attached an interpretive declaration to Article II of the Genocide Convention: "[T]he phrase 'intent to destroy in whole or in part, a national, ethnical, racial, or religious group as such' appearing in Article II means the specific intent to destroy, in whole or *substantial* part."[39] So from all of these sources, the idea seems clear enough that the individual person must intend to destroy a substantial part of a group, not merely intend to destroy an individual person who happens to be a member of the group even if the point of killing that member is because of that person's group membership. One must participate in such a plan and intend to do so, but one need not have directly committed the harm – for instance, the killing of members of a group – that is at issue, as we saw in the last section.

Individuals can hate whole groups, and even intend to discriminate against all of the members of a group. But individuals generally do not intend to destroy whole groups. Individuals may wish that whole groups would be destroyed. Yet intending their destruction is a different matter. To intend to destroy a group, it must be plausible to think that one could do so. It does not make sense to say that one intends to do what one knows one could not do, only perhaps that one intended to do what turns out to be impossible to do unbeknownst to the actor. It is generally implausible for one person to be able to destroy an entire group, and hence it is also implausible for that person to intend to do so. It is plausible for a person to destroy a group in part, depending on the size of the part. Hence it is plausible to intend knowingly to destroy a group in part.[40]

It is plausible for an individual to intend to destroy a part of a group since, at the limit, an individual is part of a group, and one individual can destroy another individual. It is nonetheless generally implausible to intend to destroy a group by planning to kill just one member of that group. But if one intends to destroy a part of a group, and the part that one intends to destroy is itself a "substantial" part of the group, then it can plausibly be said that the intent was to destroy the group. And this is something that individuals can both intend and accomplish, but only with the help of many others. Again, this is why the United States made the qualification to the Genocide Convention that the "in part" aspect of the intent element must refer to a "substantial part."

The emerging jurisprudence on the crime of genocide distinguishes between "the collective genocidal intent underlying the plan" and the "genocidal intent of the individual."[41] The Jelisic court looked for "an affirmed resolve to destroy in whole or in part a group as such."[42] This was the link thought to be necessary between the collective and the individual genocidal intent. Actually, this is sometimes a difficult standard to meet, and the ICTY Trial Chamber said that it was not met in the Jelisic case since Jelisic appeared to use a random selection mechanism in his killing. Indeed, the ICTY held that "it will be very difficult in practice to provide proof of the genocidal intent of an individual if the crimes committed were not widespread and if the crime charged is not backed by an organization or a system."[43] Hence the emerging jurisprudence is that there must be more than a plan; also a group, normally an organized group, of which the defendant is a part, must attempt to carry out this plan. Whereas it may be possible for an individual, on his or her own, to hatch a plan to destroy a group, and carry out that plan, it will be very difficult in practice to prove genocide in such a case.

We might wonder further why intending to destroy a part of a group is the same as intending to destroy the group. One possible answer is that while that is not strictly so, the larger the part of the group one intends to destroy, the greater is the likelihood that one is intending to destroy the group.[44] But what of the parts of groups that are geographically confined and isolated? If the relevant part of the group is confined geographically, is it really true that the intent to destroy this part of the group should count as the intent to destroy the group? And why should it matter that one does not intend to destroy the part of the group that is not in a particular geographical locale? The answer to these questions turns on the empirical claim that the larger the part of a group one intends to destroy, the greater is the likelihood that one intends to destroy the whole group.

This brings us to the requirement that the crime of genocide must involve the intent to destroy a group "as such." The intent to destroy only a part of a group must be in furtherance of the destruction of the group as such. It thus seems that the individual genocidal intent element is a complex requirement. Along with the actions of others, either the defendant must have an intent to destroy a whole group as such, or the defendant must have an intent to destroy a part of a group, and have the further aim of ultimately destroying the group as such. It thus appears that even the "in part" aspect of the genocidal intent element must be accompanied by the further intent ultimately to destroy the group. It is not enough to intend ultimately to destroy only this particular geographically isolated part of a group, even though it is enough to intend *at the moment* only to destroy that part of the group. The "as such" requirement means that one must also intend, by destroying the part of the group, that one thereby ultimately aims to contribute to the destruction of the group.[45] Here we might think again of the International Law Commission's statement that "the intention must be to destroy the group 'as such' meaning as a separate and distinct entity" and that the way to accomplish this was to commit an act against an individual because of his or her membership in a group "as an incremental step in the overall objective of destroying the group."[46]

In this section and the previous sections, we have seen various ways of understanding how an individual's act and intent could be connected to the group or political crime of genocide. I have followed current international criminal jurisprudence in attempting to specify what should be required of an individual's act and intent in order to prove that individual guilty of genocide. The individual's act must in some sense be connected to the larger act of group destruction by being able, together with the acts of others, plausibly to accomplish the group's goal. And the individual's intent must be not only to destroy a part of a group, but also to aim at the ultimate destruction of the larger group. In the next two sections, I make the case for thinking that such a linkage between what the individual does and the political crime can, and often should, be a basis for *individual* guilt and punishment.

V. Sharing Responsibility for Political Crimes

In this section, I will argue that it is *plausible* for individuals to be prosecuted for political crimes. In the final section, I will provide positive advantages that show that individuals *should* sometimes be prosecuted and punished for political crimes such as genocide. In this section, I develop further the argument that prosecutions of individuals for political crimes such as genocide are plausible when they are based primarily on the individual's intention to participate in harm rather than on their directly harmful acts. I will also argue that prosecutions of individuals for political crimes such as genocide are plausible when they provide a means to hold someone responsible and punishable for that person's complicity in clearly horrendous harms.

A political crime is a crime that is committed by people the bulk of whom do not have to do anything directly harmful themselves. So, to call something a political crime is to say that it is a crime committed by a collectivity, typically by a State or by an organized group of people in some way acting systematically. Typically, the group that commits a political crime has a structure that endures over time, and it might make sense to say of the group that it is responsible for what has occurred even though no current members played a role in the harm for which the group is held responsible.[47] Arendt's position, discussed earlier, was that it was not plausible to hold individuals accountable for what organizations do, especially since organizations have a life of their own that does not correspond to the life of the individual, and since current members will then be held responsible for what earlier members have done.

To see how political crimes relate to legal or moral ones, let us look at a similar distinction between *political* guilt versus *legal* and *moral* guilt in Karl Jasper's writings.[48]

Political guilt: This, involving the deeds of statesmen and of the citizenry of a state, results in my having to bear the consequences of the deeds of the state whose power governs me and under whose laws I live. Everybody is co-responsible for the way he is governed. Jurisdiction rests with the power and the will of the victor, in both domestic and foreign politics.[49]

Political guilt is to be contrasted with legal guilt, which Jaspers says involves crimes that are "capable of objective proof and violate unequivocal laws," and with moral guilt, which involves my judgment of my own deeds. In legal guilt, jurisdiction lies with the courts; in moral guilt, jurisdiction lies with conscience. But in the case of political guilt, "success decides," and "natural and international law, serve to mitigate arbitrary power."

It is interesting to note that Jaspers mentions international law, which in his day (writing in the 1940s) had only begun to include international criminal tribunals. Indeed, international criminal law would have been a kind of oxymoron for Jaspers. But today we are faced with this blending of categories, in which political crimes such as genocide are indeed judged not by victors' success but by judges acting according to international law, and determining legal guilt. Nonetheless, Jaspers's main point is still relevant – namely, in political crimes where we seek to establish political guilt, many people, if not everyone, in a political society is co-responsible. But how that political co-responsibility translates into legal guilt remains a deeply divisive matter, even if not the purely subjective matter Jaspers thought it was.

For Arendt, personal responsibility, rather than legal guilt, can be determined on the basis of what each individual person did or didn't do in participating in political crimes.[50] Arendt admitted that the key question was whether a person "participated" in a given political crime. This is significant because such crimes would not occur if "enough people would act 'irresponsibly' enough and refuse support, even without active resistance and rebellion."[51] According to Arendt, the question should not be merely whether one obeyed orders, the question we will take up in the next chapter, but simply whether one participated. And one's personal responsibility could then be based on that participation. But what Arendt failed to see was the importance of intention here as well as in allowing us to talk not only of personal or moral responsibility but also of legal guilt. For legal guilt and punishment, the question is not merely whether one was following orders, or participating, but whether one was intentionally participating.

In normative terms, we can speak plausibly of shared criminal responsibility of those individual members of organizations who commit political crimes. The main insight that I shall proceed from, and that I believe Arendt and Jaspers would support, is that crimes of States and other organizations involve acts of many individuals, (1) many of whom are merely blindly following orders, but (2) some of whom are giving those orders, and (3) others of whom are following orders but share the goals of those who are giving the orders. For this reason, it is plausible, especially concerning people in the second and third categories here, that individuals be held criminally liable for their roles in these so-called political crimes. There is normative implausibility only when an individual is held criminally liable for all that a State has done. If we are speaking of shared rather than sole responsibility or liability, the evident normative implausibility does not arise.

Shared responsibility involves responsibility not merely of those who directly cause harm but also those who cause harm indirectly and in other ways are complicit in a crime. A person is complicit in a crime if he intentionally participates in a collective endeavor that brings about the crime. All those people who are complicit in a crime can plausibly be said to share in responsibility for the crime. For once one plays a role or generally participates in an event, and does so intentionally, one is then normatively a proper subject of responsibility.[52] Not only those who directly cause harm, but also those who do so indirectly, can be plausibly said to be responsible for that harm.

Indirect causation of harm that is nonetheless intentional is a plausible basis for responsibility ascriptions, even ascriptions of criminal liability, if it is intentional. The element of direct causation of harm is necessary in order to create responsibility when we are asking about who might have sole responsibility for a harm. But even in that case, it is curious indeed that one person should be forced to shoulder all of the responsibility when there were others whose indirect help also made them complicit in the harm. If normative plausibility of responsibility ascriptions is connected to what people did, then we should not stop with direct causation, but should also hold people accountable for indirect causation, since this is also what they did. In this sense, shared responsibility is much more plausible than sole responsibility, when more than one person participates in a harm. Hence it is normatively plausible that individuals who are complicit but not the direct causes of harm be held liable for their share in these harms.

Another issue separating Arendt and Jaspers's view on the one side, and my view on the other, concerns whether something resembling objective proof can be obtained in the case of political crimes. For while it may be conceptually and normatively plausible to assign guilt or blame for each person's role in a political crime such as genocide, there may be overwhelming practical difficulties with doing so as in conspiracy cases, and because of this it may be nearly inconceivable that such trials could ever take place. There are difficult practical problems with legally proving intent, and in establishing the kind of intent that seems necessary for genocide to occur. But these practical difficulties can be overcome.

Recall that in the Jelisic case, what mattered was whether his acts were random or designed to be part of a larger genocidal plan. If his aim was to be part of a genocidal plan already shown to exist, then he is complicit in it and he is plausibly responsible for it. In the Akayesu case, what mattered was whether his omissions were designed to allow the genocide to continue, or not. Given that Akayesu was a high-ranking political leader, his intentional failure to act definitely allowed a plan to be carried out that otherwise he could have stopped. He was thus responsible for the role he played in the ensuing mass harms. In the Jelisic case, the evidence turned out to be inconclusive, and hence Jelisic was exonerated of genocide charges. In the Akayesu case, the evidence was conclusive, and Akayesu was convicted of genocide. In both cases, it was plausible for these individual defendants to be prosecuted for genocide.

Leaders such as Akayesu will be easier to convict – and should be – since their leadership roles in the society mean that they are more influential in the setting and maintaining of mass plans. The relatively minor players such as Jelisic are, and should be, harder to convict, and when convicted given lesser punishments than the leaders, since the minor players' roles in the setting and maintaining of the plans are much less influential, as we also saw in the discussion of Tadic in Chapter 7 and the discussion of Pinochet in Chapter 8. But even the minor players can sometimes plausibly be held responsible for the part they played in a political crime such as genocide. In the next section, I will present the positive advantages in favor of thinking that prosecutions of individuals for political crimes such as genocide *should* occur, not merely that they are plausibly conducted.

VI. Responsibility and Punishment for Genocide

In the last section, I contended that individual political responsibility should be seen as a form of shared responsibility. Shared responsibility is that form of responsibility according to which the individual is responsible for the contribution that he or she has made to a larger plan of crime, or the contribution that he or she makes to a continued pattern of behavior that makes certain crimes more likely than not to occur. So there are both active and passive contributions that can be counted as contributions to a larger plan of crime. As I said earlier, the leaders of a group especially are appropriately held accountable for collective crimes based on their passive contributions as well as their active contributions. Shared responsibility generally makes the most sense for concerted efforts undertaken by a number of people, each intentionally participating, and where one can talk of a collective action.[53]

The major normative advantage of employing individual criminal punishment for political crimes such as genocide is that we highlight the fact that it is ultimately individuals who are the perpetrators of these collective crimes. Punishment is normally a fitting response when individuals are responsible for having done, or contributed to, harm. When individuals share in the responsibility for harm, they should also share in the punishment. To do less than this in response to harm is to succumb to the temptation to let people off the hook merely because there are a lot of them, and they are all complicit. Even if all members of society share at least some of the blame for harm, there is nothing wrong in principle with having each member of a society experience some punishment, although prison time is almost surely excluded in any reasonably large-sized society. In such situations, we will have to be creative in thinking about what might replace prison time as a sufficiently stringent form of punishment for egregious political crimes such as genocide.

Contrary to what Jaspers and Arendt claim, an international criminal tribunal that metes out punishment need not be a form of victor's justice, where success in battle is the determiner of who gets to judge whom. Generally, the States from which the judges of the new International Criminal Court will be drawn have not themselves been engaged in any form of war, nor has the United Nations, which sponsors that court. But this does not mean that bias on the part of those who are judging will be easily eliminated.[54] My point is that it is plausible that an international criminal tribunal could truly represent the world's interests rather than simply the interests of the victorious parties in a particular war. Hence it will not necessarily be true that success or strength must be the basis for judging in international criminal tribunals.

Nonetheless, politics (in another sense of that term from its use in "political" crime) may still intrude into the judicial process. Especially when political crimes are alleged, with their hard-to-pin-down emphasis on intentions and attitudes of individuals, considerations of ideology will often surface. Although the form that politics will take does not necessarily equate with so-called victor's justice, a strong Western bias, for instance, is readily apparent in the ICC, where Western-style cross-examination and the adversarial method are generally the order of the day. Defense lawyers trained in non-Western legal systems sometimes find it difficult to operate in international criminal courts. And this problem is unlikely to go away, since courts must follow some model, whether Western or non-Western, and hence someone will be disadvantaged.

One of the reasons why convictions are so hard to obtain is that genocide – the intent to destroy a group or a people – is ultimately a collective crime rather than an individual crime. Courts are generally not well set up for such crimes. Perhaps more importantly, many people's moral intuitions are offended by the thought of collective responsibility or collective punishment. Even if we can judge that a State is responsible for perpetrating a harm against a group, it is unsettling to think that the members of a State would be held responsible for the harm that has clearly been done by their State. We recoil from the idea that no matter what one has done, then each individual member is guilty if one's group does harm. But we do not have to support such a view in order to defend the position that criminal tribunals can appropriately judge individual guilt for political crimes such as genocide.

In this context, let us return to Adolf Eichmann. I have set the stage here for thinking that leaders such as Eichmann, rather than minor players, should be the prime defendants in genocide prosecutions and, if convicted, should indeed be punished severely. International crimes such as genocide are prosecuted against individuals, not against the organized groups that largely perpetrate these crimes. What we are really doing is holding individuals responsible for their roles or parts in these larger organized efforts. Yet it is not at all clear what would amount to a similar harm to an individual in the form of a punishment that would fit the crime.

So, should Eichmann have been executed, as indeed he was? At the very end of the Epilogue to her book on the Eichmann trial, Arendt has hypothetical judges declare their judgment on Eichmann as follows: "[W]e find that no one, that is, no member of the human race can be expected to want to share the earth with you. This is the reason, and the only reason, you must hang."[55] Perhaps we can take Arendt quite literally: Executing Eichmann removed from our midst someone who had said by word and deed that he did not want to share the earth with the rest of us. The problem is that this is not clearly what Eichmann said. He was no indiscriminate killer. If he did indeed say he did not want to share the earth with anyone, it seems to have been restricted to the Jews and a few other groups.

Because of the role that Eichmann played in the Holocaust, he should be punished. But he was not truly unfit for our company, any more than we are unfit for our own company, as Arendt herself demonstrated so well. Perhaps we could say of Hitler that he was unfit for sharing the earth with us, especially if one is a Jew or a gypsy. But on Arendt's own account, Eichmann was simply a victim of misfortune, someone whose exercise of loyalty and bureaucratic skills would normally have been praised. He was unlucky enough to have been a high-ranking bureaucrat in Nazi Germany rather than at General Motors – but that surely does not make him unfit to share the earth with us. Yet, given that he intentionally participated in this mass atrocity,[56] it makes sense to punish him, just as it also makes sense to mitigate that punishment because of the similarity of what Eichmann did to what so many others did, or would have done, in similar circumstances. Eichmann should have been punished, but on Arendt's own grounds, he should surely not have been executed.

In this chapter, I have argued that international prosecutions for genocide should focus primarily on political leaders rather than on minor players, and that much more attention needs to be given to *mens rea* than to *actus reus*, as is actually reflected in a proper reading of the elements of the crime of genocide in the 1948 Genocide Convention and in the way the new ICC has interpreted the criminal elements of genocide. By focusing on criminal intention, it will be possible to overcome the justificatory hurdle involved in prosecuting an individual for what is principally a political crime. Responsibility for such a crime is best seen as a form of shared responsibility, in which the leaders of the group or institution are singled out for their intentional acts of planning the mass human rights abuse. Although it is difficult for criminal tribunals to deal with political crimes, it is not, as Arendt claimed, conceptually or normatively "inconceivable" or implausible.

Mass human rights abuses, such as genocide, involve the participation at many levels of large segments of a population, and are not normally the single isolated acts of an individual perpetrator. But it does not follow from this that it is implausible to establish individual legal guilt for political crimes. The difficulty is that individuals seem to be held liable for what others have done. But where many participate in harm, it is at least conceivable that we could assign criminal guilt and punishment for precisely what each one did and for what each intended to do. Although practical difficulties abound, it is plausible to apportion guilt to contributions in the collective enterprise. Hence, in some cases the international community should prosecute leaders, and sometimes minor players, for political crimes such as genocide. The extent to which they should be punished will be determined by considering possible excuses, a topic we have begun to explore here, and that will be the focus of our next chapter.

PART D

DEFENSES AND ALTERNATIVES

10

Superior Orders, Duress, and Moral Perception

The next two chapters consider various defenses that can be offered by those who are accused of genocide, crimes against humanity, and war crimes. I make no attempt to be comprehensive in examining possible defenses. Instead, I focus on those that are the most interesting from a philosophical point of view in light of our earlier discussions. Hence, in this chapter, I begin by examining the defense of superior orders (that one was just following orders), and eventually turn to the related defense of duress (that one had no reasonable choice). In Chapter 11, I examine several procedural "defenses" that would nullify the trial itself – that the trial involved an ex post facto proceeding, that the defendant had been singled out for selective prosecution, and that the punishment did not fit the crime for which the defendant had been charged. A consideration of these procedural defenses will lead to an examination of the rule of law in international prosecutions. In general, I argue for an expanded understanding of these defenses.

In 1946, the Nuremberg Trials were begun, attempting to bring to justice the perpetrators of the Holocaust, among others. Politically, what was groundbreaking was that the trials were based on international norms rather than the laws of any particular country, and that most of the defendants were former members of the German military forces being tried on German soil largely by non-Germans. Philosophically, one of the most interesting things about these trials was that an attempt was made to define and justify the defense of "superior orders," the defense that exculpated individual soldiers, and some other minor players, from responsibility if they were merely following duly authorized orders. Legally, what has come to be called the "Nuremberg defense" is the result of the attempt to provide a set of limitations for the "superior orders" defense by reference to concepts of moral perception and moral choice.

The courts at Nuremberg subscribed to the relatively new idea that it was not sufficient for soldiers to show that they were following orders in order to be relieved from personal responsibility for what they did. In addition, these courts held that soldiers must show that they believed their actions to be (1) morally and legally permissible, and (2) the only morally reasonable action available in the circumstances. In the first two sections of this chapter, I will be mainly interested in seeing whether the Nuremberg defense is a normatively plausible and serviceable basis for deciding when "following orders" should excuse one from responsibility. I will then consider the change in these conceptions, developed shortly after Nuremberg, that stressed the idea that the test for superior orders is to be drawn in terms of the "moral sentiments of humankind,"[1] the chief way that the notions of natural law and human rights insert themselves into these deliberations about superior orders. Finally, I will tackle the most recent attempts to define superior orders – before the Yugoslav appellate tribunal and in the drafting of the Rome Statute establishing a permanent International Criminal Court. Throughout, I will argue that the Nuremberg defense provides a normatively justifiable and workable defense, and indeed a more difficult one to rebut than is normally recognized, for many of the crimes that could be prosecuted in an international criminal court. To defend this claim, I will often traverse the difficult and philosophically rich terrain of the moral psychology of human beings who are in hostile circumstances.

In the first three sections of the chapter, I will examine the key ingredient in the Nuremberg defense – the idea that if a normal person would have known that a given order was morally or legally impermissible, then the fact that the order was given cannot be grounds for exculpation. Instead, the person[2] will remain individually responsible for what was done, even though he or she was only following orders. Underlying such a view is the notion that there is a normal moral perception of a certain set of circumstances, and that such a perception is necessary for the ascription of responsibility. From my moral minimalist position, I will challenge this view.

In the fourth section, I will examine the way limitations on one's moral choices as well as the costs of non-compliance should affect this defense. I will also examine one of the main ideas underlying this view – namely, that it makes sense to hold individuals responsible, to see them as collectively guilty, for what their groups have chosen to do. This will provide us with another dimension of the group-based analysis I have been providing throughout the previous chapters.

In the final section, I will consider the application of this defense to recent cases concerning war crimes and crimes against humanity. Here I will argue that taking the Nuremberg defense seriously, in conjunction with the defense of duress, should make it much more difficult to get convictions than some prosecutors presently believe. In this sense, the Nuremberg defense, properly understood, will shield many defendants, especially minor players, from punishment at the hands of international tribunals today.

I. The Nuremberg Defense

The Charter of the International Military Tribunal, ratified in 1945, governed the war crimes tribunals that sat in Nuremberg, Germany.[3] The Charter established principles of individual responsibility for the consequences of the actions of military personnel during World War II.[4] Most controversially, it also specified conditions under which soldiers could be relieved of responsibility when carrying out duly authorized orders from their superiors. The idea underlying the traditional superior orders defense, which the Nuremberg defense replaced, was that soldiers do not really plan and intend to kill, but only intend to do what they are ordered to do. It is those who make the orders, not those who merely carry them out, who should be held responsible for what occurs in wartime. Such an idea is consistent with what I argued in the last three chapters – that minor players should rarely be prosecuted for group-based crimes, and that prosecutions should focus instead on heads of State and other leaders.

At Nuremberg, the superior orders defense was codified, and also changed from its previous meaning. What is now called the "Nuremberg defense" is based on the following interpretation of the Charter made by the Nuremberg Tribunal:

> The true test, which is found in varying degrees in the criminal law of most nations, is not the existence of the order, but whether moral choice was in fact possible . . . A soldier could be relieved of personal responsibility for the soldier's acts only if the soldier could show that he or she did not have a moral choice to disobey his or her superior's orders.[5]

Thus the Nuremberg defense changed the traditional superior orders defense, which had relieved nearly all soldiers of responsibility for following orders, by stipulating that a soldier was only to be relieved of responsibility if the soldier had no moral choice but to obey the orders, a topic that is fraught with philosophical problems, as we will see.

As I indicated earlier, there are two aspects of moral choice that are of importance in the Nuremberg defense. The first is that the soldier reasonably believes that the superior's order was legally and morally valid. The second is that the soldier believes that following the superior's order was the only morally reasonable course of action open to him or her. In this section, I will examine the first of these conditions. Here it is assumed that a soldier, or other minor player, can subject his or her superior's orders to critical moral scrutiny and thereby ascertain what is morally and legally permissible in a given situation. In this sense, the Nuremberg defense assumes that a certain capacity of moral perception, normally thought to be necessary for personal responsibility, is also necessary for establishing an excuse from personal responsibility on the battlefield.

If a defendant lacks the capacity to understand that his or her actions are wrong, at the very least that person is said to have diminished responsibility for those actions. In addition, if that person only *contributes* to a given result, then we often assign only partial responsibility for what occurs. Both of these diminutions of responsibility are based on the idea that a person should be held responsible only for those consequences that were known to be wrong, and personally caused. In criminal law as we have seen, generally only those people are held liable who had the capacity to understand, and intended, the wrongness of their acts (*mens rea*) and whose acts causally contributed to a harm (*actus reus*).

I will begin by examining why only soldiers, as opposed to civilians, are held personally responsible for what they collectively bring about. One standard way to approach this issue is to think of soldiers as involved in a kind of conspiracy, where each displays complicity insofar as he or she contributes to a particular result under the direction of someone in authority who stands above him or her in a chain of command. Although soldiers are often thought of as mere cogs in a larger "war machine," or as representatives for the entire nation that employs them, they are surely not really automatons either. The defense of "superior orders" is meant to allow some of these soldiers to diminish or eliminate their personal responsibility, but only under fairly restricted conditions. And the main reason for this restriction is that, after all, it is the soldiers who are actually doing the killing or destroying of property. Although it is true that the soldiers are ordered to act, they are themselves also actors who should normally bear at least some of the responsibility for what they do, even while in the uniform of their respective States. The modern changes in the superior orders defense reflect the view that soldiers are normally to be considered autonomous agents, not mere cogs in a machine.

Many of the versions of the superior orders defense rely on something like a conspiracy model of understanding group behavior. The conspiracy model of responsibility is especially appropriate since soldiers truly do conspire to accomplish various objectives. An army unit is able to do things that individual soldiers would not normally be able to do because of the relationships that exist within the group, most importantly because some are leaders and others are followers. Both groups are often acting at risk to their own individual lives. Because of the structure of these military relationships, there are common goals and objectives that all of the members of the unit seek to accomplish; most importantly, there is normally not disagreement about what those goals or objectives are. Of course, the chief reason for this nearly undisputed commonality of objective and goal is that there is a chain of command running from soldiers to their leaders, who are the nearly sovereign determiners of what goals and objectives should be pursued.

The traditional version of the superior orders defense was premised on the idea that soldiers do not generally give orders to themselves, but are ordered to act by their superiors. The soldiers have strong institutional role responsibilities to follow what they have been ordered to do. In the Middle Ages, even lords of the manor used the superior orders defense, arguing that they were duty bound to do what the prince commanded. In one famous case, a medieval court rejected this version of the superior orders defense concerning Peter of Hagenbach, Charles of Burgundy's Governor of Breisach. The court seemingly thought that a lord of the manor was autonomous enough to be held responsible for what he did, even when ordered by his prince to do so. But this medieval court generally did acknowledge the legitimacy of such a defense for slightly lower-ranking members of a hierarchical structure.[6] For many centuries thereafter, soldiers were not held responsible for what they did, since it was their leaders, not they, who had intentionally set out on a path of a certain sort by issuing various orders.

The Nuremberg defense brings about a sea change in our understanding of the idea of choice in a soldier's actions. After Nuremberg, it was thought that soldiers should be able to see that some of the orders they had been given were clearly immoral or illegal, and if the orders were seen as clearly immoral or illegal, then those soldiers should not be excused for following those orders. The Nuremberg Trials put soldiers on notice that they would not necessarily be relieved of responsibility for their acts merely because they were ordered to act. The idea behind the Nuremberg Trials was that there are higher moral rules than those issued by commanding officers, and that the higher rules should be obeyed, at least in some circumstances, even when they are countermanded by the orders of a commanding officer.

In previous chapters, we examined the supposed basis for having higher norms in international law. Because it is so hard to determine what is morally required across cultures, a minimalist approach that stressed the relatively uncontroversial basic security interests of people was adopted. When we now come to the moral rules that soldiers should obey, it is even harder to ascertain what is truly universal and what is merely based on customary ways of proceeding. One of the chief difficulties here is that supporters of a clear moral norm that goes beyond a certain minimum rely on knowledge that any foot soldier should have known, even in the most distracting and demanding of circumstances. The fact of extremely distracting circumstances will make it very hard to specify what every soldier must be supposed to know, although there certainly are some easy cases.

In one notorious case from World War I that had a profound impact on the Nuremberg Trials, Lieutenant Patzig, a commander of a German U-Boat, "sunk a hospital ship and then destroyed two lifeboats with survivors." After the war, charges were brought against two of the U-boat's crew members when Lieutenant Patzig could not be found. "The court ruled that [the crew members] well knew that Patzig's order to attack the lifeboats was unlawful." Both were convicted of manslaughter, but both soon escaped "apparently with the connivance of the jailers."[7] The court did not challenge the fact that the original order to sink the hospital ship may have been properly issued. Instead, the German court held that no reasonable person could think that it is morally or legally justifiable to sink lifeboats carrying medical personnel and patients.

This case is easy to understand from our moral minimalist perspective. It is clear that those who are in hospital ships are those most at risk of loss of basic security. Firing on hospital ships is a clear violation of the security interests of these people. It is even clearer that there is a violation of a moral minimum if these already badly off people are no longer on ships but are now in lifeboats. Shooting at lifeboats filled with sick people, who are not a threat to anyone, is surely a violation of the moral minimum of acceptable behavior.

In another case, greatly influenced by the Nuremberg proceedings, Lieutenant William Calley of the United States Army was tried for what came to be known as the "My Lai massacre." On March 16, 1968, hundreds of unarmed women, children, and elderly male Vietnamese were rounded up and killed by the soldiers of Charlie Company, 1st Battalion, 20th Infantry Division of the United States Army under Calley's direction. Calley declared that he himself was only following orders to kill everyone in the hamlet.[8] But Judge Kennedy, a United States military court judge, held that "'a man of ordinary sense and understanding' would see that it was unlawful to kill civilians as at My Lai."[9] According to the court, even if Calley had been ordered to lead his men against the civilians of My Lai, he should have been able to see that such orders were illegal and immoral. As we will see in subsequent sections, it is perhaps not as clear that Calley should have seen these acts to be immoral as that the U-boat crew should have seen their acts to be immoral, and this is because it was not clear that in the Calley case the security of the victims was the only security issue worthy of consideration.

It is interesting that in both of these cases, the imagery of "seeing" what is morally right is crucial. If it is self-evident to any normal person who perceives a certain situation that following an order is immoral, then that person cannot claim to be excused from responsibility in such cases merely because he or she was ordered to do a certain thing. But the question to ask is why an individual's responsibility turns on what a normal person would see as morally right or wrong. In the context of wartime cases, should we hold people to standards set for normal people given the abnormal conditions of the battlefield? The Nuremberg Trials stand for the proposition that it is indeed just this standard of normalcy that should be applied in some cases to the abnormal circumstances of war. In the next section, philosophical problems with this approach will be explored.

II. Normal Perception in Abnormal Times

"Moral perception" generally refers to the ability to ascertain what is morally salient in a given set of circumstances.[10] Moral sensitivity is that part of moral perception that concerns the ability to ascertain an appropriate response to these circumstances given the moral character of these circumstances and the expected moral reactions of others.[11] "Normal" moral sensitivity, if there is such a thing, seems to involve some average or general way of ascertaining what is morally salient. But does it make sense to judge people in terms of what the normal or average person would see to be morally right or wrong? If this judgment is to make sense, it should recognize that people's moral perceptions vary based on character and circumstance.

It could be argued that the concept of moral negligence is applicable here. Perhaps from the moral minimalist position sketched in the first chapters there are moral perceptions that are thought to be so basic that when they are lacking it is considered a fault of the agent. Aristotle was the first to set out a principle of moral negligence. In the *Nicomachean Ethics*, he says that it makes sense to punish those who are ignorant of what they ought to know about in the law. The reason for this is that "we assume that it is in their power not to be ignorant, since they have the power to take care."[12] And, according to Aristotle, people should take care that they are not ignorant of what is required of them. Ignorance can be a sign of a lack of basic moral perception and, at least on Aristotle's view, something that in light of we might punish.[13] It is plausible to think that those who fail to display care in terms of their moral perceptions cannot easily be relieved of responsibility for their negligence.

In this context, Aristotle brings up the example of a person who engages in harmful conduct while drunk. Aristotle says that although we cannot hold a person responsible for what he or she has done while drunk, since the action was not voluntary, we can hold the person responsible for getting drunk. It is then only a small step to holding that person responsible for actions that he or she could have foreseen while drunk. This is the kind of situation where we can speak of "moral negligence." We assume that it was in that person's power not to get drunk, and we might be able to punish on the basis of what that person knew or should have known to be illegal behavior after getting drunk. Is there a parallel with soldiers? I will explore this issue in some detail later. Here it is worth noting that some argue that the various excuses and defenses we will consider are blocked because by becoming soldiers they realized, or should have realized, that they would have to do immoral and illegal things.[14] The problem with such an argument is that it is not at all clear that soldiers should indeed expect to be given immoral and illegal orders, or at least this is a highly controversial assumption that would need a fair amount of argumentation to overcome its counter-intuitiveness.

Notice that Aristotle says that legal punishment must be premised on a failure to see what any person would know is "illegal," not merely immoral. In this sense, even Aristotle's view is more like a *moral minimalist* position rather than a full-blooded *natural law* position. The Nuremberg court, differing from Aristotle, seemed to say that it was sufficient for punishment that the knowledge one lacked, but should have had, was *moral* knowledge. The reader may wish to return to the discussions of the problems with such a view presented in the first few chapters of this book. Even if we follow this natural law approach, there are still very serious philosophical problems that result.

In an earlier book, I sketched an account of moral sensitivity as involving four overlapping components. Moral sensitivity involves (1) perceptiveness of the needs or feelings of others, (2) caring about the effects of one's action, (3) critical appreciation for what is morally relevant about the situation of those who are affected by one's behavior, and (4) motivation to act so as to minimize the harms and offenses that might result from one's behavior.[15] Although critical appreciation is the main moral motivator, it is at least a rudimentary moral perceptiveness that is absolutely necessary for sensitivity. One must be able to see what is, and is not, morally salient about a certain situation in order to be able to judge properly what the right thing to do is.

Part of moral sensitivity involves the sharing of perspectives where it is not sufficient for a person merely to perceive the world from his or her own "normal" perspective. It can make sense, in certain cases, to think of the morally perceptive act as potentially average or general, but relying on this type of moral perception in all, or even most, cases would not be sensitive to the differences among people. I may justifiably believe that any normal person would not take offense at a remark of mine, and yet, knowing that you are not normal, I will have failed in moral sensitivity if I continue to think that you are like normal people and will not be offended by that remark. It would be insufficiently attentive to who you are to base my reactions solely on how a normal person would react.

Similarly, the Nuremberg defense asks us to postulate a normal moral perception in abnormal times when there may be, perhaps because of the times, abnormal people. There are several ways of understanding what is postulated by the Nuremberg defense. It may be that what we are asked to do is to imagine what a normal person, unexposed to the vagaries of war, would think about the moral and legal permissibility of killing civilians in certain situations. Or, perhaps more plausibly, it may be that what we are asked is how someone who had been exposed to just what the soldier in question had been exposed to would think about killing civilians in certain situations. Or, finally, it may be that what we should be asking is whether someone just like this soldier, exposed to just what this soldier had been exposed to in wartime, would think about the killing of civilians in circumstances just like these. Of course, the last of these three alternatives would not get us very far since presumably someone just like the soldier in question *would* react just as the soldier in question *did* react. So we are left with the first two possibilities, to which I will now turn in more detail.

In the Anglo-American legal tradition, it is common to ask jury members to place themselves in the shoes of the defendant and then ask themselves whether they think the defendant's behavior was reasonable. The assumption is that any person on the street can tell whether some other person on the street is acting reasonably or not. This is because it is assumed that all humans have roughly the same capacities of moral perception and judgment. But what this seemingly fails to take into account is that even slight changes in the circumstances one faces, and even slight changes in the experiences through which one filters these circumstances, can make a profound difference in moral perception and judgment, perhaps making one person's moral situation opaque to that of another person.

In the discussion of wartime situations, differences in experience will make even a bigger difference in moral perceptions than would normally be true of two different people. Specifically, there is little in a person's normal experiences that can compare to being in the military uniform of a country that is at war with the country on whose soil one is currently trespassing. It is no exaggeration to say that a person's whole outlook changes when on enemy soil.[16] The normal reaction to strangers, where it is assumed that the stranger is trustworthy until proven otherwise, is turned on its head, so that the burden of proof is on the stranger to demonstrate trustworthiness, otherwise distrust will be the "norm."

Thomas Hobbes well illustrated the problem when he pointed out, more than 300 years ago, that "when taking a journey, [a man] arms himself, and seeks to go well accompanied."[17] When in foreign lands, especially when one is the enemy of the peoples of that land, one acts differently from when one is in the "normal" circumstances of one's home country. Such considerations lead me to think of the normal moral perceiver as someone who is deeply enmeshed in the particularities of given circumstances. We cannot plausibly ask whether a given person's battlefield response is reasonable without considering the specific battlefield circumstances that such a person faced.

We need to ascertain whether someone on the battlefield would have the moral perception to see an order as immoral or illegal and be able to exercise the moral choice to resist the order. The drafters of the Nuremberg defense seem to have contemplated just this eventuality, and chose generally not to prosecute ordinary soldiers, but instead to prosecute those officers in the Third Reich who were not blinded by the rhetoric of the Fuhrer or who did not feel coerced by the circumstances of their circumscribed roles.[18] The United Nations tried to codify this view when it established its own War Crimes Commission in 1948. For soldiers to be held responsible, it would have to be clear that "they commit[ted] acts which both violate unchallenged rules of warfare and outrage the general sentiment of mankind."[19] Here we have a version of the Nuremberg defense that once again calls for an assessment of what seems to violate the conscience of humanity, a topic we have already addressed, and that we will next explore in greater detail.

III. Outrage and the Sentiments of Humanity

The International Military Tribunal at Nuremberg was established to prosecute individuals for three kinds of action: (1) crimes against peace, including starting an unjust war, (2) war crimes, including murder or ill-treatment of prisoners of war, and (3) crimes against humanity, including an attack on a civilian population that involves the killing of innocent civilians and other human rights abuses.[20] This second category is the one that I have been focusing on in this chapter, and that I will now explore in greater detail in the rest of this section. For all three categories of action, the crimes are thought to be of sufficient importance and scope to warrant an international prosecution. These acts have in common the idea that something has been done that offends a basic human sense of justice, not merely a localized sense of what is fair or just.

The appeal to what would cause outrage in the general sentiments of humanity is a common way to think about the elements of normal moral perception of which each person is thought to be capable. Certain things are thought to be so heinous that any person would be outraged when perceiving them. The killing of civilians during wartime is one of the most commonly cited examples of just this kind of heinous act. But consider, for a moment, the conditions of warfare when one is acting in enemy territory. In some wartime situations, every person, soldier or civilian, is a potential threat. If the civilians seem to be unarmed, and the soldiers are armed, then the idea of the civilians as potential threats is only partially blunted, because the soldiers often do not know which civilians are members of the enemy forces.

Is it clearly an outrage against the sentiments of humanity for soldiers at My Lai to kill civilian men, women, and children? Initially it seems that the answer would be clearly "yes," as in fact was held by the American military tribunal that convicted Lieutenant Calley. The shooting of seemingly unarmed civilians, especially children, at point-blank range, appeared to be morally outrageous. Virtually all societies have had strong moral prohibitions against the taking of innocent life. The standard morally acceptable bases for justified killing – self-defense or defense of others – cannot be seen to justify killing those who do not have the capacity to harm or kill a well-armed, typically male, adult soldier. Soldiers have been trained to kill. When soldiers follow their training, and kill, it is not as much of an outrage as it would be for a non-soldier to engage in such killing. But when a soldier or non-soldier kills an innocent person, especially a child, this is considered to be enough of an outrage to our civilized instincts to think that it should be heavily sanctioned so as to prevent future acts of this sort at almost any cost.

In the My Lai massacre, it is uncontested that Lieutenant Calley and his men killed more than 100 unarmed civilian men, women, and children. But as one reads through the various court opinions in the case, there is quite a lot of disagreement of how best to characterize these killings. As I said, the military tribunal found Calley guilty of war crimes, and the Court of Military Review upheld the conviction. But the first civilian court to consider the case took a very different position. Here is how the U.S. District Court characterized some of the facts:

Petitioner was 25 years of age and ... had been an enlisted man for approximately 14 months ... The petitioner's first assignment in Vietnam was at Doc Pho. He had a short series of classes there and most of the instruction was given by ARVN instructors. This was his first indoctrination about the character of the potential enemy. He was told that women were as dangerous as men, and that children were even more dangerous because they were unsuspected. He was also informed that women were frequently better shots than the men and that the children were used to plant mines and booby traps.[21]

During Calley's earlier limited missions (the U.S. District Court continued),

the unit was continually subject to fire from unknown and unseen individuals. A number of men in the company had been killed or wounded and prior to the operation at My Lai Four they had never seen the persons responsible for the death or injuries of their buddies. Consequently, they formed the opinion that civilians were in part responsible.[22]

When Calley was supposedly told to go to My Lai and kill everyone there, his background assumption seems to have been that all of the people in the village, including men, women, and children, were enemies and potential threats. This U.S. District Court granted Calley's petition for habeas corpus relief in part because of how it understood the facts.

The U.S. Court of Appeals for the Fifth Circuit reversed the U.S. District Court, also at least in part because of its very different construal of the factual record. Here is how the Circuit Court of Appeals viewed some of the relevant facts:

Lieutenant Calley was the 1st platoon leader in Company C ... and had been stationed in Vietnam since December of 1967. Prior to March 16, 1968, his unit had received little combat experience. On March 15, members of the unit were briefed that they were to engage the enemy in an offensive action in the area of My Lai (4). The troops were informed that the area had long been controlled by the Viet Cong, and that they could expect heavy resistance ... .[23]

This report was fairly close to the lower court opinion, but then an account of the massacre was given:

The attack began early in the morning of March 16. Calley's platoon was landed on the outskirts of My Lai after about five minutes of artillery and gunship fire. The assault met little resistance of hostile fire. After cautiously approaching My Lai (4), C Company discovered only unarmed, unresisting old men, women and children eating breakfast or beginning the day's chores although intelligence reports had indicated that the villagers would be gone to market. Encountering only civilians and no enemy soldiers, Calley's platoon, which was to lead the sweep through the hamlet, quickly became disorganized.

Some soldiers undertook the destruction of livestock, foodstuffs and buildings as ordered. Others collected and evacuated the Vietnamese civilians and then proceeded systematically to slaughter the villagers.[24]

In reversing the U.S. District Court, the Circuit Court of Appeals seemed to see the My Lai incident as nothing other than a "slaughter" of "unarmed, unresisting old men, women and children eating breakfast."

What complicated the picture in My Lai was that the distinction between civilian and combatant had become blurred, with even fairly small children being used to transport weapons. So while there may be strong sentiments against the killing of civilians, especially children, there was a possible defense in the case of My Lai that might have been an exception to the moral judgment about what was normally acceptable or appropriate behavior. For there was reason, according to the US District Court, to believe that some civilians, and even some children, could be trying to inflict injury or death on the American soldiers in this Vietnamese hamlet. At Calley's military trial, and also in the U.S. Circuit Court of Appeals, such reasons were indeed considered and rejected, after much discussion and debate. But the U.S. District Court seemed to believe that some of the civilians who were killed might have been thought to be threats to the soldiers in Lieutenant Calley's unit.

In retrospect, it seems to many that the District Court opinion was seriously flawed. For even if Calley had feared that the civilians in the My Lai hamlet might be enemy soldiers in disguise, they gave no indication that they were armed or that they were posing an immediate threat to Calley and his men.[25] But in partial defense of the District Court, I would point out that we do not always require that soldiers prove that enemy soldiers pose an immediate threat before it is considered justifiable to kill them. It may be too late by the time it is discovered that suspected enemy soldiers are concealing not only their identities but also their weapons. Although I remain suspicious of such an argument, it is not utterly implausible when applied to civilians for the District Court judges to have come to this conclusion. The point here is not to argue that Calley should have been relieved of responsibility, but only to indicate that even in this seemingly clear case, two courts came to very different conclusions about how to regard this "massacre," based on how they reconstructed the threat faced by Calley and his men in Vietnam.

This discussion does not call into question the normal sentiment that innocent life should be preserved. Rather, what is uncertain is the very judgment that a certain adult, or even a child, is to be seen as an innocent person. And yet it is this judgment, really a matter of moral perception, that is crucial to the determination of whether it was indeed an outrage for Lieutenant Calley's unit to kill civilians in the hamlet of My Lai in Vietnam. Normally, things would be clearer. But here we are dealing with several levels of abnormality. First, of course, it was wartime and not the normality of peacetime. Second, even for a wartime situation, things were abnormal given that the members of the enemy forces were often disguised as average-looking civilians. And there had been widespread reports of these "civilians" attacking U.S. army regulars. For these reasons, the perception that killing people who appear to be civilians is wrong was called into question.

We can contrast the My Lai case with the German U-Boat case. In the latter case, we have the bombing of a hospital ship, and then the bombing of the lifeboats that had been lowered to try to rescue those injured and sick patients who were on board the hospital ship. There is no narrative that I am aware of concerning a possible justification here, and no court discovered such a possibility. It is possible that the hospital ship was really a masquerading enemy warship. Mere possibility is not sufficient, and yet this was all there was in this case. After the ship had been bombed, and the lifeboats were clearly filled with sick and injured patients, none of whom posed a threat to the people on the U-Boat, there is no reasonable debate about the wrongness of sinking those lifeboats. They could not possibly have posed a risk to the U-Boat or to others in the waters around them. Here, the appeal to the outraged sentiments of humanity seems apt.

Moral choice is dependent on the moral perception of alternative courses of action. If someone has a gun to your head, you will react by reflex to the threat as if you literally have no choice. When soldiers are threatened, or feel threatened, by enemy troops and "civilians," as well as when they are threatened by their superiors, choice may indeed be limited. This is at least in part because they do not perceive reasonable alternative forms of action to those that they have been commanded to perform. Moral choice is the sub-category of choice that concerns those alternative possibilities that are seen as morally acceptable and appropriate. Here is where moral perception becomes motivationally important, for one may feel that one has alternatives but not perceive any of them to be acceptable given what one perceives to be salient in the situation at hand. In the next section, I will turn to the question of whether our conceptual worries about the appeal to what would be outrageous to the sentiments of humanity will help set a reasonable limit to what is expected of people, especially soldiers and other minor players.

IV. Restricted Moral Choices

As mentioned earlier, there are two parts to the Nuremberg defense. The first part, which we have just been exploring, concerns the assessment of what is perceived to be the morally or legally permissible thing to do in the circumstances. Moral perception here is filtered through the lens of what humanity would consider outrageous. But the second part concerns whether there was a moral choice to act differently than the soldiers acted. We might also appeal to the moral sentiments of humanity here. In the most extreme cases, such an appeal to the sentiments of humanity will help, but this will not be true in most of the cases.

In U.S. tort law, one way to make sense of whether one is liable for a given harm that one did not intend to cause is to ask whether one violated a duty of care owed to the person harmed. To ascertain if one had such a duty, one looks, among other things, at what the burden would have been to the agent if the agent had conformed to the duty.[26] If the crucial issue before us concerns the possible culpable ignorance or moral negligence of soldiers, then the tort analysis of duty and negligence becomes relevant.[27] What makes many battlefield situations so tragic is that the cost of acting with due care toward civilians is often that the soldiers risk death to themselves. In non-battlefield situations, one is hardly ever faced with imminent death if one exercises due care toward others in one's life. It is for this reason that the superior orders defense shows up most commonly in battlefield situations, and not very often off the battlefield.

Think again of the conspiracy as a model of most types of shared or collective responsibility. If Jones, Smith, and Rodriguez recruit Green to drive the getaway car in a bank robbery scheme Jones has cooked up, then it makes sense to think of all four as collectively responsible for the resulting bank robbery. This is especially apparent if Green is paid well for her contribution and understands full well how her contribution to this joint venture will aid in its successful completion. The driver, Green, is a cog in a machine-like enterprise that will make the robbery possible in ways that would not be true if any of the four people involved were acting on their own, or in only a loosely connected manner. For this reason, they are collectively responsible for the results of their joint undertaking. And their individual responsibility will depend on the role that each played in the joint venture.[28]

Suppose that while Green is driving away from the scene of the crime, a pedestrian steps off a curb in the path of the gang's fleeing car. Green, a generally compassionate person, begins to apply the brakes, but Jones, the insensitive ringleader, puts a gun to Green's head and says, "Drive on! If we slow down now, we'll all be caught." Should Green be held responsible for the injuries to the pedestrian as well as for the robbery? On the assumption that no one held a gun to Green's head to get her to join the conspiracy in the first place, Green seems to be in a different moral position with respect to the pedestrian's injuries than with respect to the robbery itself. Certainly Green appeared to have a choice of whether or not to join the robbery conspiracy, but not much of a choice, if she had a choice at all, about whether to run down the pedestrian. Was it a moral choice of Green's to ignore the order given by Jones? There are many parallel cases in international law, such as when a soldier or subordinate feels that his or her life is threatened if he or she does not follow orders; the same considerations should be operative, making us reluctant to say that, in such situations, there is a moral choice available to the soldier.

Now consider a second scenario. Imagine that Green had agreed to join the robbery conspiracy, only to find that Jones was a tyrant who threatened and physically abused his cohorts if they did not do exactly what he told them to do. In fact, Jones had shot and killed a previous getaway driver who had disobeyed Jones's orders. Does our assessment of Green's responsibility change if in this scenario, Jones merely orders Green not to slow down? Interestingly, I think that most people's intuitions would change in this case even though Green will probably pay a high price for disregarding Jones's orders. What has changed is the probability that Green will have to pay this price for acting in a responsible manner.

In the first scenario, with the gun pointed at Green's head, the probability that serious harm will befall Green for not complying with Jones's orders is very high. In the second scenario, with Jones merely ordering Green not to stop, against the backdrop of serious injury befalling previous people who disobeyed Jones, the probability that Green will have to pay a serious price for non-compliance is not as high as in the first scenario. As the probability decreases that Green will be forced to pay a high price for failing to follow Jones's orders, it becomes more reasonable to hold Green responsible for the injuries to the pedestrian.

When we speak of whether a person had a moral choice or not, normally we mean whether the alternatives open included ones that were morally permissible. In addition, at least part of the concept of moral choice concerns whether there were alternatives open that could be considered reasonable. In most situations, it is not part of one's moral choices, and hence too much to expect, that one should have done something highly dangerous, or otherwise unreasonable. If the only way we can avoid harming another person is to put our own lives in grave jeopardy, then it is not a moral choice to avoid harming this other person. For this reason, we need to explore the limits of unreasonable behavior.

As the probability increases that one will pay a high price for non-compliance with an order, then non-compliance becomes less and less reasonable, and we are less and less inclined to say that one had a reasonable moral choice not to comply. As the probability decreases that one will have to pay a high price for non-compliance, then it makes sense to begin to speak of a reasonable moral choice open to the agent in question. On the assumption that people should only be held responsible for their actions where they have a choice, the assessment of whether an agent is responsible will depend on whether reasonable alternatives are open – that is, whether the agent had alternatives that did not involve a high probability that there would be a high price to pay for choosing that alternative course of action.[29]

This analysis is drawn from a tort law model, as I indicated, first proposed by Judge Learned Hand. It could be objected that it is inappropriate to use this tort model for criminal guilt, or at least that the model needs to be adjusted, because the criminal law normally deals with more serious harms than does tort law. I would generally agree with this criticism. Although we want to deter accidents, we have an even stronger desire to deter criminal behavior. But we also recognize that criminal guilt carries with it a greater penalty than does tort liability. For this reason, there are generally more defenses available to the criminal defendant than the tort defendant. So, all things considered, Learned Hand's analysis may need to be adjusted when we are dealing with criminal cases, but the adjustment need not be severe.

In cases of collective guilt, subtleties of context are still relevant in determining how to apportion blame to the members of the group, especially concerning legal blame and guilt. But I am not proposing a purely subjective standard. We are not held to what a given person actually believed in a certain situation, but rather to what a reasonable person would have believed. But we do need to modify the standard "reasonable person" test in that we need to place the reasonable person into the specific context that the actual person was faced with. And to do that, it is often necessary to bring in some of the beliefs of the actual person in considering what a "reasonable person" would have done. Battlefield situations are so abnormal that it will often be hard merely to drop a "reasonable person" into that situation without taking into account how the actual person in question reacted to that situation.

War crimes tribunals have had to decide what price is too high to pay in order to expect people reasonably to exercise due care not to injure one another. In the case of Lieutenant Calley, it may be true that he and his soldiers feared for their own lives if they did not do what they thought they had been legitimately ordered to do. But was this more like the first bank robbery scenario or more like the second, described earlier? Calley never claimed that someone literally had a gun to his head, forcing him to shoot the civilians. And even his concern that the seemingly innocent civilians might be enemies in disguise was not sufficient to establish the proposition that he had no other moral choice but to follow orders, for it is important to consider what sort of threat those civilians posed. If the killing of civilians had been clearly and unambiguously wrong, then Calley would have needed a very strong showing that he had no moral choice but to do what was clearly and unambiguously wrong. The question to be asked, and one I am not in a position to answer, is whether a reasonable person in Calley's situation would believe that these civilians posed a threat to his safety, and that of his troops. If so, then perhaps even here moral choice was restricted.

Next, let us consider briefly what to make of the Nuremberg revisions to the superior-orders defense for those who are not in battlefield situations. This will have special relevance to the use of the superior orders defense in crimes against humanity where the nexus to war is very tenuous, or missing altogether. One thing seems clear from the outset – namely, if it is hard to find situations in wartime where moral choice is so restricted that one has no legitimate options but to act immorally, in peacetime there are likely to be even fewer such cases.

What will be needed is a case in which the costs of doing what is right are very high and where the probabilities are also very high that one will have to bear these costs. And it is the probability criterion that will often be the hardest to meet – for both the probability and the cost of non-compliance must be very high. Moral choice must be greatly restricted in order for us to excuse a person from responsibility for actions done with full knowledge that it was wrong so to act.

Consider the case of someone who is threatened with loss of his job if he does not do something that risks harm to another.[30] Certainly loss of a job is sometimes almost as important a cost as is loss of life on the battlefield, especially if one has to support not just oneself but also other family members. For this reason, the moral sentiments of humanity will not always unambiguously say that it is wrong to risk injury to others. Indeed, it is my view that we should not ignore the conflicts that many professionals face in which they are threatened with job loss for not complying with a superior's orders to act in morally questionable ways.[31] Of course, the threat must be real, and there must be very little prospect of finding another source of employment, as well as a serious likelihood that one would be made as worse off as is the harm that one risks causing to others.

Non-battlefield situations are important to international criminal law, since the war nexus is no longer required for crimes against humanity. Indeed, many cases before the Yugoslav Tribunal concern the actions of camp guards who were not engaged in battlefield situations.[32] The most difficult part of trying to use the superior orders defense in non-battlefield situations concerns the question of whether the probability is indeed high that the threatened harms will befall a person if he or she does not comply with his or her superior's orders. Unlike the battlefield situation, there is often much less predictability about what will happen in situations of non-compliance in the non-wartime cases. And the number of known options that one has is also much greater than in wartime cases. In the non-wartime cases, there is much greater recourse to the legal process or the media as a way to prevent one's superior from retaliating for one's non-compliance. So while the harms risked by non-compliance in the non-wartime cases may be just as grave as in wartime, the probability that the harms will befall the non-complying agent are not normally nearly as high as would be true in the battlefield cases. Of course, if there is a civil war, as in some of the Balkan cases, then crimes against humanity can be treated very similarly to war crimes, since there will also be battlefield situations as well.

If battlefield situations become less and less like the state of nature, where men fought with all of their strength for their very lives, and more and more like computer video games, the applicability of the superior orders defense even to wartime situations will likewise be lessened, just as is true of non-wartime cases. The Persian Gulf War of 1991 saw commanders giving orders for bombs to be dropped from very high altitudes or from ships hundreds of miles from their targets. It was generally not true that the majority of these soldiers risked personal loss of life or liberty at the hands of the enemy soldiers. Soldiers were much more likely to be technicians who did their jobs far from enemy lines than to be embroiled in life-threatening trench warfare. For this reason, some wartime situations now more closely resemble normal than abnormal situations.

But there are still cases where the Nuremberg version of the superior orders defense will be applicable. Consider the case of paramilitary forces existing in the former Yugoslavia. These forces were often more brutal than were the regular army units in past military operations. Also consider that regular army units will increasingly deal with peacekeeping missions that will take place in hostile civilian populations, where the considerations that applied to Calley's men will be even more apparent and dangerous. Nonetheless, it should be obvious that the Nuremberg revisions to the superior orders defense make it harder than in previous centuries for defendants to justify their battlefield actions. In the next section, we will consider more recent revisions to the superior orders defense that seemingly return somewhat to the older version of the defense. We will also briefly explore what by now should be apparent – that the various conceptualizations thought to be central to the superior orders defense are not synonymous with one another, indeed often clashing with one another. Even when considering the most recent revisions of the superior orders defense, conceptual problems are rampant.

V. Articles 31 and 33 of the ICC Charter

I will now discuss the further refinement to the superior orders defense that has been incorporated into the statute of the permanent International Criminal Court. Article 33 of the ICC Charter reads as follows:

1. The fact that a crime within the jurisdiction of the Court has been committed by a person pursuant to an order of a Government or of a superior, whether military or civilian, shall not relieve that person of criminal responsibility unless:
   (a) The person was under a legal obligation to obey orders of the Government of the superior in question;
   (b) The person did not know that the order was unlawful; and
   (c) The order was not manifestly unlawful.
2. For the purposes of this article, orders to commit genocide or crimes against humanity are manifestly unlawful.[33]

It will be recalled that the two prongs of the Nuremberg defense were:

1. That the soldier reasonably believes that a superior's order was legally and morally valid, and
2. That the soldier believes that following a superior's order was the only morally reasonable course of action open.

And it will also be recalled that the pre-Nuremberg version of the defense simply said that if orders were given to a soldier, then following those orders was a defense to that soldier's supposed criminal behavior.

The three versions of the superior-orders defense span the spectrum of ways to view the claim that one was just following orders. Before Nuremberg, proving such a claim in most cases was sufficient to relieve one of responsibility for war crimes. Instead, it was the person issuing the order who was held responsible. At Nuremberg, the defense was weakened in that claims were rejected when the soldier knew the order was illegal or immoral and should not have followed it even though it had been duly issued. As we have seen, the Nuremberg defense of superior orders required quite complex matters of moral perception. In some respects, the ICC statute seems to go one step further along the continuum toward eliminating the defense altogether, putting even more hurdles in the way of the successful use of the defense in that certain orders should be known to be illegal, regardless of what the soldier actually knew.

The new wording of the ICC Statute seemingly removes any reference to the morality of the order – or to the moral choices of the agent – from the defense. These new changes seemingly construe the defense solely in terms of what the soldier was legally obligated to do, thereby moving away from the Nuremberg superior orders defense. The only remaining oblique reference to the Nuremberg defense's criteria of moral choices and perceptions of the soldier is to be found in the claim that the court will assume that it is "manifestly unlawful" for a soldier to be ordered to commit acts of genocide or crimes against humanity. The reference to what is manifest is a carryover from the Nuremberg ideas, but even here there is no explicit reference to morality. Nonetheless, there does appear to be something beyond the legality of the posited order that the soldier must consider. Thus it appears that the ICC version of the superior orders defense is only a partial moral retreat from the Nuremberg defense.

"Manifest illegality" is a term that has been in use since the early part of the twentieth century to denote the most important members of the class of exceptions to the superior orders defense that we have been considering.[34] Generally, "manifest illegality" refers to "the most transparent forms of illegality."[35] As could have been predicted, the term was not well-defined, and interpretations ran the gamut from including all illegal acts to including none at all. The latter option was embraced when it seemed that for something to be manifest it must be the case that no reasonable soldier could fail to see it as a limit on his or her behavior in all situations, and yet battlefield conditions were so varied as to negate the category.[36] As we have seen, this interpretation is a mistake, for the idea of what is unreasonable in battlefield situations can be understood to include many things, including the bombing of hospital ships and life rafts. The ICC Statute anticipates this problem by spelling out at least two forms of manifest illegality – crimes against humanity and genocide. Even though the term refers to *illegal* and not *immoral* acts, there seems to be a partial convergence with the Nuremberg defense, since ascertaining what is manifest requires use of moral perception.

Although there seems to be some reference to the appropriate perceptions of the soldier, insofar as the soldier is expected to be aware of certain manifest legal norms, all reference to moral choice has dropped out of the ICC version of the superior orders defense. Defendants cannot claim the defense by showing that they were unaware that a given order was immoral, or that no other morally reasonable choices were open to them at the time. But, conceptually, the new ICC standard is hard to make sense of without some additional reference to moral perceptions, as was also true of the Nuremberg defense. For what is manifestly illegal depends on what it was indeed reasonable to do in a given situation, as was shown earlier, and such an assessment turns on whether, in a given situation, a reasonable person's moral perceptions would indicate manifest illegality. It is not at all clear what "manifestly illegal" would even mean in this context, unless it is to be interpreted as a kind of strict liability.

Some of this difficulty may be solved by the fact that the ICC statute also has a clearly recognized defense of "duress" to charges of international criminality. Article 31 specifies that criminal responsibility will be excluded where the conduct

has been caused by duress resulting from a threat of imminent death or of continuing or imminent serious bodily harm against that person or another person, and the person acts necessarily and reasonably to avoid the threat, provided that the person does not intend to cause a greater harm than the one sought to be avoided. Such a threat may either be:

(i) Made by other persons; or
(ii) Constituted by other circumstances beyond the person's control.[37]

Thus, if the defendant does have evidence showing that moral choices were eliminated, the consideration of moral choice, while no longer explicitly linked to the superior orders defense, could arise again in a different defense option – concerning duress. The duress defense could reopen important moral avenues of defense that were seemingly closed by the ICC's new superior orders defense.

In a 1997 case from the Yugoslav tribunal, Prosecutor v. Erdemovic, Judges McDonald and Vohrah, writing for the majority, denied "the availability of duress as a complete defense to combatants who have killed innocent persons."[38] Their argument was buttressed by policy considerations. If duress were to be allowed for cases of killing innocent civilians, then this would be "tantamount to both encouraging the subordinate under duress to kill such persons with impunity . . . and also helping the superior in his attempt to kill them."[39] But these judges were willing to consider duress as a mitigating factor in the assessment of punishment in such cases.[40] We saw earlier that allowing defenses to the killing of civilians does not necessarily encourage such acts or send the signal that such killing can be done with impunity.

Judge Cassese dissented, arguing that there was no basis in international law for such policy considerations.[41] Rather, he strongly argued that there is a general rule of international criminal law permitting the defense of duress even in cases of killing innocent civilians. Nonetheless, there was a restriction based on the principle of proportionality, so that one could not use the defense in such cases unless one's own life was indeed threatened.[42] This is similar to the conclusion reached in earlier sections of this chapter, especially as we considered variations on the bank robbery example. Cassese seems on the right track in recognizing the importance of the security interests of the defendant.

If the ICC follows the precedent of the Yugoslav Tribunal's majority opinion in the Erdemovic case, then Article 31 will not allow duress to be used as a defense to the charge of murder, except in those cases where the supposedly "innocent" victim had clearly threatened the life of the defendant. But it may be allowed for lesser charges, and will in any event be available as a mitigating factor for sentencing. Thus the ICC will not allow duress, or duress in combination with superior orders, to be a defense to the charge of killing innocent civilians. But it will still be open for defendants to argue that the supposedly "innocent" civilians were not truly innocent. As I indicated earlier, it may even be possible to consider such defenses as duress in cases such as that of Lieutenant Calley, as the U.S. District Court seemingly did.

I believe that the ICC should follow Cassese's dissent. The ICC Statute should expand the duress defense to include the killing of "innocent" civilians. While it is unclear whether the ICC will allow a combination of Articles 33 and 31 together to form a defense for such cases as well as murder and less serious crimes, I believe that the ICC should do so. If so, the recent revisions, embodied in the ICC statute, have not moved us further toward eliminating the superior orders defense. Following Cassese's dissent is consistent with the general ideas behind the security principle that I developed in earlier chapters. If a soldier is placed in a battlefield situation and fears for his or her life, we should be slow to apply rules that are designed for normal people in normal situations. The security principle, now applied to defendants and not to victims, would mean that our expectations for these defendants should be lowered since they had effectively entered a kind of state of nature.

I believe that regardless of how the ICC Statute is interpreted, international criminal defendants have several options available that should make it harder for prosecutors to get convictions. The salient question is how the ICC should view the second prong of the duress defense – that concerning threats "constituted by circumstances beyond the person's control." For instance, is the sheer scope and hostility of the ethnic cleansing campaign something that itself acted to coerce various Serbs by duress into harming Muslims and Croats in Bosnia and Kosovo? The Yugoslav Appellate Tribunal said "no." But I believe that the ICC should follow the lead of Judge Cassese's dissent. If the ICC follows Cassese's lead, the duress defense will be available to those accused of crimes against humanity, even though they are otherwise barred from using the superior orders defense for such crimes.

I have indicated in this chapter that the refinements of the superior orders defense that were worked out at the Nuremberg trials, and in subsequent proceedings, pose various conceptual puzzles. Nonetheless, the Nuremberg version of the superior orders defense does provide a largely justifiable and workable way to assess wartime cases concerning people who acted wrongly because they were ordered to do so. In some cases, what has happened is that the refinement of the standards has made it harder for soldiers to show that they really were blocked by their superior's orders from doing the right thing. But in other cases, it will still be possible for soldiers to mount a defense, perhaps based on duress, since the world has generally not become less hostile to soldiers. The modern wartime superior orders defense recognizes that in most situations, soldiers are not automatons, nor does fear eliminate all alternative actions; but fear may still be a legitimate basis for urging that one be excused from responsibility. Soldiers and non-soldiers alike need to be held to a standard of responsibility that is appropriate for autonomous agents whose world is often hostile. In the next chapter, we turn to various procedural "defenses" that should be given greater weight than they have been given by international criminal tribunals if there is to be anything that can be called an "international rule of law."

11

The International Rule of Law

"The rule of law" has come to stand for the requirement that law be governed by procedures that are applied fairly and without bias in favor of one group or another, not even in favor of the lawmakers themselves. On this view, authority is to be based on rules and not on the wills of particular persons. The rule of law is opposed to the arbitrary exercise of power, what is sometimes called "the rule of man." In the international arena, the exercise of control by the powerful has often been claimed to be the basis of a kind of authority. The legitimacy of international tribunals, even more than domestic tribunals, depends on law's being based on the rule of law and not on the rule of a powerful State. The common charge of victors' justice, made in nearly every international prosecution, calls attention to the need for an international rule of law. The procedural restraints on authority are aimed at reducing the likelihood, and even the appearance, of bias on the part of those who judge. For this reason, international tribunals should, among other things, only apply laws prospectively, only apply laws in a way that is evenhanded concerning all who committed the offenses, and only mete out punishments that are clearly deserved.

In this chapter, I consider some procedural safeguards that should be given great weight in international criminal law. A consideration of these safeguards will make us proceed with caution in responding to the growing demand to expand international prosecutions. I advance the argument that international criminal law needs to respond to the demands of the rule of law, and that this demand should be given much greater weight than the more common demands for quicker trials and more prosecutions made by victims' rights groups. Responding to the rule of law does not mean that there is no room for considerations of discretion on the part of judges, but only that arbitrariness and bias be eliminated as much as possible. Because of the precarious status of international law, the *international* rule of law is even more in need of protection than is the *domestic* rule of law.

In section I, I discuss the general issue of what is involved in the rule of law. Then, in Sections II and III, I address the classic procedural problems of retroactivity and selective prosecution. Section IV involves a discussion of the hardest of all the conceptual problems facing international criminal prosecutions, the problem of how the penalty is supposed to fit the international crime. This last issue is especially difficult because there has been no tradition of punishing international criminals according to a consistent rationale. In Section V, I return to a Hobbesian approach to issues of authority and sovereignty, developed in the earlier chapters of the book, in order to give fuller philosophical justification to the international rule of law. The international rule of law is always a contentious matter, on which a great deal of good conceptual work needs to be done both to clarify and to render respectable the domain of international criminal law. In addition, defendants' rights depend crucially on a fully worked out set of procedural guarantees in order for international prosecutions to be considered legitimate.

I. The Concept of the Rule of Law

The rule of law needs to be conceptualized somewhat differently in international law than in domestic law. In this section, I will explore the idea of a rule of law in detail, and respond to several recent attempts to articulate a rule of law for the international arena. I will also provide a sketch of what the rule of law means in its procedural sense,[1] thereby offering a framework for considering the specific defenses based on the rule of law to be discussed in the following sections. The rule of law is especially important for international law since international law is not immediately seen as deserving of fidelity and respect.

The rule of law can be understood either *procedurally* or *substantively*. In this chapter, I will be mainly concerned with the procedural rule of law. In general, the "rule of law" is supposed to be contrasted with the "rule of man." When individual humans engage in unfettered rule, there is a high likelihood that they will make decisions based on their own interests and those of their friends and acquaintances. When individual rulers are restrained by laws, setting the proper limits of individual human action and decision-making, there is less likelihood of bias and arbitrariness. Procedurally, the rule of law guarantees that similar cases will be treated in a similarly fair manner.[2] Substantively, the rule of law guarantees that decision-making will conform to standards of justice, such as that punishment be awarded only where it is actually due, that are for serious matters of wrongdoing (crimes *mala in se*). At the international level, there is even greater possibility of abuse than in the domestic sphere since there is less individual accountability because of the lack of democratic procedures and coordinated oversight.

The international rule of law is often equated with the thwarting of impunity – that is, with the guarantee that all wrongdoers will be convicted and punished. But conviction and punishment is surely only one part of what would count as an international rule of law. We want to make sure that *wrongdoers* are not allowed to walk free merely because of who they are or who their friends and family members are. We also want to make sure that prosecutions do not occur because of an undue concern for who the *victims* are or who their friends and family members are. The rule of law does not play favorites, but in its neutrality it often appears in practice to favor defendants, when it corrects for bias against defendants caused by the strong power differential in favor of prosecutors. This is even more the case in the international arena, where the knowledge, skill, and resources of the prosecutors often dwarf those of the defendants.

The rule of law is the rallying cry that aims to defeat all forms of personal and group bias in the administration of government and law. To accomplish this goal, the advocates of the rule of law generally propose procedures that must be followed in all cases of a certain sort, and that minimize divergence from these procedures, minimizing especially the exercise of discretion by judges and prosecutors that could allow in bias and arbitrariness. The rule of law is often associated with a set of rights and rules that protect defendants and victims alike. The institution of courts, with impartial judges, is often seen as the cornerstone of the rule of law. It is thus not surprising that defenders of the international rule of law have been at the forefront of those who pay careful attention to procedural constraints in international criminal prosecutions.

Throughout the next few pages, I will summarize some of the restraints most commonly listed in discussions of the rule of law. There is wide consensus among theorists about many of these restraints, although, as we will see, there is also some disagreement, especially when we move to more substantive provisions of the rule of law. There are four major categories of procedural restraints that are thought to be necessary for law to be properly binding. Those restraints are based on the following minimal requirements: for there to be rules, for there to be a coherent system of rules, for there to be fair administration of rules, and for there to be fair interpretation of rules. In addition, more substantively, it is thought that law must conform to a minimal sense of justice, or a broader conception of moral principles such as the moral rights articulated in various constitutional documents.[3] I will discuss each of these categories of restraint in turn.

First, there are procedural restraints based on the nature of rules. Some of these restraints are merely the articulation of what it means minimally to have rule-governed human behavior. This aspect of the rule of law is probably the least controversial. Here are five restraints commonly mentioned under this label:

1. The rules must be general, not specific.
2. The rules must be prospective, not retrospective.
3. The rules must be public, not secret.
4. The rules must be knowable, not obscure.
5. The rules must require behavior that is performable, not impossible to perform.

In all five cases, it is often said that there could not be true rule-governed behavior if any of these features were missing. If these restraints were not in place, there would be such a strong possibility of arbitrariness as to make it unlikely that rules were the basis of decisions. When rules are secret, for instance, there is no possibility of public accountability. Nonetheless, in Section II of this chapter, we will see that some of these seemingly uncontroversial restraints, such as the prohibition on retroactivity, are actually more controversial than might appear at first.

Second, there are procedural restraints based on the minimal systematicity of rules. For there to be a system of rules, restraints must be placed on the rules in order to make sure that the rules form a coherent body. There are three more restraints commonly listed under this heading:

6. The rules must be consistent with each other, not conflicting.
7. The rules must cohere, not be unconnected to each other.
8. The rules must not be arbitrarily changed.

In these three cases, if any of these features were missing, there would not really be a system of rules, but at most only a set or loose collection of rules. Systems entail that the members be related to each other in a way that identifies them all as of the same sort.

Third, there are procedural restraints based on what it means for a system of rules to be fairly administered, or even to be said to be administered at all. If there is no fair administration of the rules, there is also no system of rules that would constitute law. Here are three more commonly mentioned procedural restraints:

9. The rules must not be selectively enforced.
10. The rules must be reflected in what the administrators are doing.
11. Penalties or punishments must be proportionate to the offense.

These restraints begin to define a procedurally fair system of rules. Again, the key concern is that arbitrariness be minimized in the application or administration of these rules.

Fourth, there are procedural restraints based on the fair interpretation of rules. These procedural restraints are probably the most controversial of all of the aspects of the rule of law. Three procedural restraints are sometimes proposed:

12. Disputes about the interpretation of rules must be resolved by public hearings.
13. Disputes about interpretation must be resolved by the acts of independent judges.
14. Disputes about interpretation must be subject to appellate review.

These aspects of the rule of law have indeed been definitive of the Western, Anglo-American model of law, but may not be necessary for the rule of law in general. It remains deeply controversial, for instance, as to whether independent appellate review of the interpretation of rules is necessary for the rule of law, or merely a good thing to have, all other things being equal. Military tribunals often lack these features. Some contend that this makes military tribunals not truly legal, but merely extra-legal. Others contend that military tribunals are legal proceedings that conform to the rule of law, but that they are not as fair as tribunals that have these additional restraints and procedures in place.

For the sake of completeness, I should now mention that there are various commonly voiced challenges to the procedural rule of law. I will summarize three criticisms that can be raised against the idea of the rule of law, leaving until later a discussion of particular aspects of the rule of law discussed above. First, certain provisions of the rule of law, even those uncontroversial provisions, seem to conflict with other provisions, making the rule of law an ideal, but not always a realizable threshold or required minimum for binding law. The requirement that laws must be knowable (rule 4) seems to conflict with the requirement that laws must be general (rule 1). The generality of law will mean that there will be many instances where it is unclear whether or not a case falls under the rule. But if we must wait for the ultimate determination of a judge to clear up this uncertainty, then the law was, at the time the defendant acted, unknowable by a layperson.[4]

Second, there are also challenges to the procedural rule of law based on a perceived conflict between the rule of law and popular democratic rule. Legislators change quite frequently, and new laws will be enacted without the current legislators, who are themselves often different from the legislators who enacted the old laws, ensuring that the new laws do not conflict with old laws. In addition, because of the way that legislative compromises are reached, it will not be clear, until a court rules, what the binding rule in a particular case is. Yet the messiness of legislation is a necessary feature of popular sovereignty. And judges who try to uphold the rule of law by resolving these inconsistencies will be acting against popular democratic sovereignty. Consider, for example, a 2001 dispute in Thailand in which the Constitutional Court ruled that the very popular Prime Minister, Thaksin Shinawatra, had to step down from elected office because he had violated financial disclosure laws.[5]

Third, there is a challenge to the rule of law brought by those who support the principles of equity, as well as forms of equitable relief such as pardons and amnesties, that are seen to be at odds with the rule of law. Since the rule of law demands that there be strict conformity to public rules, there is little room for the kind of discretion that is necessary for the application of the principles of equity. Since equity requires a certain flexibility and discretion so that judges can fit the law to concrete cases, often not contemplated by the lawmakers, it will not be possible for interpretive rules to be adhered to. For equity to remain a function of legal systems, it may be that the rule of law cannot be conceived as providing unbending procedural restraints.[6] We will present a more detailed examination of this issue in the final chapter (Chapter 13).

As we now turn to the so-called international rule of law, we find that one of the main problems, first voiced by H. L. A. Hart, is that international law is at best a set of rules, not a system of rules, since there is no master rule (or rule of recognition). We can return to the three features mentioned under this heading (rules 6–8). Codification of law projects, such as the recent Rome Convention setting out a list of crimes that are proscribed in international law, help relieve some of the sting of Hart's criticism. But his main point is untouched by codes of law, since these codes do not necessarily cohere, and in any event, codes do not generally supply the rule of recognition that Hart finds missing in international law. As we have seen in previous chapters, as long as international law continues to be driven by customary norms, with *opinio juris* so hard to define, customary international rule of law will remain generally problematical.

All of the criticisms of the rule of law mentioned here are even more appropriately placed at the door of international law than at the door of domestic law. International law is in many respects still in its infancy in terms of the fidelity and respect that people display toward it. It is too often said that international law cannot be separated from politics, especially the political disputes between developed and developing states. When an international court such as the Yugoslav Tribunal acts, its decisions are often challenged as blatantly political – that is, as the expressions of the biases of the Western powers, or perhaps only of the United States. For this reason, there is a great need for the clear establishment of the features of the rule of law in the international domain. The international rule of law would have to display similar features as the domestic rule of law, but perhaps these features would have to be more scrupulously followed in order to overcome the reluctance by many to grant even basic respect to international law.

In the field of international criminal law, conforming to the provisions of the rule of law is even more important than in other areas of international law. Since there is no single international sovereign, and a disparate international community, it is often unclear what entity international crimes harm, as we saw in previous chapters. It is too easy for the critics of international criminal law to say, as was even said at Nuremberg, that the trials were simply victors' justice.[7] Partially to rebut this claim, it must be shown that international law is deserving of fidelity and respect because of the procedural fairness in the administration of international law. The concept of an international rule of law that would follow the provisions of the domestic rule of law addresses just these worries. The international rule of law, then, is that set of procedural and substantive considerations that will make it less likely that international courts will act arbitrarily.

In the next sections, I will single out three violations of the rule of law that pose especially difficult problems for international criminal law: retroactivity, selective enforcement, and lack of proportionality of punishment. Any of these violations of the rule of law could be used as significant procedural defenses by defendants accused of international crimes. Indeed, international tribunals have discussed each of these defenses in recent years, although international tribunals, in my opinion, have not given these procedural defenses their due. I begin with one of the most serious charges – that international criminal prosecutions may violate the prohibition against retroactivity in the rule of law.

II. Retroactivity

At the time of the Nuremberg Trials, the issue of retroactivity played a key role in the challenges by the defense to the legitimacy of the Nuremberg Tribunal and to the legitimacy of the charges brought against the defendants. The Nuremberg Tribunal held that The Hague and Geneva Conventions were its guiding law. But it was far from clear that "crimes against humanity," recognized really for the first time at the Nuremberg Trials, were somehow contained in these conventions. Similarly, in the first of the early cases argued before the Yugoslav Tribunal, the issue of retroactivity was also discussed. I will argue, though, that the issue of retroactivity has not been sufficiently dealt with by the Yugoslav Appellate Tribunal. Before looking at the Yugoslav Tribunal's attempt to deal with the retroactivity issue, I will briefly consider Lon Fuller's contribution to our understanding of the importance of retroactivity.

In *The Morality of Law*, Fuller lists the institution of retroactive statutes as one of the eight ways that the rule of law can be disrupted. He argues that:

Law has to do with the governance of human conduct by rules. To speak of governing or directing conduct today by rules that will be enacted tomorrow is to talk in blank prose. To ask how we should appraise an imaginary legal system consisting exclusively of laws that are retroactive, and retroactive only, is like asking how much air pressure there is in a perfect vacuum.[8]

Fuller then suggests that the only intelligible system of rules containing *retroactive* law is one in which the majority of laws were *prospective*.

Fuller argues that there are some cases where a retroactive law may be justified, and hence argues that we should restrict the scope of this feature of the rule of law. Fuller urges that the rule of law feature requiring only the prospective application of laws can be waived when we are dealing with civil matters, and where either justice seems to require retroactivity or where the law is so unclear that one of two conflicting interpretations has to be given credence so as to clear up the ambiguity in the law. Consider, for example, a law that says that marriages must have an official stamp affixed to the marriage certificate in order to be valid. Now suppose that the stamps are not available when the law goes into effect. Time passes, and many people are "married," but without the stamps, which simply were not available. Fuller argues in favor of a retroactive law that said that marriages without stamps were nonetheless valid during the period when the stamps were not available. Such a retroactive law seems anything but monstrous. As Fuller says, "when things go wrong . . . the retroactive statute often becomes indispensable as a curative measure."[9]

Nonetheless, Fuller does not urge this kind of exception to retroactivity where criminal laws are concerned. Indeed, Fuller advocates the following principle: "[A] defendant should not be held guilty of crime where the statute, as applied to his particular situation, was so unclear that, had it been equally unclear in all applications, it would have been held void for uncertainty."[10] Since defendants face serious deprivation of liberty in criminal law proceedings, we should be less willing to allow retroactive laws, even as corrective measures, than we are in the domain of civil law. Fuller defends the claim that retroactivity in criminal law is unjustified by referring to a kind of moral absurdity. "It is the retrospective criminal statute that calls most directly to mind the brutal absurdity of commanding a man today to do something yesterday."[11] If people can be subjected to criminal punishment for laws that were not yet passed, then a very significant arbitrariness and abuse has pervaded a legal system, since the punishment is meted out for proscribed activity that could not have been anticipated by the accused.

Fuller's approach gives us a good start at understanding the reason to favor prospective laws over retrospective laws, but it does not quite go far enough. For Fuller does not really explain why retroactive criminal laws could not also serve broader curative functions in an extant legal system. We find just such problems rampant in international criminal law. For example, consider mass rape. Until very recently, no international treaty or court case had considered mass rape to be a violation of international criminal law. Yet surely this was merely an omission that was based on the fact that the largely male authors and judges had not considered rape to be anything but a personal assault, not a means of group coercion. According to Fuller's view, it would not seem clearly unfair to subject State leaders to international prosecution if they orchestrate campaigns of mass rape – for the purposes of ethnic cleansing, for instance. Prosecution based on retroactive criminal statutes in this case is like a curative act, making up for an obvious omission in the law.

In criminal law, it is generally assumed, as it was by Fuller, that it is patently unfair to punish someone for committing an act that that person could not have known was proscribed at the time he or she acted. Yet, as we have seen earlier, many aspects of international law are contested and highly uncertain until courts have ruled. This would not be such a problem in the civil domain, where people expect that close calls may go against them in contract or property disputes. But is it true in international criminal law that lack of clarity concerning what a person is required to do to avoid international prosecution is a sign that the law supposedly in effect simply was not binding on the defendant? While we may want to be very careful about the possibility of abuse here, in many cases it seems to be too strong a reaction to this lacuna merely to let the defendant go free.

We now turn to the Yugoslav Tribunal's prosecution of Tadic and others for crimes that were only codified after his acts took place – namely, when the Tribunal was established by the UN Security Council. In Tadic's appeal, the putatively retroactive law in question is Article 3 of the Yugoslav Tribunal's statute. According to this article, it is considered to be a war crime to engage in various specified acts (of torture, rape, murder, and so on) "regardless of whether they were committed in internal or international armed conflicts."[12] The main basis for thinking that Article 3 was merely a codification of existing international legal norms had to do with the Appeals Chamber's reading of customary international law:

> The first rules that evolved in this area were aimed at protecting the civilian population from the hostilities. As early as the Spanish Civil War (1936–1939), State practice revealed a tendency to disregard the distinction between international and internal wars and to apply certain general principles of humanitarian law, at least to those internal conflicts that constituted large-scale civil wars.[13]

The difficult part of this justification is that it turns on the "tendency" of international customary law, while not citing any authority that clearly articulated this change in customary law. The rule of law's prohibition of retroactivity seems to be compromised by this argument from a "tendency," especially when the International Red Cross had so vocally disagreed with what the tendency in customary international law was in this domain.[14]

Seemingly recognizing the shaky ground on which it had acted, the Appellate Court also made the following normative argument:

> [I]n the area of armed conflict, the distinction between interstate wars and civil wars is losing its value as far as human beings are concerned. Why protect individuals from belligerent violence, or ban rape, torture, or wanton destruction of hospitals, churches, museums, or private property, as well as proscribe weapons causing unnecessary suffering when two sovereign States are engaged in war, and yet refrain from enacting the same bans or providing the same protection when armed violence has erupted "only" within the territory of a sovereign State. If international law, while of course duly safeguarding the legitimate interests of States, must gradually turn to the protection of human beings, it is only natural that the aforementioned dichotomy should gradually lose its weight.[15]

Unfortunately, this kind of normative argument does not dispel the feeling that the ICTY has unjustifiably acted in contravention of the prohibition against retroactivity. If the dichotomy were only gradually losing its weight when the defendant acted, how could Tadic have known what was required of him in international law? This is not a mere lacuna being filled, but a change in customary international law that rendered the defendant unaware that he would be acting in violation of international law.

It is not plausible to say that the ICTY statute performed a curative act in recognizing international crimes that were not committed during an interstate war. It seems clear that the ICTY was making new law, and then applying it retroactively. It may be true that Tadic could see that his acts were illegal, since murder is considered illegal in every domestic jurisdiction. But as we saw earlier, the harder question is whether a particular act of murder is a violation of international law, not just a violation of domestic law. In order for a defendant to be properly tried before an international tribunal in a way that does not run afoul of the rule of law, either the international law the defendant is accused of violating must have been knowable at the time the defendant acted, or the law must have been easily inferable from what was known of international law. Reference to customary international law does not seem to help on either count.

A better argument was hinted at when the Appellate Tribunal said: "What is inhumane, and consequently proscribed, in international wars, cannot but be inhumane and inadmissible in civil strife."[16] Here the tribunal could have, but did not, argue that the various crimes of which Tadic was accused were violations of *jus cogens* norms, and hence known or knowable by everyone. Such an additional claim could have blunted the concerns about retroactivity. In addition, the tribunal argued that there was indeed a settled *opinio juris* condemning murder, rape, and torture during civil war. "Of great relevance to the formation of *opinio juris* to the effect that violations of general international humanitarian law governing internal armed conflicts entail the criminal responsibility of those committing or ordering those violations are certain resolutions adopted by the Security Council."[17] Of course, earlier we raised serious questions about the appeal to *opinio juris* to establish binding international law.

Fuller calls such things as the prohibition on retroactive laws "the inner morality of law."[18] The inner morality of law is very much like what Hart characterized as the minimal content of the natural law. Indeed, Hart drew the connection between these two concepts directly in *The Concept of Law*.[19] There are procedural restraints on law-making that are so fundamental as to become at least minimally moral. But, as Hart points out, such procedural restraints are nonetheless "compatible with very great iniquity."[20] Nonetheless, as both Fuller and Hart acknowledged, principles that prohibit retroactive statutes are part of the principles of natural justice, the conformity to which is necessary for a system of law that is minimally moral.

Law is not merely something that is promulgated and routinely obeyed. Law is generally thought to be something that deserves our fidelity and respect, as something that we are morally obligated to obey. If international law is to stand on a par with domestic law, international law must also be deserving of fidelity and respect. The mere fact that most of international law is customary law does not necessarily make all of it retroactive. But the customary basis of international law must conform to stricter standards of clarity in the criminal domain than in other aspects of international law, because it is the liberty of defendants that is principally at stake rather than merely monetary penalties for breach of international law. Defendants must be able to anticipate that by behaving a certain way their conduct will be judged to have violated international criminal norms and that they will risk serious loss of liberty. This is what the prohibition on retroactivity is supposed to guarantee. International tribunals need to be clearer than they have been so far about meeting this requirement. When the international norms are not clear, then we should follow Fuller in thinking that these various provisions of international law may be void because of their vagueness. In general, it is likely to be a violation of the inner morality of international law for defendants to be prosecuted for violating norms that they could not have anticipated. International courts must take the charge of retroactivity much more seriously than they have so far.

III. Selective Prosecution

Rarely is it contended that selective prosecution of the laws is consistent with the rule of law. The rule of law is supposed to guarantee that arbitrariness and bias of individual officials is not substituted for proper rule enforcement – that is, for equal justice under the law. When official conduct is at odds with what the law requires, then the rule of law has been undermined. And when the laws are only selectively enforced, there is the kind of room for arbitrariness and bias that the rule of law is supposed to prevent. Given the serious challenges that have been made to international criminal tribunals, we need to be especially worried about this particular abuse. We begin with a discussion of the challenges made at Nuremberg based on selective enforcement, and then turn to similar charges at the Yugoslav Tribunal.

The Nuremberg Trials were inaugurated with one of the most famous attempts to justify international tribunals, Justice Robert Jackson's opening statement on behalf of the prosecution. Jackson contrasted the Nuremberg Trials with the vengeance that would otherwise surely have been the defendants' fate. Jackson made it clear, though, that the Nuremberg Trials were indeed a form of victors' justice. He said: "Either the victors must judge the vanquished or we must leave the defeated to judge themselves." Jackson then offered two reasons for not letting the Germans judge themselves. First, "[a]fter the first World War, we learned the futility of the latter course." And second, Jackson asked, "[d]id we spend American lives to capture them only to save them from punishment."[21] With so candid an admission, it is not surprising that many have said that the Nuremberg Trials were little more than victors' justice.

The charge that the Nuremberg Trials, the first truly international criminal trials, were tainted is not an implausible charge. At the trials, there was no discussion of any putative war crimes by members of the Allied forces. Yet it seems clear that there could have been prosecutions for the bombing of Hiroshima and Nagasaki by the United States, for the bombing of Dresden by England and the United States, or for the many atrocities committed in Eastern Europe by the Soviet army. This is not to deny that those who were put in the dock at the first Nuremberg Trial – the high-ranking Nazi leadership – did not deserve to be prosecuted. Rather, this is merely to suggest that there was indeed selective prosecution at the Nuremberg Trials.[22]

Some forms of selective prosecution may be justifiable, as is arguably true in some respects of the Nuremberg Trials. One has to start somewhere, and when there are an enormous number of criminal acts to choose from, and limited prosecutorial resources, some selectivity is inevitable. What is not inevitable is that the selection of cases to be prosecuted will exclude whole categories of persons, and where what categorized the type of person had nothing to do with the degree of guilt or ease of capture. Selective prosecution is only justified – if it is at all – when the selection of cases is based on administrative issues rather than the characteristics of the victims or perpetrators. For, of course, prosecutors regularly, and justifiably, select for prosecution the cases that are most serious, or that have the clearest and most complete factual record. But to choose to prosecute on the basis of whether one was an Allied or an Axis leader is just the kind of selective prosecution that is proscribed by the rule of law. It is indeed unfortunate that so important an occasion as the Nuremberg Trials should have been tarnished by the plausible charge of selective prosecution.

It might be argued that world public opinion at the time would not have allowed for trials of the Allied leaders, since these same leaders were "flush with victory," as Justice Jackson said.[23] But this is just the point. If trials are going to occur so close in time to major atrocities, those trials cannot be driven by public opinion without risking violations of the rule of law. There is also the concern about appearances that should have caused the Nuremberg prosecutors to be more evenhanded in selecting those to be prosecuted. Yet the fact that the prosecutors were drawn only from the major Allied countries made it unrealistic that prosecutions would be conducted against Allied soldiers or leaders.

When prosecutors and judges are drawn, perhaps of necessity, only from certain specific States where nationalism often runs high, the concern about selective prosecution takes on an urgency. Of course, judges – and prosecutors – are supposed to be impartial in the way they make their decisions. Loyalty to the larger community is supposed to overcome loyalty to particular locales. But in the international arena, loyalty to the world community (what is often called "cosmopolitanism") is normally an inadequate sentiment to override the sentiments of loyalty to home country. National loyalty is deeply engrained, whereas cosmopolitan loyalty is generally quite weak. Although it is certainly undeniable that we are all "citizens of the world" in some sense of this phrase, it is unclear how much weight is to be given to this metaphorical citizenship in comparison to the often hard-won citizenship of a given State. Because of this, the judges on international tribunals may appear to favor people from their own States and nations. In Nuremberg, the judges were all drawn from Allied States, and the charge of selective prosecution was given more credence than if the judges had been drawn from the Axis States as well, although there would certainly have been practical problems in meeting this objective.

In the Yugoslav trials, charges of selective prosecution have taken two forms. First, there is the charge that the prosecutors have not been evenhanded in prosecuting non-Serbs, many of whom committed equally egregious crimes as those of the Serbs, and yet Serbs have primarily been the focus of prosecution. In addition, it has recently been charged that the prosecutor has not investigated the allegations of atrocities committed by the NATO forces that waged war against Serbs in Bosnia and Kosovo, and then bombed Belgrade. Indeed, this was the main charge, heard over and over, in the early days as former Yugoslav President Slobodan Milosovic defended himself before the Yugoslav Tribunal. In addition, none of the prosecutors or judges at the Yugoslav Tribunal is a Serb, raising once again the same charge of victor's justice that was heard at the time of the Nuremberg Trials.[24]

Second, there is the charge that selective prosecution occurred when minor players rather than leaders were put in the dock. Richard Goldstone, the first chief prosecutor of the Yugoslav Tribunal, says that the prosecution's "strategy includes the investigation of lower-level persons, directly involved in carrying out the crimes in order to build effective cases against the military and civilian leaders who were party to the overall planning and organization of those crimes."[25] But should prosecutors be allowed to engage in such selective prosecutions? The issue of fairness that arises as a result of selective prosecution will indeed be hard to combat. The leaders who promulgated and coordinated the ethnic cleansing campaign are often clearly more fairly prosecuted than the "minor players" who were mere cogs in the larger ethnic cleansing machine.[26] One possible response to this point is that it is important to begin the process against someone in the ethnic cleansing campaign.[27] It is indeed important to start the process of holding individuals accountable for the atrocities committed in the former Yugoslavia. But concerns about fairness can potentially undermine the importance of the tribunal's work if they are not properly addressed.[28]

It is important to recognize the political reality of how difficult it has been for the Yugoslav Tribunal's prosecutors to secure the capture of indicted war criminals so that they can put a more representative sample of the wrongdoers on trial. Richard Goldstone asked the United States "to make the surrender of indicted suspects a condition for any peace accord" at the Dayton peace talks aimed at negotiating a cease-fire in the Balkans.[29] Goldstone was ultimately unsuccessful in this venture, and as a result it has taken many years to get significant leaders into the dock. This further underscores how dependent international prosecutions have been on political decision-makers. Selective prosecution becomes an even more serious restraint on the international rule of law when there is such a possibility of political manipulation of the prosecutorial process.

Selective prosecution will remain one of the main legitimate bases for challenging international prosecutions, at least until there is a much stronger sense of cosmopolitanism than exists today. But even cosmopolitanism will not solve all of the problems discussed in this section. Problems will remain when strong State governments engage in political protection of certain defendants, forcing prosecutors to proceed against those who were often considerably less responsible for what occurred than those who remain at large. Indeed, because of the rise in importance of the defenses of "superior orders" and "duress," these minor players will be harder and harder to convict in any event, bringing with it the possibility of general impunity in the face of large-scale atrocities.

IV. Let the Punishment Fit the Crime

It is typical in discussions of proportionality in criminal law to make a distinction between legal and moral guilt. U.S. Supreme Court Justice Antonin Scalia has put the point this way:

[T]wo equally blameworthy criminal defendants may be guilty of different offenses solely because their acts cause differing amounts of harm. "If a bank robber aims his gun at a guard, pulls the trigger, and kills his target, he may be put to death. If the gun unexpectedly misfires he may not. His moral guilt in both cases is identical, but his [legal] responsibility in the former is greater."[30]

It is attractive to draw this distinction in domestic law, for then the question of proportionality of punishment can be addressed purely in legal rather than moral terms. Even if it is possible to draw this distinction in domestic criminal law, it is hopeless to draw it in international criminal law. Justice Jackson seemingly admitted this when he said in his opening statement at the Nuremberg Trials, that "[w]e charge guilt on planned and intended conduct that involves moral as well as legal wrong."

As we have also seen, one of the tests for whether an act of the defendant violates international criminal law is whether that act shocks the conscience of humanity. Even on my moral minimalist account of the normative justification of international law, there is a minimal overlap of law and morality, and as a result there is some relevance of moral matters to questions of whether the punishment fits the crime in international criminal law. And we also have one of the best explanations for why proportionality is such an important restraint on international criminal law. Proportionality is necessary in order to make sure that the moral outrage often expressed at the sight of atrocities does not cloud moral judgment, and so that we can indeed "stay the hand of vengeance."[31]

"Let the punishment fit the crime" is a key provision of the rule of law. Fittingness is a relative concept that must be measured against two different standards. First, there is a standard based on previous similar cases: Is the punishment meted out in this case consistent with the punishment in other similar cases? Second, there is another standard: Does the seriousness of the form of punishment mesh with the seriousness of the type of crime? Both of these ways to understand fittingness, or proportionality, are problematical in international criminal law. The former is problematical because there is not at present a single court system for international criminal law. Without a single system of courts, it is unlikely that consistency of punishment for similar offenses can be maintained. This problem will be partially addressed now that the ICC has come into being, but there will still be many international criminal law proceedings that are not conducted in the ICC but rather in domestic or ad hoc tribunals. There would have to be serious international appellate review of all of these cases to make sure that there is consistency of sentencing at the trial court level, something that is unlikely to happen soon, and in any event is not mandated by the ICC Statute.

For proportionality to make sense as a restraint imposed by the rule of law, there must be some way to assess what a reasonable punishment is for violating international criminal law in the first place. In this respect, it might be useful to consider the aggravating factors mentioned in a 1999 case to come before the Yugoslav tribunal. "Among aggravating factors, [the Yugoslav tribunal] has noted the terrorizing of victims, sadism, cruelty and humiliation, espousal of ethnic and religious discrimination, and the number of victims."[32] In serious criminal trials, especially capital trials in the United States, the guilt of the defendant is separated from the type of punishment the defendant deserves. The problem is that when such separations are made, it is hard to keep the punishment proportional to the type of crime in question, since emotional reactions will vary greatly based on how emotionally compelling the prosecutor's presentation is. Strong emotional appeals are more likely to make sentencing decisions quite idiosyncratic. Of course, since international trials are largely not conducted with juries but with panels of judges, perhaps the adverse effects of emotional appeals can be muted. But, even so, factors such as "espousal of ethnic and religious discrimination and the number of victims" seem more relevant to the international crime for which the defendant stands accused than the character of the accused. These factors are certainly easier to consider objectively when trying to decide if the punishment is proportional to that in other cases, and that it fits the crime.

Proportionality is one of the most important restraints on those judges who would let emotional factors influence their sentencing decisions. The fact that ad hoc international criminal trials arise in response to "the horror of the crimes" makes it especially difficult to determine what would be appropriate restraints so that these proceedings can be consistent with a "traditionally humane view of sentencing and the rights of prisoners."[33] These humane considerations have led to the abolition of the death penalty in contemporary international law.[34]

The Nuremberg Tribunals issued quite a number of death sentences, largely grounded on the two-pronged need for deterrence and retribution. The international community has moved progressively toward the elimination of the death penalty primarily as it has moved away from both retribution and deterrence. But how then is proportionality in sentencing to be assessed when both of these justifications for punishment have been diminished?

The Yugoslav Tribunal has declared that although prevention has not been completely eliminated as a goal in sentencing, it must be modified by reference to considerations of "collective reconciliation."[35] It is also important to note that the Universal Declaration of Human Rights prohibits punishment that is "cruel, inhuman, and degrading."[36] These two goals – of looking to collective reconciliation, and of prohibiting cruel, inhuman, or degrading punishment – point us toward the beginning of an answer to the question of how to understand proportionality. Sentencing should not be so severe as to constitute cruelty or to undermine efforts at reconciliation after large-scale violence has ravaged a particular region. I will return to this topic in the final chapter of this book. One principle that could support this understanding is that international criminal law is aimed at holding individuals accountable, but only for group-based crimes. Hence, in the end it is not the character of individuals that should be the main concern of international criminal norms.

In looking at proportionality, we should realize that the proper purview of international criminal law is the group-based crime. Those who can be truly said to have masterminded or instigated these crimes are the ones who deserve to be punished, since these people are fittingly seen as responsible for those group-based crimes. The leaders of an ethnic cleansing campaign, for instance, might be fittingly subject to severe punishment (short of the death penalty), since they were the ones whose criminal acts were the most important from the standpoint of the international community. "Let the punishment fit the crime" in international criminal law will thus call for much more lenient sentences for those who are merely minor players, and may call for more severe punishments for those who are the leaders of a group-based crime. In any event, this provision of the international rule of law will also require greater scrutiny than has been recently provided by international tribunals.

V. A Hobbesian Approach to the International Rule of Law

In Chapter 1, I presented some of Hobbes's concerns about international law, and also a possible Hobbesian solution to the problems of sovereignty and tolerance. In Chapters 1 and 4, I suggested that Hobbes should be seen as laying the foundation for the version of moral minimalism that I embraced. Now, while considering the rule of law, I wish to return to Hobbes, or at least to Hobbesian arguments, that will allow us to connect our discussion of the rule of law with moral minimalism. From a Hobbesian perspective, the question arises: Why would people ever give up their natural liberty and agree to be restrained in the sense that they were obligated to act as others thought they should? The Hobbesian answer is that this only makes sense insofar as people would see that it is in their long-run interest to do so rather than be subject to the whim and power of unruled others.[37] This analysis leads us directly into the debate about the rule of law, for it is often said that the "rule of law" is better than the "rule of men," and it is better yet than the state of nature. It certainly is prudentially better, but is it sufficiently morally better so that subscribing to the rule of law is somehow morally binding on us? And can we make sense of the rule of law in international society that is largely governed by democratic procedures?

Hobbes famously argued that a human person can only be ruled by another person's will, not by an abstraction such as law. The sovereign was that person whose will was strongest in the sense that no one else ruled over him or her. So what becomes of the rule of law in a democracy, on this account? Jean Hampton argued that an answer can be provided only if there is a form of democracy in which the people are the ones who rule over themselves, through their laws.[38] Laws cannot really rule over anyone, at least not without those people agreeing, for whatever reason, to be ruled by the laws. Yet democracy appears to have the problem that if the people literally rule over themselves, even through their laws, the people can change the rules any time they do not want to follow them, thereby negating the idea that the people are ultimately bound by rules or law at all. This has been called the "regress problem": Democracy is inconsistent with the rule of law because any law, in a democracy, is ultimately changeable at will by the people, and hence the people are not really ruled by the law. We saw a version of this problem when we considered how it can be that custom, which starts out being largely consensual, can nonetheless bind into the future.

There are several ways to solve the regress problem. Jean Hampton tries to solve the problem by distinguishing between two roles: When the people sit as legislators, they act as rulers; when they sit as subjects, they are ruled.[39] This stratification of roles allows for the people to rule themselves through laws, and to avoid the sense that they are merely being ruled by themselves, as a form of "the rule of men." Hampton doesn't admit it, but this particular solution is distinctly Hobbesian itself. For Hobbes talks about the different personas of people when he discusses (1) the difference between natural and artificial persons, and (2) the key concept of authority and the act of authorizing another to act in one's behalf.[40]

In the international arena, the regress problem is seemingly even harder to solve. From a Hobbesian perspective, a democratic international rule of law would also have to involve some kind of rule by people, under one description, over themselves, under another description. Since the people in the international arena are not truly subjects of any one sovereign, then it appears that they do not have the dual stratification on which a resolution of the regress problem could be based. At present, there is no status of "citizen" or "subject" of a world government. And hence it appears that if people do rule themselves in the international arena, they will not also be ruled by law. Indeed, as we saw at the beginning of the book, it is conceptually unclear what the very idea of law becomes in the international arena where there is no law-giving sovereign. In subsequent chapters, I also provided a Hobbesian resolution to this problem of sovereignty in the international arena, to which we now return.

In an earlier chapter (Chapter 3), we encountered this puzzle when discussing the problem of the persistent objector. Just as customary international law gets its strength from the test of time, so it must be admitted that those who refuse to accede to that custom also derive strength from the test of time. Indeed, customary norms seem to be consensual in the sense that the people who are bound by a custom can merely decide not to accept that custom, and then, at least after a period of time, become unbound by that custom. Hence it appears, especially in the international realm, that people are not bound by the rule of law so much as having bound themselves. In this sense, the international domain is one dominated by the rule of "States," not by the rule of law. But this problem can be solved, just as it was solved in the domestic case.

The international rule of law can be understood, like the domestic rule of law, as involving a form of self-rule by people, but a form of self-rule that is importantly mediated by law. International law is that set of rules which States agree to enforce. People feel bound to obey these rules for the usual reasons having to do with coercion and fidelity, both linked to the need for security. Ultimately, people are most clearly morally bound only by what they themselves have agreed to regard as binding, or what they would find acceptable. In the context of international law, this will occur largely, but not exclusively, in terms of what people have consented, or would consent, to allow their home States to set as international restraints on their liberty.

Once people have consented, or would consent, to be bound, and to have States enforce those obligations, then people are no longer free to disregard the law. For this reason, people in democratically elected States are not truly living under the rule of "man." A similar argument can help us see how the international realm can be governed by the rule of "law," not the rule of "States." Once people have agreed, or would agree, to let States enforce an international legal regimen, then those people are no longer subject to the rule of "States." If States are required either to prosecute offenders or to extradite them to a State that will prosecute them, there is the beginning of an international rule of law.[41] Of course, in a democratic international order, the people can change international law, but they must do so according to established procedures, not merely at their own whim. If this latter condition is not met, then there is not yet a rule of law. As in the domestic case, there must be a stage at which people are forced to put on different hats when they *change* the law as opposed to the hats they wear while being *bound to obey* the law. The procedural restraints discussed in this chapter are crucial for establishing just such different stages that create different personas for the people who make international law and the people who are bound by international law.

Even for those States that are not democratically organized, the members of these States can contribute to and influence international law through a kind of civil society that non-government organizations provide.[42] Without such influence, it appears that States act on the basis of a different rule of "man": rule by one or a small number of "men" – namely, rule by elites. If it appears that elites or powerful individuals create international "law," then normal individuals will not feel bound to obey international law out of a sense of fidelity to that law. Of course, many people now living in poverty and in non-democratic States are still internationally disenfranchised from the process of international law-making. Until such problems can be solved, the international rule of law will remain conceptually and pragmatically infirm. International law is pragmatically infirm when people do not feel bound by it; international law is conceptually infirm when the bindingness of international law is unrestrained by the procedural matters we have discussed in this chapter. I remind the reader here of the arguments advanced by anti-colonialists that we discussed in Chapter 2.

Nonetheless, we can often still speak of an international rule of law that places restrictions on what international legal, and quasi-legal, bodies can legitimately do to individual people. Such considerations have special weight when we are discussing – as we are in this book – international *criminal* legal sanctions, since those sanctions require even greater vigilance in order to root out sources of arbitrariness. For this reason, we need to be especially sensitive to the restrictions on law-making and law-adjudication that the literature on the rule of law has traditionally stressed in the domestic arena, applying those restrictions even more vigorously in the realm of international law. Indeed, as I have suggested, the international rule of law remains infirm as a result of questions about sovereignty, and hence there remain problems about fidelity and respect to international law that will require very strong restraints, especially on criminal law sanctions.

In this chapter, I have provided reasons for thinking that courts need to exercise considerable restraint in prosecuting, convicting, and sentencing individuals for international crimes. My reasons have been based on a concern for the rule of law, especially for the emerging notion of the international rule of law. In this chapter and the preceding one, I have set out various considerations that taken together support what might be called "defendants' procedural rights" in international criminal law. In the final two chapters, I will explain why the claims of victims should not be given the credence that is currently provided in discussions of international criminal law, and why amnesty programs may be legitimate alternatives to international prosecutions, convictions, and punishments. Criminal trials are not always the best remedy for mass crimes for which groups of people share responsibility.

12

Victims and Convictions

Victims wish for some form of closure, and sometimes also for retribution against those who have harmed them. Victims and their family members also often make a very distinct demand for what can be called "final justice." Especially when the perpetrators of crimes are in hiding, victims often have a sense of righteous indignation that the perpetrators are free and unharmed, while the victims may be dead or seriously injured and their families thrown into a state of emotional upheaval. The victims and their families will call out for justice, and this will most readily lead them to demand prosecution in criminal trials, where the perpetrators are confronted by their deeds, publicly proclaimed to be guilty by a representative (group or individual) of the society, and punished appropriately by significant loss of liberty or life for the harms they have caused. International criminal law is motivated by such concerns, as it should be.

Advocates for truth commissions and amnesty programs in international law face some of the same problems as Anglo-American criminal defense lawyers. First, they face the strongly voiced objection that they impede the goal of retribution, not allowing the victims to get their due. Second, there is a concern that lawyers become complicit in the destruction of the "rule of law," since people who have done wrong will escape punishment, thereby achieving the kind of impunity that marks non-rule-governed societies. In this chapter, I offer reasons to reject both of these objections. I argue that victims are not owed convictions; rather it is the larger society,[1] if anyone, that has the right to pursue convictions. And I argue that the rule of law is not necessarily destroyed when a society decides to forego criminal trials and to provide alternative means for facilitating the return to normalcy in that society. Victims should have their due, but so also should defendants, as well as the larger society in which the victims live.

In both international and domestic law, prosecutors who claim to represent victims often say that justice for these victims demands that there be convictions with serious punishments. In prosecutions for crimes against humanity, prosecutors claim that they seek retribution for the victims and act to support the rule of law, and for this reason they reject pleas for amnesty, even when civil strife will surely be intensified by the trials.[2] In the guilt phase of capital murder cases in the United States, prosecutors appeal strongly to the jury's sense of retribution. And in the penalty phase, prosecutors are quite explicit in attempting to appeal to the emotions of the jurors to vote for the death penalty by asking the jurors to step into the shoes of the victim's family (often showing "day in the life" films of the victim)[3] in arguing that the victim is owed not only a guilty conviction but also a death sentence for the defendant.[4]

In one of the clearest statements of this problem, the relatives of Steve Biko challenged the legitimacy of the amnesty program of the South African Truth and Reconciliation Commission (the TRC). The Report of the TRC stated:

The effect of section 20 (7) [of the Promotion of National Unity and Reconciliation Act], read with other sections of the Act, is to permit the Amnesty Committee to grant amnesty to a perpetrator... A perpetrator cannot be criminally or civilly liable for an act or acts for which he or she has received amnesty. Similarly, neither the state, nor any other body, organization nor person that would ordinarily have been vicariously liable for such acts can be liable in law.[5]

The TRC "limited the applicant's right... to 'have justiciable disputes settled by a court of law or... other independent or impartial forum.'"[6] Biko's family argued that they were prevented from seeking proper retribution or recompense for what murderers and torturers did to their loved one.[7] In addition, many expressed the view that the TRC was not supportive of the rule of law. Critics of such commissions wondered whether lawyers violated their ethical duties by agreeing not to prosecute.[8]

I will examine several arguments in support of the claim that victims' rights are violated when there are no criminal trials. The first two arguments concern retribution and substantive justice. In the first section, I consider the purely retributive argument that victims are owed convictions so as to right the wrong that has been done to them. In the second section, I consider the argument that the State represents the interests of the victims, and that the State should press for convictions on behalf of the victims so as to express its condemnation of the perpetrator's act. I will argue that these arguments either should be recast as claims about what society is owed, or that they represent a category mistake in that these arguments mistake punishment for compensation.

The second set of arguments concerns the rule of law, understood largely as a procedural constraint. In the third section, I take up the argument that respect for the rule of law demands that the State seek convictions for the victims. In the fourth section, I consider the claim that the unique nature of the international rule of law demands such convictions. I argue that these arguments miss the mark because trials are not mandated by the rule of law, even by the international rule of law. Other procedures can guarantee that decisions are not biased or arbitrary, and other procedures can fulfill the function of public condemnation of the perpetrator and public vindication of the victim.

In the final chapter, I will return to substantive issues and discuss the argument that even considerations of reconciliation should not be allowed to move us from the pursuit of convictions. In general, I argue that none of these arguments is necessarily fatal to the work of truth commissions, amnesty programs, or other non-conviction ways of dealing with the perpetrators of crimes.

I. Restoring the Right

In *The Philosophy of Right*, G. W. F. Hegel famously claimed that punishment is necessary "to annul the crime, which otherwise would be held valid, and to restore the right."[9] Hegel argued in general that "crime is to be annulled, not because it is the producing of an evil, but because it is the infringement of the right as right."[10] The original infringement of right is of course the harm done to the victim by the defendant, the putative wrongdoer. Hegel claims that the retributive theory of punishment is better able to represent this idea that right must be restored than are theories of punishment based on "a preventive, a deterrent, a threat, or a reformative" model of punishment.[11] The criminal "deserves punishment" since "as the criminal has done, so should it be done to him."[12]

For Hegel, the only good justification for punishment of the criminal refers to an objective state of affairs, not to a subjective one. The victim has been wronged, and now objectively this wrong needs to be righted so that we can return to a point of stability, perhaps of global justice. And the only thing that can right a wrong is another wrong, now committed in the form of a punishment directed at the perpetrator of the original wrong. The "demand for a justice freed from subjective interest and a subjective form no longer contingent on might . . . is the demand for justice not as revenge but as punishment."[13] Ultimately, the perpetrator of a crime has coerced the victim, and thereby annulled the freedom of that victim. But consider this question: Does Hegel's reference to the objective as opposed to the subjective basis for prosecution of the wrongdoer mean that the original victim's subjective interests should not count, or merely that those interests are to be decontextualized but still seen as interests of the victim?

Hegel recognized that retribution must be distinguished from simple revenge. If we place too much emphasis on the claims of the victim for vengeance, then we seem to countenance the sort of blood-feud revenge-seeking that the institution of criminal law was supposed to end. On the other hand, if we take the subjective interests of the victim off the table altogether, then the whole basis for retribution loses, at least for some, its chief intuitive appeal. If it is merely society that has the right to seek convictions and punishment, the strong emotional support for responding to what has happened to the victim is lost.

Hegel offers two arguments that appeal to objectivity rather than subjectivity to justify the view that wrongs must be righted by "wronging" the wrongdoer. First, Hegel is explicit in analogizing criminal punishment to the civil righting of wrongs in such cases as theft. We wrong the wrongdoer so as to return to the victim what was lost. And, second, there is also the implicit argument for global justice mentioned earlier. We wrong the wrongdoer so as to return the world to the place it was in before the wrong was done. But it is my view that neither of these arguments will support the right of the victim to have the perpetrator convicted or punished.

Let us first consider the analogy between harms to property and harms to persons. If one person seizes and takes possession of something that is not his or her own, he or she has taken something to which he or she has no right. Instead, the person who has had the object taken is the "party who has the right to it."[14] The law steps in to return the object to its rightful owner. Similarly, one can think of a person's body as also something that that person owns. Coercion is wrong because it "is an exercise of force against the existence of my freedom . . ."[15] The law steps in to punish so as to right the wrong. Just as one has coerced, so shall he or she be coerced.

Hegel's first strategy does indeed justify the victim's claim that he or she is owed something, but we have here a classic confusion of compensation with punishment. In the case of theft – now seen as a tort, not as a crime – the victim is owed compensation, normally in the from of the return of the thing that has been taken by the thief, or the paying of an equivalent value to the victim by the wrongdoer. Such compensation is owed to the victim as a private law remedy for what has been done. This analogy will indeed work well to explain why we compensate someone in private tort law where there has been an assault or battery against a person. But what is justified is the payment of compensation for the harm, normally calculated in terms of the money equivalent necessary to make the victim whole again – that is, medical expenses, lost wages, lost future earning power, and so on. The analogy is properly between the torts of harm to property and of harm to person, not between the tort of harm to property and the crime of assault or battery.

Punishment is not a form of compensation. It does not make the victim whole by returning what it is that the victim has lost. The act of punishment does not restore anything to the victim, since the act of punishment does not give to the victim, or the victim's family, anything other than a sense of vengeance. Assuming, with Hegel, that retribution and vengeance are to be distinguished, and that the victim has not had control over the wrongdoer's life taken from him or her, the wrongdoer's punishment does not restore to the victim anything comparable to what the victim has lost.

Hegel's second strategy also does not support the right of the victim to have the defendant convicted and punished, since the argument for global justice is not addressed from the perspective of the victim but of the world. Perhaps Hegel means that there has been a tear in the seam of the global rights of people, and that the conviction and punishment of the person responsible for that tear should repair that seam. Even if we hold this metaphysical understanding of global justice, we are still faced with the question of why it is the victim, as opposed to society at large, that is owed the repairing of the tear. Yes, it is true that the tear is primarily the victim's tear insofar as the tear occurred because the victim's rights were violated. But in another important sense, it isn't anything of the victim's in the abstract that is now being repaired, as we saw earlier. Neither of these strategies supports the victim's claim for conviction or punishment of the wrongdoer.

Yet another strategy open to Hegel is to think of each person as merely an instantiation of the larger societal whole. In this case, it might make sense to say that the victim, as an instantiation of the society, is owed the conviction of the wrongdoer. It will then not be clear how the victim's right, as right, has been restored, since we would have lost any personal sense of righting a wrong or any corresponding sense of being owed convictions by the victim. The victim, as an instantiation of the society, is not the kind of entity that could have strong claims against the wrongdoer.[16] Nonetheless, we should investigate how it is that the claims of the victim are related to claims of the society. We will do this in the next section.

II. Expressing Condemnation

Several of the problems mentioned earlier, especially concerning blood-feud revenge, as well as what could possibly be owed to a deceased victim, are answered by the strategy of saying that victims are owed convictions, but that this claim is passed onto the larger society, which then presses for conviction, as an expression of condemnation of the perpetrator, in the victim's name. Virtually every prosecutor has begun his or her opening statement to the jury with an appeal for justice on behalf of the victim. Most prosecutors also claim that the victim has a right to a conviction as an expression of condemnation, which the State, as the victim's representative, is seeking to secure. In this section, I challenge this common dogma.

As noted earlier, what was wrong with allowing the victims to avenge their wrong is that it created a cycle of blood feuds, where vengeance for a wrongdoing was followed by vengeance for the act of vengeance, etc. The folk history of law has it as a dictum that criminal law was invented to stop the blood feud. If it is the State that seeks vengeance for the wrong done to the victim, then it will be clearer to the members of the family of the wrongdoer that they do not have any reasonable claim of vengeance against the State for what it has done to their loved one, thereby blocking the perpetuation of blood feuds. Similarly, at the international level, if one State tries to prosecute the members of another State, a similar blood feud can develop that can be prevented by having an international tribunal, rather than a State, do the prosecuting. Let us consider three variations of this argument.

Some philosophers, such as Immanuel Kant, have suggested that the State acts on behalf of the victim when it convicts and punishes the wrongdoer, and that a failure to act in this way on the part of the State makes the State, or the people who comprise it, complicit in the crime of the wrongdoer. Kant argued that if a murderer is not executed, even when he is the only one left in jail at the end of a revolution, a serious wrong has occurred:

[T]he last murderer remaining in prison must first be executed, so that everyone will duly receive what his actions are worth and so that the bloodguilt thereof will not be fixed on the people because they failed to insist on carrying out the punishment; for if they fail to do so they may be regarded as accomplices in this public violation of legal justice.[17]

For Kant, the blood feud will be continued against the people if the people, standing in for the victim,[18] fail to convict and punish the murderer. In addition, the State for Kant has a moral duty to stand in for the victim. And such a duty is based on universal justice, much as it was for Hegel. But for Kant, there is an important limitation. If the crime has been committed against the State, then the sovereign has the right to grant a pardon. But if the crime is committed by one subject against another, the sovereign "absolutely cannot exercise this right" to pardon, "for in such cases, exemption from punishment constitutes the greatest injustice toward his subjects."[19]

Social contract theory provides another basis for the proposition that it is the duty of the State to convict and punish as a stand-in for the victim. When a subject agrees to obey the law, that subject gives up the right to private vengeance, and the State agrees to protect the subject's rights by now acting in the place of the subject. Here we have another important argument for thinking that victims are owed convictions. The victim as subject has ceded to the sovereign the right to seek vengeance against the wrongdoer. In exchange for the obedience of the subject, the sovereign agrees to protect that subject. Part of this protection involves the prosecution, conviction, and punishment of wrongdoers. If the sovereign does not convict and punish, then the sovereign acts as an accomplice with the wrongdoer. And if the sovereign pardons the wrongdoer, the sovereign has committed an injustice toward the subject, who, on this view, retains a residual (natural) right that wrongdoers be convicted and punished.

We can ask several questions about this analysis from the Hobbesian perspective we have adopted in this book. First, what right has been violated when a sovereign pardons a wrongdoer? Is there a violation of the right that the subject has to be protected by the sovereign? Or is it the original right to avenge a wrong committed? Universal justice does not easily support the idea that victims must retain a right to convict and punish their attackers. Even for those theorists who base the sovereign's rights on the agreement of the subject, it would be a classic mistake to think that the subject retains a right to avenge those wrongs that he or she does not prosecute and punish. For allowing the subject to retain a right to avenge a wrong is to retain the state of nature and thereby to destabilize civil society. The subject would then be allowed to second-guess the sovereign, which will undermine the sovereign's authority. Allowing the subject to retain the right to avenge, especially in a situation where the sovereign has decided to pardon the wrongdoer, allows for the sovereign's decision to be overridden, hence making it no longer truly the act of a sovereign.[20]

Second, saying that the subject retains a right to be protected by the sovereign does not pose the same concerns as the first strategy. Such a retained right, though, will not support strong claims against the sovereign's right to pardon. For it is certainly conceivable that a sovereign would judge that maintaining the overall peace of the society requires that certain wrongdoers not be prosecuted and punished. We might disagree with the bases of these decisions, and wonder whether public safety really would be jeopardized by criminal trials, but it is certainly conceivable that these sovereign rulers would be correct in their decisions. And if these sovereigns had the duty to maintain public safety, the case can hardly be supported that they committed injustice against their subjects by not convicting and punishing wrongdoers as long as such sovereigns did something else reasonably designed to advance the safety of the people.

There could also be other ways for the society, domestic or international, to express or demonstrate its condemnation for what the perpetrator has done, than by pursuing conviction and punishment. Indeed, there is no obvious reason why the society cannot express such condemnation by public shaming of the wrongdoer, followed by a pardon. The shaming would need to be done by the society in a way that was clearly the expression of the society's condemnation. There is no reason to think that a public trial, with convictions and prison time as the punishment, is the only way society can meet the goal of expressing condemnation.

When the society represents the victim, the society is not bound to do just what the victim would want to do. For the very purpose of having such representation is to break the cycle of vengeance-taking, which means in part that the society must do what it can to defuse the hostility that exists between the victim and the wrongdoer. The society is thus not a surrogate for the victim, not a mere stand-in doing what the victim wants done, but the victim's representative. This means that the society has to exercise independent judgment to figure out how best to advance the interests of the victim, as well as the interests of the rest of the society, which it must also represent.

Just as a society must see itself as representing the victim in expressing condemnation for what the perpetrator has done to the victim, the society must also see itself as representing the rest of the members of the community. The society must see itself as representing the defendant, since both victim and defendant are its members. This does not mean that the society cannot punish the defendant, but only that it cannot act merely on the wishes of the victim. From the social contract perspective, the rights and interests of the parties in the state of nature are transformed into civil rights and interests. Even though one might think that as a matter of natural (or human) right, victims are owed convictions in the state of nature, once people enter into civil society their *natural* rights are transformed into *civil* rights. And as a matter of civil right, victims are not owed convictions, since the sovereigns are the ones who now have that right and can choose to exercise it or not, based on the goal of advancing the interests of all of their subjects.

III. Trials and the International Rule of Law

Michael Scharf, in his 1996 essay "Swapping Amnesty for Peace: Was There a Duty to Prosecute International Crimes in Haiti?" argues that victims are owed convictions because respect for the rule of law demands it.[21] When wrongdoers are not prosecuted, convicted, and punished, they are given a kind of impunity that suggests they are above the law. The idea here is that the rule of law requires that no person be above the law in that all are subjected to the same treatment at the hands of the law. In this section, I will consider general issues concerning what is owed to victims out of respect for the rule of law. I leave to the next section a more elaborate discussion of conceptual problems and arguments based on the international rule of law.

Martha Minow has provided a very good starting point for a discussion of the rule of law as a basis for understanding what victims are owed.

To respond to mass atrocity with legal prosecutions is to embrace the rule of law. This common phrase combines several elements. First, there is a commitment to redress harms with the application of general, preexisting norms. Second, the rule of law calls for administration by a formal system itself committed to fairness and opportunities for individuals to be heard both in accusation and defense. Further, a government proceeding under the rule of law aims to treat each individual person in light of particular, demonstrated evidence. In the Western legal tradition the rule of law also entails the presumption of innocence, litigation under the adversary system, and the ideal of government by laws, rather than by persons. No one is above or outside the law, and no one should be legally condemned or sanctioned outside legal procedures.[22]

This provides us with a good framework for beginning to understand why respect for the rule of law is thought to give victims a basis for saying that they are owed convictions.[23]

The rule of law is indeed a very powerful image in democratic societies. Is it a violation of the rule of law for wrongdoers not to be convicted and punished for their crimes? I will address two related issues. First, is it a violation of the rule of law if the formal procedures for dealing with crimes do not involve trials, with their attendant notions of conviction and punishment? Second, is it a violation of the rule of law if some wrongdoers are convicted in court proceedings, and others are treated in a parallel system that trades amnesty or pardon for a truthful account of their role in a wrongdoing coupled with a sincere apology?

I take it as almost uncontroversial that a system of law that subjected all wrongdoers to the same rule – one that traded amnesty or pardon for truthfulness and apology – is not a violation of the rule of law. Minow's account does say that in the Western tradition, adversarial litigation with both parties well represented and treated by the same rules of evidence is *normally* presumed to be necessary. But Minow herself leaves open the possibility that this is merely a Western assumption, and hence one that could be rebutted by substituting something non-Western in its place. Indeed, Scharf says that it is the countering of impunity that is crucial to the rule of law, although he says that trials are necessary for that. I wish to draw out this distinction between what has customarily been done in Western societies and what is necessary for the countering of impunity. In a society where there is a formal system for identifying wrongdoers and forcing them to make public apologies, but where no trials are conducted, it is not necessarily true that wrongdoers are granted impunity.

The term impunity suggests that a wrongdoer is allowed to remain free from "punishment, harm, or loss."[24] On this common understanding, there are obviously other ways to avoid the charge of impunity than by the use of trials and formal punishments. As Lon Fuller has argued: "It is important to note that a system for governing human conduct by formally enacted rules does not of necessity require courts or any other institutional procedure for deciding disputes about the meaning of rules."[25] What is required are some rules that allow for the identification of wrongdoers. If this is not considered as self-evident, then one need only consider the arguments advanced in the earlier sections of this chapter to see that there is no freestanding argument that these trials should occur. I will confine myself here to the situation in which there is a system in place that subjects some wrongdoers to trials but in which others are not subjected to trials. In such situations, is there a claim, based on the rule of law, that victims should be able to have their cases taken to trial – as was claimed by the family of Steve Biko – rather than being treated by an alternative amnesty for truth process?

When the topic is so confined, it is not immediately obvious how to respond. For the discussion of the rule of law almost always considers arbitrary exceptions that are made to the normal procedures, where there is no alternative set of procedures, and where a trial does not take place simply because of a kind of favoritism displayed to one putative wrongdoer. Lon Fuller is one of the few thinkers to address the question of whether there can be two systems of rules operating within a society, and yet for there to be respect for the rule of law. Fuller argues that there are more instances of societies that have multiple systems, including our own federal system, than of societies that do not.[26] And Michael Walzer points out that even in Biblical times, people operated with three very different systems of rules, and yet there was still the rule of law.[27] So, it does not seem that the mere existence of two different procedural systems of rules will violate the rule of law.

Of course, if there is no in-principle way to decide which system of rules is to be used in a particular case, then an arbitrariness creeps in that could be a violation of the rule of law that is similar to what we saw in the previous chapter in the discussion of the problem of selective enforcement of the law. In the brouhaha about President Clinton's pardons at the end of his term, one of the main questions was whether he was influenced in granting pardons to some people by an exchange of money for favors. If there is no procedural basis for ascertaining when pardons can be appropriately given, and when punishments should be meted out, the distinct possibility of arbitrariness and unfairness creeps into the system of rules in violation of the core principles that are supposed to be protected by the rule of law. But this will not necessarily happen simply because trials do not take place. Pardons or amnesty programs do not necessarily mean impunity for the wrongdoer, as long as there are procedures in place, and they are followed.

It could be claimed that trials are the best means available for making sure that arbitrariness and bias do not enter into the decisions about how to treat wrongdoers. Arbitrariness and bias need to be guarded against so as to guarantee that all parties achieve procedural fairness. In the literature on the rule of law, it is the transparency of the procedures that seems to be the most obvious bar to arbitrariness and bias.[28] A system of procedural constraints on the discretion of the pardoner, especially constraints that demand full openness of the proceedings, should make it much harder for arbitrariness and bias to creep into the system of pardons and amnesty programs. Such transparency can be had in non-trial proceedings.

It might also be claimed that once trials begin, it is a violation of the rule of law for prosecutors not to press for convictions. This is indeed one of the hardest issues, and one to which I will only be able to sketch an answer. The issue is hard because the system of rules that includes trials is premised on the idea that the parties to the trial will all be scrupulous in following their roles. Even if a prosecutor has sympathy for a defendant, or if a defense lawyer believes that his or her client is guilty, both lawyers should pursue the interests of their respective clients.[29] The issue is somewhat different if the question is whether a judge should show mercy toward a defendant, and effectively pardon the defendant. This issue cannot be easily resolved by reference to the judge's role morality, for the judge, at least in the Anglo-American system of law, often has discretion to do just this – namely, suspend the sentence.

But does the judge have the discretion, within the confines of the rule of law, to prevent conviction? In answer, I can only point out that there is a technical basis for doing so within the U.S. system of law, normally not thought to be in violation of the rule of law. A judge can overturn a jury's verdict of guilt by ruling favorably on a properly filed motion – a motion for an acquittal, the criminal equivalent of a "judgment as a matter of law" in civil cases – if the judge believes that the evidence does not support a conviction.[30] As long as this is built into the system of procedures, once again there is no clear-cut violation of the rule of law allowing the judge to block a conviction. This would seem to indicate that the rule of law does not provide victims a basis for claiming that they are owed convictions.

IV. The Failure to Convict International Criminals

The right of the victim to have someone convicted for the harms done to him or her is a thoroughly reasonable sounding right. According to this view, the victim, and the victim's family, have a right to know who has committed the act that has so disrupted their lives. Such a right is indeed easily justified by reference to universal justice, or social contract, considerations, or expressivist concerns about condemning what the wrongdoer has done. The family members also need to get closure, and to know who the wrongdoer is, so they are aware who may be out there waiting to harm them again.

Yet it seems clear to me that a concern for finding the identity of the wrong-doer does not support the right to a conviction. To illustrate this point, consider how the South African Truth and Reconciliation Commission operated. To qualify for amnesty, a person had to admit publicly what role he or she had played in apartheid. The admission of guilt did not come after a trial but as a free act given to the victims by the person who had done the harm to the victim and the members of the victim's family. The admission of guilt had to be done publicly, often in front of the victim's family. Because the admission of guilt was not extracted after an adversarial trial, many victims and their family members felt that the admission was more heartfelt, and this helped them achieve closure to their victimization better than after a trial.[31]

This helps us see why truth commissions and amnesty proceedings are often more conducive to reconciliation than are public trials. Trials do provide a forum for the victim (or victim's family) and the putative wrongdoer to meet in a relatively civilized manner. And the trial does have a terminus where both victim and wrongdoer are treated fairly. But especially because of the accusatory nature of the proceedings, there are often ill feelings left at the end of the trial, at least in part because of the confrontational way the lawyers normally conduct themselves on behalf of their clients. While trials are often the best way for a resolution to be achieved for a matter under dispute, trials also often can move the parties farther apart rather than bring them closer together. Divorce lawyers have learned this fact, and many have argued for alternative, less adversarial methods to reach a resolution in such conflicts, especially where the two parties need to retain a relationship, perhaps for the sake of their children.[32]

Owen Fiss has argued that formal adjudication through trials, not alternative dispute resolution, is often in the best interest of victims. Alternatives to trials often produce a peaceful resolution between the parties "while leaving justice undone."[33] In the adversarial adjudication process, the parties often stand in for larger social groups who have been harmed in the society, where both retribution and deterrence may conflict with the goal of providing a kind of private settlement for one perpetrator. When a settlement is reached out of court, other, unnamed but affected parties do not have a say in what occurs. Fiss argues that, for this reason, going through with the trial is often the only way to make clear what the various interests at stake are. Hence, some have argued that lawyers violate their duty to serve justice when they work instead for peace or truth. But as we will see in greater detail in the final chapter, there is no incompatibility between pursuing peace and pursuing justice. As long as the victim gets a public acknowledgment of the identity of the wrongdoer, and the perpetrator is publicly condemned, the victim has his or her due in a way that exposes things to the light of public scrutiny and diminishes the private settlement problem identified by Fiss.

I wish to return here to the claims made by the family of Steve Biko against the amnesties granted by the South African Truth and Reconciliation Commission. As I indicated earlier, it is important to note that those responsible for the murder of Steve Biko were not allowed to act with impunity by the TRC. In South Africa, amnesties were only granted to those who came forward and confessed their role in apartheid. Because the TRC demanded more than cursory explanations of the roles played in apartheid, the parties who came forward were subjected to the public embarrassment of having to confess in detail precisely what they had done. Was this enough to satisfy the rule of law? In this final section, I will argue for a qualified affirmative answer.

Since the people of South Africa overwhelmingly approved the TRC in a referendum as a procedure for dealing with the perpetrators of apartheid, it seems at least prima facie reasonable to think that the TRC was consistent with the domestic rule of law. Indeed, many commentators argued that the TRC was the instantiation of the domestic rule of law after the legal system that fostered apartheid had been dismantled. If a set of procedures has been put in place for ensuring that wrongdoers cannot escape with impunity, and this set of procedures has been accepted by the society in which the procedures are to function, then a prima facie case has been made that the rule of law has been satisfied. And if the people of South Africa have indicated that this is what they want as the basis for dealing with those responsible for the wrongs of apartheid, then it seems that it will be hard for the victims to claim that nonetheless they are owed domestic convictions. So, in the remainder of this section, I will address the more common claim – namely, that the TRC violated the international rule of law.

We must first return to the discussion in the previous chapter of what is meant by the international rule of law. In the context of international criminal law, the rule of law requires that wrongdoers not have impunity, and that there be formal international procedures in place for ascertaining who these wrongdoers are. We have already seen that these conditions, in a domestic setting, do not require that trials, with corresponding convictions and punishments, occur. The question then becomes: Is the rule of law significantly different – in respect to the right of victims to have perpetrators convicted and punished – in the international sphere as opposed to the domestic sphere?

It could be claimed that international law protects human rights, not merely the civil rights that are the proper sphere of domestic law. The protection of human rights could be justified by reference to *jus cogens* norms[34] – universal human rights that stipulate how States must treat their citizens. Then it could be said that the international rule of law protected people from human rights abuses, even in those cases where the human right in question was not recognized in the domestic jurisdiction in which the abuse took place. And on this basis it might be said that the international rule of law is different from the domestic rule of law. Given this scenario, does the international rule of law provide the victims of human rights abuses with the claim that they are owed convictions?

Why might the international rule of law, regardless of what it protects, place higher demands on what victims are owed procedurally than would the domestic rule of law? If domestic tribunals would not otherwise prosecute a given wrongdoing, then it is probably fair to assume that the society at large would not be all that willing to cooperate in establishing who is the wrongdoer. For this reason, greater international procedural safeguards need to be in place than would be necessary in the domestic setting in order to guarantee that victims are given what they are owed – a reasonable likelihood of finding out who the wrongdoer is and some sort of public condemnation of the wrongdoer for having violated the rights of the victim. In addition, the international community is very fragile, so greater vigilance is needed in protecting rights than would be necessary for a more stable domestic order. The fragility of the international order is largely, although not exclusively, traceable to the fact that we lack a single international sovereign, as we saw in Chapter 1.

The lack of cohesion and stability in the international community does indeed give a different color to the international rule of law as opposed to the domestic rule of law. I admit that more vigilance is needed in protecting rights internationally than domestically. But this does not establish that the international rule of law requires that victims are owed convictions. I would argue that the international community is generally not well set up to deal with international trials in the first place. The recent experiences in Yugoslavia and Rwanda have high-lighted how hard it is to secure the interdiction and extradition of defendants. Because of the difficulty in apprehending defendants and in securing evidence, it is necessary that people find the international remedies acceptable. Unfortu-nately, international trials are often seen as an affront to the peoples living in the region where the trials are held, or where the defendants are hiding. Alterna-tives to trials, such as amnesty for truth programs, are sometimes seen as more conciliatory and less likely to disrupt the fragile international order, and more likely to secure the cooperation of the locals in identifying the perpetrators in the first place.

Another strategy is to claim that the rule of law is weakened because of amnesty programs, although stopping short of claiming that amnesty programs are prohibited by the rule of law. Here is what Michael Scharf, a prominent international law scholar, has said on this idea:

[F]ailure to punish former leaders responsible for widespread human rights abuses en-courages cynicism about the rule of law and distrust toward the political process.[35]

The rule of law is weakened, in this view, because of a deep suspicion that the reason these officials have been pardoned is that they were able to evade the normal legal procedures. If one is subject to those often highly public pro-cedures, such suspicion is minimized when possibly dark secret dealings are subjected to the light of public scrutiny. Yet, as was argued earlier, trials are not the only way to maintain procedural guarantees – especially concerning transparency – that will make it less likely that the appearance of arbitrariness will creep into a system of law, and thereby encourage cynicism.

Victims may not be owed convictions, but the society at large can legit-imately demand that peace be restored and that justice be done in response to wrongdoing. It is sometimes said that justice and truth cannot coexist.[36] We will see next that there is no incompatibility between these two values as long as the truth is conjoined with some form of public acknowledgment of wrongdoing. The normal tendency is to think that if wrongdoers are not convicted and punished, they have been let off the hook, and justice has not been done. But this is too narrow a way to conceive of justice as the pro-tector of rights violations. Impunity only occurs when wrongdoers are truly let off the hook, not when they are subjected to alternative systems for as-certaining who is the wrongdoer and for publicly condemning the acts of the wrongdoers.

Throughout this chapter, I have argued that victims are not owed convic-tions. Nonetheless, victims should be respected and their pain should not be ignored. Those, like me, who urge that we respect defendants' rights and that we should sometimes seek alternative means for dealing with wrongdoers than is normally countenanced in trial and punishment, do not see this as a zero-sum game. We can, and must, respect both victims and defendants. Our common humanity demands this much. So, although victims are not owed convictions, their suffering should be recognized and the perpetrators of their harms should be identified and publicly condemned. My point is that we should think more creatively about how to understand the charge that wrongdoers not be granted impunity. And we must construct those alternatives with an eye to the rights of defendants, and to the needs of the societies in question, not merely to the rights of victims. This is the task, but one I can only begin, in the final chapter.

13

Reconciliation and Amnesty Programs

Many mass crimes, such as genocide or ethnic cleansing, involve criminal acts perpetrated on such a large scale and so gruesomely and methodically executed as to be literally unbelievable. Surely, we hope, humans would not do such things to other humans. If even just some of the crimes reported in Rwanda, Cambodia, South Africa, Guatemala, Nigeria, or the Balkans are true, the very idea of not prosecuting the perpetrators, and of granting them amnesty, seems also unbelievable. Not prosecuting people for these crimes seems to be the ultimate in impunity, allowing people to escape accountability for the worst things they could do to their fellow humans.

In the last chapter, I argued that victims are not owed prosecutions, convictions, and punishment of perpetrators. In this chapter, I will argue that it is sometimes justifiable to employ amnesty programs, instead of trials, as a response to some cases of mass atrocity. I will employ the concept of reconciliation in this attempt to show that criminal trials are not necessarily required, even in horrific cases of mass crime.

I will argue that in some cases, the idea of amnesty to secure peace is not unreasonable. The justification for amnesty, or pardon, is based on the claim that we should look beyond the wrongful act in question to the person's character, to his or her other acts, or, even more importantly, to the societal good. And, in some cases, this seems to be both the right strategy and the best indication of our humanity. For example, in South Africa, amnesty programs seem to have had the desired effect of moving the country forward toward a true democracy, whereas conducting criminal trials for those responsible for apartheid might have made achieving that goal impossible. In the last chapter, I argued that in some cases, trials are not required by justice or the rule of law. In this chapter, I provide a positive moral argument in favor of amnesties and pardons over criminal trials in certain cases.

In what follows, I provide a conceptual basis for such a defense by drawing on considerations of equity, forgiveness, and collective responsibility. Equity and forgiveness are intimately entwined concepts that are deeply rooted in Greek moral philosophy and the Anglo-American legal tradition. I do not argue for a general, unrestricted amnesty for all international crimes. Rather, I propose that we follow Aristotle in narrowly construing equity, not as the voice of conscience of the judge but as a gap-filler to correct for certain injustices so as to promote reconciliation. I argue that such a rationale can be extended to some cases of group-based harm that could be the subject of international criminal trials. I then connect reconciliatory goals to considerations of collective responsibility: If many aspects of a society are implicated in mass crimes, then group-based, rather than individualized, remedies become appropriate. In this sense, I complement my earlier argument that international crimes are best seen as group-based crimes with the argument that in some cases, group-based remedies are the most appropriate responses to these international crimes.

In the first section, I explore the goals of reconciliation. Reconciliation is an important idea for my moral minimalist analysis because its chief goal is to return a society to a situation of stable security where inter-group tensions have been diminished. In the next three sections, I take up three of the most important objections to employing remedies other than criminal trials when mass harm has occurred. In the second section, I consider the nature of equity, arguing that there are good reasons for thinking that the display of mercy should sometimes be employed. In the third section, I examine the nature of forgiveness, arguing that forgiving, and even temporarily forgetting, past harms can be justified in some cases. In the fourth section, I consider the concept of collective responsibility, and argue that when many people in a society have shared responsibility or where there is collective responsibility for mass harms, establishing which individuals are most guilty is not always the best strategy. In the fifth section, I return to the more general issue of what would justify reconciliatory strategies, instead of criminal trials, in cases of group-harm. I argue that in some cases, collective remedies are appropriate, and also even preferable in order to satisfy the demands of justice.

I. The Goals of Reconciliation

Victims often have a sense of righteous indignation that the perpetrators are free and unharmed while the victims may be dead or seriously injured and their families thrown into a state of emotional upheaval. But the larger society in which mass crimes have occurred may have other goals that are just as important as the goals of the victims. Key among these goals is that the society be healed, so that, for instance, (1) the various groups in the society can return to a time when they were at peace with each other, or (2) martial law can be ended and democracy restored, or (3) a transition to a new equitable arrangement within the society can more easily be established. This is especially true when a large cross-section of the population participated, in some form or other, in the harms.

Trials are best at dealing with individuals who are responsible, not with groups that are responsible, especially large groups. As Hannah Arendt once said, "[W]here all are guilty, nobody in the last analysis can be judged."[1] What I think she meant is that it makes little sense to look for the responsible individual in a context in which most of the members of the society, at least by complicity, participated in a harm. In response to Arendt, I argued in Chapter 9 that trials that focused on the most guilty people, normally political and military leaders, could be conducted. Going beyond these leaders to others in the society who are guilty, when many others in that same society are guilty, raises problems for the rule of law, as I indicated in Chapter 11.

So here we have the following puzzle. International criminal trials are most clearly justified when harms are group-based, but trials themselves are most problematical when large groups participate, or are complicit, in mass harms. The result is that in some situations, we may do better with various alternative remedies to criminal punishment, such as those remedies provided by truth commissions and amnesty programs. These alternatives to trials may better advance the goals of reconciliation than would criminal trials, with their heightening of adversarial tensions. We can see the roots of this problem in that even when there are just two possible perpetrators, there is a great likelihood that each will try to portray the other as the only one responsible. There are rule of law issues concerning selectivity if one perpetrator, and not the other, is prosecuted. With even larger groups, tensions are intensified, and the group of perpetrators comes to see itself at odds with the group of victims, or worse, where some parties are both perpetrators *and* victims. Whereas *compensatory*, or rectificatory, justice may not be done, *distributive* justice may nonetheless best be accomplished if certain alternatives to trials are pursued.

Distributive justice becomes important in cases of mass crime since there are normally also mass perpetrators. Whenever many people are all potentially guilty, serious questions arise about who should be blamed most, who should be blamed least, or who not at all. Justice, as fairness, becomes an important concern in deciding who should receive what share of the blame for such mass crimes. Compensatory justice involves the idea of a proper return to one who has been harmed. Distributive justice is centered on the idea that if more than one party is owed something, we must determine how to divide things up in such a way that although not all are satisfied, no one can claim that from an impartial standpoint the distribution is unfair. Reconciliation is closer to distributive justice than to compensatory justice. Indeed, in order to accomplish a peaceful settlement of differences, it may not be possible fully to compensate those who have been harmed. This is the price of reconciliation, and the rationale could be either that distributing burdens and benefits fairly could not otherwise be achieved, or that the future consequences of achieving reconciliatory peace for all dictate that some people not be compensated at the present.

As we saw in the last chapter, it is also not clear that compensatory justice should be the proper goal of the criminal law. The criminal law aims at making things right for the society after a horrendous crime has been committed. Individual compensation for victims is largely a matter of the civil law, not of the criminal law. For this reason, it could also be argued that reconciliatory strategies that failed to provide compensatory justice for victims should not be so easily dismissed. Since it is the society that is owed something after criminal acts, reconciliation can be seen as at least as legitimate a goal as providing closure for victims. And if the society needs reconciliation, and that reconciliation will not involve further oppression, and if the only way to achieve reconciliation is to forego trials, then the society might be justified in not holding criminal trials at all.

It is important to note that I have focused on defendants' rights in criminal law in this book. This should not be interpreted to mean that I am unsympathetic to the victims. We need to do much more than is presently done, in either domestic or international law, to compensate victims, especially in mass atrocities. Direct civil compensation schemes are the most obvious way to make up for the structural lack of attention to victim compensation in criminal law. But it is also important, as we will see, that social conditions be changed so that the likelihood of mass violence to victims is diminished. We owe victims this much. Unfortunately, this compensation is not the proper purview of the criminal law.

Martha Minow has argued that "reconciliation is not the goal of trials except in the most abstract sense . . . The trial works in the key of formal justice, sounding closure through a full and final hearing, a verdict."[2] One example of reconciliation occurs when two or more warring factions are brought together again as a means to mend a tear in the fabric of society. This is seen most clearly in the case of the Balkans, although it may not be the best way to characterize other cases of reconciliation, such as in post-apartheid South Africa. That such a tear be mended is often crucial for the end of war, and the turning away from martial law and toward the rule of law. This appears to present another puzzle. Some forms of reconciliation are crucial for moving toward establishing the conditions necessary for a democratic order, indeed for a return to the rule of law itself, and yet it is often thought that amnesty programs aimed at reconciliation are themselves clear violations of the rule of law. In the last chapter, though, I argued that this need not necessarily be true, especially in cases where amnesty is granted in exchange for public acknowledgment of guilt and acceptance of public condemnation. In such cases, as was true with the South African Truth and Reconciliation Commission, procedures can be put in place that make arbitrariness and impunity no more likely than in the case of trials. In any event, this is only part of the picture. If reconciliation cannot be achieved – as, for instance, in the contemporary situation in the Balkans – the very possibility of a stable court system, the hallmark of the rule of law, is jeopardized.

Sometimes, reconciliation can only be achieved through something like a criminal trial, where once and for all a guilty party is identified. Only when this determination has been made can the two warring sides stop their mutual recriminations. This is the idea that I discussed in previous chapters when I suggested that the international community take a special interest in those harms that are group-based, since the security of the international community will be jeopardized unless there is some criminal trial. So my position is not that criminal trials are never appropriate, or that reconciliation is somehow opposed to criminal trials. Rather, I only argue that in some cases, reconciliatory goals may require that criminal trials not be engaged in, for there to be a better chance at long-term peace and stability in a given region of the world. But in other cases, justice will demand that trials occur. In these latter cases, attention needs to be paid nonetheless to the variety of claims of justice.

From my moral minimalist perspective, the defense of reconciliation is linked to the establishment of a stable and secure order – that is, in bringing people to a position of relative harmony with one another. The goals of reconciliation all concern the attainment of that peace and security among peoples that we all seek. Criminal trials sometimes exacerbate rather than diminish the tensions and divisions among peoples. In those situations, it makes sense to consider alternatives to criminal trials, such as amnesties or truth commissions. In the next three sections, I will consider the main arguments advanced against amnesties and other alternatives to criminal trials. For each set of arguments, I will argue that there are some cases where avoiding a criminal trial is justifiable. At the end of this chapter, I will return to the discussion of the drawbacks of criminal trials in a world that is trying to repair rather than compensate.

II. The Concept of Equity

One of the most often-heard objections to amnesties and pardons is that they violate the rule of law, especially concerning the provision that law must be administered equitably. We saw some reasons to reject this view in the last chapter, largely negative in character, arguing that victims are not owed convictions or punishments as a procedural right. Now we turn to the positive argument. And here we will explain first why it is that a judge, or even a whole society, can justifiably choose to ignore the clear prescripts of the criminal law, and show mercy. It matters, of course, whether amnesty is granted before there has been a trial, or whether a pardon is given at the end of a trial.[3] But in both cases, it appears that amnesties and pardons violate the rule of law in that the perpetrators of criminal acts seemingly "get off 'scot-free.'"[4] In addition, the amnesties seem to be problematical since the judges or legislatures that decide in favor of them often consider the effects of such amnesties only on their own States and not also on the world community that is itself the subject of the international harm. Only when judges or legislatures take into account the larger international harms can amnesties rise above obtaining merely local justification. In this section, I will focus mainly on the criticism concerning the rule of law applied to judges who effectively grant pardons and legislatures that grant more generalized amnesties.[5]

Since at least the time of the ancient Greeks, it has been recognized that strict adherence to the letter of the law will sometimes result in inequity and even injustice. In the *Nicomachean Ethics*, Aristotle says of equity: "The legislator having left a gap, and committed an error, by making an unqualified proposition, we must correct his omission; we must say for him what he would have said himself if he had been present, and what he would have put into law if only he had known." Since laws are universal in form, and cases are particular, it will sometimes turn out that the law has been correctly applied to the case, but that justice dictates that the case not fall under the law. In such cases, the court should make a correction in accordance with the principles of equity. In this context, Aristotle gives the classic definition of equity as "a correction of law where law is defective owing to its universality."[6]

There are two ways that law can be in need of correction on grounds of equity. First, an unanticipated case could arise, which, if anticipated, would have caused the legislature, or the parties to a treaty, to change the law so that it would apply differently to the case. Correction is needed here because of the limits on imagination in predicting what cases that would fall under the law might arise. The correction is justified because the lawmakers *would* have wanted the case not to fall under the law. Second, even if anticipated, there are cases that should not fall under the law because a clear injustice will arise. This is the more problematical side of equity. There is still a defect in the law, "owing to its universality," but the defect is in need of correction regardless of whether the lawmakers would have wanted such a correction. Correction is needed because the lawmakers are bound by general principles of justice, and without correction, the law would be applied to this case. In this second way, the correction is justified because the lawmakers *should* have wanted the case not to fall under the law. As will be indicated later, this second basis for equity has been hotly debated since Aristotle's time.

Aristotle employs the analogy of "the leaden rule used in making the Lesbian mouldings." If we were to use a rule that was unbending, it would not conform to the shape of the stone. Instead, the leaden "rule adapts itself to the shape of the stone and is not rigid." Analogously in law, an equitable "decree is adapted to the facts."[7] Here, Aristotle is clearly talking about equity as a form of discretionary power of the judge. But that power is still carefully circumscribed, just as is the "leaden rule" that can bend to the shape of the stone, but no further. Similarly, equity involves a discretionary power to bend the rules of law in a way that conforms to the facts of an unusual case so as to achieve justice. But the rules nonetheless have a fixed elasticity, circumscribed by the general principles of justice that supported the rule in the first place. In this sense, equity is already important in the act of the legislature in setting out rules that are flexible enough to be bent by judges to fit the facts of particular cases. Aristotle contends that equity is, to a certain extent, superior to legal justice, since it is "a correction of legal justice."[8]

Equity was of central concern to Roman law and also to the early development of Anglo-Saxon law. In both contexts, equity was given a broader meaning than Aristotle had given it, so that equity came to be seen as the correction of law based on broad principles of morality, largely having to do with the conscience-based judgments of judges. Frederick Pollock and Frederic William Maitland tell us that by the time of Henry Bracton, the thirteenth-century English legal scholar, judges conceived of themselves as having equitable powers with wide discretionary purview.[9] But this is not at all what Aristotle had in mind, and not what equity has come to mean in recent Anglo-American jurisprudence, and certainly not the kind of equity I would support from my moral minimalist position.

Theodore Plucknett argues that the "need for a supplement to the common law procedure was very evident in the fourteenth century."[10] By the sixteenth century, the Star Chamber courts had already carved out their own domain, quite distinct from common law courts, and formed what Pluncknett calls a court of "criminal equity." As common law courts saw themselves to be more and more bound by precedent, and less and less able to exercise discretion, the need arose for separate courts. These courts were established to correct for the possible unfairness of the strict application of previous legal authority to contemporary cases that was not contemplated in the earlier decisions and statutes, or where a clear injustice would occur by such an application. In effect, one court system engaged in the rigorous interpretation and application of the law, and the other court system took a broader view of what would be best for all of the parties to a dispute, including the society at large.

By the early sixteenth century, the barrister and legal philosopher Christopher St. Germaine urged a reining-in of the courts of equity, and thereby a return to Aristotle, saying that "the lord chancellor must order his conscience after the rules and grounds of the law of the realm."[11] In other words, St. Germaine urged that judges not be allowed to exercise what had become their nearly unbridled discretion in courts of equity. Over the next few centuries, the extent of discretion for the conscientious judgments of judges in equity courts became greatly circumscribed, but without losing the idea that equity was to involve the application of limited moral principles to legal judgments. For our purposes, courts of equity continued to allow the application of mercy to situations that otherwise clearly called for strict penalties or punishments.

The difficulty with the more expansive view of equity that had pervaded the English courts prior to the sixteenth century was that conscience is an unstable basis on which to correct or change a legal decision, since one person's conscience may differ quite considerably from another person's conscience.[12]

Hence, one judge's conception of mercy might be quite broad, but another's quite narrow. The black letter law will be subject to nullification by a judge whose conscience tells him that the law is morally wrong, or that morally the law should not be applied in a case, whereas, for another judge, the law *will* be applied in that case. The resolution of this problem by seventeenth-century philosophers such as Thomas Hobbes is quite different from that of Roman and medieval natural law theorists, in that the conscience in question is a kind of artificial conscience, not the natural conscience of the person who happens to occupy the position of Lord Chancellor.[13]

Natural conscience is the conscience of the judge or chancellor *as a person*, whereas artificial conscience is the conscience of the judge or chancellor in his or her limited role *as an office-holder*. For the judge as office-holder, conscientious judgments should be based on the specific principles of justice found in a given society. For the judge as natural person, conscientious judgments are based on broader moral principles. When equity is restricted to artificial conscientious judgments, the judgments will, at least in principle, be predictable by anyone who thinks about the case in question in light of the more specific principles of justice that underlie any legal system. The discretion of judges sitting in courts of equity should be restricted when equity is understood as involving artificial, not natural, conscience.

In more recent times, various legal theorists have continued to worry that equity seems to give judges such a wide discretionary power that they are able to base their judgments on their consciences without consideration of what the law says. This is what seemed to worry Oliver Wendell Holmes, Jr., at the end of the nineteenth century when he railed against judges who display "a confusion between morality and law" in deciding cases.[14] Holmes seemed to think that equity should not be a basis for a ruling when it is in direct conflict with a clear rule of law. Yet one can place limits on conscience by restricting it to what is part of institutional "conscience." Indeed, a system of law needs to be connected with morality in some respects, as was shown in the first chapters of this book, for that system of law to be deserving of respect at all. So Holmes's criticism is misplaced – the issue is not whether judges should base their decisions on morality, but what type and extent of moral judgments should be allowed to affect the legal decisions of judges. As in earlier chapters of this book, I will take a moral minimalist approach.

The very function of equity is to correct the law; thus, equity will necessarily conflict directly with a clear rule of law. The criticism of equity by Holmes is instructive nonetheless. Surely if equity is an area of overlap between law and morality, it must involve a narrow and highly circumscribed overlap, otherwise no one will be able to predict how judges sitting in equity will rule. This is the institutional sense of equity – namely, conscience restricted by past institutional practice. The moral minimalist position that I endorsed in earlier chapters is strongly supportive of only a minimum of overlap between law and morality.

As we saw in Chapter 2, my position embraces a moral minimum, which we can now see as itself supporting mercy in some cases, and even overriding the application of particular legal rules that do not seem to advance a broader conception of justice.

As I have indicated, equity is not the same as legal justice, and can conflict with it in a narrow sense; but in a broader sense, equity is an essential condition of justice that corrects the law. As a result, appeals to equity will justify the kind of appeal to mercy and broader social good that is involved when amnesties are granted instead of holding criminal trials, or when pardons are granted after those trials are held. Support for this view comes from tradition in Anglo-American law going back hundreds of years, in the philosophical tradition dating back to Aristotle, and also from the burden of the arguments advanced in this section. If it is recognized that peace will be jeopardized by holding a criminal trial, a legislature, or the parties to a treaty, would have, or at least should have, allowed for a different remedy than merely following the law and holding a trial. Hence equity can support amnesties or pardons even when amnesty seems to be a clear violation of the application of "black letter law."

III. Forgiveness and Amnesty

A related objection to not conducting criminal trials is that the perpetrators will be allowed to forget what they have done. And once this has occurred, there is a greater likelihood that these perpetrators, or others in the society, will be allowed to repeat the past injustices. One of the main advantages of alternatives to criminal trials is that the members of the society might come to forget the cause of their animosities toward one another. In this section, I confront the problem that reconciliation often involves some form of forgetting, and yet risks leaving the members of society without both a strong memory of the horrors that have been caused, and are to be avoided in the future, and a basis for deterrence of future crimes of this sort. What criminal trials provide is an acknowledgment and condemnation of the perpetrators. When equity and forgiveness are mixed with too much forgetting, there is a loss of the kind of recognition of wrongdoing that is crucial for justice.[15]

The word "amnesty" is derived from the Greek word *amnestia*, which is closely linked with another Greek term *amnestikakeia*, which means forgetting and forgiving legally wrongful acts. Indeed, the Athenian Greeks were famous for having declared one of the world's first general amnesties, in 403 B.C., when all of the rebels in a bloody civil uprising were pardoned after they had surrendered. The Athenians were praised for forgetting the injuries they had sustained in the uprising, for forgiving their enemies, and for having resisted the contemporary custom of executing or exiling rebels.[16] The praise for this amnesty recalls the words of Justice Jackson at the start of the Nuremberg

Trials. Jackson said that the Allied countries were similarly to be praised for staying the hand of vengeance by conducting trials rather than summary executions. Jackson did not seem to realize that there are several other alternatives to summary executions. Indeed, the Greek amnesty is one of the oldest known examples of staying the hand of vengeance.

Forgiveness is a virtue of persons and institutions. On some accounts, forgiveness is deserved or merited once a person has somehow atoned for his or her initial wrong.[17] Sometimes the offender deserves to be pardoned, either because of who he or she is, or because of the circumstances of the offense, or because of what would likely occur after punishment is inflicted. Surely, differences in circumstance should matter – relevantly different cases should not be treated alike. This equitable principle, integral to systems of law of any sort, should guide us into taking account of special circumstances. As we saw earlier, to disregard all considerations other than the guilt of the accused is sometimes to deny basic equity. Here again we see what Aristotle described as the gap that can open because of a mismatch between the generality of law and the specificity of the case. If the accused is a child, or is mentally incompetent, or possessed of good intentions, mercy and forgiveness may dictate that amnesty or pardon is the appropriate basis for response.

Like pardons for capital offenders, amnesties for criminal wrongdoing do not appear to fit well within a system of courts and trials. Amnesty programs stand in stark contrast to the adversarial confrontation and punishment of lawbreakers that satisfies a society's desire for retribution, but that also might thwart reconciliation.[18] But retribution is not the only morally legitimate response to harm and wrongdoing.[19] There is also what has been called "transitional" or "restorative" justice.[20] Restorative justice is that form of justice that corresponds to reconciliation, in that restorative justice seeks to remedy the effects of injustice by restoring the society to order. In this sense, restorative justice recalls Hegel's idea of global justice. We return to this idea, now stripped of the idea that it is something victims can demand as their right, but rather something that society can demand so as to heal from the tear in the fabric of society that is produced especially by mass crimes. But unlike in Hegel's discussion of this point, convictions and punishments are not necessarily owed as a matter of "global" justice.

Amnesties or, properly, pardons, can be a legitimate form of remedy, even after there has been a formal trial. As I have indicated, this is because one of the main functions of courts since the time of the Greeks has been to take account of gaps that open in the normal administration of strict legal justice, and to deal in a fair way with cases that do not easily fit under a given black letter law. Equity is a matter of broader justice, and a court is the traditional forum in which disputes about justice are adjudicated. Indeed, Justice William O. Douglas has written that "[t]he qualities of mercy and practicality have made equity the instrument for nice adjustment and reconciliation between the public interest and private needs . . . "[21] Notice that in Douglas's view, there is a clear relationship between equity and reconciliation that operates especially through the moral category of mercy.

U.S. courts regularly use equitable remedies to enforce *oral* agreements that cannot be enforced at law because they violate the Statute of Frauds, and where equality of treatment would require them to be enforced just as their relevantly similar cousins, *written* agreements, are enforced. The gap left for equity in oral agreement cases is that, for some reason, the people in question never committed the terms of their agreement to writing. In the oral agreement case, the possibility of fraud needs to be guarded against. But if there is no reason to suspect fraud, then it would violate principles of equity to treat the oral agreement case differently from the case of a non-fraudulent written agreement, even though, from a strict legal perspective requiring that contracts be written, there is no agreement to be enforced because there is no written contract.

A related objection contends that the granting of amnesties or pardons goes against one of the canons of equity – "Equity follows the Law." Following this maxim would mean restricting equity to truly filling in the gaps – that is, providing equitable remedies only where the law is truly silent. But there is another maxim of equity that can be cited to the contrary – "Equity will not Suffice a Wrong to be Without a Remedy,"[22] that it is inequitable for some wrongs to be punished and others not. The tradition of equity I have traced from Aristotle until the present recognizes that some wrongs should not be punished even though punishment seems to be called for, since there could be, or has been, an application of clearly applicable law to a case. This is another way of filling the gaps, but one in which courts will sometimes have to "forget" what the law strictly requires, perhaps by granting pardons or amnesty, so as to follow justice in its broader sense. Such a traditional understanding of equity makes it a part of justice without its being the same as legal justice, and we can see how forgetting can be consistent, in some cases, with justice.

Amnesty programs are typically established extra-judicially – that is, by some act of legislature or comparable body. And here we return to our original problem. Amnesty programs seem to require the kind of forgetting of past offenses that risks leaving the members of a given society without a clear memory of the horrors of mass violence. In this context, though, consider a situation such as that in present-day Burundi, where "ethnic Tutsi leaders have reportedly expressed fear of prosecution for their part in the civil war there, a clear disincentive to leave office soon." Or also consider a 2001 amnesty proposal in Kenya that was offered as a way to persuade the strong-arm leader, Daniel arap Moi, finally to step down in favor of elections.[23] In both cases, at least temporary forgetting does seem to be necessary for the democratic process to be restored.

In order to achieve peace and return to democratic rule, it is sometimes necessary that the members of society not only forgive but also, at least temporarily, forget horrible atrocities. One could argue that this is precisely what has not happened in hot spots that continue to experience bloodshed and unrest, such as Palestine, Ireland, Kashmir, and the Balkans. Temporary amnesia is indeed what the people in these regions need if they are ever to experience a lasting peace. Dwelling on the past, especially dwelling on who was at fault for past wrongs, seems to be just what has produced such instability. Reconciliation between groups does not generally require forgetting, but it does require a kind of forgiving that is sometimes made considerably easier if it is linked with temporary forgetting. In addition, the social conditions have to change so that what caused the violence is not repeated, otherwise we risk repeating the past. As I have been arguing, the difficult part is inducing the temporary amnesia of certain wrongs in a way that does not lead to permanent collective amnesia from which we are likely to repeat past injustices.

Forgiveness and mercy are themselves part of an enlarged background of justice. It is a form of injustice to treat all cases according to the same standard. And it is also a form of injustice to ignore the factors that would call for lesser, or no punishment, due to special circumstances. Legal justice is often understood as strict conformity to the rules of law. But there are always gaps in formal legal justice, or areas where there should be gaps, and cases that fall into those gaps can be treated in terms of mercy and forgiveness when it is warranted, instead of by strict adherence to the legal framework. The broader construal of justice that takes into account background conditions fits the remedy to the case, and as we have seen, this means that sometimes there will not be strict conformity to legal rules. In some cases, especially when there are important societal goals to be accomplished, amnesties and pardons are warranted, even though criminal acts have occurred that otherwise should be prosecuted.[24] Indeed, it is sometimes precisely because there have been criminal acts that otherwise should be prosecuted that forgiving and temporary forgetting are important in order for peace and democracy to be restored.

IV. Collective Responsibility

A third objection to amnesties or pardons as alternatives to prosecution and punishment is that the idea of individual responsibility is lost. When individual perpetrators are pardoned, they are let off the hook in a way that seems to give them a kind of impunity. The individual perpetrator is treated as if he or she is not responsible for what has occurred – hence it appears that individual responsibility is lost. Yet what is sometimes gained is also related to responsibility – namely, a greater sense of collective responsibility for what has occurred. And as we will see, collective responsibility can sometimes be more productive of societal healing and harmony than is the accusation and counter-accusation of the criminal trial's attempt to establish individual responsibility.

Amnesties in the past have been vehicles for achieving reconciliation that also attempt to preserve individual responsibility. Aristotle's discussion of the Athenian Constitution mentions amnesty as a correction of the law concerning those who have offended against the law "if they render account" of themselves.[25] In some amnesty programs, we maintain this sense of personal accountability by requiring a public confession of the role the perpetrator played in the harm as a condition of receiving amnesty. Even where individual responsibility is weakened, other responsibility considerations may justify the amnesty program. In this section, I will argue that there are good reasons, based on notions of collective responsibility, for amnesties and pardons to be declared even where criminal trials could have taken place, and despite the fact that individual responsibility might, in a certain sense, be weakened.

One of the most recent general amnesties in the United States was extended to undocumented aliens who had entered the United States prior to 1982.[26] The United States Congress was praised for having forgiven those who had broken the law by entering the United States illegally or by overstaying the limits of their visas. In addition, amnesty was thought to be appropriate for trying to heal the wounds of racial divisiveness swirling around the issue of the inequitable treatment of "illegal" aliens, many of whom are Hispanic.[27] Such amnesty programs can be justified as a reconciliation remedy, especially as a remedy for injustices that result from a collective harm, and where it might be said that an organized group is collectively responsible for that harm.

Collective responsibility is a highly contested subject in moral and legal philosophy.[28] In these debates, "collective" refers to some sort of grouping or assembling of people into a single unit, and "responsibility" refers to some form of accountability to another party for what the unit has done. Collective responsibility can be understood in either a distributive sense, referring to aggregated individual responsibilities, or in a non-distributive sense, referring to the responsibility of a group itself. When collective responsibility is used in its distributive sense, it is not thought to be especially problematic. If I am responsible for what I have done, and you are responsible for what you have done, then when you and I act together, we are responsible for what we have done. I am responsible for my part, and you for yours. Difficulties arise when it is not possible to pry apart what each of us has contributed. In that case, there is a temptation to say that we are responsible in a non-distributive sense: The unit – the "we" – is responsible for what the unit has done.[29] Here, the responsibility is based on some action or feature of the group that is not reducible to a feature or action of the group's members.

Various forms of collective responsibility have been recognized in law. In primitive legal systems, "the unit is not the individual but the kin. The individual is but part of the kin. If he be injured, it is the kin which is injured. If he be slain, it is the blood of the kin that has been shed, and the kin is entitled to compensation or to vengeance."[30] In modern times, collective responsibility turns up in both criminal and tort actions. The doctrine of criminal conspiracy allows an individual to be held liable for what another individual did when both individuals were acting in concert, as we saw in earlier chapters. Vicarious liability in tort law allows employers to be held liable for what their employees did, and for corporations to be held liable for what their officers did. Thus, even in that most individualistic field of law, collective responsibility is not unknown. Collective responsibility in criminal law makes the most sense where there has been a mass crime of the sort that could only have been committed with the participation of a large number of people in the society, and where there was some sort of coordination, such as in the case of ethnic cleansing or genocide campaigns.

Reconciliation remedies, such as amnesties, are most clearly called for when there has been a fissure in the society caused by a collective mistreatment of a group by the larger society, and when such a fissure has caused the mistreated minority to engage in illegal acts. In such cases, the larger society is collectively responsible for finding a remedy for the illegal acts of the minority that will take into account the majority's own complicity in these "illegal acts." When the majority contributes to the "illegal" acts of the minority, the majority bears a collective responsibility to provide a fair remedy that does not merely mete out retribution against the minority's members.[31] Consider a nation that conducts an illegal war, causing many men and women to disobey military draft laws. The nation owes the war resisters a fair remedy for their illegal acts that will facilitate reconciliation. In a similar case, U.S. draft resisters were granted amnesty to return home from Canada, where they had sought asylum during the Vietnam War.[32]

Consider also the case of an ethnic war in which both sides have antagonized the other for many years, perhaps harming individuals of the other group merely because they were group members. When mass harms of this sort occur, it is likely that both sides to the conflict have been complicit in these harms.[33] This is not always true, for one group may merely assault another group without provocation or involvement in the group harm. Even in the case of the Holocaust, there is evidence to suggest that Jewish leaders were complicit in some of these harms.[34] Or consider the case of so-called illegal aliens in the United States, where the larger society is complicit in enticing these aliens into our society as a form of cheap labor. In some cases, collective responsibility would seem to support the idea that some sort of amnesty or pardon be granted to those who were in the wrong, given that those who were wronged were at least somewhat responsible for the situation that generated the harm. This would follow the general practice in legal theory of seeing "contributory fault" as a bar to recovery, or at least as a basis for diminishing the amount of compensation that can be recovered in tort actions.

In cases of mass crime, such as genocide and ethnic cleansing, there is some-times a similar involvement by most of the rest of the larger society. Recently, in the Balkans and Palestine, we have seen how few have escaped with clean hands. For this reason, it makes sense to talk of collective responsibility and to consider collective remedies, even when those collective remedies might in some sense diminish individual responsibility. For in another sense, we will be calling attention to the complicity of many others – where complicity is a form of individual responsibility – and hence also acknowledging their individual responsibility, now understood in a somewhat different sense. Collective responsibility is not to be shunned or ignored in such cases. Collective responsibility need not be based on "guilt by association" but rather on the obvious fact that mass crimes often occur as a result of the complicity of many members of a society, even those who are members of the victimized group.

The argument of this section is that in some situations of group-based harm, many members of the society may have chosen to play a role in the climate that has been instrumental in nurturing the harmful conduct.[35] As we will see next, when many members of a society share responsibility for the conditions that spurred some individuals to cause harm, the line between perpetrator and bystander (and sometimes even the line between perpetrator and victim) is harder to draw, resulting in an ascription of collective, or shared, responsibility. When this occurs, amnesties or pardons may then be justified as a replacement for criminal trials and individual punishments, even though there is in some sense a loss of individual responsibility. Here I am not talking about a defense against, or even a diminishment of, individual responsibility, but an alternative remedy altogether that hopefully, as we will see next, will still preserve much of individual responsibility.

V. Collective Remedies

The standard criminal remedy of imprisonment will obviously not work when a large group, especially the majority of the members of a society, is collectively responsible for a harmful situation. And once imprisonment is ruled out, most people think that other standard remedies are also ruled out as a basis for settling such disputes. But this is not necessarily true. Think, for a moment, of how corporations are dealt with at law, even at criminal law. Courts have ordered corporations to pay stiff fines, or, in several celebrated cases in Australia, pay for adverse publicity against themselves.[36] And when courts have not been involved, legislatures and similar entities have ordered amnesties or pardons in exchange for admissions of guilt.[37] In these contexts, the idea of collective remedies seems obviously to be relevant to our deliberations about mass crimes and reconciliation.

Since the Nuremberg Trials, there has been much discussion about what form of remedy is appropriate when a group is collectively responsible for a given harm. In such cases, it seems intuitively appealing to look for some kind of collective remedy that secures peace between the two groups. When one sub-group of a society engages in harmful conduct against another sub-group of that society, it seems appropriate to try to reconcile the two groups. The sub-group that is collectively responsible might begin this process by expressing remorse or regret and by asking the larger group for forgiveness. If the larger sub-group – the majority – is engaged in collectively harmful actions against a minority sub-group, it may be the case that the larger unit is the one to ask for forgiveness, as was true when the United States government publicly apologized and asked for forgiveness for unjustly incarcerating Japanese Americans during World War II.

One strategy that is open to us, though, is to think of the feelings of guilt or shame of a group as being distributed and vicariously expressed by a representative member of the group.[38] Just as a collective decision can be expressed in the representative actions of the leader of a group, or even in the actions of a minor player in the group, so it may be possible for a representative member of the group to express the group's collective feelings of regret or apology. This strategy has the advantage over more robustly metaphysical solutions to the problem in that it does not have to reify the group or convey the idea that there is some kind of group feeling that transcends the feelings of the individual members.[39] So it may be that by acting through a representative member, one group can apologize to another for a collective wrong it has caused. And this collective apology, perhaps along with expressions of individual remorse for what each member of the group has done to contribute to the harm, may be a reasonable form of collective remedy for group harms.

What if the harm is in some sense a harm to humanity, as we discussed in previous chapters? Can amnesty programs have any hope of redressing harm to humanity? It seems quite likely that granting amnesty to Pinochet, for instance, does not redress anything, and makes the harms to humanity that Pinochet perpetrated worse rather than better, especially if his amnesty was a calculated way to get him off the hook, and perpetrated by his political cronies. Now, if the society had voted to grant such an amnesty, paying special attention to the voices of those who were victimized by Pinochet, things might be different. But the pardon or amnesty granted by cronies to one another does not redress anything. Rather, the kind of case in which amnesty might partially redress mass atrocities is, as I said earlier, one in which a large proportion of the society was complicit in the mass harms, perhaps where many people were both victims and perpetrators, or at least bystanders. In such cases, a process that promotes positive social change and healing may indeed redress the harm to humanity.

Any collective remedy, such as collective responsibility itself, is often subject to the charge of unfairness. For it is almost always true that the members of a group do not all act in the same guilty way, or even at all. Treating individuals collectively seemingly makes no exceptions, and in effect forces all of the members of the group to suffer the consequences for what some members of the group have done. This is often referred to as "guilt by association." The main response to the charge of unfairness is that although it is rare for all the members of a group to be equally responsible, it is also rare that all non-participating members of the group are powerless to prevent the group from so acting, or at least able to distance themselves from the harmful effects of the collective action. There is no reason to think that the distribution of responsibility to the members of a group must be done in a way that is unfair, since that distribution could be based on the actual contribution to the harm that each has made, or it could be based on the leadership role played or the extent of benefit received by the members. In cases in which amnesty is tailored rather than blanket, as was true in the Vietnam War protestors' case mentioned earlier, it will be possible to spread responsibility without necessarily violating principles of fairness.[40]

Various international documents decry the attempt to talk about collective remedies in legal or even quasi-legal terms.[41] The idea here is that collective remedies fail to treat people according to what they have done. In collective remedy arrangements, one must treat the individual according to his or her status, merely as a group member – hence the charge of guilt by association. But this is only true of *blanket* amnesties and pardons, not of those types of amnesties that require the individual member to admit his specific role in a given harm, and then to demonstrate sincere remorse for what the person has specifically done.[42] So we return to the idea we started with. The wronged minority group could press for some kind of amnesty coupled with public disclosure of the specific wrongs committed by the members of the majority, along with some kind of vicarious expression of sincere apology or public condemnation, as a collective remedy for the wrongs.

Amnesties and pardons can be justifiably used in those situations of group-based harm in which reconciliation will be more clearly advanced by this route than by criminal trials (and where the perpetrators still must admit their role and guilt).[43] Amy Guttman and Dennis Thompson rightly caution, though, that only certain forms of reconciliation can justify amnesty programs – namely, those reconciliation plans that do not purchase stability at the cost of repression.[44] There are many stable societies that are morally odious. Amnesties and pardons are justified only when the reconciliation makes things better for those who were the object of harm. For once we move outside the normal avenues of criminal prosecution, the rights of the victims should again be at center stage, and no amnesty or reconciliation plan should be allowed to go forward unless repression is diminished, not merely that stability is achieved.

One reason why amnesties may be a good collective remedy has to do itself with the core idea underlying collective and shared responsibility. The poet Joy Kazama has laid the groundwork for this idea, expressing it better than I could, when she said: "[B]ystanders and perpetrators are on the same side."[45] Most members of a society, including most victims, are also bystanders, or, as it is often put, somehow complicit. Are any of us all that different from one well-known Yugoslav philosopher who was previously known for his moral courage and who now is known for his support of ethnic cleansing – both apparently on principled grounds? Are our own attitudes all that different from his? If we acted as he did, given how much alike he and we are, is it inconceivable that he (that we) should be pardoned, that our acts should be forgiven and even forgotten as if there were a collective temporary amnesia, so that we can heal?

I remain bothered by this suggestion, as I imagine is true for most of my readers. For this reason, throughout this book I have generally supported criminal trials for group-based and mass harms. What is worrisome about amnesties and pardons is that they can sweep too broadly, exculpating those who did monstrous things for terrible motives, and instead treating them just like those who merely looked the other way. Surely these people are not all complicit in the same way, even if it is true that they are all "on the same side." So what I favor is a limited form of amnesty or pardon, granted in some cases where a large number of people in the society have participated in the climate that gave rise to the crimes. And I also favor an amnesty or pardon program that calls for a sincere admission of the role and guilt on the part of the person to be pardoned.

Those of us raised in the Western legal tradition often have a visceral reaction to attempts to sidestep legal trials. We worry about the rule of law, among other things. I share those worries. Criminal trials can be used to express the outrage of humanity, but it is difficult to do so, given that there is an individual in the dock, not an "ism," to recall Hannah Arendt's point about the Eichmann trial.[46] The goals of reconciliation can sometimes make it justifiable to circumvent the criminal process. To see this, we need to suspend our faith in the notion that only trials can achieve justice. And to do so, we need to recognize that justice comes in different forms, and that each form may be best served by a different set of institutional arrangements. In some cases, amnesties and pardons are the best institutional forms for dealing with harmful conduct. In other cases, as long as we proceed cautiously to protect the rights of defendants, international criminal trials may be justifiable as well.

The goals of reconciliation sometimes take precedence over other important concerns, such as the goal for victims and their families to attain closure and emotional renewal. But, as I have argued, reconciliation need not be seen as opposed to justice, at least where justice is understood in a wide sense to include distributional as well as compensatory concerns. Nonetheless, amnesties are not very often justified. They are sometimes justified when societies have been torn apart by group conflict, and where attaining reconciliatory or distributive justice among groups is as important as providing compensatory justice for victims and their families. But in such cases, trials may still be appropriate, at least for political and military leaders, even as amnesty is provided for minor players. This is because the international community may have a strong stake in seeing that the "most guilty" of the perpetrators are still brought to justice.

But since victims are not owed criminal trials, convictions, and the punishment of their attackers, the door is open for alternative forms of remedy from that provided by criminal trials. What I have shown in this chapter is that in some cases, amnesties and pardons can be plausibly defended insofar as they advance reconciliation.

Conclusions

Throughout this book, I have argued that international criminal law is in need of conceptual clarification and normative support, especially so that it can better take into account the rights of the defendants. The point of this book has not been to add fuel for those who wish to burn down the still "under construction" edifice of international criminal law.[1] I do not agree that we are better off without, than with, an International Criminal Court. Indeed, I support the effort to add new international institutions generally.[2] Instead, this book has attempted to investigate the normative foundations of such institutions. That the normative support has been found to be partially wanting in various ways is no reason to reject the whole project. Rather it is reason to scale back the project, and focus on those defendants who have clearly violated international criminal law and who cannot support a defense of superior orders or duress.

International justice is not an oxymoron; it can be philosophically explicated and defended. There are indeed *jus cogens* norms of international criminal law, norms that proscribe genocide, apartheid, slavery, and discrimination, as well as group-based torture, murder, and rape. But the list of international crimes does not extend so far as to include all supposed human rights abuses, especially those that are not group-based. International tribunals should not prosecute individualized human-rights abuses as crimes against humanity. And minor players should not be prosecuted unless discriminatory intent can be shown, thereby linking the individual to the larger group-based crime. International justice does not *demand* that victims get the convictions they request, nor does international justice *demand* that there be convictions rather than of amnesty for peace plans. When we stay the hand of vengeance, there is no reason why only criminal convictions can substitute for the victors' justice that the winning side in war has thirsted after.[3]

I have proposed that we adopt a moral minimalist philosophical position concerning international criminal law. One of the advantages of such a position is that it forces us to think about international law as a putative system of rules that must achieve a sense of bindingness out of the practices of that system of rules. Legal positivism generally reconstructs law as a system of coherent principles, where the authority of law is internal rather than external to that system. In a highly contentious field such as international criminal law, it is an advantage to be forced to think about the issue of obligation and bindingness from within the system itself, at least initially. This makes us try to find justificatory principles for international criminal law that are not derived from contentious external sources and that would be even more controversial than the field of international criminal law itself. When moral or natural law principles are incorporated into this system of law, such matters should be highly circumscribed so as not to jeopardize the legitimacy of the whole system of law.

In order for international criminal law to attain the sense of fidelity and respect that is afforded to domestic law, it is vitally important that there be a firm commitment to the international rule of law. Here we need to be especially concerned about retroactivity and selective punishment. History gives us one of the best reasons to be worried about these aspects of the rule of law since even some of the staunchest defenders of the Nuremberg Trials consider these trials to have failed to live up to the ideals of the rule of law.[4] The Nuremberg Statute that codified the crimes that were the basis of the trials of the Nazi leaders was established *after* the acts to be prosecuted had occurred. And it was clear that not only the leaders of the military forces of the Axis, but also some of those of the Allies, should have been subject to prosecution.

Many detractors of the new International Criminal Court worry that serious intrusions into domestic sovereignty will be the norm for that court. But even on my group-based way of conceptualizing *jus cogens* norms, the ICC would have no basis on which to prosecute organizations such as the American Nazi Party or the Ku Klux Klan when they engage in racially motivated violence. For, remember, my model ideally prefers those prosecutions where there is both group-based harm and State action. Whatever one thinks of the present U.S. government leaders, it is very hard to see them as colluding with the KKK. Only if the U.S. government consistently fails to prosecute the KKK, thereby negligently condoning what it does, is there anything like State action in such a case. And if there is such failure to prosecute in domestic tribunals, it becomes much more plausible to think that an international court should prosecute these crimes.

Another objection is that my view still allows a lot of unprosecuted discriminatory conduct to occur in the world, and hence for there still to be too much global injustice. The basis for this objection is that risks to the security of the international community – the cornerstone of what makes something an international crime, in my view – is not strong enough to form a basis for the prosecution of all forms of discrimination. My response here has two prongs. First, I think that a lot of the serious discrimination that affects ethnic, racial, and gender groups will indeed be covered by my proposal. I have tried to show that certain group-based harms are also harmful to humanity. Second, those forms of discrimination that do not rise to the level of international crimes will either be covered by domestic tribunals or will simply not be prosecuted, as part of the cost of having a strongly justified international criminal court. Domestic courts also have their limits. For example, in many Western societies, hatred that does not clearly rise to the level of harming a given person, other than the person doing the hating, is not normally subject to criminal prosecution.

Can international criminal law rise above the expectations of its detractors? On one level, the prospects do not look good. Since the exemplar of international criminal trials, the Nuremberg prosecutions, have been so widely criticized, what hope is there that future international tribunals will be able to avoid the appearance of victor's justice? On another level, there is considerable room for hope in light of the fact that the new International Criminal Court will not be burdened with the appearance of having been set up specifically by the victors at the end of a war. Rather, the ICC, as a freestanding court, will have resources and judges from areas that are not involved in a particular international conflict. I am perhaps more hopeful about the ICC than most of those who believe that there are, and will remain, serious conceptual and normative problems in international criminal law. My hopefulness is based on the fact that so many well-intentioned people have come together to make the ICC and the general idea of international criminal law a fair and decent alternative to vengeance in the international community.

My deep respect for those who have devoted their lives to supporting the idea of an international criminal court does not sweep so far as to make me less vigilant in defending the rights of the accused in international criminal tribunals. International criminal courts have an astounding potential for abuse, especially regarding those who are otherwise too weak to defend themselves. When criminal trials take place after bitter ethnic conflicts, there is a strong motivation for the members of one side of the conflict to try to embarrass publicly the members of the other side. Witnesses will be members of one or another ethnic group, as will also be true of many of the defendants and their lawyers. Criminal proceedings will not necessarily temper ethnic hatred. Indeed, there is reason to think that ethnic hatred will be intensified by some of these proceedings. Procedures must be clearly in place in order to ward off the potential for abuse that these conditions might trigger.

This book has perhaps provided a curious mixture of abstract philosophical theorizing and contemporary legal analysis. Its enduring effect will no doubt come from the former, since the latter may prove to have expressed premature judgments, not ones that will stand the test of time. But it is my view that good philosophical work must be done against the backdrop of concrete, real-world cases. What better cases to consider than those that we are currently living through? When I started working on this topic six years ago, it was not such a hot topic. Now, news about international criminal law is reported daily in such periodicals as *The New York Times*, and even my local paper, *The St. Louis*

Post-Dispatch. The philosophical underpinnings of international law are also being debated regularly, but unfortunately not as well reported as is news about current high-profile international trials. Philosophical argumentation about international criminal law is still in its infancy, despite the widespread popular interest.

I hope this book will encourage those working in international criminal law to think more carefully about the theoretical underpinnings of what they are doing. And I hope that philosophers working in moral and political philosophy will take more seriously the events that are unfolding on the stage of international criminal law. My book will be a success, though, if even a few people who work in either field are inspired to think harder than they have about the momentous changes in international criminal law that are occurring. As I write these final lines, the world is witnessing the trial in The Hague of Slobodan Milosevic, the first major head of State to be tried for crimes against humanity in an international criminal tribunal. I hope that this book will set the stage for a serious philosophical debate about such trials so that we are not judged by later generations to have merely settled for victors' justice.

Notes

Chapter 1

1. Charter of the International Military Tribunal at Nuremberg, Annex to the London Agreement, 8 Aug. 1945, 82 U.N.T.S. 279, Article 6.
2. Rome Statute of the International Criminal Court, Adopted by the U.N. Diplomatic Conference, July 17, 1998, Art. 5: "Crimes Within the Jurisdiction of the Court."
3. I am very grateful to David Luban for discussions of this category of international crime.
4. Throughout the book, I will use the phrase "cross state border," sometimes in a literal manner, sometimes in a figurative manner. Here, I use the phrase literally. I will say more about this concept in later chapters.
5. Hugo Grotius, *The Law of War and Peace*, 1625, Francis W. Kelsey, trans., Oxford: Clarendon Press, 1925. Hein, 1997, p. 20.
6. Ibid., p. 102.
7. Ibid., p 15.
8. Ibid., p. 12.
9. Ibid., p. 15.
10. Ibid., p. 18.
11. Ibid., p. 19.
12. Ibid., p. 21.
13. Ibid., p. 157.
14. Ibid., p. 158.
15. Ibid., p. 17.
16. See Allen Buchanan's new book, *Justice, Legitimacy and Self-Determination*, Oxford: Oxford University Press, 2004.
17. For a very good treatment of this other aspect of international law, see Buchanan, op. cit.
18. John Rawls, *The Law of Peoples*, Cambridge, MA: Harvard University Press, 1999. The one exception to Rawls's nearly exclusive focus on peoples is his discussion of human rights. On p. 79, Rawls says that considerations of human rights "restrict the justifying reasons for war and its conduct, and they specify limits to a regime's internal autonomy." Rawls devotes only three pages to such considerations. Yet, increasingly, international law and politics concern such "human rights" issues. My entire book is meant to address the philosophical underpinnings of this topic.

19. Ibid., p. 59.
20. Ibid., p. 65.
21. Ibid., p. 81.
22. John Stuart Mill, *On Liberty*, ch. 1, Stefan Collini, ed., Cambridge: Cambridge University Press, 1989, p. 13.
23. Michael Walzer, *On Toleration*, New Haven: Yale University Press, 1997, p. 14.
24. Of course, there might not be a need for much toleration for there to be bare survival, as in the case of Native Americans in North America.
25. Simon Blackburn, *Ruling Passions*, Oxford: Clarendon Press, 1998, p. 13.
26. Anthony Clark Arend and Robert J. Beck, *International Law and the Use of Force*, New York: Routledge, 1993, p. 16.
27. Thomas Hobbes, *Leviathan* (1651), *The English Works of Thomas Hobbes*, London: John Bohn. Second reprint, Scientia Verlag Aalen, 1966, vol. 3, p. 115.
28. Ibid., p. 342.
29. Ibid., p. 117 (Hobbes's italics).
30. Ibid.
31. See Larry May, "Hobbes on the Attitude of Pacifism," in *Thomas Hobbes: De La Metaphysique A La Politique*, M. Bertman and M. Malherbe, eds., Paris: J. Vrin, 1989.
32. See Larry May, "Hobbes on Fidelity to Law," *Hobbes Studies*, vol. 5, 1992, pp. 77–89.
33. Hobbes, *Leviathan*, pp. 124–5.
34. Ibid., pp. 116–17.
35. Ibid., p. 113.
36. Ibid., p. 159.
37. Ibid., p. 117.
38. Ibid., p. 147.
39. Ibid., p. 145.
40. For more on the relationship between natural law and international law, see Larry May, "*Jus Cogens* Norms and International Criminal Law" (translated into Italian), *Ars Interpretandi*, vol. 6, 2001, pp. 223–48.
41. Hobbes, *Leviathan*, p. 120.
42. See Larry May, "Hobbes on Equity and Justice," in *Hobbes's Science of Natural Justice*, C. Walton and P. J. Johnson, eds., Dordrecht: Martinus Nijhoff, 1987; Larry May, "Hobbes's Contract Theory," *Journal of the History of Philosophy*, vol. 18, pp. 195–208, 1980; and Larry May, "Hobbes," in *Ethics in the History of Western Philosophy*, R. J. Cavalier, J. Guinlock, and J. P. Sterba, eds., New York: Macmillan, 1989.
43. John Austin, *The Province of Jurisprudence Determined*, Cambridge: Cambridge University Press, 1832, Lecture One.
44. M. Cherif Bassiouni and Edward M. Wise, *Aut Dedere Aut Judicare: The Duty to Prosecute or Extradite in International Law*, Dordrecht: Martinus Nijhoff, 1995.

Chapter 2

1. In general, my approach is to treat international crimes as group-based rather than individual crimes. I defend this strategy explicitly in Chapters 4 and 5. Here, I would just note that this is a fairly common way to think of the most egregious international crimes in international law.

2. *Jus cogens* norms are non-consensual, universal norms concerning what is required of states in international law. See Jerzy Sztucki, *Jus Cogens and the Vienna Convention on the Law of Treaties*, Vienna: Springer Verlag, 1974, for an excellent discussion of the historical development of the concept of *jus cogens* in international law.

3. Article 53 of the Vienna Convention on the Law of Treaties of 23 May 1969, UN doc A/CONF. 39/27. I set out some of the conceptual confusions in this construal of *jus cogens* norms at the end of this chapter and in the next chapter.

4. *Black's Law Dictionary*, 4th ed., St. Paul, MN: West Publishing, 1979, p. 1023.

5. Not all international norms have universal scope. Indeed, most have quite limited scope, since they are dependent on the consent of a given State to be bound by that norm.

6. M. Cherif Bassiouni, *Crimes Against Humanity in International Criminal Law*, The Hague: Kluwer Law International, 2nd ed., 1999, p. 496, quoting the International Court of Justice's Advisory Opinion: *Concerning Reservations to the Genocide Convention*. I will also remark later on the conceptual confusion in this definition of *jus cogens* norms.

7. For an excellent discussion of these two concepts, see Maurizio Ragazzi, *The Concept of International Obligations Erga Omnes*, Oxford: Clarendon Press, 1997. See also Andre de Hoogh, *Obligations Erga Omnes and International Crimes*, The Hague: Kluwer Law International, 1996.

8. Grotius often refers to a similar principle as being embodied in "the law of nature." See Hugo Grotius, *The Law of War and Peace*, 1625, Francis Kelsey, trans., Oxford: Clarendon Press, 1925, p. 13.

9. Vienna Convention on the Law of Treaties, May 23, 1969, 1155 U.N.T.S. 331, 8 International Legal Materials 679 (1969), Art. 53.

10. Barcelona Traction Case, case concerning the Barcelona Traction, Light and Power Co., Limited, Second Phase, Belgium v. Spain, 1970 I.C.J. 3, 1970 WL 1.

11. There is some dispute about whether the Barcelona Traction case concerned *jus cogens* norms. The ICJ speaks of "obligations *erga omnes*" rather than *jus cogens* norms. But even if these concepts can be made conceptually distinct, they are closely enough related for us to learn something about *jus cogens* norms from this case.

12. Barcelona Traction Case, para. 33.

13. Ibid.

14. Ibid., para. 34.

15. Of course, this conceptual problem could be averted if a State were not able to withdraw its consent at a later time. But there are both conceptual and, more importantly, practical concerns that militate against this position, as we will see in the next chapter.

16. Ragazzi, *The Concept of International Obligations Erga Omnes*, p. 60.

17. See Filartiga v. Pena-Irala, 630 F.2d 876 (2d Cir. 1980) for a discussion of what would happen if the prohibition against torture were seen as a consensual norm.

18. John Austin, *The Province of Jurisprudence Determined*, 1832, Cambridge: Cambridge University Press, 1995, William E. Rumble, ed., Lecture I.

19. H. L. A. Hart, *The Concept of Law*, Oxford: Clarendon Press, 2nd ed., 1991, p. 189.

20. Ibid., p. 191.

21. Ibid., p. 193.

22. Ibid., p. 193: "[W]ithout a minimum of cooperation given voluntarily by those who find that it is in their interest to submit to and maintain the rules, coercion of others who would not voluntarily conform would be impossible."

23. Ibid.
24. Ibid., p. 236 and elsewhere.
25. Ibid., pp. 228–30.
26. Ibid., p. 230.
27. I am grateful to Carl Wellman for helping me on this point. For Hart, the minimum content of the natural law was not itself a moral basis for legal norms; rather, it is best seen as only a prudential basis for both legal and moral norms.
28. Ragazzi, *The Concept of International Obligation Erga Omnes*, p. 48.
29. *Terra nullius* is land that was not previously occupied or claimed by another State.
30. Alfred von Verdross, "Forbidden Treaties in International Law," *American Journal of International Law*, vol. 31, 1937, p. 571. Even though it may not appear so, Verdross thought of care for the spiritual well-being of a State's citizens as also quite minimalist.
31. Hart is unclear about whether there is a common natural basis for norms that are both legal and moral, or whether the natural norms are themselves, at least in some rudimentary way, moral. See H. L. A. Hart, *Essays in Jurisprudence and Philosophy*, Oxford: Clarendon Press, 1983, pp. 79–81. Also see Neil MacCormick, *H. L. A. Hart*, Stanford: Stanford University Press, 1981, pp. 21–4; and Michael D. Bayles, *Hart's Legal Philosophy*, Dordrecht: Kluwer Academic Publishers, 1992, pp. 117–22, for interpretations of Hart on this point. On the other hand, Verdross is clear about this, but so clear that some have wondered whether he correctly labeled himself as a legal positivist at all.
32. See Hart, *The Concept of Law*, pp. 190–1.
33. H. L. A. Hart, "Are There Any Natural Rights?" in *Political Philosophy*, Oxford: Oxford University Press, 1967, Anthony Quinton, ed., p. 53.
34. Hobbes, *Leviathan* (1651), *The English Works of Thomas Hobbes*, vol. 3, London: John Bohn. Second reprint, Scientia Verlag Aalen, 1966, p. 164.
35. Ibid., p. 147.
36. Ibid., p. 133.
37. The debate over the justification of prosecuting individuals for international crimes begins after World War I. Unlike in more recent discussions, it was the American delegates to the 1919 Preliminary Peace Conference who were skeptical of the idea of universal norms or laws of humanity. They issued a statement saying that the concept of laws of humanity is "not the subject of punishment by a court of justice," since it involved merely a question of "moral law" and hence lacked any "fixed and universal standard." Commission on the Responsibility of the Authors of the War and on Enforcement of Penalties, "Report Presented to the Preliminary Peace Conference," March 29, 1919, reprinted in *American Journal of International Law*, vol. 14, 1929, p. 115. The United States no longer voices these objections, although there are other objections that prevented the United States from signing the 1998 Rome Treaty establishing the permanent International Criminal Court. See Phyllis Hwong, "Defining Crimes Against Humanity," *Fordham International Law Journal*, vol. 22, 1998, p. 457.
38. Report of Robert H. Jackson, United States Representative to the International Conference on Military Trials 50, 1945.
39. Convention (No. IV) Respecting the Laws and Customs of War on Land, With Annex of Regulations, Oct. 18, 1907, Preamble, 36 Stat. 2277, T.S. No. 539, 1 Bevans 631.
40. Sztucki, p. 62.

41. See Filartiga v. Pena-Irala, 630 F.2d 876 (2d Cir. 1980), where Judge Irving R. Kaufman says that even though the right not to be tortured is often violated, nonetheless all governments affirm the validity of this right.

42. See Matthew Lippman, "Crimes Against Humanity," *Boston College Third World Law Journal*, vol. 17, 1997, p. 187, for a good account of the Soviet disagreements with the French and Americans on this point.

43. Grigory I. Tunkin, "The Contemporary Soviet Theory of International Law," *Current Legal Problems*, 1978, p. 185.

44. Ibid., p. 181.

45. Grigory I. Tunkin, "*Jus Cogens* in Contemporary International Law," *Toledo Law Review*, Fall/Winter, 1971, p. 115.

46. Ibid., p. 117.

47. Ibid., p. 118.

48. Ibid., p. 113.

49. This is similar to the debate between Catholic and Marxist humanists. The Marxists insisted that the concept of human nature be replaced with "species being," which was specific to historical periods and not universal to all humanity over time.

50. See Carol Gould, *Rethinking Democracy*, Cambridge: Cambridge University Press, 1988.

Chapter 3

1. The reader may skip this chapter, especially if one has already been convinced by the last chapter that *jus cogens* norms need a philosophical grounding. The point of this chapter is to provide a negative argument for the same thesis as presented in the last chapter.

2. Jordan J. Paust, M. Cherif Bassiouni, Michael Scharf, Jimmy Gurule, Leila Sadat, Bruce Zagaris, and Sharon A. Williams, *International Criminal Law: Cases and Materials*, Durham, NC: Carolina Academic Press, 2nd edition, 2000, p. 4.

3. I am very grateful to Andrew Altman and William Edmundson for helpful discussion of these points.

4. See Jerzy Sztucki, *Jus Cogens and the Vienna Convention on the Law of Treaties*, Vienna: Springer Verlag, 1974, for an excellent discussion of the historical development of the concept of *jus cogens* in international law.

5. North Sea Continental Shelf Cases, 1969 I.C.J. Reports 3, para. 37.

6. Texaco v. Libya, 17 International Legal Materials 1, 1978.

7. Kuwait v. Aminoil, 21 International Legal Materials 976, 1982.

8. David Hume, "Of the Original Contract," in *Hume's Ethical Writings*, Alasdair MacIntyre, ed., Notre Dame, IN: University of Notre Dame Press, 1979.

9. Ibid., p. 256.

10. Ibid., p. 257.

11. Ibid., p. 259.

12. Ibid., p. 264.

13. I am grateful to Kit Wellman for discussion of this point.

14. Hume, op. cit., p. 267.

15. Texaco/Libya Arbitration, Award of 19 January 1977, 17 International Legal Materials 1, 1978, para. 2.

16. Ibid., para. 7.

17. Ibid., para. 80.
18. Ibid., para. 83–4.
19. The international legal rights and duties of the United Nations come from the consent of its members. In the Reparations case, the ICJ held that the UN has both political and legal personality. Specifically, the court held that the UN "could not carry out the intentions of its founders if it was devoid of international personality." See *Reparations for Injuries Suffered in the Service of the United Nations*, Advisory Opinion, 11 April 1949, ICJ Reports, para. 174. The UN's legal capacity to act is based on the power vested in it by its members. To distinguish the UN from the unsuccessful League of Nations, the founding members of the UN gave to the Security Council, but not to the General Assembly, the power to initiate actions to promote international peace, including authorizing armed attacks. Until the 1990s, the Security Council was embroiled in ideological disputes between Communist and non-Communist countries that prevented it from acting according to its mandate. The end of the Cold War changed things – at least for the moment.
20. Liamco v. Libya, 20 International Legal Materials, 1, 1981.
21. It is interesting to note that the second Liamco nationalization occurred on the same day that Texaco's concessions were also nationalized.
22. Liamco v. Libya, para. 113.
23. Ibid., para. 47.
24. Ibid.
25. Ibid., para. 48.
26. Ibid., para. 48–9.
27. Ibid., para. 50.
28. The UN's swift and successful response to Iraq's invasion of Kuwait seems to be just what the UN was founded to do. The first sentence of Article 1(1) of the UN Charter says that the main goal of the UN is "[t]o maintain international peace and security." The Charter specifically calls for "the prevention and removal of threats to the peace, and for the suppression of acts of aggression." The swift action of the UN in enlisting member States to confront Iraq and force it to stop exploiting Kuwait is arguably the kind of "removal of threats to the peace" and "suppression of acts of aggression" that are the hallmark goals of the UN. See Charter of the United Nations, 1945, Article 1(1).
29. Frederic J. Kirgis, *International Organizations*, St. Paul, MN: West Publishing, 2nd ed., 1993, p. 651.
30. Eugene Rostow, "Until What? Enforcement Action or Collective Self-Defense," *American Journal of International Law*, vol. 85, 1991, p. 506, contends that in any such Article 51 action, the key is to act on the basis of the provision of Article 51 that allows for "the inherent right of individual or collective self-defense . . . until the Security Council has taken measures necessary to maintain international peace and security."
31. Case Concerning Military and Paramilitary Activities in and against Nicaragua (Nicaragua v. United States), 1986, ICJ, 14, para. 190.
32. The Security Council claimed to be authorized to take these actions, and those actions proved to be important. Article 2(6) of the Charter says that the UN "shall ensure that states which are not members of the United Nations act in accordance with these principles so far as may be necessary for the maintenance of international peace and security." So, if the UN determines that an action requires conformity from non-members for its success in maintaining international peace and security, non-members can be required to act. This proposition can also be supported by reference to Article 35 of the Vienna Convention on

the Law of Treaties, although Article 35 says that the third-party State must "expressly accept the obligation in writing."

33. Quoted in Kirgis, p. 678.
34. Advisory Opinion on the Legality of the Threat or Use of Nuclear Weapons, 1997 I.L.M. 814, ICJ, July 8, 1996, para. 105 E.
35. Ibid., Schwebel dissent, para. 10–12.
36. Ibid., Schwebel dissent, para. 12–13.
37. Ibid., Weeramantry dissent, para. 1.
38. Ibid., Weeramantry dissent, para. 11.
39. Ibid., Weeramantry dissent, para. 37.
40. Ibid., Weeramantry dissent, para. 40.
41. Ibid., Weeramantry dissent, para. 42.
42. Ibid., Majority Opinion, para. 87.
43. North Sea Continental Shelf Cases, 1969, ICJ Reports, 3, 44, quoted in Mark Janis, *An Introduction to International Law*, 1993, p. 46.
44. Ibid., p. 47–8.
45. The most obvious way to show this is by the words uttered by the leaders of the State at the time the State acts. Another way, but much more controversial, is to look at how publicists and jurists interpret what the State's motivations are.
46. North Sea Continental Shelf Cases, 1969, ICJ Reports 3, para. 37. What the court seems to have meant by "a priori" is that states feel they cannot disregard the norm for reasons of self-interest.
47. Ibid., para. 55.
48. Ibid., para. 61.
49. Paust, Bassiouni et al., *International Criminal Law*, p. 5.
50. Even if we regard custom as a kind of tacit treaty, it will be the kind of treaty that States can "unsign," as happened when the United States decided to unsign the Rome Treaty establishing the ICC.
51. See John Ladd's entry, "Custom," in *The Encyclopedia of Philosophy*, New York: Macmillan, vol. 2, 1967.
52. See the discussion of this idea in Maurizio Ragazzi, *The Concept of International Obligations Erga Omnes*, Oxford: Oxford University Press, 1997, pp. 60–67. As Ragazzi notes, international law today only allows for the persistent objector to evade the bindingness of a custom if no "fundamental principles" are at stake. Of course, the topic of whether *jus cogens* norms are customary is deeply embedded in the discussion of whether a persistent objector can evade the bindingness of a custom.
53. See the final chapter of H. L. A. Hart's *The Concept of Law*, 2nd ed., Oxford: Oxford University Press, 1991.
54. This is not to say that such a moral grounding will be easy to achieve, or that this moral grounding will be universally acknowledged by everyone. We might need to settle for less than this, but we need to be clear that what is short of moral grounding will not truly justify.
55. Mark Janis argues in a similar vein that *jus cogens* norms should not be seen as grounded in customary international law. See Mark Janis, "The Nature of *Jus Cogens*," *Connecticut Law Review*, vol. 3, 1988, p. 360. Janis thinks that the only way to justify non-consensual *jus cogens* norms is through natural law theory. As should be obvious by now, I have reservations about that view.

56. See Allen Wertheimer, "Unconscionability and Contracts," *Business Ethics Quarterly*, vol. 2, no. 4, October 1992, pp. 479–96, for a very good conceptual analysis of the basis, and limitations, of unconscionability in contracts in U.S. law.

Chapter 4

1. See M. Cherif Bassiouni and Edward M. Wise, *Aut Dedere Aut Judicare: The Duty to Prosecute or Extradite in International Law*, Dordrecht: Martinus Nijhoff, 1995.
2. M. Cherif Bassiouni, "The Sources and Content of International Criminal Law: A Theoretical Framework," *International Criminal Law*, Vol. I, Crimes, 2nd ed., M. Cherif Bassiouni, ed., NJ: Transaction Press, 1999, p. 55.
3. Ibid., p. 31.
4. John Stuart Mill, *On Liberty*, 1859, Stefan Collini, ed., Cambridge: Cambridge University Press, 1989.
5. Joel Feinberg, *The Moral Limits of the Criminal Law*, Vol. I: *Harm to Others*, Oxford: Oxford University Press, 1984, p. 6.
6. See Tony Honore, *Making Law Bind*, Oxford: Oxford University Press, 1987, pp. 12–16, who argues that fear of sanctions must at least remain a background concern for law to have a binding force. But Honore recognizes that fear of sanctions is only a partial basis for binding law in the international arena. If international laws are pointless or tyrannical, there is no moral bindingness, and therefore the laws are not properly binding at all.
7. See Lon Fuller, *The Morality of Law*, New Haven: Yale University Press, 1964, 1969.
8. Ibid., 184–6. Fuller presents a similar argument, but does not connect the "internal morality of law" to the concept of fairness. Fuller also points out that one can be a natural law theorist, at least a procedural one, and support just this idea that I am attributing to moral minimalism.
9. As we have seen, Hart argues against seeing international law as a system of law, because it lacks a rule of recognition, although he also thinks that international laws are no less binding for lacking this dimension. See H. L. A. Hart, *The Concept of Law*, Oxford: Oxford University Press, 1961, 1994, pp. 214 and 231.
10. Bassiouni, "The Sources and Content of International Law," p. 44.
11. See Joel Feinberg, *The Moral Limits of the Criminal Law*, Vol. IV, *Harmless Wrongdoing*, Oxford: Oxford University Press, 1988.
12. See H. L. A. Hart, *Law, Liberty, and Morality*, Stanford: Stanford University Press, 1962.
13. An exception to this may occur when racial or ethnic hatred is expressed by one's words. See Mari J. Matsuda, Charles R. Lawrence III, Richard Delgado, and Kimberle Williams Crenshaw, *Words That Wound*, Boulder, CO: Westview Press, 1993.
14. All three of these principles, along with others, are generally collected together under the label "the rule of law." I discuss the international rule of law in Chapter 11.
15. Feinberg, *Harm to Others*, pp. 105–6.
16. James Crawford made this point to me in private conversation, Saturday, October 21, 2000, at a conference at St. Louis University's Law School. As I indicated in Chapter 1, I will not attempt to find a rationale for international crimes that includes piracy, leaving this category of crime to stand in a set of amorphous crimes that have sometimes been prosecuted, but that are also not of central concern to international criminal law.

17. Bassiouni, "The Sources and Content of International Criminal Law," p. 39.
18. As explained in Chapter 1, by "crossing its borders" I mean to include many forms of *actually* intruding into another State, or *metaphorically* intruding by instituting legal proceedings on behalf of those who have been harmed but that are not explicitly sanctioned by the host State.
19. I am very grateful to Gerald Postema for forcefully pressing me on this issue.
20. Henry Shue, *Basic Rights: Subsistence, Affluence, and U.S. Foreign Policy*, Princeton: Princeton University Press, 1980, p. 21. Shue also makes a similar argument in defense of subsistence rights.
21. See Irving Thalberg and Deborah Pellow, "Imagining Alternatives," *Philosophical Forum*, vol. 11, 1979, pp. 1–17.
22. Myres McDougal, Harold Lasswell, and Lung-Chu Chen, *Human Rights and World Public Order*, New Haven: Yale University Press, 1976.
23. Ibid., xvii.
24. Ibid.
25. Ibid., p. xx.
26. Ibid., p. 3.
27. Alfred von Verdross, "Forbidden Treaties in International Law," *American Journal of International Law*, vol. 31, 1937, p. 571.
28. McDougal et al., p. 7.
29. I will draw such a distinction in later sections of this chapter.
30. McDougal et al., pp. 7–14.
31. Universal Declaration of Human Rights, Article 24.
32. See Thomas Hobbes, *Leviathan* (1651), *The English Works of Thomas Hobbes*, vol. 3, London: John Bohn. Second reprint, Scientia Verlag Aalen, 1966, Chapter 30.
33. Ibid, p. 322.
34. Ibid.
35. I am grateful for discussions with Richard Vernon on this topic. See his paper, "What Is Crime Against Humanity," *Journal of Political Philosophy*, vol. 10, no. 3, Sept. 2002, pp. 231–49.
36. Hobbes, *Leviathan*, p. 204.
37. Ibid.
38. Ibid., p. 208.
39. See Larry May, "Hobbes on Fidelity to Law," *Hobbes Studies*, vol. 5, 1992, pp. 82–3.
40. Hobbes, *Leviathan*, p. 205.
41. Although I will not discuss this point further, it seems clear that the security principle could also justify secession, and even revolution.
42. For a good discussion of the various jurisdictional principles, see Paust, Bassiouni et al., *International Criminal Law: Cases and Materials*, Durham, NC: Carolina Academic Press, 2nd ed., 2000, pp. 180–7.
43. Rome Statute, Article 5, para. 1.
44. See Chapter 7 for an account of this case.
45. See Chapter 8 for an account of this case.
46. See Chapter 9 for an account of this case.
47. Rome Statute, Preamble, Article 1, para. 10.
48. Ibid., Article 17.

Chapter 5

1. See Joel Feinberg, *Harm to Others*, New York, NY: Oxford University Press, 1984, chapter 1.
2. M. Cherif Bassiouni, "International Crimes: *Jus Cogens* and *Obligatio Erga Omnes*," *Law and Contemporary Problems*, vol. 59, 1996, p. 69.
3. M. Cherif Bassiouni, "The Sources and Content of International Criminal Law: A Theoretical Framework," *International Criminal Law*, Vol. I, Crimes, 2nd ed., M. Cherif Bassiouni, ed., NJ: Transaction Press, 1999.
4. See especially the Rome Treaty ("... when committed as part of a widespread or systematic attack"). The ICTY Statute has also been interpreted by the Tadic Trial Chamber to require that rape or murder be part of a widespread or systematic attack. In contrast, the first definition of crimes against humanity in the Nuremberg Tribunal did not require a group connection, but also did not recognize highly individualized crimes such as rape as a crime against humanity. See Charter of the International Military Tribunal at Nuremberg and Agreement for the Prosecution and Punishment of the Major War Criminals of the European Axis Powers and Charter of the International Military Tribunal, August 8, 1945, Article 6(c) (requiring only that the act be committed "before or during the war").
5. See Larry May, "On Conscience," *American Philosophical Quarterly*, vol. 20, 1, 1983, for a general discussion of the nature of conscience.
6. See Bernard Boxill, *Blacks and Social Justice*, Totowa, NJ: Rowman and Littlefield, 1984, arguing that treating people on the basis of characteristics they did not choose to acquire is a serious injustice.
7. See Larry May, *The Morality of Groups*, Notre Dame, IN: University of Notre Dame Press, 1987, pp. 116–19, for an analysis of the idea of a group-based harm.
8. State v. Ferguson, 20 SW 3rd 485 (2000) at 500.
9. We might think of the parallel with the United States government when it enters into what would otherwise be a state matter when there is a "federal issue" – that is, a matter that affects the whole of the United States. In a sense, the whole nation enters into the state matter so as to vindicate the national community.
10. Prosecutor v. Dusko Tadic, Case No. IT-94-1-T (May 7, 1997), para. 644.
11. I am grateful to the students in the advanced class on punishment taught by Thad Metz at University of Missouri, St. Louis, who forcefully pushed me to think about such examples.
12. See Maurizio Ragazzi, *The Concept of International Obligations Erga Omnes*, Oxford: Oxford University Press, 1997, p. 72, for a discussion of the similarities between *jus cogens* norms and obligations *erga omnes*.
13. M. Cherif Bassiouni, "International Crimes: *Jus Cogens and Obligatio Erga Omnes*," p. 69. Here, Bassiouni says that *jus cogens* crimes are "characterized explicitly or implicitly by state policy or conduct."
14. Tadic Trial Chamber, para. 697.
15. On this point, see the parallel analysis of sexual harassment in Larry May and Marilyn Friedman, "Harming Women as a Group," *Social Theory and Practice*, vol. 11, no. 2, Summer 1985.
16. Rome Statute, Article 5, paragraph 1.
17. Ibid.

Chapter 6

1. M. Cherif Bassiouni, for instance, began his very influential 1992 book on crimes against humanity by pointing out the incongruity of international criminal law, which must use "technical legal terms" to criticize that which conscience already so eloquently condemns. Yet even so sensitive a theorist as Bassiouni wrote only one sentence about rape in all the 820 pages of the first edition of his book on crimes against humanity. See M. Cherif Bassiouni, *Crimes Against Humanity in International Criminal Law*, The Hague: Kluwer Law International, 1992, p. x. When Bassiouni published the second edition in 1999, he came down squarely in favor of the use of international tribunals such as the ICC to prosecute rape. But here, Bassiouni does not provide any basis for limiting the international prosecution of rape and other forms of sexual violence. See M. Cherif Bassiouni, *Crimes Against Humanity in International Criminal Law*, The Hague: Kluwer Law International, 2nd ed., 1999, pp. 361–2.

2. See Anthony Lewis, "U.S. Denied its Heritage in Failing to Embrace World Court," *The St. Louis Post-Dispatch*, July 21, 1998, p. B1. Also see James Podgers, "War Crimes Court Under Fire," *ABA Journal*, September 1998, pp. 64–9.

3. See Kelly Dawn Askin, *War Crimes Against Women*, The Hague: Kluwer Law International, 1997.

4. Recently, the high profile "Foca case" has been prosecuted by the Yugoslav Tribunal. See Jerome Socolovsky, "Landmark Rape Case Opens Today at Yugoslav Tribunal on War Crimes," *The St. Louis Post-Dispatch*, March 20, 2000, pp. A1, A7.

5. Prosecutor v. Dusko Tadic, Case No. IT-94-1-T, May 7, 1997, International Criminal Tribunal for the Former Yugoslavia [hereinafter ICTY] Trial Chamber; Prosecutor v. Anto Furundzija, Case No. IT-9517/1-T (December 1998) ICTY Trial Chamber.

6. See Margaret E. Galey, "International Enforcement of Women's Rights," *Human Rights Quarterly*, vol. 6, 1984, p. 463; Hilary Charlesworth and Christine Chinkin, "The Gender of *Jus Cogens*," *Human Rights Quarterly*, vol. 15, 1993, p. 63; and Theodor Meron, "Rape as a Crime Under International Humanitarian Law," *American Journal of International Law*, vol. 87, 1993, p. 424.

7. Hugo Grotius, *The Law of War and Peace*, 1625, Francis W. Kelsey, trans., Oxford: Clarendon Press, 1925. Although the quotation does not say so directly, Grotius had in mind the idea that international action might be needed to redress mass rape.

8. My next project is to write about war crimes, a topic certainly deserving of a book-length philosophical treatment in its own right.

9. Grotius, *The Law of War and Peace*, p. 723.

10. Ibid., p. 733.

11. See Aryeh Neier, *War Crimes*, New York: New York Times Books, 1998, especially ch. 11.

12. In 1993, a UN-sponsored conference on human rights said that violence against women, in both public and private life, violates women's human rights. See UN World Conference on Human Rights: Vienna Declaration and Programme of Action, U.N. Doc. A/Conf. 157/24, Part I, 1993, reprinted in I.L.M. 1661, 1678–80, 1993.

13. These are the words of the famous Martens Clause of The Hague Convention of 1907, which Justice Jackson employed as a source of international law for the Nuremberg prosecutions. See Report of Robert H. Jackson, United States Representative to the International

Conference on Military Trials 50 (1945) quoting Convention (No. V) Respecting the Laws and Customs of War on Land, With Annex and Regulations, Oct. 18, 1907, Preamble, 36 Stat. 2277, T.S. No. 539, 1 Bevans 631.

14. Statute for the International Tribunal for the Prosecution of Persons Responsible for Genocide and Other Serious Violations of International Humanitarian Law Committed in the Territory of Rwanda, S.C. Res. 955, art. 3(g), Nov. 8, 1994, reprinted in 33 I.L.M. 1598, 1994; Rome Statute for the International Criminal Court, A/Conf. July 17, 1998, art. 7.

15. Prosecutor v. Anto Furundzija, Case No. IT-9517/1-T, December 1998, ICTY Trial Chamber.

16. Ibid., para. 39–41.

17. Ibid., para. 168.

18. Ibid., para. 153–7.

19. Askin, *War Crimes Against Women*, p. 93.

20. In Chapter 7, I argue that discriminatory intent is the key consideration that must be proved for morally justifiable international criminal prosecutions.

21. See Larry May and Marilyn Friedman, "Harming Women as a Group," *Social Theory and Practice*, vol. 11, 1985, p. 207, for an argument showing how a charge of group-based harm could be made for women in a particular society.

22. See Krishna R. Patel, "Recognizing the Rape of Bosnian Women as Gender-Based Persecution," *Brooklyn Law Review*, vol. 60, 1994, p. 948, for an argument on how to understand mass rape as indeed a group-based crime against women.

23. See Keith Burgess-Jackson, "A Crime Against Women: Calhoun on the Wrongness of Rape," *Journal of Social Philosophy*, vol. 30, 2000, p. 286, for a similar argument.

24. INA sec. 101(a)(42) [8 U.S.C.A. sec. 1101].

25. Lazo-Majano v. INS, 813 F.2d 1432, 1433 (9th Cir. 1987).

26. Ibid, at 1435.

27. Ibid.

28. Catherine MacKinnon, "Crimes of War, Crimes of Peace," in *On Human Rights*, Stephen Shute and Susan Hurley, eds., Boston: Basic Books, 1993, p. 108.

29. See Larry May, *Sharing Responsibility*, Chicago: University of Chicago Press, 1992, pp. 36–55, for an argument that omissions can implicate an institution in harms such as those associated with racism.

30. I also discuss this issue in great detail in the next chapter.

31. The comfort women were raped by Japanese soldiers. Furundzija was a commander of a local Bosnian Serb police force. Zuniga was a sergeant in the Salvadoran army.

32. In Chapter 5, I discuss the systematicity, as well as the widespreadness, criterion in much more detail.

33. On this point, see chapter 16 of Thomas Hobbes's *Leviathan* (1651), *The English Works of Thomas Hobbes*, vol. 3, London: John Bohn. Second reprint, Scientia Verlag Aalen, 1966.

34. Mass rape and sexual violence are also condemnable by natural law theory's dictates of public conscience, since the group-based nature of the assaults fails to treat these women as unique individuals. Even less controversial is the fact that this characterization is in line with the anti-colonialist's view of *jus cogens* norms as protecting colonial and disadvantaged populations from aggression by the more powerful.

35. See Steven R. Ratner and Jason S. Abrams, *Accountability for Human Rights Atrocities in International Law*, Oxford: Oxford University Press, 1997.

36. These defenders of individual rights of victims can of course turn to the codification of international crime as a basis for international prosecution, but this, as I argued earlier, does not give them a moral basis for international prosecutions.

37. This is a historically contingent response. I am quite willing to allow that what I have said so far also might set the stage for a much more ambitious understanding of an international criminal regime in the distant future.

38. Hart, *The Concept of Law*, pp. 228–30.

39. There is a serious concern, raised by some, that the ICC list of international crimes reflects the disproportionate influence of certain interest groups. Indeed, the Rome Conference gave extraordinary and unprecedented powers to non-governmental organizations. While most NGOs are engaged in good works at the international level, they are not representative of the peoples of the world, and they are frequently blinded by the zealousness with which they pursue their often single-issue agendas.

40. See Patricia Wald's speech at Washington University's School of Law on November 17, 2000.

41. See Chapter 11 for more discussion of the international rule of law.

Chapter 7

1. On July 11, 1996, international indictments against Radovan Karadzic and Ratko Mladic were issued. International Criminal Tribunal for the Former Yugoslavia (ICTY): International Arrest Warrants and Orders for Surrender for Radovan Karadzic and Ratko Mladic, 36 I.L.M. 92 (1997). Then, on May 27, 1999, Louise Arbour, the second chief prosecutor of the ICTY announced that indictments had been issued against President Slobodan Milosevic and four other high-ranking Yugoslav and Serbian officials. Statement by Justice Louise Arbour, The Hague, May 27, 1999, JL/PIU/404-E. Carla Del Ponte, the recently installed third chief prosecutor of the ICTY, described her main mission as prosecuting these leaders. "[T]he primary focus of the Office of the Prosecutor must be the investigation and prosecution of the five leaders of the Federal Republic of Yugoslavia and the Republic of Serbia, who have already been indicted, and who are alleged to be responsible for the crimes described in the indictment." Statement by Carla Del Ponte, The Hague, September 29, 1999, PR/P.I.S./437-E. On June 29, 2001, Slobodan Milosevic was extradited to The Hague.

2. Throughout this discussion, I will use the term "minor players" fairly broadly to include most soldiers and other purveyors of violence who are not in charge of the larger plans their acts are a part of.

3. See Jorg Friedrich, "Nuremberg and the Germans," in *War Crimes: The Legacy of Nuremberg*, Belinda Cooper, ed., NY: TV Books, 1999, p. 87, arguing that the decision to prosecute the leaders of the Third Reich was made to counter the resentment of the average German, who thought that the war crimes tribunal was merely victors' justice perpetrated against the whole German people [hereinafter War Crimes.]

4. See Michael Scharf, *Balkan Justice*, Durham, NC: Carolina Academic Press, 1997, pp. 84–90, explaining why the leaders of the ethnic cleansing campaign were not the first to be prosecuted [hereinafter Scharf].

5. The general issue of who can justifiably be prosecuted is several thousand years old. Plato discussed a trial in ancient Greece of military leaders who were accused of not rescuing civilians in a naval battle. Plato protested that they were all tried together, with no consideration for who had given the orders and who had merely carried them out. See Plato, *The Apology* 32b.

6. I will mainly be looking at crimes against humanity, and extrapolating to all international crimes. But, of course, there may be international crimes that are not best understood using the model of crimes against humanity.

7. In this context, it is especially interesting to recall Justice Jackson's famous Opening Address for the United States, November 21, 1945, at the Nuremberg Trials. Jackson said, "[L]aw should not stop with the punishment of petty crimes by little people. It must also reach men who possess themselves of great power and make deliberate and concerted use of it to set in motion evils which leave no home in the world untouched." Reprinted in *The Nuremberg War Crimes Trial 1945–46: A Documentary History*, Michael R. Marrus, ed., 1997, p. 80 [hereinafter *Nuremberg War Crimes Trial*].

8. Rather than focusing on the "ex post facto" fairness problem, this chapter will instead focus on the problem of prosecuting those who did not plan the events that mainly constituted the international crime. See Larry May, "Socialization and Institutional Evil," in *Hannah Arendt: Twenty Years Later*, Cambridge, MA: MIT Press, Jerome Kohn and Larry May, eds., 1996, p. 132, where I argue that the excuse that one was merely a cog in a machine is not well-supported.

9. The prosecution sought to blunt this criticism by portraying Tadic as an especially sadistic character. See Scharf, p. 118.

10. John Quigley has argued that ethnic cleansing should be prosecuted against a State. See John Quigley, "State Responsibility for Ethnic Cleansing," *U.C. Davis Law Review*, vol. 32, 1999, pp. 341, 350. Unlike Quigley, the current chapter looks at how to conceptualize ethnic cleansing as a crime of individuals, rather than as a State crime. Many of the conclusions reached throughout this chapter, though, should make one increasingly sympathetic to Quigley's focus on the State, rather than the individuals, as the object of international legal action.

11. This issue is explored most recently in Beth Van Schaack, "The Definition of Crimes Against Humanity: Resolving the Incoherence," *Columbia Journal of Transnational Law*, vol. 37, 1999, p. 787, arguing that the ICTY should not have required the element of discriminatory intent as an element in crimes against humanity [hereinafter Van Schaack]. Van Schaack's view will be criticized in the third part of this chapter.

12. Justice Jackson, the chief prosecutor at the Nuremberg trials, said in his "Report to the President" that "it became more and more felt that these were crimes that were committed against us, and the whole society of civilized nations by a band of brigands who had seized the instrumentality of a state." See Robert H. Jackson, Report to the President, June 6, 1945, reprinted in *Nuremberg War Crimes Trial*, p. 43.

13. In Prosecutor v. Dusko Tadic, the Trial Chamber said that a single act can be prosecutable as a crime against humanity. See Prosecutor v. Dusko Tadic, Case No. IT-94-1-T (May 7, 1997), para. 649, Opinion and Judgment, ICTY Trial Chamber [hereinafter Tadic Trial Chamber].

14. This is how Tadic is characterized in Scharf, p. 118.

15. The Final Report of the Commission of Experts Established Pursuant to Security Council Resolution 780 (1992), May 27, 1994, UN Doc. S/1994/674, at 33. See Steven R. Ratner

and Jason S. Abrams, *Accountability for Human Rights Atrocities in International Law*, Oxford: Oxford University Press, 1997, p. 30, for a discussion of this definition [hereinafter Ratner & Abrams].

16. The Final Report of the Commission of Experts, ibid.

17. Ibid.

18. See UN Doc. E/1992/22, E/CN.4/1992/84/Add. 1, 1992, articulating the General Assembly's condemnation of ethnic cleansing in the Balkans, and 1/1992/S-1/1 Annex, 1992, articulating the Security Council's condemnation of ethnic cleansing in the former Yugoslavia, cited in Natan Lerner, "Ethnic Cleansing," in *War Crimes in International Law*, Yoram Dinstein and Mala Taroy, eds. The Hague: Martinus Nijhoff Publishers, 1996, pp. 107, 110 [hereinafter Lerner].

19. Report of the Secretary-General Pursuant to Paragraph 15 of Security Council Resolution 757, 1992, and Paragraph 10 of Security Council Resolution 758, 1992, S/24100, 15 June 1992, reprinted in *The "Yugoslav" Crisis in International Law: General Issues*, Daniel Bethlehem and Marc Wheeler eds., 1997, p. 523.

20. Ibid.

21. Statute for the International Tribunal for the Prosecution of Persons Responsible for Serious Violations of International Humanitarian Law Committed in the Territory of the Former Yugoslavia since 1991, Annex to the Report of the Secretary-General Pursuant to Paragraph 2 of Security Council Resolution 808 (1993), UN Doc. S/25704, 3 May 1993, Annex, at 36–48. 32 *I.L.M.* 1192–1201 (1993), devoting 21 pages to the elements of crimes against humanity, but fewer pages to an analysis of the legal basis of the other crimes [hereinafter ICTY Statute].

22. M. Cherif Bassiouni, *Crimes Against Humanity in International Criminal Law*, 2nd ed., Dordrecht: Kluwer Law, 1999, pp. 60–1, arguing that the term "laws against humanity" was first used in 1899, and the term "crimes against humanity" was first used in the Nuremberg Charter [hereinafter Bassiouni].

23. See Sharon Anderson-Gold, "Crimes Against Humanity: A Kantian Perspective on International Law," in *Autonomy and Community*, Jane Kneller and Sidney Axinn, eds., 1998, p. 103, using the writing of Immanuel Kant to provide a justification for prosecuting individuals for such large-scale human rights abuses as ethnic cleansing.

24. See Andrew Bell-Fialkoff, *Ethnic Cleansing*, New York: St. Martin's, 1996, pp. 7–49, providing an excellent history of the idea of ethnic cleansing, and tracing the idea of ethnic cleansing back to Assyrian attempts forcibly to resettle various conquered peoples from 883–859 B.C. Also see Norman Cigar, *Genocide in Bosnia: The Policy of Ethnic-Cleansing*, College Station, TX: Texas A & M University Press, 1995, pp. 11–21, providing the historical background for the ethnic cleansing campaign in the Balkans, including its roots in various forms of persecution during the time of the Ottoman empire [hereinafter Cigar].

25. See ICTY Statute for a listing of these acts.

26. This was in fact the way that criminal conduct was understood prior to the Nuremberg Trials. See Ruth Teitel, "Nuremberg and Its Legacy: Fifty Years Later," in *War Crimes*, p. 44.

27. The International Military Tribunal at Nuremberg was a turning point in the history of international law in that individuals were prosecuted for crimes for which only States had previously been prosecuted. See Ratner & Abrams, pp. 2–8.

28. Tadic was also charged with violations of war crimes and violations of the Geneva Convention. See Prosecutor v. Dusko Tadic, Tadic Trial Chamber, para. 559.
29. For an excellent account of Tadic's background and his crimes, see Scharf, pp. 93–109. Also see William W. Horne, "The Real Trial of the Century," in War Crimes, p. 120, discussing events that led up to Tadic's arrest, including the important role played by Richard Goldstone, the first chief prosecutor of the ICTY.
30. Tadic Trial Chamber, para. 38.
31. Ibid., para. 39.
32. Ibid., para. 40.
33. Ibid., para. 42.
34. Ibid., para. 49.
35. Ibid., para. 45.
36. Scharf, p. 205.
37. Ibid., pp. 97–101, discussing the importance of Tadic's fleeing to Germany, where he was easier to capture than if he had stayed in Bosnia.
38. Quoted in Scharf, ibid., p. 118.
39. Ibid., at 119. Although the statements from the prosecution and defense show that each side thought the trial was about larger issues, it is also true that both sides characterized that larger issue differently. I am grateful to Frances Foster for this point.
40. Tadic Trial Chamber, para. 683.
41. These are the words of Graham Blewitt, deputy prosecutor of the ICTY, quoted in Scharf, p. 96.
42. The full text reads as follows: "CRIMES AGAINST HUMANITY: namely, murder, extermination, enslavement, deportation, and other inhumane acts committed against any civilian population, before or during the war, or persecutions on political, racial or religious grounds in execution of or in connection with any crime within the jurisdiction of the Tribunal, whether or not in violation of the domestic law of the country where perpetrated." Agreement for the Prosecution and Punishment of the Major War Criminals of the European Axis Powers and Charter of the International Military Tribunal, Aug. 8, 1945, art. 6(c), 59 Stat. 1544, 82 U.N.T.S. 279 [hereinafter Nuremberg Charter].
43. The full text of the ICTY Statute, Article 5, Crimes Against Humanity, reads as follows: "The International Tribunal shall have the power to prosecute persons responsible for the following crimes when committed in armed conflict, whether international or internal in character, and directed against any civilian population: (a) murder; (b) extermination; (c) enslavement; (d) deportation; (e) imprisonment; (f) torture; (g) rape; (h) persecutions on political, racial and religious grounds; (i) other inhumane acts." Statute for the International Tribunal for the Prosecution of Persons Responsible for Serious Violations of International Humanitarian Law Committed in the Territory of the Former Yugoslavia Since 1991, Annex to the Report of the Secretary-General Pursuant to Paragraph 2 of Security Council Resolution 808 (1993), UN Doc. S/25704, 3 May 1993, Annex at 36–48. 32 I.L.M. 1192–1201 (1993).
44. Here is a longer edited version: "For purposes of this Statute, 'crimes against humanity' means any of the following acts when committed as part of a widespread or systematic attack directed against any civilian population, with knowledge of the attack: (a) Murder; (b) Extermination; (c) Enslavement; (d) Deportation...; (e) Imprisonment...; (f) Torture; (g) Rape...; (h) Persecution...; (i) Enforced disappearance of persons; (j) The crime of apartheid; (k) Other inhumane acts of a similar character intentionally

causing great suffering, or serious injury to body or to mental or physical health." Rome Statute of the International Criminal Court, A/Conf. July 17, 1998, art. 7 [hereinafter Rome Statute].

45. By 1996, Ratner and Abrams, in *Accountability for Human Rights Atrocities in International Law*, Oxford University Press, 1997, p. 55, could state that "the vast majority of states considered [the nexus between crimes against humanity and war crimes] unnecessary, and nearly all definitions submitted to the [General Assembly's Preparatory Commission on the Establishment of an International Criminal Court] lacked the nexus; but a handful of important states, such as Russia, China, and India, continued to argue for the nexus."

46. Prosecutor v. Dusko Tadic, Case No. IT-94-1-T, Para. 141 (October 2, 1995), Decision of the Appeals Chamber on the Defense Motion for Interlocutory Appeal on Jurisdiction, ICTY Appeals Chamber.

47. Prosecutor v. Dusko Tadic, Case No. IT-94-1-T (May 7, 1997), para. 649, Opinion and Judgment, ICTY Trial Chamber [hereinafter Tadic Trial Chamber], para 627. Here is a summary of the history of this case. The Trial Chamber began its deliberations in 1995. The defense launched a three-pronged attack on the Chamber's jurisdiction to hear the Tadic case. The Trial Chamber issued judgment against the defense motions on August 10, 1995. Tadic appealed this ruling to the Appeals Chamber. On October 2, 1995, the Appeals Chamber rejected Tadic's main jurisdiction motions. At this point, the Trial Chamber continued its deliberations, resulting in judgment on May 7, 1997.

48. See Ratner and Abrams, pp. 49–57, for a good discussion of this point.

49. This is not to suggest that there are no conceptual problems concerning the prosecution of leaders who have orchestrated crimes against humanity. It is always difficult to determine how much control an individual leader had versus how much that leader was compelled to act by forces beyond his or her control. See Hannah Arendt, *Eichmann in Jerusalem*, NY: Viking Books, 1963, discussing Eichmann's claim that he was forced to do what he did by his upbringing, but arguing that Eichmann was nonetheless properly prosecuted for his central role in planning the Holocaust.

50. There remains a major controversy in international criminal law, as mentioned in the previous chapters, about whether the requirement should be that the prosecution show widespreadness *and* systematicity, or merely widespreadness *or* systematictity. I employ the latter formulation as the least controversial of the two.

51. The second of these elements is the most likely to accomplish the task of linking the individual to the collective crime but, as we will see, participation in the plan may be unintentional and hence not something that provides a normative basis for blaming that individual.

52. See Nuremberg Statute, "committed against any civilian population"; ICTY Statute, "directed against any civilian population"; and Rome Statute, "directed against any civilian population."

53. Tadic Trial Chamber, para. 644, italics added.

54. Ibid., para. 649. A single act could constitute a crime against humanity as long as there is a link to a widespread or systematic attack.

55. See Gary Komarow, "Individual Responsibility Under International Law: The Nuremberg Principles in Domestic Legal Systems," *International and Comparative Law Quarterly*, 1980, p. 21, arguing that under international law, individuals do have a duty not to engage in human rights abuses, and that prosecutions for violations of those duties are justified.

56. It might be contended that the acts of many scholars writing about a single subject is more like a "class of individual acts." It is a collective act when the individuals coordinate their activities for a common goal, such as advancing the understanding of a concept like crimes against humanity. I am grateful to Carl Wellman for drawing my attention to this distinction.

57. See Lu-in Wang, "The Transforming Power of 'Hate': Social Cognition Theory and the Harms of Bias-Related Crime," *Southern California Law Review*, 1997, p. 47, arguing that in hate crimes, "[t]he perpetrator is conscious of his motivation for selecting the victim – he knows that he is hostile toward the social group in question and on that basis intentionally targets members of that group to victimize."

58. Tadic Trial Chamber, para. 644. "The 'population' element is intended to imply crimes of a collective nature and thus exclude single isolated acts which . . . do not rise to the level of crimes against humanity."

59. Ibid. The population element "has been interpreted to mean . . . that there must be some form of a governmental, organizational, or group policy."

60. Ibid., para. 653. "Traditionally this requirement was understood to mean that there must be some form of policy to commit these acts." See Phyllis Hwong, "Defining Crimes Against Humanity," *Fordham International Law Journal*, vol. 22, 1998, p. 495, questioning the wisdom of including this element as a distinct element since it can be inferred from the other elements.

61. ICTY Statute. From the context, it is clear that "directed at" implies an intentional act.

62. Tadic Trial Chamber, para. 653.

63. Ibid., para. 655.

64. Ibid.

65. I am grateful to Trudy Govier for suggesting this example.

66. See letter dated 24 May 1994, from the Secretary General to the President of the Security Council, UN Doc. S/1994/674, para. 21, setting out the importance of the element of widespread and systematic attack.

67. Tadic Trial Chamber, para. 648.

68. Ibid., para. 645.

69. I will use these terms somewhat differently here than in Chapter 5.

70. It is assumed here that grammaticality is indicative of conceptual truth. If this is thought to be too controversial, then it is sufficient for the reader to agree that the "plain meaning" of a term is initially a good indication of how that term should be understood. See Lawrence M. Solum, "Learning Our Limits: The Decline of Textualism in Statutory Cases," *Wisconsin Law Review*, 1997, p. 235, discussing Justice Scalia's method of textual interpretation that begins with the "plain meaning" or commonsense approach to the terms of a statute.

71. Conceptually, widespreadness can of course be disconnected from systematicity. But both need to be understood against a background of other acts. A single act cannot be widespread – there must be other acts of the same sort for them to be spread widely over a given terrain. And a single act cannot be systematic – there must be other acts that either do or do not form a system with this act.

72. See Tadic Trial Chamber, para. 649. "Crimes against humanity" can refer to individual acts, but only those that are part of a larger plan.

73. The most significant debate about these concepts is whether they are to be understood conjunctively or disjunctively – that is, whether the act must manifest both widespreadness and systematicity, or whether merely one of these is sufficient. See Darryl Robinson,

"Defining 'Crimes Against Humanity' at the Rome Conference," *American Journal of International Law*, vol. 93, 1999, p. 47, for a good discussion of recent debates about this issue [hereinafter Robinson].

74. Ratner and Abrams, p. 76.
75. Ibid., p. 60, arguing that group intimidation caused by an individual act also manifests widespreadness and systematicity.
76. Ibid., p. 76.
77. *Vukovar Hospital Rule 61 Decision*, para. 30, U.N. Doc. IT-95-13-R61 (1996), quoted in Tadic Trial Chamber, para. 649. See Ronald C. Slye, "Apartheid as a Crime Against Humanity," *Michigan Journal of International Law*, 1999, pp. 284–5, for discussion of this case.
78. In the last chapter, I explained the rationale for this condition. It might be possible to meet the spirit of this condition if the plan were aimed at having widespread and systematic effects but had not yet reached that level. Because of the very difficult problems of proof, I do not pursue this option in what follows.
79. Ratner and Abrams, pp. 76–7, arguing that the international community should sharpen its consensus that the scale and systematicity of a crime make it a violation of international law.
80. Recall that in discussing the Vukovar Hospital decision, the ICTY Trial Chamber said that widespreadness and systematicity were meant to show that there was an attack against a civilian population.
81. Van Schaack, p. 840.
82. Van Schaack refers to this element as a "discriminatory motive" element, yet the ICTY calls it "discriminatory intent." See Tadic Trial Chamber, para. 650. Since Van Schaack is clearly arguing against the ICTY, this chapter will follow the ICTY's terminology.
83. I am grateful to Thad Metz for helping me clarify my position in this respect.
84. See Robinson, "Defining 'Crimes Against Humanity' at the Rome Conference," *American Journal of International Law*, vol. 93, 1999, discussing the debate about the inclusion of a discriminatory intent element in crimes against humanity.
85. Provisional Verbatim Record of the 3217th Meeting, U.N. Doc. S/PV.3217 (25 May 1993), quoted in Tadic Trial Chamber, para. 652.
86. See Phyllis Hwong, "Defining Crimes Against Humanity," *Fordham International Law Journal*, vol. 22, 1998, p. 495, hypothesizing that the rest of the international community had decided to drop the "discriminatory intent" element because it was proving difficult for prosecutors to meet [hereinafter Hwong].
87. But the idea of discriminatory intent remains important in the crime of persecution, one of the most important of the crimes against humanity, even though the Rome Statute no longer considers it an element in crimes against humanity generally. See Hwong, pp. 494–501, for a good discussion of the debates about this idea in the Rome Conference.
88. ICTY Statute.
89. Tadic Trial Chamber, para. 652.
90. Ibid., para. 650–1. The aim of this chapter is to show that in some cases, the knowledge element is not sufficient without being paired with the intent element.
91. Prosecutor v. Touvier, 100 I.L.R. 341, 358, 1992, Court of Cassation, Criminal Chamber 1992.
92. Regina v. Finta [1994] 1 S.C.R. 701, 813 (Can.).
93. Ibid., 820.

94. In this respect, crimes against humanity are like hate crimes. Hate crimes also involve raising an act of murder, for instance, to a more serious level – namely, a hate crime. A 1999 essay has made some preliminary connections between the additional element in hate crimes and crimes against humanity, especially concerning the similarity of requiring an additional mental element. See Jose E. Alvarez, "Crimes of States/Crimes of Hate: Lessons from Rwanda," *Yale Journal of International Law,"* 1999, vol. 24, pp. 365–437.

95. Recall the ICTY's claim that crimes against humanity manifest the collective nature of individual acts, para. 644.

96. See Carlos Santiago Nino, *Radical Evil on Trial*, New Haven: Yale University Press, 1996, chapter 1, arguing forcefully for criminal punishment as a response to mass human rights violations.

97. Yet a third possibility is that the person is merely exploiting the larger campaign of ethnic intimidation to hide his or her own act of revengeful or sadistic killing. As explained later, this person's act should not be considered a crime against humanity.

98. A leader is normally also linked, in terms of act and not intention, by the fact that most leaders are also agents of a State or State-like entity.

99. See Larry May, *Sharing Responsibility*, Chicago: University of Chicago Press, 1992, chapter 2, explaining how individuals can come to share responsibility for large-scale harms such as racism.

100. See Tadic Trial Chamber, para. 644. "The population element is intended to imply crimes of a collective nature . . . the emphasis is not on the individual victim but rather on the collective."

101. See Larry May, *The Morality of Groups*, Notre Dame, IN: University of Notre Dame Press, 1987, pp. 113–15, for more on the idea of group-based categories of assessment. I also discuss the conspiracy model in greater detail in the next chapter.

102. Ibid., p. 116, for more of the details of this idea.

103. See John Biggs, Jr., *The Guilty Mind*, Baltimore, MD: The Johns Hopkins University Press, 1955, citing evidence to show that an individual mental element was necessary for criminal responsibility in Biblical, Chinese, Mohammedan, Greek, and Roman systems of law, as well as in the contemporary legal systems of France, Germany, China, Japan, and Great Britain.

104. See Norman D. Lattin, *On Corporations*, Mineola, NY: The Foundation Press, 2nd ed., 1971, p. 65, where Lattin explains that a legal corporation is treated as a single entity, an institution that is liable for what its employees do, and whose suits must be brought in its corporate name.

105. See Larry May, *The Morality of Groups*, pp. 141–2, for more on this topic.

106. Ibid., p. 140, for more on this topic.

107. Also see Douglas N. Husak, "Motive and Criminal Law," *Criminal Justice Ethics*, vol. 3, pp. 3–14, 1989, arguing that there are no principled reasons for confining the element of motive to sentencing considerations, and arguing that motive has been almost as important as intent in the elements of Anglo-American criminal law.

108. The major concern when one moves away from an individualistic model is that one risks "guilt by association." On this point, see Larry May, *Sharing Responsibility*, chapter 1.

109. Wayne R. LaFave and Austin W. Scott, Jr., *Criminal Law*, 2nd ed., St. Paul, MN: West Publishing, 1986, p. 7.

110. See Martin R. Gardner, "The *Mens Rea* Enigma: Observations on the Role of Motive in the Criminal Law Past and Present," *Utah Law Review*, 1993, pp. 651–81, describing the history of traditional psychological elements in Anglo-American criminal law, and arguing that from the earliest times, an individual mental element was required for criminal culpability.

111. I am grateful to David Luban for forcefully pressing this objection.

112. For an excellent analysis of such cases, see Mark J. Osiel, *Obeying Orders*, New Brunswick, NJ: Transaction Press, 1999.

113. Jeremy Bentham, *An Introduction to the Principles of Morals and Legislation* [1789], J. H. Burns and H. L. A. Hart, eds., Oxford: Oxford University Press, 1996, p. 86.

114. Tadic Trial Chamber, para. 650.

115. See Matthew Lippman, "Crimes Against Humanity," *Boston College Third World Law Journal*, vol. 17, 1997, pp. 177–9, discussing the Holocaust as the inspiration for the first use of the term "crimes against humanity."

116. See Cigar, pp. 3–10, documenting genocide in Bosnia-Herzegovina.

117. See Quigley, pp. 343–7, discussing the acts of State that constituted ethnic cleansing in Bosnia-Herzegovina.

118. UN General Assembly Resolution 47/80 of 16 December 1992, quoted in Lerner, p. 116.

119. See ICTY Statute, "when committed in armed conflict whether international or internal in character, and directed against any civilian population."

120. See Tadic Trial Chamber, para. 652. "The Trial Chamber adopts the requirement of discriminatory intent for all crimes against humanity."

121. See James Nickel, "What's Wrong With Ethnic Cleansing?" *Journal of Social Philosophy*, vol. 25, 1994, pp. 5–15, describing multiple types and motivations for ethnic cleansing.

122. Tadic Trial Chamber, para. 53–126.

123. Ibid., para. 127–79.

124. See ibid., para. 180, beginning the discussion of who Tadic was and what he did.

125. Ibid., para. 574–5.

126. Ibid., para. 574.

127. Ibid., "acts of the accused are related to the armed conflict in two distinct ways."

128. Ibid., para. 575.

129. Ibid.

130. Ibid., para. 2.

131. Ibid., para. 574–5.

132. Ibid., para. 625.

133. Ibid., para. 659.

134. Ibid., italics added.

135. See Larry May, *The Morality of Groups*, for an analysis of this concept.

136. Tadic Trial Chamber, para. 683.

137. Ibid., para. 714.

138. See ibid., para. 649–50, where the ICTY Trial Chamber has listed as its section heading: "b. The necessity of discriminatory intent."

139. Ibid., para. 652, contending that the requirement of "discriminatory grounds . . . is satisfied by the evidence . . . that the attack on the civilian population was conducted only against the non-Serb portion of the population because they were non-Serbs."

140. See ibid., para. 683, "nor has the Prosecution proved that the accused was engaged in the operation of the camps."
141. See Bassiouni, p. 563, arguing that murder, rape and torture are proscribed by every civilized society.
142. Tadic Trial Chamber, para. 644, "that the actions be taken on discriminatory intent."
143. Ibid., para. 273.
144. Ibid., para. 272.
145. Ibid., para. 271.
146. Ibid., para. 268.
147. Ibid.
148. Ibid., para. 277.
149. Ibid., para. 253.
150. Ibid., para. 254.
151. Convention on the Prevention and Punishment of the Crime of Genocide, 78 U.N.T.S. 277 (1948), Article II.
152. See Van Schaack, arguing that the difficulty of proving discriminatory intent should lead the international community to drop this element in crimes against humanity.
153. See Hwong for an excellent discussion of this issue.
154. The decision to require only a "knowledge" element is probably driven by the pragmatic consideration that such an element is easier to prove than is a "discriminatory intent" element. But conceptually, this strategy undermines the justifiability of the prosecution, as I have been arguing.
155. Ratner and Abrams, pp. 3–6.
156. See James Bohman, "The Rule of Law Outside of Borders: The International Criminal Court and Cosmopolitan Democracy," unpublished manuscript arguing that international criminal institutions are necessary for the rule of law.
157. See Martha Minow, *Between Vengeance and Forgiveness*, Boston: Beacon Press, 1998, exploring the advantages and disadvantages of international criminal tribunals and truth commissions. I explore these issues in Chapters 9 and 10.

Chapter 8

1. Bassiouni contends that the practice of putting Japanese into concentration camps in Canada and the United States during World War II was not a crime against humanity since both countries were not trying to persecute the Japanese, "even though [these countries] discriminated against an identifiable group." M. Cherif Bassiouni, *Crimes Against Humanity in International Criminal Law*, 2nd ed., Dordrecht: Kluwer, 1999, p. 261, [hereinafter Crimes Against Humanity].
2. Ibid. p. 563.
3. LaFave and Scott, *Criminal Law*, 2nd edition, St. Paul, MN: West Publishing, p. 32.
4. Bassiouni, Crimes Against Humanity, p. 563.
5. LaFave and Scott, p. 33.
6. Bassiouni, Crimes Against Humanity, p. 563.
7. See "Milosevic Prepares Speech on Eve of Trials," *The St. Louis Post Dispatch*, February 12, 2002, p. A2.
8. Tadic Trial Chamber, para. 652.

9. Prosecutor v. Musema, Trial Chamber, ICTR-96-13-T (27 Jan. 2000), para. 129–130, reprinted in Paust et al., *International Criminal Law*, Durham, NC: Carolina Academic Press, 2000.

10. Ibid., para. 131.

11. See Larry May, *Sharing Responsibility*, Chicago: University of Chicago Press, 1992, ch. 5.

12. Prosecutor v. Delalic et al., IT-96-21-T, Judgment (16 November 1998), para. 334.

13. Larry May, *The Morality of Groups*, Notre Dame, IN: University of Notre Dame Press, 1987.

14. Tadic Trial Chamber, para. 644. "The population element is intended to imply crimes of a collective nature and thus exclude single or isolated acts . . . the emphasis is not on the individual victim but rather on the collective, the individual being victimized not because of his individual attributes but rather because of his membership in a targeted civilian population."

15. See "Interview with Larry May," *Corporate Crime Reporter*, vol. 2 (1988), pp. 6–11.

16. See the "Introduction" to Larry May and Stacey Hoffman, eds., *Collective Responsibility*, Lanham, MD: Rowman & Littlefield, 1991. Also see Larry May, "Collective Responsibility," *The Encyclopedia of Ethics*, Lawrence Becker and Charlotte Becker, eds., 2nd ed., New York: Routledge, 2001.

17. See Ratner and Abrams.

18. Wayne R. LaFave and Austin W. Scott, Jr., *Criminal Law*, 2nd ed., St. Paul, MN: West Publishing, 1986, p. 526.

19. Ibid. p. 532: "It can instead be inferred from the facts and circumstances of the case. It is possible for various persons to be parties to a single agreement (and thus one conspiracy) even though they have no direct dealing with one another or do not know the identity of one another, and even though they are not all aware of the details of the plan of operation or were not all in the scheme from the beginning."

20. Ibid., p. 530.

21. See Smithson v. Garth (1601) 3 Lev. 324, 38 Eng. Rep. 1150, one of the earliest English cases to deal with concerted action.

22. By conspiracy-like, I mean that although the group has not been formed to commit criminal acts, it is currently pursuing such criminal acts in the way that conspiracy groups often do.

23. U.S. v. Park, 421 U.S. 658, 660 (1975).

24. Ibid.

25. See my discussion of this issue in "Negligence and Corporate Criminality," in *Shame, Responsibility, and the Corporation*, Hugh Curtler, ed., New York: Haven Publications, pp. 139–57.

26. In the Tadic case, an exception to the rule, a relatively small fry was successfully prosecuted for crimes against humanity. Tadic was the first person prosecuted by the ICTY. He was a part-time saloon keeper who stole into various camps to inflict torture and murder on his enemies. His acts were not seen as ethnic cleansing until it was demonstrated that he had knowledge of the larger campaign and had manifested discriminatory intent. See Scharf for a good description of the Tadic case.

27. Regina v. Bartle and the Commissioner of Police for the Metropolis and others Ex Parte Pinochet (on appeal from a Divisional Court of the Queen's Bench Division) and Regina v.

Evans and another and the Commissioner of Police for the Metropolis and others Ex Parte Pinochet (on appeal from a Divisional Court of the Queen's Bench Division), November 25, 1998 [hereinafter Pinochet Trial].

28. Ibid., opinion of Lord Steyn, p. 35.
29. Ibid. pp. 35–6.
30. There remains the question of where he should have been tried. The ICC would be the best place for such trials in the future, but at the time had not yet been set up. Concerns about trying a former head of State in a foreign court are not insignificant.
31. See Larry May, "Professional Action and Liabilities of Professional Associations: ASME v. Hydrolevel," *Business and Professional Ethics Journal*, vol. 2, no. 1 (Fall 1982), for my discussion of this doctrine in one of the leading cases to consider the concept of apparent authority.
32. Pinochet Trial, p. 25.
33. Regina v. Bartle and the Commissioner of Police for the Metropolis and Others, Ex Parte Pinochet, House of Lords (24 March 1999).
34. J. L. Brierly, *The Law of Nations*, 6th ed., Oxford: Oxford University Press, 1963, p. 162.
35. Thomas Hobbes's *Leviathan*, 1651, first paragraphs of chapter 16.
36. Pinochet Trial, p. 37.
37. Ibid.
38. Ibid., p. 37.
39. Quoted in ibid., p. 11.
40. Ibid., p. 33.
41. Ibid.
42. Ibid.
43. I do not accept the "but for" test as generally sufficient fully to establish causal responsibility. I use it here only as a quick way to show how one might establish at least prima facie responsibility.
44. I could mention the debate that has taken place in philosophical circles about whether torture could be justified in order to extract information about the location of a bomb that is set to explode soon and could cause massive casualties. It is well beyond the scope of this chapter to discuss the possible excusing conditions for such acts of torture. Let it suffice to say that even those who commit torture have not been condemned in all cases.

Chapter 9

1. Group crimes are literally committed against groups by other groups, as opposed to group-based crimes, which are perpetrated against individuals for being members of groups.
2. William A. Schabas, *Genocide in International Law*, Cambridge: Cambridge University Press, 2000, p. 79, citing UN Doc. A/C.6/SR.132 (Fitzmaurice, United Kingdom).
3. Hannah Arendt, *Eichmann in Jerusalem*, NY: Viking Books, Postscript, p. 298, 1964.
4. It is not impossible, though, for one individual, especially with stolen nuclear weapons, say, to destroy a whole group. Such cases are rare. Normally, a lot of people need to participate. I am grateful to Eric Rovie for this point.
5. William A. Schabas, *Genocide in International Law*, Cambridge: Cambridge University Press, 2000, p. 79, quoting UN Doc. A/C/.6/SR.132 (Fitzmaurice, United Kingdom).
6. Quoted in Schabas, p. 91.

7. Quoted in Schabas, p. 92.

8. Schabas, p. 12.

9. Arendt did not mean that these crimes were not truly terrible, from a moral point of view.

10. Colin McGinn, "Moral Vocabulary," *The New York Times*, Arts and Ideas Section, Saturday, December 28th, 2002, p. A17. Unfortunately, genocide involves acts that are far too ordinary to be able, by our condemning them, to stiffen our resolve.

11. The "enormity" issue and the "maliciousness" issue, although of course related, are definitely not the same issue.

12. Grendt, *Eichmann in Jerusalem*, p. 20.

13. Ibid., p. 18. To look beyond Eichmann "would have demanded exposure of the complicity of all German offices and authorities in the Final Solution – of all civil servants in the state ministries, of the regular armed forces, with their General Staff, of the judiciary, and of the business world."

14. Ibid., pp. 10–11.

15. Ibid., p. 23. And there was only one bit of evidence purportedly showing that Eichmann ever gave orders for Jews to be killed: a note that someone else had scribbled on a document saying, "Eichmann proposes shooting." Eichmann said that this was based on a conversation about what to do with "rebellious Jews," not with the Final Solution.

16. Ibid., p. 26. Arendt also said that Eichmann seemed "incapable of telling right from wrong." But this is to be understood not as meaning that Eichmann was "insane," but only that he was thoughtless. See Arendt's essay, "Thinking and Moral Considerations," *Social Research*, August 1971, pp. 417–46.

17. Colin McGinn, *Ethics, Evil and Fiction*, Oxford: Oxford University Press, 1997, chapter 4. Indeed, Eichmann had several Jewish relatives, and managed to save one of them from the concentration camps.

18. See Christopher Browning, *Ordinary Men*, New York: Harper Collins, 1992; Mark Osiel's, *Mass Atrocity, Ordinary Evil, and Hannah Arendt*, New Haven: Yale University Press, 2001; and Michael Scharf, *Balkan Justice*, Durham, NC: Carolina Academic Publishers, 1997.

19. On this general point, see Douglas Husak's intriguing essay, "The 'But-Everyone-Does-That!' Defense," *Public Affairs Quarterly*, vol. 10, no. 4, October 1996.

20. Arendt, *Eichmann in Jerusalem*, p. 278.

21. Stanley Milgram, *Obedience to Authority*, New York: Harper & Row, 1974.

22. See R. M. Hare, *Moral Thinking*, Oxford: Oxford University Press, 1973.

23. Arendt, *Eichmann in Jerusalem*, p. 278.

24. Ibid., p. 278.

25. See Hervey Cleckley's *The Mask of Sanity: An Attempt to Reinterpret the So-called Psychopathic Personality*, St. Louis, MO: Mosby Publishers, 1941.

26. Convention on the Prevention and Punishment of the Crime of Genocide, adopted Dec. 9, 1948, entered into force January 12, 1951, 78 U.N.T.SW. 277, Art. II. The very same acts are listed for the crime of genocide in the Rome Statute, Article 6.

27. The Prosecutor of the Tribunal against Georges Anderson Nderubumwe Rutaganda, International Criminal Tribunal for Rwanda, Case No. ICTR-96-3, Judgment and Sentence, 6 December 1999, para. 52.

28. This is one of the main differences between the way the Rome Statute treats genocide as apposed to crimes against humanity. As we saw in Chapter 7, crimes against humanity do not at present require a second intent, but only an additional knowledge requirement.

In that chapter, I argued in favor of requiring discriminatory intent, at least in cases of the prosecution of minor players for crimes against humanity. As can now be seen, this means that I was arguing that crimes against humanity should have a similar intent requirement to that of genocide.

29. Prosecutor v. Goran Jelisic, International Tribunal for the Prosecution of Persons Responsible for Serious Violations of International Humanitarian Law Committed in the Territory of the Former Yugoslavia, Judgment of the Trial Chamber, 14 December 1999.

30. The Prosecutor of the Tribunal Against Jean Paul Akayesu, International Criminal Tribunal for Rwanda, Case No. ICTR-96-4, Judgment of the Trial Chamber, 2 September 1998.

31. Jelisic Trial Chamber Judgment, para. 100.

32. Jelisic Appeals Chamber Judgment, para. 48.

33. Akayesu Trial Chamber Judgment, para. 523.

34. Genocide Convention, Article II.

35. Akayesu Trial Chamber Judgment, para. 497.

36. Report of the International Law Commission on the Work of its 48th Session, U.N.GAOR, 51st Sess., Supp. No. 10, at 87, UN Doc. A/51/10 (1996) at 88.

37. Akayesu Trial Chamber Judgment, para. 469.

38. See Alexander K. A. Greenawalt, "Rethinking Genocidal Intent: The Case for a Knowledge-Based Interpretation," *Columbia Law Review*, vol. 99, no. 8, December 1999, pp. 2259–94.

39. My italics, quoted in Guglielmo Verdirame, "The Genocide Definition in the Jurisprudence of the *Ad Hoc* Tribunals," *International and Comparative Law Quarterly*, vol. 49, no. 3, July 2000, p. 580.

40. "Intending" is like "promising" – it has a performative aspect. Normally, one cannot promise to do something and yet not have any plan to do so; similarly, one cannot intend to do something and yet not have a plan to do so. Of course, one could have a plan that was doomed from the start. But normally one cannot have an intention to do something that one knows has a doomed plan for its accomplishment. It simply would not be intending. And just as one cannot make a promise that one intends not to keep, one cannot intend to do something that one knows one cannot accomplish. "Intending" is different from "attempting." In the case of attempting, there is some sense to the concept of attempting to do the impossible. If I know in advance that I will not be able to influence my Dean, I may attempt to do so anyway, and my colleagues would not be talking nonsense when they said that I had made a valiant attempt. But it would be nearly inconceivable to say that I would have intended to do the impossible. This is one of the reasons why it made sense to add the phrase "in part" to the intent element of the crime of genocide.

41. See Verdirame, p. 588.

42. Jelisic Trial Chamber Judgment, para. 107.

43. Ibid., para. 101.

44. See William A. Schabas, "Was Genocide Committed in Bosnia and Herzegovina? First Judgments of the International Criminal Tribunal for the Former Yugoslavia," *Fordham International Law Journal*, vol. 25, no. 1, November 2001, p. 40.

45. Perhaps it could be argued that the destruction of a whole group is different from the destruction of a group as such. Intending to destroy a whole group might mean doing what is necessary to bring about the group's end all at once, by somehow assaulting the entire group. Intending to destroy a part of a group would be less than this – that is, intending to do what is necessary to bring about part of a group's demise by assaulting

part of the group. Both forms would involve the ultimate aim of destroying the group as such, not merely ending the lives of the individual members of the group. Even if we take this route, it remains unclear what it would mean to destroy a group in whole as such.

46. Cited in Greenawalt, p. 2265.

47. A surprising result of all of this is that some groups, such as the mafia, can commit political crimes. This is one reason why I explore the analogy between conspiracy law and the international law concerning genocide.

48. While Hannah Arendt and Karl Jaspers held somewhat different views of these matters, I will ignore their differences here and treat them as if they had roughly the same view, as they themselves maintained.

49. Karl Jaspers, *The Question of German Guilt*, New York: Capricorn Books, 1947, p. 31.

50. Hannah Arendt, "Personal Responsibility Under Dictatorship," *The Listener*, vol. 72, no. 1845, August 6, 1964, p. 186.

51. Ibid., p. 205.

52. See Kutz, *Complicity*, New York: Cambridge University Press, 2000.

53. For an analysis of collective action, see chapter 2 of Larry May, *The Morality of Groups*, Notre Dame, IN: University of Notre Dame Press, 1987. For more on the nature of shared responsibility and how it is related to collective action, see also Larry May, *Sharing Responsibility*, Chicago: University of Chicago Press, 1992.

54. The major disadvantage of trials for political crimes is that it is very difficult to find unbiased witnesses and impartial judges when nearly everyone in a society is one of the perpetrators of the crime. When all, or almost all, are guilty, there is little possibility of having the non-guilty as judges, and hence little possibility in that society of having impartial trials. In addition, when all are guilty, the testimony of one's neighbors or co-workers will often not be believable since it is so likely to be biased by self-interest. Of course, one way to get around the first of these problems is to have the judging party be selected from outside the society in question, which is what international criminal tribunals have been primarily constructed to do. Unfortunately, these tribunals have yet to figure out an answer to the latter problem, since even when a trial is held far away from the society where the crime occurred, it will still need witnesses from that society, and bringing them hundreds or thousands of miles from home does not necessarily make their testimony any more trustworthy.

55. Hannah Arendt, *Eichmann in Jerusalem*, New York: Viking Press, revised edition 1964, Epilogue, p. 279.

56. I do not have the space to go into this issue here, but Eichmann in his memoirs clearly indicates that he acted with the intention of participating in a plan of genocide against the Jews, not merely to follow orders.

Chapter 10

1. Recall that a similar term – namely, what offends the "conscience of humanity" – was used in explicating the idea of universal, or *jus cogens*, norms of international law.

2. Throughout this chapter, I will mainly talk of "soldiers" as the defendants, but other minor players who are in a chain of command, such as camp guards and perhaps even people like Tadic, might also be able to avail themselves of this defense.

3. The Tribunal considered three types of crime: war crimes, crimes against humanity, and crimes against peace, even though the Tribunal was only called a "war crimes" tribunal.

4. As it turned out, only the actions of soldiers of the German army were considered, even though soldiers from many other armies took part in World War II.

5. *The Judgment of the International Tribunal at Nuremberg*, Washington, DC: United States Government Printing Office, 1947, p. 53, reprinted in *War and Morality*, Richard Wasserstrom, ed., Belmont, CA: Wadsworth Publishing, 1970, p. 109.

6. See "The Breisach Trial of 1474," in G. Schwarzenberger, *International Law*, vol. II, London: Stevens and Sons, 1968, p. 462.

7. Telford Taylor, *The Anatomy of the Nuremberg Trials*, Boston: Little, Brown, 1992, p. 17.

8. There is considerable disagreement about exactly what orders Calley was given.

9. Quoted in Richard Hammer, *The Court Martial of Lt. Calley*, NY: Coward, McCann, and Geoghegan, 1971, 337. See also David Cooper, "Responsibility and the System," in Peter French, ed., *Individual and Collective Responsibility: The Massacre at My Lai*, Cambridge, MA: Schenkman Publishing, 1972; Burleigh Wilkins, "Responsibility for the My Lai Massacre," in his book *Terrorism and Collective Responsibility*, New York: Routledge, 1992, p. 88; and Calley v. Callaway, 519 F.2d 184 (5th Cir. 1975), where a federal circuit court upheld Calley's conviction, reversing a lower federal court ruling.

10. See Lawrence Blum, *Moral Perception and Particularity*, Cambridge: Cambridge University Press, 1994.

11. See Larry May, *Sharing Responsibility*, Chicago: University of Chicago Press, 1992.

12. Aristotle, *Nicomachean Ethics*, 1113b30–1114a.

13. See Ronald Milo's discussion of this point in his *Immorality*, Princeton: Princeton University Press, 1984, chapter 4.

14. I am grateful to George Rainbolt for discussion of this objection.

15. See Larry May, *Sharing Responsibility*, chapter 3.

16. See J. Glenn Gray's evocative descriptions of these experiences in *The Warriors: Reflection on Men in Battle*, New York: Harcourt Brace, 1959, especially chapter 5.

17. Thomas Hobbes, *Leviathan* (1651), *The English Works of Thomas Hobbes*, vol. 3, London: John Bohn. Second reprint, Scientia Verlag Aalen, 1966, p. 114.

18. On this point, see Guenther Lewy, "Superior Orders, Nuclear Warfare, and the Dictates of Conscience," *American Political Science Review*, vol. 55, 1961, reprinted in *War and Morality*, Richard Wasserstrom, ed., pp. 119–20.

19. United Nations War Crimes Commission, *History of the United Nations War Crime Commission and the Development of the Laws of War*, London, 1948, Article 443, p. 282, quoted in Lewy, p. 116.

20. *The Judgment of the International Tribunal at Nuremberg*, p. 102.

21. Calley v. Callaway, 382 F.Supp.650, 654.

22. Ibid.

23. Calley v. Callaway, 519 F.2d 184, 191.

24. Ibid., 191–92.

25. I am grateful to William Edmundson for this point.

26. This is roughly the way Justice Learned Hand advised that negligence be understood. See Hand's discussion in United States v. Carroll Towing Co., 159 F.2d 169, 2d Cir. 1947, where the formula was expressed as follows: "If the probability be called P; the injury, L; and the burden, B; liability depends upon whether B is less than L, multiplied by P: i.e., whether B [is less than] PL," at 173.

27. The tort analysis of negligence "applies to only a relatively few modern statutory crimes" in the United States. "More often, it is a concept that is applicable to a defense to crime,

rather than an element in the crime itself, as in the defense of self-defense." See the discussion of the distinction between *tort* negligence and *criminal* negligence in Wayne R. LaFave and Austin Scott, *Criminal Law*, 2nd ed., St. Paul, MN: West Publishing, 1986, pp. 233–35.

28. For an analysis of the conditions of collective responsibility, see Larry May, "Collective Responsibility," in *The Encyclopedia of Ethics*, 2nd ed., Lawrence and Charlotte Becker, eds., New York: Garland Press, 2001.

29. On this point, see chapter 1 of Larry May, *Sharing Responsibility*.

30. See my discussion of such cases in chapter 10 of Larry May, *The Socially Responsive Self*, Chicago: University of Chicago Press, 1996.

31. On this point, see Hannah Arendt's discussion of how Eichmann felt he had few choices because of his need to be the supporter of his family, in Arendt, *Eichmann in Jerusalem*, New York: Viking Books, 1963.

32. Recall the earlier discussion of the Tadic case, the case that has set the pattern for most of the jurisprudence for the Yugoslav Tribunal.

33. Rome Statute for the International Criminal Court, reprinted in vol. III of M. Cherif Bassiouni, *International Criminal Law*, 2nd ed., New York: Transactional Publishers, 1999, p. 736.

34. See Mark Osiel, *Obeying Orders*, New Brunswick, NJ: Transaction Press, 1999, p. 61.

35. Ibid., p. 55. Osiel says that this is generally seen as a class of atrocities.

36. Ibid., pp. 77–83.

37. Ibid., p. 735.

38. Prosecutor v. Erdemovic, Judgment. Case No. IT-96-22-A. International Criminal Tribunal for the Former Yugoslavia, Appeals Chamber, October 7, 1997 (Cassese, McDonald, Li, Stephen, Vohrah, JJ.) para. 80.

39. Ibid., para. 8.

40. Ibid., para. 80.

41. Prosecutor v. Erdemovic, No. IT-96-22-A, separate and dissenting opinion of Judge Cassese, para. 11.

42. Ibid., para. 3. See also Olivia Swaak-Goldman's "Note on Erdemovic Case," *The American Journal of International Law*, vol. 92, 1998, p. 286.

Chapter 11

1. See Lon Fuller, *The Morality of Law*, New Haven: Yale University Press, 1964, 1967, chapter 2, for a discussion of the procedural basis of the rule of law [hereinafter Fuller].

2. For more elaboration on many of these procedural restraints, see Cass R. Sunstein, *Legal Reasoning and Political Conflict*, Oxford: Oxford University Press, 1996, chapter 4.

3. Ibid., chapter 3.

4. See William S. Eskridge, Jr., and John Ferejohn, "Politics, Interpretation, and the Rule of Law," *NOMOS XXXVI: The Rule of Law*, New York: New York Univerisity Press, 1994.

5. See Seth Mydans, "New Rule of Law in Thailand May Be a Leader's Downfall," *The New York Times*, July 30, 2001, p. A8.

6. See Lawrence B. Solum, "Equity and the Rule of Law," *NOMOS XXXVI: The Rule of Law*, New York: New York University Press, 1994.

7. On this point, see Telford Taylor's wonderful book, *The Anatomy of the Nuremberg Trials*, Boston: Little Brown, 1992.

8. Fuller, p. 53.
9. Ibid.
10. Ibid., p. 58.
11. Ibid., p. 59.
12. ICTY Appeals Chamber, Decision on the Defense Motion for Interlocutory Appeal on Jurisdiction, 2 October 1995, IT Doc. IT-94-1-AR72, para. 68.
13. Ibid., para. 100.
14. See Preliminary Remarks of the International Committee of the Red Cross, 22 February 1993, reproduced in Virginia Morris and Michael Scharf, *An Insider's Guide to the International Criminal Tribunal for the Former Yugoslavia*, vol. 2 (1995), p. 391.
15. ICTY Tadic Appeals Chamber, para. 89.
16. Ibid., para. 119.
17. Ibid., para. 133.
18. Fuller, p. 42.
19. H. L. A. Hart, *The Concept of Law*, Oxford: Oxford University Press, 1961, 3rd ed., 1994, p. 207.
20. Ibid.
21. Robert H. Jackson, Chief of Counsel for the United States, Opening Statement for the United States at the Palace of Justice, Nuremberg, Germany, November 21, 1945.
22. See remarks by M. Cherif Bassiouni, Richard Falk, and Yasuaki Onuma in "Forty Years After The Nuremberg and Tokyo Tribunals: The Impact of the War Crimes Trials on International and National Law," *Proceedings of the 80th Annual Meeting, American Society of International Law*, Washington, D.C., April 9–12, 1986.
23. Robert H. Jackson, Opening Statement, third sentence.
24. Despite these very serious charges, I remain a strong defender of the Yugoslav Tribunal – a flawed court that has stepped into the breach where otherwise there would simply be nothing resembling justice at all.
25. Press statement by the Prosecutor, Justice Richard Goldstone, in conjunction with the Announcement of the Indictments on 25 July 1995, quoted in Scharf, p. 85.
26. Quoted in Scharf, ibid.
27. This is the position taken by Louise Arbour, the second chief prosecutor at the ICTY. Her views were expressed to me in a private communication, October 28, 1998. A similar position was taken by Richard Goldstone, the first chief prosecutor of the ICTY, also in a private communication, June 4, 1999.
28. Thomas Franck says that the fairness will be measured by looking at the procedures of such tribunals. He worries specifically about trials conducted in absentia. See Franck, Thomas p. 280. *Fairness in International Law*, Oxford: Oxford University Press, 1995.
29. Stephen Engelberg, "Panel Seeks U.S. Pledge on Bosnia War Criminals," *The New York Times*, November 3, 1995, p. A1.
30. Payne v. Tennessee, 501 U.S. 808, 818, 1991, Scalia dissenting, quoting Booth, 482 U.S. at 519.
31. This phrase was made famous by its inclusion in Justice Jackson's opening statement at the Nuremberg Trials.
32. William A. Schabas, "International Sentencing: From Leipzig (1923) to Arusha (1996)," in *International Criminal Law*, 2nd ed., vol. III, M. Cherif Bassiouni, ed., Transnational Publishers, 1999, p. 182, citing Prosecutor v. Tadic, paras. 16, 20, 32, 44, 47, 55, 56, 59.
33. Ibid., p. 193.

34. See William A. Schabas, *The Abolition of the Death Penalty in International Law*, 2nd ed., Cambridge: Cambridge University Press, 1997.

35. Prosecutor v. Erdemovic, Case No. IT-96-22-T, Sentencing Judgment of Trial Chamber I, Nov. 29, 1996, para. 58. We return to the issue of reconciliation in Chapter 13.

36. Universal Declaration of Human Rights, GA Res. 217 A (III), U.N. Doc. A/810.

37. See Gregory Kavka, *Hobbesian Moral and Political Theory*, Princeton: Princeton University Press, 1986, for an excellent discussion of Hobbesian views of the sort I am discussing in this section.

38. Jean Hampton, "Democracy and the Rule of Law," in *NOMOS XXXVI: The Rule of Law*, Ian Shapiro, ed., New York: New York University Press, 1994.

39. Ibid., p. 25.

40. See Thomas Hobbes, *Leviathan* (1651), *The English Works of Thomas Hobbes*, vol. 3, London: John Bohn. Second reprint, Scientia Verlag Aalen, 1966, chapter 16.

41. See M. Cherif Bassiouni and Edward M. Wise, *Aut Dedere, Aut Judicare: The Duty to Extradite or Prosecute in International Law*, Dordrecht: Martinus Nijhoff Publishers, 1995.

42. I am grateful to Jim Bohman for very helpful discussions of this point.

Chapter 12

1. I want to leave open the question of what sort of society might have this right. My point is simply that criminal law concerns a larger group than just those immediately affected by the victim's plight.

2. See Richard Goldstone's sensitive defense of this position in his book, *For Humanity: Reflections of a War Crimes Investigator*, New Haven: Yale University Press, 2000. In the Foreword to that book, Justice Sandra Day O'Connor says that the "rule of law is generally vindicated by holding transgressors accountable for their actions through prosecution and punishment," p. xi.

3. In the case of *Payne v. Tennessee*, 501 U.S. 808 (1990), Chief Justice Rehnquist, writing for the majority, overruled previous Supreme Court opinions, and held that victim-impact evidence during the penalty phase of capital murder cases did not violate the Eighth Amendment to the United States Constitution.

4. See John Gibeaut, "Deadly Choices," *ABA Journal*, May 2001, pp. 38–45, for a good account of the unfairness that results when prosecutors are driven by the victims' families to seek the death penalty.

5. See Azanian Peoples Organization, *Report of the Truth and Reconciliation Commission*, presented to President Nelson Mandela on October 29, 1998, Cape Town: Groves Press, 1999, vol. 1, p. 175.

6. Ibid., p. 175.

7. Judge Mahomed is quite lucid in articulating the concerns of these family members, even as he rejects their claims in the case of Azanian Peoples Organization, Ms. N. M. Biko, Mr. C. H. Mxenge, and Mr. C. Ribeiro v. President of the Republic of South Africa . . . and the Chairperson of the Commission, in the Constitutional Court, 1 Case No. CCT 17/96, reported in ibid, p. 176.

8. See Michael Scharf, "Swapping Amnesty for Peace: Was There a Duty to Prosecute International Crimes in Haiti," *Texas International Law Journal*, vol. 31, 1996, p. 1.

9. G. W. F. Hegel, *Philosophy of Right* (1821), T. M. Knox, trans., 1952, para. 99, p. 70.

10. Ibid., p. 70.
11. Hegel generally holds to a restorative theory of justice, but he believes that retribution is one of the best means available to aid in restoration of the right. Although this view is itself highly controversial, I will not pursue it here, but focus instead only on what Hegel says about retribution.
12. Hegel, *Philosophy of Right*, para. 101, p. 71.
13. Ibid., para. 103, p. 73.
14. Ibid., para. 85, p. 65.
15. Ibid., para. 94, p. 67.
16. On this point, see the discussion in Chapter 13 on the topic of whether institutions can feel forgiveness.
17. Immanuel Kant, *Metaphysical Elements of Justice* (1797), John Ladd, ed., 2nd ed., 1999, p. 140.
18. Ibid., pp. 114–115.
19. Ibid., p. 144.
20. In Hobbes's *Leviathan* (1651), *The English Works of Thomas Hobbes*, vol. 3, London: John Bohn, second reprint, Scientia Verlag Aalen, 1966, especially chapter 26, very powerful arguments are advanced in support of this claim.
21. Scharf, *Texas International Law Journal*, 1996.
22. Martha Minow, *Between Vengeance and Forgiveness*, Boston: Beacon Press, 1998, p. 25.
23. Although we did raise critical questions in Chapter 11 about whether these features really were necessary for the rule of law as opposed to being merely part of a Western conception of procedural justice.
24. *Webster's Third International Dictionary*, 1986, p. 1138.
25. Lon Fuller, *The Morality of Law*, New Haven: Yale University Press, 1964, 1969, p. 55.
26. Ibid., p. 123.
27. Michael Walzer, "The Legal Codes of Ancient Israel," *NOMOS XXXVI: The Rule of Law*, New York: New York University Press, 1994, pp. 101–19.
28. For a good summary of the various perspectives on the rule of law, see Lawrence B. Solum, "Equity and the Rule of Law," and Stephen Macedo, "The Rule of Law, Justice, and the Politics of Moderation," in *NOMOS XXXVI*, ibid.
29. On this point, see Larry May, "Single-Mindedness and Professional Roles," delivered as the 1st James Lapaglia Lecture on Ethics at Carnegie Mellon University, February 2001, and as a keynote address at a professional ethics conference at the University of Dayton, April 2001.
30. Federal Rules of Criminal Procedure 29; Federal Rules of Civil Procedure 50. I am grateful to Mark Tushnet for clarifying this point.
31. See Yazir Henry, "Where Healing Begins," in Charles Villa-Vicencio and Wilhelm Verwoerd, eds., *Looking Back, Reaching Forward*, Cape Town: University of Cape Town Press, 2000.
32. See my discussion of this issue in "Legal Advocacy," chapter 8 of Larry May, *The Socially Responsive Self*, Chicago: University of Chicago Press, 1996.
33. Owen Fiss, "Against Settlement," *Yale Law Journal*, vol. 93, 1984, p. 1085.
34. See Chapter 2 for a thorough discussion of these non-consensual norms in international law.
35. Michael Scharf, "Swapping Amnesty for Peace: Was There a Duty to Prosecute International Crimes in Haiti," *Texas International Law Journal*, vol. 31, 1996, p. 14.

36. A recent book of essays on this topic is *Truth v. Justice*, Amy Guttman and Dennis Thompson (Rotberg and Thompson, eds.), Princeton: Princeton University Press, 2000. The use of the "v." makes it seem that there might be a zero-sum game here.

Chapter 13

1. Hannah Arendt, "Organized Guilt and Universal Responsibility," *Jewish Frontiers*, 1948, reprinted in *Collective Responsibility*, Larry May and Stacey Hoffman, eds., Lanham, MD: Rowman and Littlefield, 1991, p. 278.

2. Martha Minow, *Between Vengeance and Forgiveness*, Boston: Beacon Press, 1998, p. 26.

3. In most cases, I will use the term "pardon" for the mercy that is shown after a trial has occurred, or at least after there has been a preliminary indication of guilt, and the term "amnesty" for the mercy that is shown prior to a trial, or other determination of guilt. I will sometimes use the term "amnesty" to cover both situations.

4. Elizabeth Kiss, "Moral Ambition Within and Beyond Political Constraints: Reflections on Restorative Justice," in *Truth v. Justice*, Robert I. Rotberg and Dennis Thompson, eds., Princeton: Princeton University Press, 2000, p. 68.

5. See Kent Greenawalt, "Amnesty's Justice," in ibid., pp. 189ff, for a good discussion of the difference between pre-prosecution and post-prosecution amnesties.

6. Aristotle, *Nicomachean Ethics*, W. D. Ross, trans., NY: Oxford University Press, 1925, 1137b5–6.

7. Ibid., 1137b30–32.

8. Ibid., 1137b23.

9. Frederick Pollock and Frederic William Maitland, *History of English Law*, vol. 2, Boston: Little Brown, 1909, p. 671.

10. Theodore F. T. Pluncknett, *A Concise History of the Common Law*, 5th ed., Boston: Little Brown, 1956, p. 675.

11. Christopher St. Germaine, *Doctor and Student*, 1535, p. 50, quoted in Steven J. Prall, "The Development of Equity in Tudor England," *American Journal of Legal History*, vol. 8, 1964, p. 4.

12. For a contemporary attempt to defend a more expansive conception of equity see Peter Charles Hoffer, *The Law's Conscience: Equitable Constitutionalism in America*, Chapel Hill, NC: University of North Carolina Press, 1990.

13. Thomas Hobbes develops the distinction between artificial and natural persons in chapter 16 of *Leviathan*. See Thomas Hobbes, *Leviathan* (1651), *The English Works of Thomas Hobbes*, vol. 3, London: John Bohn. Second reprint, Scientia Verlag Aalen, 1966, p. 147. And Hobbes develops this idea and relates it to equity in his *Dialogue*. See Thomas Hobbes, *A Dialogue Between a Philosopher and a Student of the Common Laws of England*, 1681, Joseph Cropsey, ed., Chicago: University of Chicago Press, 1971.

14. Oliver Wendell Holmes, "The Path of the Law," *Harvard Law Review*, vol. 10, 1897, p. 458.

15. See André Du Toit, "The Moral Foundations of the South African TRC: Truth as Acknowledgement and Justice as Recognition," in Rotberg and Thompson, pp. 122ff. Also see Wilhelm Verwoerd, "Toward the Recognition of our Past Injustices," in *Looking Back, Reaching Forward: Reflections on the Truth and Reconciliation Commission in South Africa*, Charles Villa-Vicencio and Wilhelm Verwoerd, eds., Cape Town: University of Cape Town Press, 2000.

16. See Alfred Dorjahn, *Political Forgiveness in Old Athens: The Amnesty of 403 B.C.*, Evanston, IL: Northwestern University Press, 1946.

17. See Jeffrie G. Murphy and Jean Hampton, *Forgiveness and Mercy*, Cambridge: Cambridge University Press, 1988, for an excellent debate about the meaning of these terms, and their moral limits.

18. See Naomi Roht-Arriaza and Lauren Gibson, "The Developing Jurisprudence on Amnesty," *Human Rights Quarterly*, vol. 20, 1998, p. 843.

19. See Elizabeth Kiss for a good discussion of this point.

20. See David Crocker, "Truth Commissions, Transitional Justice and Civil Society," in Rotberg and Thompson, pp. 99ff.

21. Hecht Co. v. Bowles, 321 U.S. 321, 329–30 (1944), quoted in Pangilinan v. INS, 796 F.2d 1102. See also Martha C. Nussbaum, "Equity and Mercy," *Philosophy and Public Affairs*, vol. 22, 1993, p. 83.

22. Zachariah Chaffe and Edward D. Re, *Cases and Materials on Equity*, Brooklyn, NY: Foundation Press, 5th ed., 1967, p. 12.

23. See Ian Fisher, "Where Justice Takes a Back Seat to Just Ending War," *The New York Times*, Sunday, July 15, 2001, sec. 4, p. 5.

24. See the excellent discussion of these issues in Trudy Govier, *Forgiveness and Revenge*, New York: Routledge, 2002, especially chapter 8.

25. Aristotle, *The Athenian Constitution*, H. Rachham, trans., Cambridge, MA: Harvard University Press, 1935, 39.6.

26. One of the most recent non-general amnesties only affects certain groups. "On November 12, 1997, Congress approved, and November 19, 1997, President Clinton signed into law, the Nicaraguan Adjustment and Central American Relief Act ("NACARA") which provides blanket eligibility for adjustment of status for many Cubans and Nicaraguans, and allows Salvadorans, Guatemalans, and certain East Europeans to apply for suspension of deportation . . ." Mario M. Lovo, "Nicaraguan Adjustment And Central American Relief Act 'NACARA,'" *Immigration Briefings*, vol. 1, November 1998.

27. See Karen Leaf, "Legalizing the Illegals," *Columbia Human Rights Law Review*, vol 12, 1980, pp. 65–89. Leaf.

28. See Larry May and Stacey Hoffman, eds., *Collective Responsibility: Five Decades of Debate in Theoretical and Applied Ethics*, Lanham, MD: Rowman and Littlefield, 1991.

29. I have a lengthy discussion and defense of collective responsibility in Larry May, *The Morality of Groups*, Notre Dame, IN: University of Notre Dame Press, 1987, pp. 73–111.

30. E. Sidney Hartland, *Primitive Law*, New York: Kennikat Press, 1924, p. 42.

31. See Daniel Kanstroom, "Judicial Review of Amnesty Denials: Must Aliens Bet their Lives to Get into Court?" *Harvard Civil Rights – Civil Liberties Law Review*, vol. 25, 1990, p. 53.

32. See Alfonso Damico, *Democracy and the Case for Amnesty*, Gainesville, FL: University Presses of Florida, 1975; Lawrence Barkir and William Strauss, *Reconciliation After Vietnam*, Notre Dame, IN: University of Notre Dame Press, 1977. Also see Jonathan Dorris, *Pardon and Amnesty Under Lincoln and Johnson*, Westport, CT: Greenwood Press, 1953.

33. See Christopher Kutz, *Complicity*, New York/Cambridge: Cambridge University Press, 2000, for an excellent analysis of the general concept of complicity.

34. See Hannah Arendt, *Eichmann in Jerusalem*, NY: Viking Press, 1963.
35. See Larry May, *Sharing Responsibility*, Chicago: University of Chicago Press, 1992, especially chapter 2, for a discussion of how the nurturing of a climate that makes harm more likely means that many people share responsibility for the harms other than those who directly perpetrate them.
36. See Brent Fisse and John Braithwaite, *The Impact of Publicity on Corporate Offenders*, Albany, NY: State University of New York Press, 1983.
37. See note 26 and accompanying text, for a discussion about NACARA. This was an act of the United States Congress that effectively granted amnesty for illegal immigrants from various Central American countries.
38. Trudy Govier, "Collective Responsibility and the Fallacies of Composition and Division," unpublished manuscript, 2001.
39. See Margaret Gilbert's recent work on this topic, especially "Group Wrongs and Guilt Feelings," *The Journal of Ethics*, vol. 1, no. 1, 1997.
40. See chapter 4 of Larry May, *The Morality of Groups*.
41. Most prominently, some have said that the Universal Declaration of Human Rights, Article 1, with its recognition of the status of "person before the law," would prohibit punishing one person for the acts of another. *See* Paust et al., *International Criminal Law: Cases and Materials*, 2nd ed., Durham, NC: Carolina Academic Publishers, 2000, p. 45.
42. See Ronald Slye, "Justice and Amnesty," in Villa-Vicencio and Verwoerd, pp. 174ff, for a good discussion of why the South African TRC does not fall prey to the standard objections against amnesty programs.
43. These amnesty and pardon programs of course must also conform to the rule of law. There is a very good practical question, which I will not address in this chapter, as to who should administer amnesty or pardon programs concerning international crimes. Perhaps this will end up being one of the functions of the Security Council, or one of its sub-divisions, after the ICC is functional. Regardless of who administers these programs, it must be done in a way that does not erode respect for law and, generally, the rule of law.
44. Amy Guttman and Dennis Thompson, "The Moral Foundations of Truth Commissions," in Rotberg and Thompson, p. 23.
45. Joy Kogawa, remarks at conference on reconciliation at University of Calgary in June of 1999. Also see Joy Kogawa, *The Rain Ascends*, Toronto: Vintage Canada, 1995.
46. Hannah Arendt, "Personal Responsibility under Dictatorship," *The Listener*, vol. 72, no. 1845, August 6, 1964, p. 186.

Conclusions

1. Some clearly want to do just this. See Alfred Rubin, *Ethics and Authority in International Law*, 1997; and Jovan Babic, "War Crimes: Moral, Legal, or Simply Political?" in *War Crimes and Collective Wrongdoing*, Aleksandar Jokic, ed., London: Blackwell, 2001.
2. See Aryeh Neier, *War Crimes*, NY: Times Books, 1998. Although I disagree with Neier about amnesty programs, I certainly agree that international tribunals are needed.

3. See Tzvetan Todorov, "In Search of Lost Crime: Tribunals, Apologies, Reparations, and the Search for Justice," *The New Republic*, January 29, 2001.

4. See remarks by M. Cherif Bassiouni, Richard Falk, and Yasuaki Onuma in "Forty Years After The Nuremberg and Tokyo Tribunals: The Impact of the War Crimes Trials on International and National Law," *Proceedings of the 80th Annual Meeting, American Society of International Law*, Washington, D.C., April 9–12, 1986.

Bibliography

Advisory Opinion on the Legality of the Threat or Use of Nuclear Weapons, 1997 I.L.M. 814, International Court of Justice, July 8, 1996.

Advisory Opinion on Reparations for Injuries Suffered in the Service of the United Nations, International Court of Justice, April 11, 1949.

Advisory Opinion on Reservations to the Genocide Convention, ICJ Reports 16, International Court of Justice, 1951.

Alvarez, Jose E. "Crimes of States/Crimes of Hate: Lessons from Rwanda," *Yale Journal of International Law*, vol. 24, pp. 365–437, 1999.

Anderson-Gold, Sharon. "Crimes Against Humanity: A Kantian Perspective on International Law," in *Autonomy and Community*, Jane Kneller and Sidney Axinn, eds., Albany, NY: State University of New York Press, 1998.

Arend, Anthony Clark, and Robert J. Beck. *International Law and the Use of Force*, New York: Routledge, 1993.

Arendt, Hannah. *Eichmann in Jerusalem*, New York: Viking Press, 1963.

Arendt, Hannah. "Organized Guilt and Universal Responsibility," *Jewish Frontiers*, 1948, reprinted in *Collective Responsibility*, Larry May and Stacey Hoffman, eds., Lanham, MD: Rowman and Littlefield, 1991, p. 278.

Arendt, Hannah. "Personal Responsibility Under Dictatorship," *The Listener*, vol. 72, no. 1845, August 6, 1964.

Arendt, Hannah. "Thinking and Moral Considerations," *Social Research*, August 1971, pp. 417–46.

Aristotle, *The Athenian Constitution*, H. Rachham, trans., Cambridge, MA: Harvard University Press, 1935.

Aristotle, *Nicomachean Ethics*, W. D. Ross, trans., New York: Oxford University Press, 1925.

Askin, Kelly Dawn. *War Crimes Against Women*, The Hague: Kluwer Law International, 1997.

Austin, John. *The Province of Jurisprudence Determined*, Cambridge: Cambridge University Press, 1832.

Azanian Peoples Organization, Ms. N. M. Biko, Mr. C. H. Mxenge, and Mr. C. Ribeiro v. President of the Republic of South Africa . . . and the Chairperson of the Commission, in the Constitutional Court, 1 Case No. CCT 17/96, reported in *Report of the Truth and*

Reconciliation Commission, presented to President Nelson Mandela on October 29, 1998, Cape Town: Groves Press, 1999, vol. 1, p. 175.

Babic, Jovan. "War Crimes: Moral, Legal, or Simply Political?" in *War Crimes and Collective Wrongdoing*, Aleksandar Jokic, ed., London: Blackwell, 2001.

Barcelona Traction, Light and Power Co., Limited, Second Phase, Belgium v. Spain, I.C.J. 3, International Court of Justice, 1970.

Barkir, Lawrence, and William Strauss, *Reconciliation After Vietnam*, Notre Dame, IN: University of Notre Dame Press, 1977.

Bassiouni, M. Cherif. *Crimes Against Humanity in International Criminal Law*, The Hague: Kluwer Law International, 1992.

Bassiouni, M. Cherif. *Crimes Against Humanity in International Criminal Law*, The Hague: Kluwer Law International, 2nd ed. 1999.

Bassiouni, M. Cherif. "International Crimes: *Jus Cogens* and *Obligatio Erga Omnes*," *Law and Contemporary Problems*, vol. 59, 1996, pp. 63–74.

Bassiouni, M. Cherif. "The Sources and Content of International Criminal Law: A Theoretical Framework," in *International Criminal Law*, Vol. I, *Crimes*, 2nd ed., M. Cherif Bassiouni, ed., NJ: Transaction Press, 1999.

Bassiouni, M. Cherif., Richard Falk, and Yasuaki Onuma, in "Forty Years After The Nuremberg and Tokyo Tribunals: The Impact of the War Crimes Trials on International and National Law," *Proceedings of the 80th Annual Meeting, American Society of International Law*, Washington, D.C., April 9–12, 1986.

Bassiouni, M. Cherif, and Edward M. Wise. *Aut Dedere Aut Judicare: The Duty to Prosecute or Extradite in International Law*, Dordrecht: Martinus Nijhoff, 1995.

Bayles, Michael D. *Hart's Legal Philosophy*, Dordrecht: Kluwer Academic Publishers, 1992.

Bell-Fialkoff, Andrew. *Ethnic Cleansing*, New York: St. Martin's, 1996.

Bentham, Jeremy. *An Introduction to the Principles of Morals and Legislation* (1789), J. H. Burns and H. L. A. Hart, eds., Oxford: Oxford University Press, 1996.

Biggs, John Jr., *The Guilty Mind*, Baltimore, MD: The Johns Hopkins University Press, 1955.

Blackburn, Simon. *Ruling Passions*, Oxford: Clarendon Press, 1998.

Blum, Lawrence. *Moral Perception and Particularity*, Cambridge: Cambridge University Press, 1994.

Boxill, Bernard. *Blacks and Social Justice*, Totowa, NJ: Rowman and Littlefield, 1984.

Brierly, J. L. *The Law of Nations*, 6th ed., Oxford: Oxford University Press, 1963.

Browning, Christopher. *Ordinary Men*, New York: Harper Collins, 1992.

Buchanan, Allen. *Justice, Legitimacy and Self-Determination*, Oxford: Oxford University Press, 2004.

Burgess-Jackson, Keith. "A Crime Against Women: Calhoun on the Wrongness of Rape," *Journal of Social Philosophy*, vol. 31, pp. 286–93, 2000.

Calley v. Callaway, 519 F.2d 184,1975.

Calley v. Callaway, 382 F.Supp.650, 1974.

Cigar, Norman. *Genocide in Bosnia: The Policy of Ethnic Cleansing*, College Station, TX: Texas A & M University Press, 1995.

Chaffe, Zachariah, and Edward D. Re, *Cases and Materials on Equity*, Brooklyn, NY: Foundation Press, 5th ed. 1967.

Charlesworth, Hilary, and Christine Chinkin, "The Gender of *Jus Cogens*," *Human Rights Quarterly*, vol. 15, 1993.

Charter of the International Military Tribunal at Nuremberg and Agreement for the Prosecution and Punishment of the Major War Criminals of the European Axis Powers, Annex to the London Agreement, 8 Aug. 1945, 59 Stat. 1544, 82 U.N.T.S. 279.

Charter of the United Nations, T.S. 993, 59 Stat. 1031, 1976, Y.B.U.N. 1043, 1945.

Cleckley, Hervey. *The Mask of Sanity: An Attempt to Reinterpret the So-Called Psychopathic Personality*, St. Louis, MO: Mosby Publishers, 1941.

Commission on the Responsibility of the Authors of the War and on Enforcement of Penalties, "Report Presented to the Preliminary Peace Conference," March 29, 1919, reprinted in *American Journal of International Law*, vol 14, 1929.

Convention on the Prevention and Punishment of the Crime of Genocide, adopted Dec. 9, 1948, entered into force Jan. 12, 1951, 78 U.N.T.SW. 277.

Cooper, David. "Responsibility and the System," in Peter French, ed., *Individual and Collective Responsibility: The Massacre at My Lai*, Cambridge, MA: Schenkman Publishing, 1972.

Crocker, David. "Truth Commissions, Transitional Justice and Civil Society," in *Truth v. Justice*, Robert I. Rotberg and Dennis Thompson, eds., Princeton: Princeton University Press, 2000.

Damico, Alfonso. *Democracy and the Case for Amnesty*, Gainesville, FL: University Presses of Florida, 1975.

Dorjahn, Alfred. *Political Forgiveness in Old Athens: The Amnesty of 403 B.C.*, Evanston, IL: Northwestern University Press, 1946.

Dorris, Jonathan. *Pardon and Amnesty Under Lincoln and Johnson*, Westport, CT: Greenwood Press, 1953.

Du Toit, André. "The Moral Foundations of the South African TRC: Truth as Acknowledgement and Justice as Recognition," in *Truth v. Justice*, Robert I. Rotberg and Dennis Thompson, eds., Princeton: Princeton University Press, 2000.

Engelberg, Stephen. "Panel Seeks U.S. Pledge on Bosnia War Criminals," *The New York Times*, November 3, 1995, p. A1.

Eskridge, William S. Jr., and John Ferejohn, "Politics, Interpretation, and the Rule of Law," *NOMOS XXXVI: The Rule of Law*, New York: New York University Press, 1994.

Federal Rules of Criminal Procedure 29.

Feinberg, Joel. *The Moral Limits of the Criminal Law*, Vol. I: *Harm to Others*, Oxford: Oxford University Press, 1984.

Feinberg, Joel. *The Moral Limits of the Criminal Law*, Vol. IV, *Harmless Wrongdoing*, Oxford: Oxford University Press, 1988.

Final Report of the Commission of Experts Established Pursuant to Security Council Resolution 780 (1992), May 27, 1994, UN Doc. S/1994/674.

Fisher, Ian. "Where Justice Takes a Back Seat to Just Ending War," *The New York Times*, Sunday, July 15, 2001, p. A1.

Fiss, Owen. "Against Settlement," *Yale Law Journal*, vol. 93, 1984, pp. 1073–90.

Fisse, Brent, and John Braithwaite, *The Impact of Publicity on Corporate Offenders*, Albany, NY: State University of New York Press, 1983.

Friedrich, Jorg. "Nuremberg and the Germans," in *War Crimes: The Legacy of Nuremberg*, Belinda Cooper, ed., New York: TV Books, 1984.

Fuller, Lon. *The Morality of Law*, New Haven: Yale University Press, 1964, 1969.

Galey, Margaret E. "International Enforcement of Women's Rights," *Human Rights Quarterly*, vol. 6, pp. 463–90, 1984.

Gardner, Martin R. "The *Mens Rea* Enigma: Observations on the Role of Motive in the Criminal Law Past and Present," *Utah Law Review*, 1993, pp. 635–81.

Gibeaut, John. "Deadly Choices," *ABA Journal*, May 2001, pp. 38–45.

Gilbert, Margaret. "Group Wrongs and Guilt Feelings," *The Journal of Ethics*, vol. 1, no. 1, 1997, pp. 65–84.

Goldstone, Richard. *For Humanity: Reflections of a War Crimes Investigator*, New Haven: Yale University Press, 2000.

Gould, Carol. *Rethinking Democracy*, Cambridge: Cambridge University Press, 1988.

Govier, Trudy. *Forgiveness and Revenge*, NY: Routledge, 2002.

Gray, J. Glenn. *The Warriors: Reflection on Men in Battle*, New York: Harcourt Brace, 1959.

Greenawalt, Alexander K. A. "Rethinking Genocidal Intent: The Case for a Knowledge-Based Interpretation," *Columbia Law Review*, vol. 99, no. 8, December 1999.

Greenawalt, Kent. "Amnesty's Justice," in *Truth v. Justice*, Robert I. Rotberg and Dennis Thompson, eds., Princeton: Princeton University Press, 2000.

Grotius, Hugo. *The Law of War and Peace* (1625), Francis W. Kelsey, trans., Oxford: Clarendon Press, 1925.

Guttman, Amy, and Dennis Thompson, "The Moral Foundations of Truth Commissions," in *Truth v. Justice*, Robert I. Rotberg and Dennis Thompson, eds., Princeton: Princeton University Press, 2000.

Hague Convention (No. IV) Respecting the Laws and Customs of War on Land, With Annex of Regulations, Preamble, 36 Stat. 2277, T.S. No. 539, 1 Bevans 631, Oct. 18, 1907.

Hammer, Richard. *The Court Martial of Lt. Calley*, New York: Coward, McCann, and Geoghegan, 1971.

Hampton, Jean. "Democracy and the Rule of Law," in *NOMOS XXXVI: The Rule of Law*, Ian Shapiro, ed., New York: New York University Press, 1994.

Hare, R. M. *Moral Thinking*, Oxford: Oxford University Press, 1973.

Hart, H. L. A. "Are There Any Natural Rights?" in *Political Philosophy*, Anthony Quinton, ed., Oxford, Oxford University Press, 1967.

Hart, H. L. A. *Law, Liberty, and Morality*, Stanford: Stanford University Press, 1962.

Hart, H. L. A. *Essays in Jurisprudence and Philosophy*, Oxford: Clarendon Press, 1983.

Hart, H. L. A. *The Concept of Law*, Oxford: Clarendon Press, 2nd ed., 1991.

Hartland, E. Sidney. *Primitive Law*, New York: Kennikat Press, 1924.

Hecht Co. v. Bowles, 321 U.S. 321, 329–30 (1944).

Hegel, G. W. F. *Philosophy of Right* (1821), T. M. Knox, trans., 1952.

Henry, Yazir. "Where Healing Begins," in Charles Villa-Vicencio and Wilhelm Verwoerd, *Looking Back, Reaching Forward*, Cape Town: University of Cape Town Press, 2000.

Hobbes, Thomas. *A Dialogue Between a Philosopher and a Student of the Common Laws of England* (1681), Joseph Cropsey, ed., Chicago: University of Chicago Press, 1971.

Hobbes, Thomas. *Leviathan* (1651), *The English Works of Thomas Hobbes*, London: John Bohn. Second reprint, Scientia Verlag Aalen, 1966.

Hoffer, Peter Charles. *The Law's Conscience: Equitable Constitutionalism in America*, Chapel Hill, NC: University of North Carolina Press, 1990.

Holmes, Oliver Wendell. "The Path of the Law," *Harvard Law Review*, vol. 10, 1897.

Honore, Tony. *Making Law Bind*, Oxford: Oxford University Press, 1987.

Hoogh, Andre de. *Obligations Erga Omnes and International Crimes*, The Hague: Kluwer Law International, 1996.

Horne, William W. "The Real Trial of the Century," in *War Crimes in International Law*, Yoram Dinstein and Mala Taroy, eds., The Hague: Martinus Nijhoff Publishers, 1996.

Hume, David. "Of the Original Contract," in *Hume's Ethical Writings*, Alasdair MacIntyre, ed., Notre Dame, IN: University of Notre Dame Press, 1979.

Husak, Douglas N. "Motive and Criminal Law," *Criminal Justice Ethics*, vol. 3, 1989, pp. 3–14.

Husak, Douglas. "The 'But-Everyone-Does-That!' Defense," *Public Affairs Quarterly*, vol. 10, no. 4, October 1996, pp. 307–34.

Hwang, Phyllis. "Defining Crimes Against Humanity," *Fordham International Law Journal*, vol. 22, 1998, pp. 457–504.

Jackson, Robert H. Opening Statement for the United States, November 21, 1945, reprinted in *The Nuremberg War Crimes Trial 1945–46: A Documentary History*, Michael R. Marrus, ed., 1997.

Jackson, Robert H. Report of United States Representative to the International Conference on Military Trials 50, June 6, 1945, reprinted in *Nuremberg War Crimes Trial*.

Janis, Mark. "The Nature of *Jus Cogens*," *Connecticut Law Review*, vol. 3, 1988.

Janis, Mark. *An Introduction to International Law*, New York: Aspen Law, 1993.

Jaspers, Karl. *The Question of German Guilt*, New York: Capricorn Books, 1947.

Kanstroom, Daniel. "Judicial Review of Amnesty Denials: Must Aliens Bet Their Lives to Get into Court?" *Harvard Civil Rights – Civil Liberties Law Review*, vol. 25, 1990, pp. 53–100.

Kant, Immanuel. *Metaphysical Elements of Justice* (1797), John Ladd, trans., 2nd ed., 1999.

Kavka, Gregory. *Hobbesian Moral and Political Theory*, Princeton: Princeton University Press, 1986.

Kirgis, Frederick J. *International Organizations*, St. Paul, MN: West Publishing, 2nd ed., 1993.

Kiss, Elizabeth. "Moral Ambition Within and Beyond Political Constraints: Reflections on Restorative Justice," in *Truth v. Justice*, Robert I. Rotberg and Dennis Thompson, eds., Princeton: Princeton University Press, 2000.

Kogawa, Joy. *The Rain Ascends*, Toronto: Vintage Canada, 1995.

Komarow, Gary. "Individual Responsibility Under International Law: The Nuremberg Principles in Domestic Legal Systems," *International and Comparative Law Quarterly*, vol. 29, 1980, pp. 21–37.

Kutz, Christopher. *Complicity*, New York/Cambridge: Cambridge University Press, 2000.

Kuwait v. Aminoil, 21 International Legal Materials 976, 1982.

Ladd, John. "Custom," in *The Encyclopedia of Philosophy*, New York: Macmillan, vol. 2, 1967.

LaFave, Wayne R., and Austin W. Scott, Jr., *Criminal Law*, 2nd ed., St. Paul, MN: West Publishing, 1986.

Lattin, Norman D. *On Corporations*, Mineola, NY: The Foundation Press, 2nd ed., 1971.

Lazo-Majano v. INS, 813 F.2d 1432, 1987.

Leaf, Karen. "Legalizing the Illegals," *Columbia Human Rights Law Review*, vol. 12, 1980, pp. 65–89.

Lerner, Natan. "Ethnic Cleansing," in *War Crimes in International Law*, Yoram Dinstein and Mala Taroy, eds., The Hague: Martinus Nijhoff Publishers, 1996.

Lewis, Anthony. "U.S. Denied its Heritage in Failing to Embrace World Court," *The St. Louis Post-Dispatch*, July 21, 1998, p. B1.

Lewy, Guenther. "Superior Orders, Nuclear Warfare, and the Dictates of Conscience," *American Political Science Review*, vol. 55, 1961.

Liamco v. Libya, 20 International Legal Materials, 1, 1981.

Lippman, Matthew "Crimes Against Humanity," *Boston College Third World Law Journal*, vol. 17, pp. 171–273. 1997

Lovo, Mario M. "Nicaraguan Adjustment and Central American Relief Act 'NACARA,'" *Immigration Briefings*, vol. 1, November 1998.

MacCormick, Neil. *H. L. A. Hart*, Stanford: Stanford University Press, 1981.

Stephen Macedo, "The Rule of Law, Justice, and the Politics of Moderation," *NOMOS XXXVI: The Rule of Law*, New York: New York University Press, 1994.

MacKinnon, Catherine. "Crimes of War, Crimes of Peace," in *On Human Rights*, Stephen Shute and Susan Hurley, eds., Boston: Basic Books, 1993.

Matsuda, Mari J., Charles R. Lawrence III, Richard Delgado, and Kimberle Williams Crenshaw, *Words That Wound*, Boulder, CO: Westview Press, 1993.

May, Larry. "Collective Responsibility," *The Encyclopedia of Ethics*, Lawrence Becker and Charlotte Becker, eds., 2nd ed., New York: Garland, 2001.

May, Larry. "Hobbes," in *Ethics in the History of Western Philosophy*, R. J. Cavalier, J. Guinlock, and J. P. Sterba, eds., New York: Macmillan, 1989.

May, Larry. "Hobbes on Equity and Justice," in *Hobbes's Science of Natural Justice*, C. Walton and P. J. Johnson, eds., Dordrecht: Martinus Nijhoff, 1987.

May, Larry. "Hobbes on Fidelity to Law," *Hobbes Studies*, vol. 5, 1992, pp. 77–89.

May, Larry. "Hobbes on the Attitude of Pacifism," *Thomas Hobbes: De La Metaphysique A La Politique*, M. Bertman and M. Malherbe, eds., Paris: J. Vrin, 1989.

May, Larry. "Hobbes's Contract Theory," *Journal of the History of Philosophy*, vol. 18, 1980, pp. 195–208.

May, Larry. "Interview with Larry May," *Corporate Crime Reporter*, vol. 2, 1988.

May, Larry. "*Jus Cogens* Norms and International Criminal Law" (translated into Italian), *Ars Interpretandi*, vol. 6, 2001, pp. 223–248.

May, Larry. "Negligence and Corporate Criminality," in *Shame, Responsibility, and the Corporation*, Hugh Curtler, ed., New York: Haven Publications.

May, Larry. "On Conscience," *American Philosophical Quarterly*, vol. 20, 1, 1983.

May, Larry. "Professional Action and Liabilities of Professional Associations: ASME v. Hydrolevel," *Business and Professional Ethics Journal*, vol. 2, no. 1, Fall 1982.

May, Larry. *Sharing Responsibility*, Chicago: University of Chicago Press, 1992.

May, Larry. "Socialization and Institutional Evil," in *Hannah Arendt: Twenty Years Later*, Cambridge, MA: MIT Press, Jerome Kohn and Larry May, eds., 1996.

May, Larry. *The Morality of Groups*, Notre Dame, IN: University of Notre Dame Press, 1987.

May, Larry. *The Socially Responsive Self*, Chicago: University of Chicago Press, 1996.

May, Larry, and Marilyn Friedman, "Harming Women as a Group," *Social Theory and Practice*, vol. 11, no. 2, Summer 1985.

May, Larry, and Stacey Hoffman, eds., *Collective Responsibility*, Lanham, MD: Rowman and Littlefield, 1991.

McDougal, Myres, Harold Lasswell, and Lung-Chu Chen, *Human Rights and World Public Order*, New Haven: Yale University Press, 1976.

McGinn, Colin. *Ethics, Evil and Fiction*, Oxford: Oxford University Press, 1997.

McGinn, Colin. "Moral Vocabulary," *The New York Times*, Arts and Ideas Section, Saturday, December 28, 2002, p. A17.

Meron, Theodor. "Rape as a Crime Under International Humanitarian Law," *American Journal of International Law*, vol. 87, 1993, pp. 424–28.

Milgram, Stanley. *Obedience to Authority*, New York: Harper & Row, 1974.

Mill, John Stuart. *On Liberty*, Stefan Collini, ed., Cambridge: Cambridge University Press, 1989.

Milo, Ronald. *Immorality*, Princeton: Princeton University Press, 1984.

Minow, Martha. *Between Vengeance and Forgiveness*, Boston: Beacon Press, 1998.

Murphy, Jeffrie G., and Jean Hampton, *Forgiveness and Mercy*, Cambridge: Cambridge University Press, 1988.

Mydans, Seth. "New Rule of Law in Thailand May be a Leader's Downfall," *The New York Times*, July 30, 2001, p. A8.

Neier, Aryeh. *War Crimes*, New York: Times Books, 1998.

Nicaragua v. United States, Concerning Military and Paramilitary Activities in and against Nicaragua, I.C.J. 14, International Court of Justice, 1986.

Nickel, James. "What's Wrong With Ethnic Cleansing?" *Journal of Social Philosophy*, vol. 26, 1995, p. 15.

Nino, Carlos Santiago. *Radical Evil on Trial*, New Haven: Yale University Press, 1996.

North Sea Continental Shelf Cases, ICJ. Reports 3, International Court of Justice, 1969.

Nussbaum, Martha C. "Equity and Mercy," *Philosophy and Public Affairs*, vol. 22, 1993, pp. 83–125.

Osiel, Mark J. *Mass Atrocity, Ordinary Evil, and Hannah Arendt*, New Haven: Yale University Press, 2001.

Osiel, Mark J. *Obeying Orders*, New Brunswick, NJ: Transaction Press, 1999.

Patel, Krishna R. "Recognizing the Rape of Bosnian Women as Gender-Based Persecution," *Brooklyn Law Review*, vol. 60, 1994, pp. 929–58.

Pangilinan v. I.N.S., 796 F.2d 1091, 1986.

Paust, Jordan J., M. Cherif Bassiouni, Michael Scharf, Jimmy Gurule, Leila Sadat, Bruce Zagaris, and Sharon A. Williams, *International Criminal Law: Cases and Materials*, Durham, NC: Carolina Academic Press, 2nd ed., 2000.

Payne v. Tennessee, 501 U.S. 808, 1991.

Plato, *The Apology*, in *Collected Dialogues*, Edith Hamilton and Huntington Cairns, eds., Princeton: Princeton University Press, 1961.

Plucknett, Theodore F.T. *A Concise History of the Common Law*, 5th ed., Boston: Little Brown, 1956.

Podgers, James. "War Crimes Court Under Fire," *ABA Journal*, September 1998, pp. 64–9.

Pollock, Frederick, and Frederic William Maitland, *History of English Law*, vol. 2, Boston: Little Brown, 1909.

Preliminary Remarks of the International Committee of the Red Cross, 22 February 1993, reproduced in Virginia Morris and Michael Scharf, *An Insider's Guide to the International Criminal Tribunal for the Former Yugoslavia*, vol. 2, 1995.

Prosecutor v. Akayesu, International Criminal Tribunal for Rwanda, Case No. ICTR-96-4, Judgment of the Trial Chamber, September 2, 1998.

Prosecutor v. Anto Furundzija, Case No. IT-9517/1-T, International Criminal Tribunal for the Former Yugoslavia, Trial Chamber, December 1998.

Prosecutor v. Delalic et al., Case No. IT-96-21-T, Judgment, International Criminal Tribunal for the Former Yugoslavia, November 16, 1998.

Prosecutor v. Dusko Tadic, Case No. IT-94-1-T, Decision of the Appeals Chamber on the Defense Motion for Interlocutory Appeal on Jurisdiction, International Criminal Tribunal for the Former Yugoslavia, Appeals Chamber, October 2, 1995.

Prosecutor v. Dusko Tadic, Case No. IT-94-1-T, Opinion and Judgment, International Criminal Tribunal for the Former Yugoslavia, Trial Chamber, May 7, 1997.

Prosecutor v. Erdemovic, Judgment. Case No. IT-96-22-A. International Criminal Tribunal for the Former Yugoslavia, Appeals Chamber, October 7, 1997.

Prosecutor v. Goran Jelisic, International Criminal Tribunal for the Former Yugoslavia, Judgment of the Trial Chamber, December 14, 1999.

Prosecutor v. Musema, Trial Chamber, Case No. ICTR-96-13-T, International Criminal Tribunal for Rwanda, January 27, 2000.

Prosecutor v. Rutaganda, International Criminal Tribunal for Rwanda, Case No. ICTR-96-3, Judgment and Sentence, December 6, 1999.

Prosecutor v. Touvier, 100 I.L.R. 341, 358, Court of Cassation, Criminal Chamber, 1992.

Quigley, John. "State Responsibility for Ethnic Cleansing," *U.C. Davis Law Review*, vol. 32, 1999, pp. 341–87.

Ragazzi, Maurizio. *The Concept of International Obligations Erga Omnes*, Oxford: Clarendon Press, 1997.

Ratner, Steven R., and Jason S. Abrams, *Accountability for Human Rights Atrocities in International Law*, Oxford: Oxford University Press, 1997.

Rawls, John. *The Law of Peoples*, Cambridge, MA: Harvard University Press, 1999.

Regina v. Bartle and the Commissioner of Police for the Metropolis and Others Ex Parte Pinochet (on appeal from a Divisional Court of the Queen's Bench Division) and Regina v. Evans and another and the Commissioner of Police for the Metropolis and others Ex Parte Pinochet (on appeal from a Divisional Court of the Queen's Bench Division), November 25, 1998.

Regina v. Bartle and the Commissioner of Police for the Metropolis and Others, Ex Parte Pinochet, House of Lords, March 24, 1999.

Regina v. Finta, 1 S.C.R. 701, 813 (Can.), 1994.

Report of the International Law Commission on the Work of its 48th Session, U.N.GAOR, 51st Sess., Supp. No. 10, at 87, U.N. Doc. A/51/10, 1996.

Report of the Secretary-General Pursuant to Paragraph 15 of Security Council Resolution 757, 1992, and Paragraph 10 of Security Council Resolution 758,1992, S/24100, 15 June 1992, reprinted in *The "Yugoslav" Crisis in International Law: General Issues*, Daniel Bethlehem and Marc Wheeler, ed., 1997.

Robinson, Darryl. "Defining 'Crimes Against Humanity' at the Rome Conference," *American Journal of International Law*, vol. 93, 1999, pp. 43–57.

Roht-Arriaza, Naomi, and Lauren Gibson, "The Developing Jurisprudence on Amnesty," *Human Rights Quarterly*, vol. 20, 1998, pp. 843–85.

Rome Statute of the International Criminal Court, Adopted by the U.N. Diplomatic Conference, July 17, 1998.

Rostow, Eugene. "Until What? Enforcement Action or Collective Self-Defense," *American Journal of International Law*, vol. 85, July 1991, pp. 506–16.

Rubin, Alfred. *Ethics and Authority in International Law*, New York: Cambridge University Press, 1997.

Schabas, William A. *Genocide in International Law*, Cambridge: Cambridge University Press, 2000.

Schabas, William A. "International Sentencing: From Leipzig (1923) to Arusha (1996)," *International Criminal Law*, 2nd ed., vol. III, *Enforcement*, M. Cherif Bassiouni, ed., Ardsley, NY: Transnational Publishers, 1999.

Schabas, William A. *The Abolition of the Death Penalty in International Law*, 2nd ed., Cambridge: Cambridge University Press, 1997.

Schabas, William A. "Was Genocide Committed in Bosnia and Herzegovina? First Judgments of the International Criminal Tribunal for the Former Yugoslavia," *Fordham International Law Journal*, vol. 25, no. 1, November 2001.

Scharf, Michael. *Balkan Justice*, Durham, NC: Carolina Academic Press, 1997.

Scharf, Michael. "Swapping Amnesty for Peace: Was There a Duty to Prosecute International Crimes in Haiti," *Texas International Law Journal*, vol. 31, 1996, pp. 1–38.

Shue, Henry. *Basic Rights: Subsistence, Affluence, and U.S. Foreign Policy*, Princeton: Princeton University Press, 1980.

Slye, Ronald. "Justice and Amnesty," in *Looking Back, Reaching Forward: Reflections on the Truth and Reconciliation Commission in South Africa*, Charles Villa-Vicencio and Wilhelm Verwoerd, eds., Cape Town: University of Cape Town Press, 2000.

Slye, Ronald C. "Apartheid as a Crime Against Humanity," *Michigan Journal of International Law*, vol. 20, 1999, pp. 267–300.

Smithson v. Garth, 3 Lev. 324, 38 Eng. Rep. 1150, 1601.

Solum, Lawrence. "Equity and the Rule of Law," *NOMOS XXXVI: The Rule of Law*, New York: New York University Press, 1994.

Solum, Lawrence. "Learning Our Limits: The Decline of Textualism in Statutory Cases," *Wisconsin Law Review*, 1997, pp. 235–83.

Socolovsky, Jerome. "Landmark Rape Case Opens Today at Yugoslav Tribunal on War Crimes," *The St. Louis Post-Dispatch*, March 20, 2000, pp. A1, A7.

St. Germaine, Christopher. *Doctor and Student*, 1535, quoted in Steven J. Prall, "The Development of Equity in Tudor England," *American Journal of Legal History*, vol. 8, 1964.

State v. Ferguson, 20 SW 3rd 485, 2000.

Statute for the International Tribunal for the Prosecution of Persons Responsible for Serious Violations of International Humanitarian Law Committed in the Territory of the Former Yugoslavia since 1991, Annex to the Report of the Secretary-General Pursuant to Paragraph 2 of Security Council Resolution 808 (1993), UN Doc. S/25704, 3 May 1993, Annex, at 36–48. 32 I.L.M. 1192–1201,1993.

Statute for the International Tribunal for the Prosecution of Persons Responsible for Genocide and Other Serious Violations of International Humanitarian Law Committed in the Territory of Rwanda, S.C. Res. 955, art. 3(g), Nov. 8, 1994, reprinted in 33 I.L.M. 1598, 1994.

Sunstein, Cass R. *Legal Reasoning and Political Conflict*, Oxford: Oxford University Press, 1996.

Swaak-Goldman, Olivia. "Note on Erdemovic Case," *The American Journal of International Law*, vol. 92, 1998, pp. 283–87.

Sztucki, Jerzy. *Jus Cogens and the Vienna Convention on the Law Of Treaties*, Vienna: Springer Verlag, 1974.

Taylor, Telford. *The Anatomy of the Nuremberg Trials*, Boston: Little Brown, 1992.

Teitel, Ruth. "Nuremberg and Its Legacy: Fifty Years Later," in *War Crimes in International Law*, Yoram Dinstein and Mala Taroy, eds., The Hague: Martinus Nijhoff Publishers, 1996.

Texaco v. Libya, 17 International Legal Materials 1 (1978).

Thalberg, Irving, and Deborah Pellow. "Imagining Alternatives," *Philosophical. Forum*, vol. 11, 1979, pp. 1–17.

Todorov, Tzvetan. "In Search of Lost Crime: Tribunals, Apologies, Reparations, and the Search for Justice," *The New Republic*, January 29, 2001, pp. 29–36.

Tunkin, Grigory I. *"Jus Cogens* in Contemporary International Law," *Toledo Law Review*, Fall/Winter, pp. 107–18. 1971.

Tunkin, Grigory I. "The Contemporary Soviet Theory of International Law," *Current Legal Problems*, 1978, pp. 177–88.

United Nations World Conference on Human Rights: Vienna Declaration and Programme of Action, U.N. Doc. A/Conf. 157/24, Part I, 1993, reprinted in I.L.M. 1661, 1993.

Universal Declaration of Human Rights, GA Res. 217 A (III), U.N. Doc. A/810, December 10, 1948.

United States v. Carroll Towing Co., 159 F.2d 169, 2d Cir. 1947.

U.S. v. Park, 421 U.S. 658, 660,1975.

Van Schaack, Beth. "The Definition of Crimes Against Humanity: Resolving the Incoherence," *Columbia Journal of Transnational Law*, vol. 37, pp. 787–850, 1999.

Verdirame, Guglielmo. "The Genocide Definition in the Jurisprudence of the *Ad Hoc* Tribunals," *International and Comparative Law Quarterly*, vol. 49, no. 3, July 2000.

Verdross, Alfred von. "Forbidden Treaties in International Law," *American Journal of International Law*, vol. 31, 1937, pp. 571–92.

Vernon, Richard. "What Is Crime Against Humanity," *Journal of Political Philosophy*, vol. 10, no. 3, Sept. 2002, pp. 231–49.

Verwoerd, Wilhelm. "Toward the Recognition of Our Past Injustices," in *Looking Back, Reaching Forward: Reflections on the Truth and Reconciliation Commission in South Africa*, Charles Villa-Vicencio and Wilhelm Verwoerd, eds., Cape Town: University of Cape Town Press, 2000.

Vienna Convention on the Law of Treaties, UN doc A/CONF. 39/27, May 23, 1969.

Vukovar Hospital Rule 61 Decision, U.N. Doc. International Criminal Tribunal for Yugoslavia, IT-95-13-R61, 1996.

Walzer, Michael. *On Toleration*, New Haven, CT: Yale University Press, 1997.

Walzer, Michael. "The Legal Codes of Ancient Israel," *NOMOS XXXVI: The Rule of Law*, New York: New York University Press, 1994.

Wang, Lu-in. "The Transforming Power of 'Hate': Social Cognition Theory and the Harms of Bias-Related Crime," *Southern California Law Review*, 1997.

Wertheimer, Allen. "Unconscionability and Contracts," *Business Ethics Quarterly*, vol. 2, no. 4, October 1992.

Wilkins, Burleigh. "Responsibility for the My Lai Massacre," in his book *Terrorism and Collective Responsibility*, New York: Routledge, 1992.

Index